Communication in the
Presidential Primaries

Recent Titles in the
Praeger Series in Political Communication
Robert E. Denton, Jr., *General Editor*

Presidential Crisis Rhetoric and the Press in the Post–Cold War World
Jim A. Kuypers

The 1996 Presidential Campaign: A Communication Perspective
Robert E. Denton, Jr., editor

Reconciling Free Trade, Fair Trade, and Interdependence: The Rhetoric of
Presidential Economic Leadership
Delia B. Conti

Politics and Politicians in American Film
Phillip L. Gianos

Electronic Whistle-Stops: The Impact of the Internet on American Politics
Gary W. Selnow

Newspapers of Record in a Digital Age: From Hot Type to Hot Link
Shannon E. Martin and Kathleen A. Hansen

Campaign '96: A Functional Analysis of Acclaiming, Attacking, and Defending
William L. Benoit, Joseph R. Blaney, and P. M. Pier

Political Communication in America, Third Edition
Robert E. Denton, Jr., editor

Reelpolitik: Political Ideologies in '30s and '40s Films
*Beverly Merrill Kelley, with John J. Pitney, Jr., Craig R. Smith, and
Herbert E. Gooch III*

World Opinion and the Emerging International Order
*Frank Louis Rusciano, with Roberta Fiske-Rusciano, Bosah Ebo, Sigfredo Hernandez,
and John Crothers Pollock*

Seeing Spots: A Functional Analysis of Presidential Television Advertisements,
1952–1996
William L. Benoit

Losing Our Democratic Spirit: Congressional Deliberation and the Dictatorship
of Propaganda
Bill Granstaff

Political Campaign Communication: Principles and Practices, Fourth Edition
Judith S. Trent and Robert V. Friedenberg

Communication in the Presidential Primaries

Candidates and the Media, 1912–2000

Kathleen E. Kendall

Praeger Series in Political Communication

PRAEGER

Westport, Connecticut
London

Library of Congress Cataloging-in-Publication Data

Kendall, Kathleen E., 1937–
   Communication in the presidential primaries : candidates and the
media, 1912–2000 / Kathleen E. Kendall.
      p.   cm.—(Praeger series in political communication, ISSN
1062–5623)
   Includes bibliographical references and index.
   ISBN 0–275–94070–5 (alk. paper).—ISBN 0–275–96897–9 (pbk. : alk. paper)
   1. Presidents—United States—Election—History—20th century.
   2. Primaries—United States—History—20th century.
   3. Communication in politics—United States—History—20th century.
   4. Rhetoric—Political aspects—United States—History—20th
century.   5. Mass media—Political aspects—United States—
History—20th century.   I. Title.   II. Series.
   E176.1.K42   2000
   324.7'0973'0904—dc21   99–22140

British Library Cataloguing in Publication Data is available.

Library of Congress Catalog Card Number: 99–22140
ISBN: 0–275–94070–5
      0–275–96897–9 (pbk.)
ISSN: 1062–5623

First published in 2000

Praeger Publishers, 88 Post Road West, Westport, CT 06881
An imprint of Greenwood Publishing Group, Inc.
www.praeger.com

Printed in the United States of America

The paper used in this book complies with the
Permanent Paper Standard issued by the National
Information Standards Organization (Z39.48–1984).

10 9 8 7 6 5 4 3 2 1

To Ronald B. Edgerton and Alice King Edgerton
for a lifetime of love and support

Contents

Series Foreword   ix
  Robert E. Denton, Jr.

Acknowledgments   xiii

1. Introduction: The Unique Rhetorical Situation of the
   Presidential Primary   1

2. Primary Rules and Their Impact on Communication   29

3. Speeches and Debates for Dozens ... and Millions   53

4. Advertising in a Multi-Candidate Field   91

5. Through Media Eyes in the Pre-Television Era: News Media
   Shaping of the Primaries, 1912–1952   129

6. Through Media Eyes in the Age of Television: News Media
   Shaping of the Primaries, 1972–1992   161

7. Communication Patterns in Presidential Primaries, 1912–2000:
   Knowing the Rules of the Game   203

Selected Bibliography   225

Index   245

Series Foreword

Those of us from the discipline of communication studies have long believed that communication is prior to all other fields of inquiry. In several other forums I have argued that the essence of politics is "talk" or human interaction.[1] Such interaction may be formal or informal, verbal or non-verbal, public or private, but it is always persuasive, forcing us consciously or subconsciously to interpret, to evaluate, and to act. Communication is the vehicle for human action.

From this perspective, it is not surprising that Aristotle recognized the natural kinship of politics and communication in his writings *Politics* and *Rhetoric*. In the former, he established that humans are "political beings [who] alone of the animals [are] furnished with the faculty of language."[2] In the latter, he began his systematic analysis of discourse by proclaiming that "rhetorical study, in its strict sense, is concerned with the modes of persuasion."[3] Thus, it was recognized over twenty-three hundred years ago that politics and communication go hand in hand because they are essential parts of human nature.

In 1981, Dan Nimmo and Keith Sanders proclaimed that political communication was an emerging field.[4] Although its origin, as noted, dates back centuries, a "self-consciously cross-disciplinary" focus began in the late 1950s. Thousands of books and articles later, colleges and universities offer a variety of graduate and undergraduate coursework in the area in such diverse departments as communication, mass communication, journalism, political science, and sociology.[5] In Nimmo and Sanders's early assessment, the "key areas of inquiry" included rhetorical analysis, propaganda analysis, attitude change studies, voting studies, government and the news media, functional and systems analyses, technological changes, media technologies, campaign techniques, and re-search techniques.[6] In a survey of the state of the field in 1983, the same authors and Lynda Kaid found additional, more specific areas of con-cerns such as the presidency, political polls, public opinion, debates, and advertising.[7] Since the first study, they have also noted a shift away from the rather strict behavioral approach.

A decade later, Dan Nimmo and David Swanson argued that "political communication has developed some identity as a more or less distinct domain of scholarly work."[8] The scope and concerns of the area have further expanded to include critical theories and cultural studies. Al-though there is no precise definition, method, or disciplinary home of the area of inquiry, its primary domain comprises the role, processes, and effects of communication within the context of politics broadly de-fined.

In 1985, the editors of *Political Communication Yearbook: 1984* noted that "more things are happening in the study, teaching, and practice of po-litical communication than can be captured within the space limitations of the relatively few publications available."[9] In addition, they argued that the backgrounds of "those involved in the field [are] so varied and pluralist in outlook and approach, . . . it [is] a mistake to adhere slavishly to any set format in shaping the content."[10] More recently, Swanson and Nimmo have called for "ways of overcoming the unhappy consequences of fragmentation within a framework that respects, encourages, and ben-efits from diverse scholarly commitments, agendas, and approaches."[11]

In agreement with these assessments of the area and with gentle en-couragement, in 1988 Praeger established the series entitled "Praeger Se-ries in Political Communication." The series is open to all qualitative and quantitative methodologies as well as contemporary and historical stud-ies. The key to characterizing the studies in the series is the focus on communication variables or activities within a political context or di-mension. As of this writing, over 70 volumes have been published and numerous impressive works are forthcoming. Scholars from the disci-plines of communication, history, journalism, political science, and so-ciology have participated in the series.

I am, without shame or modesty, a fan of the series. The joy of serving as its editor is in participating in the dialogue of the field of political communication and in reading the contributors' works. I invite you to join me.

Robert E. Denton, Jr.

NOTES

1. See Robert E. Denton, Jr., *The Symbolic Dimensions of the American Presidency* (Prospect Heights, IL: Waveland Press, 1982); Robert E. Denton, Jr., and Gary

Woodward, *Political Communication in America* (New York: Praeger, 1985; 2d ed., 1990); Robert E. Denton, Jr., and Dan Hahn, *Presidential Communication* (New York: Praeger, 1986); and Robert E. Denton, Jr., *The Primetime Presidency of Ronald Reagan* (New York: Praeger, 1988).

2. Aristotle, *The Politics of Aristotle*, trans. Ernest Barker (New York: Oxford University Press, 1970), p. 5.

3. Aristotle, *Rhetoric*, trans. W. Rhys Roberts (New York: The Modern Library, 1954), p. 22.

4. Dan D. Nimmo and Keith R. Sanders, "Introduction: The Emergence of Political Communication as a Field," in *Handbook of Political Communication*, ed. Dan D. Nimmo and Keith R. Sanders (Beverly Hills, CA: Sage, 1981), pp. 11–36.

5. Ibid., p. 15.

6. Ibid., pp. 17–27.

7. Keith Sanders, Lynda Kaid, and Dan Nimmo, eds., *Political Communication Yearbook: 1984* (Carbondale: Southern Illinois University, 1985), pp. 283–308.

8. Dan Nimmo and David Swanson, "The Field of Political Communication: Beyond the Voter Persuasion Paradigm," in *New Directions in Political Communication*, ed. David Swanson and Dan Nimmo (Beverly Hills, CA: Sage, 1990), p. 8.

9. Sanders, Kaid, and Nimmo, *Political Communication Yearbook: 1984*, p. xiv.

10. Ibid.

11. Nimmo and Swanson, "The Field of Political Communication," p. 11.

Acknowledgments

Writing this book took a lot longer than I expected and required the patience, advice, and encouragement of many people. So I wish to thank:

The librarians at the Roosevelt Library, Hyde Park, New York; the Seeley Mudd Library, Princeton University, Princeton, New Jersey; the National Archives and the Library of Congress, Washington, DC; the Nixon Project of the National Archives; and the Massachusetts Historical Society, Boston;

My colleagues in the Department of Communication, University at Albany, State University of New York, for their patience and encouragement over an eight-year period;

The University at Albany, State University of New York, for a sabbatical leave and Faculty Research Grant to work on this book;

The Joan Shorenstein Center on the Press, Politics and Public Policy, John F. Kennedy School of Government, Harvard University, which supported this project through a Research Fellowship in the fall of 1997 and a Goldsmith Award for Research in 1994;

Colleagues at the Shorenstein Center for reading early drafts of chapters and providing valuable suggestions and comments: Pippa Norris, Marvin Kalb, Tom Patterson, Richard Parker, Anna Greenberg, Marion Just, Sara Bentivegna, and Zachary Karabell;

C-SPAN and the Purdue University Public Affairs Archives for providing funding for research and videotapes;

Paul E. Corcoran, University of Adelaide, South Australia, who was so influential in the conception, research, and writing of our joint project on the 1912 primaries, which was a starting point for this book;

Judith S. Trent, University of Cincinnati, my co-researcher and companion on three New Hampshire primary trips and constant foil for ideas on the primaries and campaigns;

June Ock Yum, Towson State University, whose survey research collaboration has helped me to understand the nature of media use in the primaries;

Other colleagues and friends who have given me candid feedback on convention papers and articles related to this research and provided valuable ideas and information: Bob Meadow, David Swanson, Barbara Hinckley, Phil Lange, Lida Churchville, Mary Stuckey, Montague Kern, Eric Appleman, Craig Allen Smith, Joshua Meyrowitz, Martin Medhurst, Bob Friedenberg, Bob Rotberg, Mitchell McKinney, and Findley Cockrell;

Students who have shared with me their independent study, thesis, and research paper ideas, including Anuradha Basu, Mark Dolan, Molly Marchione, John Peterson, Jamie Gilkey, Doug Kruse, Meredith Friedman, Scott Montgomery, Larry Goldstein, Helene Dornstreich, Linda Ben Ezra, Shai Brown, Candice D'Auria, Paul Rydza, and Desare Frazier;

Research assistants Heath Boice, Gregory Wilson, and Jessica Tonn for their help in videotaping newscasts; and Anuradha Basu, Lisa Pemble, Missy Smith, Jessica Tonn, Linda Greenwood, and Sally Kolodkin for library research;

Interviewers Greta Petry and Don Fields, whose questions helped me sharpen my ideas, and reporters for the Albany *Times-Union* and the *Gazette* (Schenectady, New York), for radio stations WAMC and WABY (Albany, New York), and for television stations (Channels 6, 10, 13, and 17) in the Albany area for providing me with more opportunities to analyze the primaries;

Radio station WAMC-FM in Albany, New York, a National Public Radio affiliate, for giving me press passes for my research trips to the New Hampshire primaries in 1988, 1992, and 1996;

People who have generously let me stay in their homes for long periods of time while I was doing research: Bill, Marilyn, and Jimmy Edgerton; Lynn Gardner; and Jeff and Jane Hinck;

Dick and Zack Kendall, for their interest and encouragement;

Bill and Marilyn Edgerton, Alicelee and Bill Graf, and Ron and Becky Edgerton for their patience and for asking good questions about the book (but not *too* often);

My parents, Ronald B. Edgerton and Alice King Edgerton, always understanding and supportive and the first to read and respond to many portions of this book.

Chapter 1

Introduction:
The Unique Rhetorical Situation
of the Presidential Primary

The scene was the Chubb Insurance Company in Manchester, New Hampshire, February 1988. Former Secretary of State Alexander Haig, a Republican candidate for president, was touring the company's offices with his wife, introducing himself to the secretaries, smiling and talking with each one personally. The author stood, observing, with half a dozen people from the media. As Haig walked over to the next desk, one secretary remarked: "I never vote for anyone I haven't met. I've met three of the candidates so far this year."[1]

The scene is again Manchester, New Hampshire, this time in February 1992. People are milling around in the Tsongas for President campaign headquarters on Elm Street, the main avenue of the city. Former Senator Tsongas has just given a rousing speech, and members of the crowd are waiting to meet him personally. One young man is there with his wife and two little daughters, one in a stroller. The author asks him if he has decided how to cast his primary vote. "We haven't decided," he replied. He explained that they had been walking up and down Elm Street, visiting different campaign headquarters. "We're shopping the candidates," he said.

The secretary waiting for the candidates to woo her directly and the man "shopping" to decide which candidate to "buy" had something in common. The philosophy expressed by these two voters is the central premise of the movement that created the presidential primary system over 90 years ago: that the voters should have the power to choose the presidential nominees directly. In 1996, Democrats in 32 states and Republicans in 40 states selected their parties' nominees in presidential primaries, and the candidates who won the primaries secured their parties' nomination.

This book focuses on primaries, but it must be noted that some states use party caucuses rather than primaries to choose their delegates. The Iowa caucuses, which are the most famous, exerted an important influence on the selection of the nominee in 1976, 1980, and 1984. In 1988, the Iowa winners faltered in later contests. And in 1992 and 1996, the Iowa results were generally discounted because the winners, Senator Tom Harkin of Iowa and Senator Bob Dole of Kansas, were presumed to be regional favorites. As Mayer (1996a) reports, "Caucuses require a considerably more significant investment of time from those who participate in them, and the voter turnout is far lower than in primaries. For example, the 1988 Democratic primaries drew 30% of voting-age Democrats, while caucuses drew only 3%" (Mayer, 1996, pp. 124–125).

Some would argue that "the power to nominate is more important than the power to elect" (Eaton, 1912, pp. 109–111). Yet there is much dissatisfaction with the primary process. People regularly decry the length and bitterness of the contests, the trivialization of public discourse, and the failure to produce nominees whose qualities are commensurate with the expense, time, and effort of all concerned. Four long months of state primary elections, combined with additional pre-primary months, now dominate the quadrennial political calendar. Successful candidates, by then the inevitable party nominees, are survivors but somehow not winners. Primaries, once a "solution" to remote and unresponsive government and the control of the party bosses, have become the problem (Crotty and Jackson, 1985, pp. 62–79; Marshall, 1981, pp. 157–171).

The essence of the primary campaign process is communication: candidates try to persuade voters to select them rather than their opponents. The media report and comment upon the process, and voters respond with enthusiasm, disgust, or indifference. This book focuses on this exchange of symbols in the presidential primaries in an attempt to better understand the gap between the ideal and the real. Why is it that this effort at grassroots participation so fascinates and disappoints the public? A cartoon by Tom Meyer of the *San Francisco Chronicle* characterizes the dilemma. A strong, barrel-chested candidate strides onto a game board at the square which reads, "Begin campaign here." Ahead of him are squares reading "Appear on MacNeil/Lehrer," "First poll," "Sex scandal," "Spin control," "Misquote," and so on. Overhead are storm clouds; rain pours onto the board. By the time the candidate emerges at the end of the game at the square marked "Political convention," he looks as though he has crawled out of a dumpster, barely standing, tongue hanging out, dazed, clothes dishevelled, and flies buzzing around his head. Two voters stand off to the side, observing and frowning in disapproval.

"Jeez!" says one. "Where do we get these guys?" (reprinted in the *Washington Post*, March 28, 1992, p. A21).

RESEARCH QUESTIONS

An increasing number of works focus on the presidential primaries, but most examine recent campaigns only. In contrast, the method of this book looks at primaries from their earliest days, comparing the nature of communication in contests from 1912 through 1996, with projections to 2000. While references are occasionally made to other years, the research focuses heavily on five primary years—1912, 1932, 1952, 1972, and 1992. By selecting campaigns at intervals of 20 years over this 80-year period rather than looking back and picking the primaries according to their fame, the author sought to bring a systematic and an open-minded approach to the research as well as to limit the material to a manageable size. The goal is to discover whether generalizations can be made about the nature and quality of communication in this unique setting. Within each of these years, the key primaries are examined, particularly those that were actively contested.

There is major disagreement among observers about whether primaries are hopelessly flawed or basically sound, and about whether one can make generalizations about primaries. Political scientist Larry Bartels defends the present primary system, arguing that it is "capable of producing reasoned collective judgments even about relatively unknown candidates," and that "it is hard to point to an instance in which the existing sequential process has produced the 'wrong' nominee, at least as measured by what we can tell after the fact about the competing candidates' underlying levels of political support" (Bartels, 1988, p. 289). *Washington Post* columnist David Broder, on the other hand, argues that the primaries are in serious need of reform. While "having a few primaries is useful," he says, "when the primaries come to dominate as completely as they do now, they can become a recipe for disaster." He denounces the shift of primaries from a popular referendum to a popularity contest in the big states, proclaiming, "This is no way to pick a president" (Broder, *Washington Post National Weekly Edition*, April 27–May 3, 1992, p. 4).

A second disagreement concerns whether primaries are so bound to the context in which they occur that one should simply study them one by one, or whether they have generic constituents over time. Are there "rules of the game" that define the nature of communication in primaries? Political scientist James Ceaser has argued that "no systematic theory about primary voting is likely to develop, at least for some time, because each campaign is so different" (Ceaser, 1982, p. 65). Bartels, however, has developed a general theory of the dynamics of momentum in the primaries over time (Bartels, 1988). And Corcoran and Kendall (1992) found many fundamental similarities in the politics and communication of the 1912 primaries and those of modern times, which suggests that there may indeed be recurring patterns.

A third question hinges on the definition of the "importance" of the primaries. One position, represented by Patterson (1993), Asher (1992), and Lucy (1973), argues that before 1972 "the primaries were a small part of the contest" (Patterson, 1993, p. 91). They took place in less than one-third of the states, candidates did not have to run in them, and there were few genuine contests in the primaries. From 1972 on, however, with the structural changes introduced by the McGovern–Fraser Commission, there is little disagreement about their importance. Today, "the weekly parade of nearly forty primaries . . . overshadows everything else" (Patterson, 1993, p. 91).

A second position regarding the importance of the primaries, represented by Wattenberg (1985), Wayne (1992), and Busch (1997), is that in the years before 1972 *both* the support of party leaders and popular support in the primaries were involved in the nomination decision process. There was not an equal balance though: "the support of party leaders was clearly paramount" (Wattenberg, 1985, p. 50). Busch (1997) notes the emerging influence of specific state primaries on convention outcomes, a trend he says began in 1948 with the New Hampshire and Wisconsin contests. "Even in 1944," Busch says, "the Wisconsin primary knocked Wendell Willkie out of contention, though it seemed unlikely at the time that he would be nominated, regardless of the outcome" (189 n. 35). In 1948, Harold Stassen's poor performance in the Oregon primary debate and his subsequent loss of the Oregon primary raised serious questions about his electability, though he had won the most Republican primaries (Kirby, 1996–1997), and Thomas Dewey received the Republican nomination at the convention. Wayne (1992) points to 1952 as "the year that primaries began to be an important route to the nomination" (p. 127). Wattenberg (1985) identifies television as being "the major driving force in initiating change in the process," pointing especially to the heavy television coverage of the 1968 primaries, which gave voters the impression that primaries were crucial (p. 50).

The evidence of the effect of winning the primaries on presidential nominations before 1972 is mixed. From 1912 to 1924, the parties regularly ignored the primary winners, though sticking by the incumbents. In 1928 and 1932, the primary winners in both parties received the nominations. In the 1940–1948 period, Democrats supported their incumbent presidents, and Republicans overrode their primary results. In 1952, Democrats selected a nominee who had not entered any of the primaries, and the close primary battle between two leading Republican contenders continued onto the convention floor. From 1956 to the present, however, the winner of the most primaries each year has secured the party's nomination.[2]

A third position on the importance of the primaries adopts a strong communication perspective, arguing that consequentiality is determined by what people pay attention to and talk about. With this perspective, words are actions. Whenever the primaries are treated by the candidates or media as significant events, whenever the public discourse constructs a verbal context in which the primaries are important, they *become* significant events. Gronbeck and Miller (1994) advocate this position, saying, "We must understand that invented political realities are precisely that—realities. What is real in political society is that which is paid attention to, defined, valued, disputed, and ultimately seized powerfully by some segment or another of political society" (p. 7).

The context of the primaries seems especially well suited to persuasion. Because the primaries are held long before the general election, before many people have formed strong opinions, the candidates and media have an unparalleled opportunity to influence their perceptions and to set the agenda in this low-information setting (Patterson, 1980; Kennamer and Chaffee, 1982; Popkin, 1991). In such a situation, media agenda setting and framing can be quite powerful (Protess and McCombs, 1991), but first the public must pay attention. If voter turnout is an indication of interest, there is a problem. In 1992, only 19.6% of eligible voters voted in the primaries (Committee for the Study of the American Electorate, Albany *Times-Union*, July 2, 1992, p. A8).

Another way to determine interest is to ask people. Patterson (1980) found that in the 1976 primaries, only 20% of his respondents reported having a strong interest in the election just before the primaries began, and half said that they had no interest. By April, however, 27% said that they were strongly interested, and another 29% said that they had some interest. FitzSimon (1992) reported a similar trend of increasing interest in the 1992 primaries, though the figures were much higher: Times Mirror polls showed that while only 38% said that they were following the campaign very or fairly closely in the October 3–6, 1991, period, the number was up to 50% by February 20, 1992, and up to 75% by March 26, 1992.

Another kind of investigation concerns the effect of the results of primaries on the popularity of winners and losers. In the 1936–1972 period, Beniger (1976) found that winning in New Hampshire and Wisconsin produced the largest gains in the polls for the candidates, an 8.38 point rise after New Hampshire and a 5.06 point rise after Wisconsin. Losses in Maryland and Wisconsin tended to precipitate the most negative results, with a 3.67 point drop after Maryland, and a 3.38 point drop after Wisconsin. In general, the earlier primaries appeared to have "a greater impact on national voter preferences" (Beniger, 1976, p. 33).

Finally, Wattenberg (1991) discusses the effects of the primaries on the fall general election. He notes that "throughout the history of presidential primaries, divisive primaries have seriously hurt a party's chances of winning those same states in November." The nominee who has done well in the primaries "begins the general election campaign in that state with the image of a winner—both well known and well liked" (p. 49), while those who have done poorly have "a serious handicap" (p. 50).

These research questions about the relative success and failure of the primaries, about the possibility of finding important explanatory principles for their dynamics, and about their importance underlie this investigation.

TOPICS TO BE COVERED

Chapter 2 treats the effect on communication of the changing rules about primaries and the variable role of the political parties. Chapter 3 covers candidate speeches and debates. Chapter 4 treats the use of paid advertising. Chapter 5 discusses the role of the mass media in the primaries in the pre-television age. Chapter 6 examines the role of the media in the television age. Chapter 7 weighs the findings of the 1912–1992 period and tests the patterns found against the experience of the 1996 primaries. These conclusions form the basis for projections about the primaries of 2000 and for a discussion of proposed principles for change.

THE UNIQUE RHETORICAL SITUATION OF THE PRIMARIES

The presidential primary is a twentieth-century phenomenon that grew out of the late-nineteenth-century tradition of party primaries on the local level. Instituted as a sweeping reform in American politics, the presidential primaries were conceived in passionate democratic debate. They were seen by early reformers as a way to take away the power to nominate the president from the party bosses and give it back to "the people." As a result, the primaries became a centerpiece in the Progressive movement of the early twentieth century.

The first presidential primary law was passed in Florida in 1901, and in 1905, "Wisconsin law provided for the direct election of delegates to the national party conventions" through a primary. Oregon was the first state to adopt the preferential primary in 1910, in which voters voted for their favorite candidates, voting for convention delegates separately (Davis, 1997, pp. 14–15). By 1912, there were at least 13 primaries and as many as 21, depending on how the term was defined.[3]

From the first year of multiple primaries, 1912, the primaries created a unique rhetorical situation. They contrasted sharply with the previous situation in which the party leaders decided on the nominees at the summer conventions, and the campaign and election occurred only in the fall.

Six new situational factors now came to bear. First, because the primaries selected delegates for the conventions, they had to be held much earlier in the year than the conventions. Second, instead of there being a one-time event such as the convention, there were multiple events: a series of state primaries and conventions and a national convention. Third, there were multiple candidates openly competing against each other to gain the nomination. The fact that there were multiple candidates led to a fourth difference: the individual candidates rather than the national party took an active role in running their own campaigns. Fifth, the primary elections were intraparty events. Voters selected among candidates in their own party rather than between candidates of opposing parties. And sixth, the primaries were serial; they occurred over a period of several months rather than all at once. Each of these situational factors has influenced the nature of communication in the primaries.

The timing of the primaries is left to the state parties. From the first, the primaries have been held several months before the conventions (in 1912, they began in March; in 1992, they began in February). The trend has been for more and more states to hold their primaries early, as the power of the early primaries has become evident. Thus, while in 1968 the only primary held before mid-March was New Hampshire's, by 1988, 20 states did so (Cook, in Nelson, 1989, p. 28). This "frontloading" of the primaries pushes the planning back even earlier, with many consequences. Now the pre-primary period has become an important factor in the campaign. Candidates need to organize their staffs, raise money, announce their candidacies, conduct polls, take part in straw votes at party gatherings, and try to attract media attention months and even years before the primaries. Instead of the relatively short, two-month campaign of the general election period, from September until Election Day, the primaries lengthen the whole process to at least one year.

The effect of this long campaign on communication is enormous. Little-known candidates must raise enough money to pay staff, travel to the primary states and, through speeches and advertising, keep their names before the public for many months, while well-known candidates who hold office normally leave their jobs at frequent intervals to campaign in the primary states. By January or sooner, media organizations have assigned reporters to follow the candidates who are considered the major contenders, and as long as the candidates continue to run, they live in a fishbowl. By April, reporters are grumbling publicly about the never-ending campaign. "It has been seven weeks now since the whole presidential primary process began in New Hampshire," said ABC anchor Peter Jennings, "it only seems like seven years" (ABC, April 7, 1992).

This book focuses on the primaries mainly in the election year itself, starting with events in January.

The primary campaign calendar contains many election days, not just one, a condition that requires great organizational skill and planning. In 1912, there were between 13 and 21 primaries; in 1932, 17 primaries; in 1952, 15 primaries; in 1972, 23 primaries; and in 1992, 37 Republican and 38 Democratic primaries in the states, as well as primaries in the District of Columbia and Puerto Rico. To plan well for several primaries that are clustered together is particularly difficult. In 1992, the New Hampshire primary was held on February 18, followed by the South Dakota primary on February 25, and Colorado, Georgia, and Maryland on March 3. Three more states held primaries on March 7, one on March 8, and 12 on Super Tuesday, March 10, and they continued through June 2. In between were state caucuses. The inability to organize for many primaries and not just one proved fatal in Senator Gary Hart's 1984 campaign. When he won in an upset against Vice President Walter Mondale in New Hampshire, Hart was unprepared to capitalize on his advantage, as he had no organization in many of the later primary states.

The fact that there are multiple primary elections lends an air of confusion to the process. The primaries are a uniquely American institution. Nowhere else in the world does anyone have to go through as many as 40 distinct and geographically separated elections in a four-month period. In fact, when described that way, the idea sounds absurd.

Not only are there multiple primaries, but there are multiple candidates as well. The increase in the number of candidates was greatly encouraged by the passage of the Federal Election Campaign Act of 1974 and the 1976 amendment, which provided campaign matching funds to primary candidates, enabling people who were not wealthy to run. But even in 1912, three prominent Republicans ran in the Republican primaries, and two prominent Democrats plus favorite-son candidates ran in the Democratic primaries. In 1992, there were two Republicans and five Democrats. In 1988, with no incumbent president running, there were seven Democrats and six Republicans.

One effect of having multiple candidates is that it is much more difficult to inform the voters about the candidates. Except for the candidates who are already well known, voter knowledge is low. In 1992, none of the Democrats were well known nationally before the primaries; in 1988, the only Democrats with high national visibility were Jesse Jackson and Gary Hart, and both had high negative evaluations. Among the Republicans, in both 1988 and 1992, George Bush had a great advantage in name recognition, as did Senator Robert Dole; the other Republicans were little known.

With many candidates to follow around, members of the press are distributed rather thinly. Both for television and newspapers, the "news hole" is only so large, making it difficult to squeeze in stories about all of the candidates. Kendall (1993) found that the length of time spent covering candidates' speeches on network news averaged 18 seconds per episode in February 1992 and 17 seconds in March. In April, when only three candidates were being covered, the average time increased to 27 seconds.

A second result of the multiple candidacies is that candidates are seldom able to win a majority of votes in a primary until the field of candidates is reduced in size. They win by plurality rather than majority, and frequently the percentages are quite close. Of what significance was it, for example, that Pat Buchanan won the 1996 New Hampshire Republican primary by gaining 1% more votes than Bob Dole? Thus the *meaning* of the primary outcome can be as hotly contested as the election itself.

Given the voters' difficulty in learning enough about a long slate of primary candidates, a New Hampshire drugstore clerk's remark during the 1988 primary is not surprising. A week before the election, the author asked her how she would vote. "I've narrowed it down to three candidates," she replied. Samuel L. Popkin's research reports that in 1984, 27% to 49% of the primary voters decided for whom to vote in the campaign's last week. The results for 1988 were similar (Popkin, 1991, p. 115). In research comparing the effects of debates during the primaries and the general election in 1988, Lenart reports that while subjects found it simple to confer winner or loser status on the two candidates debating in the general election, that was not true in the primary debates, where he found a "dearth of direct debate exposure effects." He concludes that "judging comparative debate performances in a field of six candidates is much harder than in a field of two candidates" (Lenart, 1994, p. 103).

A third effect of having multiple candidates is that the majority of votes may be divided among several candidates who have similar views, resulting in a victory by a candidate who is not representative of the majority. This happened in 1972, when Governor George Wallace of Alabama won the Florida Democratic primary, and the moderate candidates divided the rest of the vote. It also happened in 1976, when Governor Jimmy Carter won the New Hampshire primary with 29% of the vote, and the four more liberal Democrats together gained 60% of the vote.

Unlike the general election, where the parties give their all to the party nominees, candidates in the primaries organize their own campaigns. They are much more dependent on their hand-picked campaign managers and staffs and their independent fund-raising efforts than they would be in the fall campaign. Even in 1912, 1932, and 1952, when the majority of states did not have primaries and the majority of convention delegates were chosen in state party conventions, most of the primary candidates relied heavily on individual campaign organizations rather than on the national party for campaign planning. The exception is in the case of the incumbent president; the national party played an influential role in the candidacies of incumbent Presidents William Howard Taft in 1912 and Herbert Hoover in 1932, and in support of former presidential candidate Al Smith in 1932.

Since the contest is strictly intraparty rather than between parties, the candidates' competing campaigns stress the personal traits of the candidates more than the party positions. They have a narrower ground for issue disagreements than if they were members of different parties, and in order to differentiate themselves, they stress their personal qualifications and ideas and attack their opponents on these grounds. Howell Raines has described Ronald Reagan's 1980 primary campaign as a "revolution by personality," in which he "marched through the primaries with such forceful, overarching personal appeal that he developed the clout to drag the party" with him on social issues ("The Future of Tolerance," New York Times, August 14, 1996, p. A20). In 1992, Clinton's attack on Tsongas for being pompous, Tsongas's suggestion that he was more honest than Clinton, and Kerrey's capitalization on Clinton's draft avoidance were the kinds of character issues typically found in the primaries rather than the broad policy disagreements of the parties.

Another way in which the intraparty nature of the primaries influences communication is that party unity is threatened. When politicians of the same party direct attacks against each other in contest after contest, the potential for causing irreparable damage is always present. In 1972, when political analyst Theodore H. White was interviewed on CBS, he said that the primaries were "rending" the Democratic Party (CBS News Special Report, April 4, 1972, Nixon Project, 5255). Wattenberg has pointed out that the party with the longest nomination campaign loses the election (Wattenberg, 1991), although this did not prove to be true in 1992.

Because the primaries occur in serial order rather than all on one day, the outcome of a primary one week has the potential of influencing subsequent primaries. This happened in 1992 when Jerry Brown won the Connecticut primary two weeks before the New York primary. This was so unexpected (Clinton had been expected to win) that the news media covered it as a major upset and suggested that Clinton's predicted win in New York was now in jeopardy. During the days between those primaries, there was an upsurge in voter doubts about Clinton's viability as a candidate.

In 1988, Senator Al Gore failed to take into account the serial influence of the primaries upon each other. He focused his campaign in the South, not campaigning as vigorously in Iowa or New Hampshire, where the first two events of the primary-caucus period occur. He did poorly in the Iowa caucuses and in the New Hampshire primary; thus he missed out on the opportunity to use these events to gain momentum for the contests that followed. By the time the Southern primaries arrived, Governor Michael Dukakis already had this momentum, and Gore's Southern victories did nothing to counteract the perception that he was only a regional candidate.

A final effect of the serial nature of the primaries is "winnowing," where, one by one, the candidates drop out of the race, narrowing the contest. If the primaries were all held on one day, presumably the losers would drop out all at once. But because these contests occur over several months and in different geographic areas, candidates hang on if possible until the primaries reach friendly terrain for them. Thus, in 1992, Iowa Senator Tom Harkin waited until a primary was held in a farm state (South Dakota) to see if he could recoup his losses. Candidates sometimes suspend their campaigning to save their resources, rejoining the battle later when they may have a better chance, as Pat Buchanan did in 1992, emerging again in the California primary.

The media contribute to this winnowing, giving the most coverage to the front-runners and to the ones who do better than expected, and giving much less coverage to those who do poorly in the primaries or those who are running far back in the polls. They use the primaries as evidence of a candidate's viability, which is of major concern to the voters and to campaign donors. Thus, as candidates flounder in the primaries, their money dries up, and one by one they withdraw, or are "winnowed," from the race.

SETTING THE SCENE: CONTEXT OF THE PRIMARIES[4]

Party primaries are a peculiarly American institution, first used for nominating candidates for local office in California and New York in 1866 and increasingly in other states in the late nineteenth century (Wolfe, 1966). The first year in which there were numerous presidential primaries was 1912, and primary laws quickly spread; there were 20 primaries in 1916. The number then declined and fluctuated between 13 and 20 through 1968 (Davis, 1997, p. 14). Presidential candidates could not afford to ignore the primaries entirely, but the majority of convention delegates were selected at state party conventions and caucuses, and the decision about who the candidate would be was made at the national convention and not in the primaries.

The resurgence in interest and power of the primaries came in 1972. The Democratic Party's McGovern–Fraser Commission prepared guidelines to ensure that state parties would select convention delegates in a fair, open, and timely fashion. These reforms were intended to correct perceived abuses of the past, particularly the control over the selection of national convention delegates by party "bosses." The Democratic state parties complied with these guidelines, and the Republicans followed suit, with the result that many states adopted new or revised presidential primary laws. The number of state presidential primaries has grown from 15 in 1968 to 32 Democratic and 40 Republican primaries in 1996 (*Congressional Quarterly Weekly Report*, August 3 and August 17, 1996). Now the American presidential pre-convention primary season has stretched into a "marathon." Candidates, convinced by studies showing that early impressions formed by voters during the primary season last "throughout the campaign" (Patterson, 1980, p. 150), "surface" early and establish campaign efforts in dozens of states.

The McGovern–Fraser Commission reforms echoed those of the redoubtable Wisconsin reformer, Senator Robert M. LaFollette, Sr., a Progressive Republican and long-standing leader of the direct democracy movement. In the early twentieth century, he too wanted to overturn the power of the bosses. By adopting the presidential primary law, he said, "No longer . . . will there stand between the voter and the official a political machine with a complicated system of caucuses and conventions, by the manipulation of which it thwarts the will of the voter and rules of official conduct" (Ranney, 1975, p. 124).

BASIC FACTS ABOUT THE PRIMARIES, 1912–1992

The 1912 Primaries

In 1912, the Republican primaries were fought out among three candidates: the incumbent president, William Howard Taft, the former president, Theodore Roosevelt, and the Wisconsin senator, Robert M. LaFollette, Sr. On the Democratic side, the battle was between New Jersey Governor Woodrow Wilson and Speaker of the House of Representatives Beauchamp ("Champ") Clark from Missouri, along with several favorite-son candidates. Since the Republicans were the dominant party, having occupied the White House with only two interruptions since the Civil War (separate terms served by Grover Cleveland), most of the attention was focused on the "battle of the giants" between Republicans Taft and Roosevelt. Roosevelt and the Progressives believed that President Taft "had 'sold out' on tariffs, antitrust, and reform in general" (Ceaser and Busch, 1997, p. 49).

Roosevelt won the majority of the primaries, including larger states such as Illinois, Pennsylvania, Maryland, Ohio, New Jersey, and California. The delegate count was Roosevelt 278, Taft 48, and LaFollette 36 (Davis, 1980, p. 47). Ultimately, however, Taft's control over state Republican organizations gained him the nomination at the June convention in Chicago, often by tactics that reversed Roosevelt's primary victories, replacing or nullifying the Roosevelt delegates with "at-large" or substitute delegations pledged to Taft. Having been denied the Republican nomination, Roosevelt forces returned to Chicago six weeks later to nominate him as the "Bull Moose" candidate for the Progressive Party. The three-way split of votes in the general election produced a Democratic victory for Wilson, with Roosevelt running second and Taft third.

Among the Democrats, the contest between Clark and Wilson was so close that it is difficult to say who won the primaries. The official record says that each of them won five primaries, with Wilson taking 45% of the vote and Clark 42% (*Guide to U.S. Elections*, 1975, p. 314). But this does not take into account other primaries alluded to in the press; there was some confusion over which contests to call "primaries." At the convention, Clark actually gained a majority of the delegates after an all-night session, but the Democrats required a two-thirds majority (Warner, 1956, p. 259).[5] After a long, hard fight "between conservatives and progressives, the Democratic National Convention . . . nominated Wilson on the forty-sixth ballot" (Hogan and Andrews, 1995, p. 113).

The reform ideal of using the primaries to ensure that the "voice of the people" would prevail over "the bosses" achieved no clear result in the Democratic Party and was clearly stymied in the Republican Party. Nor did the primaries bring forth a flush of fresh voices with intimate ties to the common citizens; instead, the candidates were major party figures and long-time holders of political office.

The 1912 primaries established precedents for future elections. While this may seem obvious or trivial, one need only reflect upon quite different, but no less plausible, precedents that might have been set. The entry of Roosevelt, with his extraordinary personality and popularity, was itself an unusual case. Having rejected another presidential term in 1908, he might well have refused to run. It is equally plausible that Taft and his rivals could have reached an agreement not to engage actively in the novel primary process, thus establishing a very different precedent. In any case, the cast of candidates is revealing, especially the leading roles played by LaFollette and Roosevelt. LaFollette had a formidable national reputation as a missionary of progressive reform. Roosevelt was a popular former president, a self-styled hero, and an internationally acclaimed man of peace and derring-do. One has to face the hypothesis that presidential primaries served as vehicles for long-established national party leaders in a struggle for power rather than as openings for new candidates to emerge from a process of democratic selection to express and represent interests previously suppressed by party organizations.

In 1912, the first primary was in North Dakota; in 1992, the first primary was in New Hampshire. In each case, the fact that these were the *first* primaries made these events extremely important. They established precedents and were instrumental in setting the agenda for the rest of the campaign. LaFollette won decisively in North Dakota after a bitter fight between his and Roosevelt's supporters, and suddenly the media and the public were speculating about the vulnerability of Roosevelt and Taft. The *New York Times* stated that "the little Badger candidate [LaFollette] has manifested unexpected staying powers" (March 21, 1912). LaFollette had campaigned actively in North Dakota, whereas Roosevelt had not, and Taft, who received only 3% of the vote, had barely a token presence.

The presidential primary had introduced a dramatically new situation: a contest of aspirants, including even the president of the United States as a mere "candidate" for the people's votes. The signal from North Dakota was that the candidate who campaigned in person would have a clear advantage, and so the candidates set off on the long campaign trail. The primaries in 1912 extended from March 19 in North Dakota until June 4 in South Dakota, and the campaign trail took its toll. In the most populous states of the East and Midwest, the candidates traveled extensively, often giving 10 to 15 whistle-stop speeches each day. Taft traveled less than Roosevelt due to presidential responsibilities in Washington. Nonetheless, the trips of the candidates grew longer as the campaign developed.

In 1912 only men voted, but women were invited to the rallies and speeches with notices such as "Galleries Reserved for Ladies and Escorts" and "Seats Reserved for the Ladies" ("Republican Mass Meeting," *Baltimore American*, May 3, 1912, p. 18; "For Woodrow Wilson," *The Salisbury Advertiser* (MD), May 4, 1912, p. 4).

As a result of the intensive campaigning by the candidates, the Republican primaries produced polling figures several times greater than the more sedate Democratic primary (Davis, 1980, pp. 279–281).

The need for candidates to publicize their cause was not new in 1912. The traditional state convention system for selecting delegates to the national convention also had required candidates to mobilize their financial and personnel resources, to legitimize their candidacies through endorsements, to publicize their public record, and to take positions on issues. But the candidate's effort to establish credibility as a leader and a winner and to activate the party leaders and factions who selected delegates was, in the state convention system, a small-scaled, narrowly focused process.

In the presidential primaries, this process was greatly magnified and expanded into a sustained appeal to the tens or hundreds of thousands of existing and potential party members. Thus the presidential primary campaign did not suddenly appear as a novel form of electoral behavior.

Yet the momentum of the primaries in 1912, in a real sense, fed upon itself. In large part, it was a campaign about whether to have a campaign. This was a dynamic that forced the candidates to improvise as the primaries unfolded. The need for improvisation is evident, for example, in the fact that when Roosevelt declared his candidacy only seven primaries were scheduled, but his supporters worked and succeeded in at least doubling that number (David et al., 1964, p. 194). Inevitably, the candidates as well as the parties were forced into novel strategies and, at least for the Republicans, catastrophic decisions. The incumbent president's party was defeated by the electoral appeal of its own greatest hero, Roosevelt, whose popularity the primaries not only demonstrated but fashioned into repudiation and humiliation for the incumbent, Taft. In November, Wilson won with 6,300,000 votes to 4,200,000 for Roosevelt and 3,500,000 for Taft.

It was obvious from the 1912 experience that the presidential primaries were not a surefire way to guarantee that the "voice of the people" would prevail over the party bosses, as the reformers had hoped. Still, that had been the first real attempt, and "by 1916 . . . presidential primary laws had been passed in twenty-five states" (Davis, 1997, p. 15). The results that year and in subsequent years established, however, that the primaries were merely advisory to the party bosses and did not determine the nominee. In the period 1912–1968, according to Geer (1989, p. 2), "In competitive races for the nomination, the top vote getter in the primaries became the nominee only about 40 percent of the time, showing that party leaders often ignored the advice offered by voters in primaries."

The next two primaries discussed, those of 1932 and 1952, came in this period of "weak primaries." Nominees were still chosen at conventions; primaries were relatively few in number and thus advisory to the party bosses. Yet many of these primaries were fiercely fought, and for the participating candidates they were seen as an important opportunity to prove their strength and electability and to prevent other candidates from getting a first-ballot victory at the convention.

The 1932 Primaries

In 1932, incumbent president Herbert Hoover had the nomination for the asking, in spite of the dire economic situation. The omens were not good for the Republican Party. In the 1930 elections, the Democrats had recaptured control of the House of Representatives and come within one vote of controlling the Senate (down from a Republican majority of 16). Democrats also captured the majority of the gubernatorial positions (18–13, with one Farmer–Labor). However, there was a strong tradition of parties giving their incumbent presidents a second nomination. In addition, although Hoover had opponents within his party, and the party feared a defeat because of the Depression, no prominent Republican would agree to run against him. Anti-Hooverites boosted the names of two possible contenders, Senator Dwight Morrow of New Jersey and former President Calvin Coolidge, but Senator Morrow died in October 1931, and during that same month, Coolidge published a long article urging Hoover's re-election (*Saturday Evening Post*, October 3, 1931).

Hoover's only opponent in the Republican primaries was former Senator Joseph I. France of Maryland, a conservative Republican, who entered and won several primaries where he was unopposed. However, in each of those states, the primaries were *nonbinding* presidential preference primaries, only advisory to the party conventions, and the party conventions committed their delegates to Hoover (Peel and Donnelly, 1935). During the primary campaign period, therefore, rather than campaigning against each other, the Republicans spent most of their energy trying to improve the president's popularity, which was extremely low, and attacking the Democrats.

On the Democratic side, Governor Franklin D. Roosevelt of New York declared his candidacy on January 23, 1932. He was seen as the front-runner, but many other Democrats wanted the nomination. They therefore worked to prevent him from getting enough delegates for a first-ballot victory at the convention, and the 17 primaries offered a way to do that. His strongest opponent was former New York Governor and 1928 Democratic Party presidential nominee Al Smith, who on February 8, 1932, said he would "make the fight" if chosen by the Democratic Convention, but that he would not "make a pre-convention campaign to secure . . . delegates" (Josephson and Josephson, 1969, p. 436).

Favorite-son candidates also emerged. For example, John Nance Garner, the Speaker of the House of Representatives from Texas, "was skyrocketed into the Democratic horizon by William Randolph Hearst, the publisher." In a New Year's address (January 1932) broadcast from Los Angeles over the National Broadcasting Company's' network, "Mr. Hearst pronounced Mr. Garner the nation's one great hope," denouncing the other Democrats as "internationalists" (Peel and Donnelly, 1935, p. 37). Garner won the California primary and the support of the Texas delegation. Of the 17 Democratic primaries, Roosevelt won 11, Smith 2, and other candidates 3, with the New York delegates uninstructed. At the convention, where support of two-thirds of the delegates was required to win the nomination, Roosevelt did not have enough votes. Hearst helped arrange the ticket: Garner gave Roosevelt his 90 delegates in exchange for the vice presidency, pushing Roosevelt over the top on the fourth ballot.

Roosevelt's advantage in both the primaries and the state conventions was due to several factors. First, he had won a dramatic victory in the

New York governor's race in 1930, winning in Republican upstate areas as well as downstate. Second, he had already achieved a leadership position in the party by being the Democratic vice-presidential candidate in 1924, and by giving two memorable convention speeches nominating Al Smith in 1924 and 1928. Third, Roosevelt had worked long and hard to become known and liked by the party leaders around the country, corresponding with them and calling them. Fourth, he had an effective campaign team in James Farley and Louis Howe.

Farley, the New York State Democratic chairman, seized the occasion of Roosevelt's 1930 victory to give a statement to the papers "in which he announced that he 'fully' expected 'that the call [for the 1932 presidential nomination] will come to Governor Roosevelt when the first Presidential primary is held' " (Warner, 1956, p. 249). He traveled around the country in 1931 meeting party leaders and praising Roosevelt, then followed up on his visits by launching a persuasive letter-writing campaign to the thousands of people he had met. Farley, Roosevelt, and Howe communicated frequently by telephone, and Howe was a close personal adviser to Roosevelt. Finally, in the campaign itself, Roosevelt made skillful use of polls and speeches.

Al Smith was not without his resources, however. He had loyal supporters from the 1928 campaign, and he had good reason to believe that "the party already knew him and what he stood for," based on his long service, and the public knew him too. He had "covered about 30,000 miles" in the 1928 campaign, he said (Smith, May 24, 1930). He had selected the chairman of the Democratic National Committee, John J. Raskob, and Mr. Raskob campaigned tirelessly for him in 1932, as did Jouett Shouse, chairman of the executive committee of the Democratic National Committee.

Smith was a strong candidate in solidly "wet" areas in large Eastern cities; though Roosevelt also favored the wet position on Prohibition, Smith advocated making this the leading issue in the campaign, rather than the economy. In addition, Smith was the beneficiary of the "stop-Roosevelt" movement, winning support from people who, for whatever reason, wanted someone other than Roosevelt. He won the Massachusetts and New Jersey primaries, and he did well in Pennsylvania; his supporters also were instrumental in deciding that the delegates selected in the New York primary would be uninstructed rather than pledged to a candidate. In contrast to the Roosevelt campaign, however, he "started very late, and really had no organization to speak of" (Robert Moses, in Josephson and Josephson, 1969, p. 441).

In the end, the primaries were not decisive in 1932. While Roosevelt won the majority of delegates selected in the primaries and in the state conventions, there were not enough primaries to enable him to win two-thirds of the delegates. Nor did Smith win the one-third he needed to prevent Roosevelt from getting the nomination. Roosevelt's nomination was negotiated at the convention. The vote in November was Roosevelt 22,800,000, Hoover 15,800,000.

The 1952 Primaries

In the 1952 primaries (13 Republican, 16 Democratic), the chief Republican contenders were General Dwight D. Eisenhower, the Supreme Commander, Europe, of the North Atlantic Treaty Organization (NATO) and World War II general (Supreme Commander of All Allied Expeditionary Forces), and the powerful Senator Robert A. Taft of Ohio, known as "Mr. Republican." Although Eisenhower agreed to have his name entered in the primaries, he remained in Europe throughout the campaign, returning only in the last week. In his absence, his entire campaign was run by other people. Taft, in contrast, campaigned actively in the primaries.

The chief Democratic contender was Senator Estes Kefauver of Tennessee, the first candidate to use a "run everywhere" strategy in the presidential primaries (Busch, 1997, p. 176). He "won twelve of fifteen preference primaries and 64 percent of the primary vote (there were also two pure delegate primaries)" (Busch, 1997, p. 133). But the Democratic picture was complicated by the fact that incumbent President Harry Truman waited to decide not to run for re-election until March 29, 1952. Thus, many would-be candidates deferred their decisions until they knew what he would do. A January Gallup poll showed that Truman had the most support (36%) among the Democrats, though this figure was hardly a vote of confidence.

In another twist in the Democratic situation, many Democrats wanted someone whose name was not entered in the primaries to run, Governor Adlai E. Stevenson of Illinois. When they prevailed upon Stevenson, he said he was a candidate for one office only, for re-election as governor of Illinois. But he did not close the door irrevocably. Some of his supporters therefore mounted a secret publicity campaign, code named "Operation Wintergreen,"[6] to promote Stevenson's name, attempting to keep his name fresh in the news throughout the primary period. Though "Wintergreen" was not a primary election campaign, but rather a campaign for attention and popularity, it is relevant to this discussion because Kefauver had to deal with the shadow of Stevenson as his secret opponent. Stevenson's name was constantly mentioned by party leaders and the media as a likely candidate, indicating that the primaries were not viewed as conclusive in any sense. There was a good excuse to do stories on him, as he was running for re-election as governor of Illinois. And President Truman frequently said positive things about him, giving him even more visibility.

Despite Kefauver's primary victories and public popularity,[7] Stevenson was selected as the party's nominee on the third ballot at the Democratic Convention.[8]

The Democrats were on the defensive in 1952. The Korean War was in progress, Republican Senator Joseph McCarthy of Wisconsin was searching for Communists in government and claiming to find them, and the Democratic administration was tarred with findings that the Reconstruction Finance Corporation had made loans under pressure from prominent Democrats. The Republicans summed up the key issues against the Democrats with the slogan "Korea, Communism, and Corruption." The famous columnist Walter Lippmann, a strong supporter of Eisenhower, declared that the "Eisenhower movement" was about "raising the standard of public life" ("The Eisenhower Movement," *New York Herald Tribune*, March 17, 1952, p. 21).

With the Republicans setting the campaign agenda as the foreign policy ineptitude and the domestic corruption of the Democrats, they needed a candidate who would be strong in both areas. A Gallup poll in the spring of 1951 suggested that Eisenhower might be that man; he led all other Republicans among Republicans polled, and among Democrats he was preferred 40% to 20% over President Truman. A poll in August 1951 pointed to potential problems with a Taft candidacy: though five-sixths of Republicans had a favorable opinion of him, over half of Independent voters disapproved (Patterson, 1972, p. 514).

Eisenhower had resisted earlier efforts by both Democrats and Republicans to get him to seek the presidential nomination. However, a group of Republicans led by Senator Henry Cabot Lodge II of Massachusetts and New York Governor Thomas E. Dewey pursued him doggedly. In addition to their personal entreaties and much positive editorial advocacy by the Eastern press, the Eisenhower advocates staged an impressive rally to convince Eisenhower that there was a real "groundswell" of support for him. As William Safire, who worked on the rally directed by Tex McCrary, recounts the story, the Northeastern liberal Republicans "put on a rally at Madison Square Garden and filled it with 18,000 screaming people calling for Ike." They got Irving Berlin to write a campaign song, "I Like Ike," and they made a kinescope of the whole event, which was flown to Paris by the famous woman pilot Jacqueline Cochrane. Now Eisenhower "could see the people—he didn't know that we got them by bus loads and brought them in—calling out for him." And then Eisenhower agreed that they could enter his name in the New Hampshire primary of March 11 (Safire, November 6, 1997, p. 26). His chief opponents there were Taft and former Minnesota Governor Harold Stassen, with a short flurry of activity for General Douglas MacArthur as well.

The 1952 New Hampshire presidential primary proved enormously important, not only in the results (Eisenhower defeated Taft and Stassen decisively, and Kefauver defeated Truman, 55% to 45%) but also in the media coverage of the primary, and in the subsequent interpretation of the results by the party and the media. Eisenhower's victory suggested that he would be able to survive the primary contests without returning to the country. It also laid to rest questions about whether he was really a candidate, as not only did he win in a large Republican turnout, but he also wrote a letter to New Hampshire Republicans expressing his gratitude for their votes, saying, "could I express to the Republican voters of New Hampshire my profound appreciation of the extraordinary compliment they have paid me?" (in David Lawrence, "Eisenhower Cable to Adams Called Proof of Frankness," *New York Herald Tribune*, March 14, 1952, p. 4).

Kefauver's victory over Truman suggested both the president's vulnerability to other Democrats in the primaries and to Republicans in the general election. Truman had not campaigned in New Hampshire, and he had pooh-poohed the importance of primaries, referring to the New Hampshire primary as "eyewash" (quoted in David Lawrence, "New Hampshire Puts Truman in Position to Insist on 'Draft,' " *New York Herald Tribune*, March 13, 1952, p. 4). It is true that New Hampshire was a Republican state, without a strong Democratic organization, and that the Democratic turnout had been small, and there were only 16 Democratic primaries in all—the majority of convention delegates would be chosen in state conventions, not in the primaries. All of these factors would suggest that Truman had no cause for concern. But as one columnist wrote, "the press and radio and television have whipped up considerable interest in the primaries" (David Lawrence, "New Hampshire Puts Truman in Position to Insist on 'Draft,' " *New York Herald Tribune*, March 13, 1952, p. 4). The New Hampshire primary was the first primary, and therefore it drew more attention; the Eisenhower candidacy had increased this attention. While the "weak primaries" system was still in effect, and no one expected the Democratic Convention to be much influenced by primary results, this dramatic and unexpected loss by the president could not have encouraged him in his decision about whether to run again.

A final significant factor about the 1952 New Hampshire primary was that Taft and Eisenhower displayed such different approaches to the media. Taft had an old-fashioned, interpersonal style, while Eisenhower's style was better adapted to the newer, electronic media. Taft campaigned in New Hampshire and in subsequent primaries, much as his father, President William Howard Taft, had campaigned in 1912, negotiating with the party leaders and making whirlwind speaking tours to meet the voters. Eisenhower, in contrast, remained in Paris and let newsreels and television beam his handsome, uniformed image back to the voters, as radio news and newspapers reported on his words and deeds. It is true that his surrogates gave speeches on his behalf and worked with the state Republican organizations; otherwise there would have been no campaign. But Eisenhower's own involvement was almost entirely mediated, until he returned to the United States in June.

In the end, the primary contest between Eisenhower and Taft was very close: Taft won six, Eisenhower won five (Mayer, 1996a). Both had support from major party leaders. The contest continued on to the Republican Convention, which selected Eisenhower. The final vote in November was Eisenhower 33,900,000, Stevenson 27,300,000.

The 1972 Primaries

In 1972, the primaries took on a much more dominant role in the selection of the presidential nominee because of their increase in numbers. There was an abrupt increase from 15 primaries in 1968 to 23 in 1972, and these races accounted for 60% of the convention delegates. This change was the result of the reforms of the Democratic Party's McGovern–Fraser Commission, which prepared guidelines to ensure that state parties would select convention delegates in a manner which was fair, open, and timely. The Democratic state parties complied with these guidelines, and the Republicans soon adopted similar rules.

While President Nixon's popularity had dropped in 1971, according to a Gallup poll, the tradition of supporting an incumbent for re-election is a strong one, and only two Republican Congressmen made any attempt to contest Nixon's renomination. One was Paul N. "Pete" McCloskey Jr. of California, who challenged Nixon in the primaries to focus attention on his opposition to the war in Vietnam. A second was conservative John Ashbrook of Ohio, who charged that "Nixon had embraced wage and price guidelines, signed arms control treaties with the Soviets, and gone soft on Red China" (Ceaser and Busch, 1993, p. 49). Neither made any headway, however. Nixon entered and won all 23 primaries, but he did not personally campaign in any of them (Magruder, 1974, pp. 171–172). Instead, he spent the primary campaign period acting "presidential," including taking much-heralded trips to China and the Soviet Union.

Among the Democrats, however, 15 candidates announced that they were running, and at least six were considered serious contenders: Senator Edmund Muskie of Maine, the only contender to enter all of the primaries (Naughton, 1972); Senator George McGovern of South Dakota; Senator Hubert Humphrey of Minnesota; Senator Henry Jackson of Washington; Governor George Wallace of Alabama; and Mayor John Lindsay of New York. Muskie was seen as the leading candidate in January 1972: the Harris poll of that month showed him tied with Nixon for 42% of the vote each, with Wallace receiving 11% of the support.

The watershed moments in the Democratic race were the primaries in New Hampshire (March 7), Florida (March 14), Wisconsin (April 4), and California (June 6), as well as the shooting of George Wallace on May 15. Each of these events had a decisive impact of some kind. In New Hampshire, front-runner Muskie failed to live up to the expectation that he would win at least 50% of the primary vote. Instead, he received 46.4% of the vote. At the same time, McGovern, who had stood at 3% in the Gallup poll in January, surged to an amazing 37.2% of the vote. The press covered the story as a major decline for the front-runner and began to pay closer attention to McGovern. Muskie plummeted fast after that, doing poorly in most of the subsequent primaries (except for Illinois), and he dropped out of the campaign on April 26.

In Florida, one week after the New Hampshire primary, Democratic primary votes were divided among 11 candidates. The issue of busing for racial balance dominated the campaign. Wallace won, outpolling the others by far, and many of the Democrats who had hoped to make their mark there—Lindsay, Jackson, and Muskie—did poorly. Within one week, then, the effects of only two primaries were to turn campaign expectations on their head and to focus public attention not only on Muskie but also on McGovern, Humphrey, and Wallace.

The Wisconsin primary was a triumph for McGovern in this state adjoining Humphrey's home state of Minnesota: the top three candidates were McGovern 30%, Wallace 22%, and Humphrey 21%. McGovern was now seen as the clear front-runner. The effectiveness of his grassroots organization was much observed and commented upon. The Wisconsin results raised questions about whether Humphrey would be able to overtake McGovern, as well as what Wallace's role would be. Wallace, at first viewed as a kind of nuisance by Democratic leaders, was fast becoming a serious candidate, winning or coming in second in primaries in the South and Midwest.

On May 15, 1972, on the eve of the Michigan and Maryland primaries, Wallace was shot by Arthur Bremer while campaigning in Maryland. The other candidates immediately suspended their campaigning, including ads, and returned to Washington (*Today*, May 16, 1972, Nixon Project, 5375). The next day, Wallace won the primaries in Michigan and Maryland. Up until this point he had led the field in primaries won (five) and votes gained in the primaries (3.4 million), although McGovern led in the delegate count. However, his shooting changed the campaign dramatically. His wife Cornelia attempted to campaign in his place and at first maintained that the campaign would go on, but it soon became apparent that he was grievously wounded, possibly even paralyzed from the waist down (which proved to be true), and that he would need a long time to recover. The shooting effectively ended his candidacy.

Now the race was down to McGovern and Humphrey. The main battleground would be in California, with its winner-take-all primary, and the question was whether Humphrey could stop McGovern from a first-ballot victory. McGovern defeated Humphrey in California, as expected, and he went on to win a first-ballot victory at the Democratic Convention. But Humphrey's all-out fight in California, as well as his biting attacks on McGovern in their debates, took its toll. McGovern's California victory was not nearly as large as expected: his 15–20 point lead shrank to an Election Day margin of only 5%, as McGovern got 44% and Humphrey 39%. Questions raised by Humphrey about McGovern's competence and judgment were used effectively by the Republicans in the fall campaign.

Polls were widely used by the candidates and the media in the 1972 primaries. According to a PBS report, 74 firms in the country dealt primarily with political polling ("Political Polls," Public Affairs, PBS, April 26, 1972, Nixon Project, 5307). Poll reports were an integral part of news stories and news conferences.

One of the big stories of the 1972 primaries was the way in which McGovern used the new party rules to his advantage. As the chairman of the McGovern–Fraser Commission, which had revised the rules, he knew what they were and how they worked. He was thus able to plan his campaign to win the largest number of delegates in each state by organizing his supporters to back delegates in each district of the state. Other candidates, particularly Wallace, lost substantial power by ignoring the new rules and aiming solely for the popular vote.

The 1992 Primaries

When the war in the Persian Gulf ended in early 1991, President George Bush's approval rating with the American public stood at an amazing 90%. Surely this was an unbeatable incumbent president. That is what most of the potential Democratic contenders seemed to think, for one by one in the summer of 1991 they opted not to run for president: Senator Bill Bradley of New Jersey, Congressman Richard Gephardt of Missouri, Senator Jay Rockefeller of West Virginia, Senator Al Gore of Tennessee, and Senator Lloyd Bentsen of Texas. The Democrats who announced their candidacy were not well known to the nation, and most of them entered the race later than usual. Former Massachusetts Senator Paul Tsongas announced on March 10, 1991, former Mayor of Irvine, California, Larry Agran announced August 22, 1991, and Iowa Senator Tom Harkin, Virginia Governor Douglas Wilder, and former governor of California Edmund (Jerry) Brown, Jr. entered in September. Senator

Bob Kerrey from Nebraska and Governor Bill Clinton of Arkansas entered in October. Two others who had been considered possible candidates announced that they would not run—Jesse Jackson in November and New York Governor Mario Cuomo in December. In January, Wilder withdrew, leaving six Democrats.

The tradition that an incumbent president of one's own party should be supported for a second term is a strong one: "Not since 1856 when James Buchanan replaced Franklin Pierce has a president who sought renomination failed to receive the approval from his party" (Denton and Woodward, 1990, p. 87). Only one prominent Republican took on President Bush in 1992: Patrick Buchanan, former speechwriter and aide to three Republican presidents and a well-known television commentator on the program *Crossfire*. He announced his candidacy on December 10, 1991, arguing that Bush had not been true to the conservative wing of the party and had broken his pledge given at the Republican Convention in 1988: "Read my lips. No new taxes."

After Bush's high point in popularity after the war, in March 1991, his approval ratings began to fall, and his disapproval ratings rose. "By January 1992, a month before the primaries began," half approved and half disapproved of George Bush as president (Baker, 1993, p. 41, citing Gallup surveys). The economy was showing signs of trouble, with unemployment up and housing starts down. The possibility that a Democrat might be able to unseat Bush now occurred to many people, and throughout the primaries there was a groundswell of discontent with the candidates who were running. Again and again in exit polls, the voters said that they wished they had other choices.

The watershed moments in the 1992 Democratic primaries were in New Hampshire, Georgia, Florida, Illinois, Michigan, and New York. Though Clinton was the front-runner going into the New Hampshire primary, questions about whether he had had an affair with a nightclub singer named Gennifer Flowers and whether he had taken steps to avoid being drafted during the Vietnam War and then lied about it seriously eroded his popular support. Tsongas, who lived a few miles across the New Hampshire border in Lowell, Massachusetts, and who had campaigned in New Hampshire day after day after day, won in New Hampshire, and Clinton came in second, with the others trailing far behind.

The Georgia primary of March 3 was more important than expected because of its timing, coming just two weeks after New Hampshire. Clinton won, 57% to 24% over Tsongas, and he went on to win the South Carolina primary on March 7 and all six Southern states on March 10, Super Tuesday, by large margins. After the scandals and his second-place finish in New Hampshire, this was a dramatic demonstration of strength. The Clinton campaign had foreseen that an early victory would be important and persuaded Governor Zell Miller of Georgia to move the Georgia primary one week earlier than Super Tuesday. The decision proved prescient.

A third important moment was in Florida on March 10. Tsongas needed to show that he could win outside of his New England base, that he was not just a regional candidate. He had won in Maryland, but a victory in Florida with its huge delegate count and its large population of transplanted Yankees would give him national stature. However, he failed. Clinton won the Florida primary, and Tsongas did poorly.

By the time of the Illinois and Michigan primaries on March 17, Kerrey and Harkin had dropped out of the race, as they failed to win primaries, and Agran was paid little attention, drawing just a trace of votes. The remaining candidates were Clinton, Brown, and Tsongas. Clinton won both of these large, industrial states, and Brown came in second, demonstrating that Tsongas had little support among the blue-collar workers in the Rust Belt, a vital constituency for the Democrats. Soon after, Tsongas withdrew from the race.

The New York primary of April 7 settled the contest between Brown and Clinton. The charges against Clinton's character resurfaced in this race, as he tried to shake his "Slick Willie" image. After a fierce fight, much intensified by the sensationalist coverage by New York's tabloids, Clinton defeated Brown handily, and he went on to win the remaining primaries and a first-ballot victory at the Democratic Convention. He had "entered 36 primary contests and won 30 of them" (Baker, 1993, p. 59).

In the Republican primaries, Buchanan charged Bush with reneging on his "No New Taxes" pledge and with favoring affirmative action policies that resulted in reverse discrimination against whites. He was most successful in New Hampshire, receiving 37% of the vote to Bush's 53% (with 10% voting for others) and attracting heavy media attention. His vigorous campaign of speeches and advertisements forced Bush out of Washington and onto the campaign trail for a time. But Buchanan never again equaled the percentage of his New Hampshire vote, and by March 17, with lopsided Bush victories in Michigan and Illinois, it was clear that Bush would secure the party's nomination. Bush "ran in 39 primaries and won all of them" (Baker, 1993, p. 59).

Texas businessman and billionaire Ross Perot became a factor in the 1992 campaign starting on February 20, 1992, when he appeared on *Larry King Live* (CNN) and said that he would consider running for president. Though he never entered any of the primaries, he began to receive substantial write-in votes in both Democratic and Republican primaries, beginning in April. According to Busch (1997), "by the time the nominating season ended, Perot write-ins had accounted for a mean of 16.5 percent in three Democratic primaries (Minnesota, Washington, and North Dakota), and 9.5 percent in four Republican primaries (Minnesota, Washington, New Jersey, and North Dakota) (p. 254). The nominations of

Clinton and Bush were never threatened by these votes, but Perot was clearly a force to be reckoned with. In May 1992, Perot led Bush and Clinton in the polls, and both candidates found themselves addressing Perot and his followers in the late primaries of May and June.

The 1992 primaries were characterized by several new and creative methods of communicating with the public, such as Clinton's town meetings, Brown's 1–800 number, and the appearance of candidates on talk shows and the youth-oriented MTV channel.

Unlike Hoover in 1932 and Nixon in 1972, the incumbent president in 1992 was not able to limit his activities to being presidential, in the knowledge that he would be renominated as a matter of course. Bush feared losing the right wing of his party as Buchanan attacked him in the primaries, and he campaigned to win back those voters. Later, near the end of the primary period when there was no doubt about his renomination, he found it necessary to fight off the verbal attacks of Perot in an attempt to limit the damage to his policies and record, and to better his position in the polls. The final vote in November was Clinton 44,900,000, Bush 39,100,000, and Perot 19,700,000.

With this brief overview of the primaries of 1912–1992 completed, we now turn to the role of the parties' rules in primary campaign communication.

NOTES

1. In 1988, 1992, and 1996, the author traveled with the media in New Hampshire during the 8 to 10 days before the New Hampshire primary on a press pass from radio station WAMC in Albany, New York, a National Public Radio affiliate. In addition to conducting research on the primary, she also called in several stories to the station during each trip.

Many of the examples used in this book are based on the author's personal observations in New Hampshire.

2. Except for the unusual occurrence in 1968, when President Lyndon B. Johnson shocked the nation by announcing on April 1 that he would not run for re-election, thereby catapulting Vice President Hubert Humphrey into a presidential candidacy. Humphrey had not entered any of the primaries, but he won the party's nomination at the Chicago convention.

3. Davis (1997) reports that there were 12 Democratic primaries and 13 Republican primaries in 1912. Contemporary newspaper accounts, however, mention 21.

4. Much of the general historical background and 1912 information appeared earlier in Corcoran and Kendall (1989, 1992).

5. The two-thirds majority rule remained until 1936 (Busch and Ceaser, 1996, p. 334).

6. The name "Wintergreen" refers to a flavor of chewing gum. It also refers to a character in the Broadway musical satire "Of Thee I Sing," which "won a

Pulitzer Prize during the Hoover–Roosevelt campaign year of 1932." John P. Wintergreen is a presidential candidate who "is so desperate for an issue that he runs on a platform of love" (Rich, 1996).

7. According to Busch (1997), "Kefauver was able to turn his primary victories into front-running status among the public at large: days before the convention opened, polls showed him with 45% to Alben Barkley with 18, Adlai Stevenson with 23, Richard Russell with 10, and Averell Harriman with 5" (p. 133).

8. In 1956, Stevenson did run in the primaries, but only after Kefauver's "stunning back-to-back primary victories in New Hampshire and in Minnesota" (Busch, 1997, p. 135). His wins in Florida and California were important in securing the Democratic nomination. According to Troy (1991), Stevenson found the primaries "undignified, 'banal,' and exhausting"; at the end, he said he was " 'squeezed and wasted' " (p. 204).

Chapter 2

Primary Rules and Their Impact on Communication

Ranney (1977, p. 4) defined the direct primary system in this way:

(1) the parties' nominees to public office are chosen directly by rank-and-file party members rather than indirectly by their representatives in caucuses and conventions; and (2) they are chosen by primary elections—that is, elections administered by *public* authorities (not party authorities) using virtually the same *statutory* rules (not party rules) for printing, distributing, casting, and counting ballots that are used in general elections.

When the presidential primaries began, however, there was no such clarity. The nature and meaning of primaries, as interpreted by reformers, party leaders, and the media, have varied widely. And the rules concerning primaries have never stood still; the parties continue to change them, right down to the present. Changes in the meaning and rules of the primaries have directly affected primary campaign communication. This chapter will focus on two important moments in the history of presidential primaries: 1912, when presidential primaries got their first major experimentation and development, and 1972, when the Democratic Party instituted reforms leading to the sudden proliferation of primaries. The nature and rules of primaries in 1932, 1952, and 1992 also will be considered briefly.

Campaign studies rarely focus on the rules;[1] as Lengle and Shafer (1976, p. 25) have said, rules are "nearly invisible when compared with the groups, issues, and personalities that are the stuff of campaign coverage." Yet they are important "unseen 'participants.'" Senator George McGovern's thorough knowledge of the new rules developed by the Mc-

Govern–Fraser Commission, which he chaired, gave him a real advantage in the 1972 presidential primaries, so much so that although George Wallace won more popular votes than McGovern in some states, McGovern won the most delegates. Rules giving "winner-take-all" privileges to the plurality winner in state primaries were a big help to George Bush in 1988; in nine Southern states with winner-take-all rules, he secured 97% of the delegates, although he had only won 59% of the popular vote (Wayne, 1992, pp. 97–99). Knowledge of these rules is vital in developing the campaign's communication plans, helping to determine where the candidate should speak and where advertisements and other resources should be targeted.

In this examination of the history of primaries, the author found a consistent conflict between the idealized vision of primary proponents and the practical execution of primaries by the state political parties. The view expounded by Wilson and LaFollette that so influenced the Progressive movement, that leadership should be based on the "voice of the people," characterized the vision of the proponents. Ceaser (1979, p. 211) has summarized these assumptions as follows: (1) "the idea that a 'closed' system of nomination controlled by a party organization is an evil," (2) "the belief that the people on their own can fully be trusted to choose leaders without the guidance of restrictive electoral institutions," and (3) "the view that no serious side effects flow from an open pursuit of the nomination."

EARLY PRIMARY VISION AND RULES, 1912–1952

The greatest confusion about what a presidential primary is and whether to have one occurred at the beginning, in 1912. It was a year of intense debate as the states considered primary legislation, and some legislatures passed enabling legislation barely one month prior to their actual primary. There were differing interpretations from state to state, with each state putting its own stamp on the rules. In 1910, Oregon had drafted its primary law on the model of Wisconsin (Eaton, 1912, pp. 108–113; Howe, 1912, p. 56) but added the new provision of a preference vote for president and vice president and bound the delegates to give their votes to the winner of the preference contest (Overacker, 1926, p. 10). In February 1912, the Kentucky General Assembly discussed a direct primary. In March, Massachusetts passed a primary bill, scheduling the election for April 30, just one month later. And in April, the governor of Maryland signed a presidential primary bill, scheduling the election for May 6.

The Maryland law provided that the winner would take all of the delegates. In Massachusetts there was a separate vote for the preferred presidential candidate and for the delegates, leading to electoral chaos.

The two leading Republican candidates (Roosevelt and Taft) split the delegate vote in half, each getting 18 delegates, while Taft won the presidential preference vote. Upon learning that Taft had won the presidential preference vote, Roosevelt called upon his pledged slate of delegates to vote for Taft at the convention. These delegates at first balked, then said that each person would vote as he saw fit (*New-York Daily Tribune*, May 2, 1912). The Democratic primary in Massachusetts yielded equally odd results. Clark "won a two-to-one victory over Governor Wilson" in the preference vote, but there were no delegates pledged to Clark on the delegate ballot. The delegates pledged to Governor Foss of Massachusetts were elected (*Baltimore American*, May 2, 1912, p. 1).

There was one area of predictability in the new primary laws, at least in Maryland: they were governed by the General Election Law, with the same judges and clerks on duty, saloons closed, and employers required to give workers "sufficient time in which to vote." It was a legal holiday ("If Business Men Will Vote Today," *Baltimore American*, May 6, 1912, p. 16).

Davis's (1997) sourcebook on the presidential primaries records that there were 12 Democratic and 13 Republican primaries in 1912, but contemporary newspaper accounts mention twenty-seven states. The confusion arises over the term itself. When is a primary a primary? The Missouri primary described in the *New-York Daily Tribune* (March 7, 1912)[2] took place in one congressional district only, for delegates to the Republican Convention. While there are no references to state-wide primaries in Michigan, the *Tribune* reports that Detroit and Wayne County were carried for Taft in primaries early in April (April 4, 1912). The Texas contest was described as "precinct primary conventions" (May 6, 1912); it is unclear what procedures were followed. The Rhode Island primary was run by the Democratic Party, not by public authorities (*Tribune*, March 6, 1912), and the New Hampshire and Minnesota primaries were for Republicans only (*Tribune*, April 22, 1912). The news reports of New Hampshire's primary used the terms *primaries* and *caucuses* interchangeably (*Tribune*, April 24, 1912). The Kansas primary also may have been for Republicans only, as only Republican winners were reported. In a sense, the states were making up the rules as they went along, and reporters also were new to the subject of primaries.

In this first year of presidential primaries on a wide scale,[3] the term *primary* became a contested symbol, one of the most hotly debated issues of the campaign. Early enthusiasm for the adoption of primaries was quickly followed by controversy. Progressive democratic ideals were one thing, but actually allowing popular participation in selecting party candidates was something else. It threatened (one might say, promised) to subvert state and local party systems and provided an opening for candidates whose popularity and resources transcended state or even national party discipline. Clearly the intrusion of so important a structural reform was a major deviation from the status quo of American party and presidential politics. On the other hand, opponents had to tread a very careful line in criticizing what they saw as "unchecked" democracy.

Far easier to trumpet in public was the "immediate benefits" put forward by the proponents of presidential primaries: closer democratic ties between voters and elected officials, the elimination of party bosses and machines, and an overthrow of back room trading in party nominations. Against these sinister forces, entrenched by party favoritism and beholden to the wealthy, the primaries would, as Nebraska's Governor Aldrich put it, "sound the death knell of corrupt political machines" (*Tribune*, February 26, 1912).

Roosevelt's supporters were strong advocates of primaries. Roosevelt campaigned actively in early 1912 to persuade more states to adopt primaries, and he favored a national presidential primary. Running as the outsider against an incumbent president of the same party, he had the most to gain from this change in the nominating procedures. Addressing the Massachusetts legislature, Roosevelt argued that the primary and other progressive reforms would "make representative government genuinely representative" (*Tribune*, February 27, 1912). When urged to run for president in a letter from seven state governors, Roosevelt replied that the people must decide. He had always stood for the "rule of the people," he said, and he expressed the hope that "so far as possible the people may be given the chance, through direct primaries, to express their preference" (*Tribune*, February 26, 1912).

In March, Taft and Roosevelt organizers confronted each other directly on the issue of primaries. Senator Joseph M. Dixon, the chairman of Roosevelt's "Executive Committee," challenged the director of the Taft re-election campaign to "a test by means of primaries in every state in the Union" (Sen. Joseph M. Dixon to Rep. William B. McKinley, *Tribune*, March 6, 1912). He asked the Taft manager, Rep. William B. McKinley, to join with him immediately in a telegram to the Republican members of three state legislatures then considering presidential primary bills, urging them to support the measures. McKinley replied that the states should make their own decisions, without interference from the candidates. He said that he did not favor "changes in the rules of the game while the game is in progress" (*Tribune*, March 8, 1912). Then Roosevelt jumped into the fray with rhetorical guns blazing:

We who stand for honest and genuine democracy . . . , genuine representative government, hold that a public contest between parties or within parties is not carried on as a game. . . . We hold that it should be carried on for the purpose of ascertaining and putting into effect the will of the people. (Letter to Senator Dixon, *Tribune*, March 11, 1912)

Roosevelt went on to lambaste the game imagery, claiming that the Taftites saw politics as a game where "the people should simply sit on the bleachers as spectators, and that no appeal lies to the people from the men who, for their own profit, are playing the game." Citing the 18-month struggle in the New York legislature over a direct primary law, he wrote:

We are fighting against intrenched privilege, both political privilege and financial privilege, [against] the spoils politicians and patronage-mongers, who are engaged in defrauding the American people out of their first and most elemental right—the right to self government. (Letter to Senator Dixon, *Tribune*, March 11, 1912)

With the battle lines clearly drawn, Taft responded with his own views on presidential primaries. In a speech to the General Court in Boston, he said that he was "glad" that Massachusetts had recently passed a presidential primary law. He saw the purpose of primaries differently from Roosevelt, however; he described them as safeguarding the privilege of party members to have a voice in the choice of their party candidates. "Volunteer primaries," on the other hand—what he called "soap box primaries"—were worse than none at all. They allowed people from the other party "to cast unfair votes," and they were "an open avenue for fraud and violence" (*Tribune*, March 19, 1912).

Roosevelt welcomed Taft's statement favoring primaries, and he called upon him to act upon those beliefs in good faith by supporting primary bills pending in Michigan, Illinois, Maryland, New York, and the District of Columbia. He questioned Taft's sincerity, however, pointing out that Taft forces were working actively to defeat primary bills (*New York Times*, March 20, 1912).

In Maine, a few days later, Roosevelt attacked Taft for paraphrasing Abraham Lincoln's belief in "government of the people, for the people, and by the people." Taft had suggested that America has a government "of the people, for the people, and by a representative part (or class) of the people." Roosevelt called this an endorsement of "minority government," of "government of the people, for the people, by the bosses" (*Tribune*, March 24, 1912). The same week he mocked Taft for "expressing his pleasure that all the Republican voters would be allowed to vote" in the newly passed New York primary bill. According to the reporter, Roosevelt "threw his voice into a falsetto on the word 'allowed,' a trick which brought a laugh" at each of the six meetings that day. When the laughter subsided, he bellowed, "It's your *right* to vote" (*Tribune*, March 26, 1912).

The most deeply symbolic terms of the American Revolution and Constitution could hardly be questioned in a frontal attack. Taft supporters gave a lukewarm endorsement to the idea of primaries, holding that the states should decide, but then proceeded to use legalistic arguments and political maneuvers to undermine primary bills in state legislatures (Davis, 1980, p. 44). They also jumped on Roosevelt for his "hypocrisy" on the issue when his supporters opposed a primary in Texas (*Tribune*, April 22, 1912).

Roosevelt won overwhelming electoral victories in the primaries, except in North Dakota and Wisconsin, which went to LaFollette; Massachusetts, where Taft and Roosevelt split the vote; and in several nonbinding primaries won by Taft. But the Republican Party in its state conventions reversed these results, either ignoring the Roosevelt majority in nonbinding primaries or awarding delegates at large to Taft supporters. As early as March 1912, Roosevelt began to consider a third-party candidacy if, after he had won the primaries, the bosses prevailed and swung the nomination to Taft (*New York Times*, March 28, 1912). His fears were well founded, and after the Republicans nominated Taft, Roosevelt founded the Bull Moose Party. In the fall election, he came in second to Democrat Woodrow Wilson.

The 1912 precedent of the primary results being ignored and overturned by the party regulars recurred in subsequent presidential campaigns, so instead of being a dramatic reform, the presidential primary proved weak and ineffectual in determining the party nominee. The primaries served an important role, nonetheless. In the 1932 Democratic primaries, one can see the candidates using the primaries as part of their wider strategy: to draw attention to themselves, to have a say in setting the agenda of issues for the campaign, to prove to influential party leaders that they were more than regional candidates, to gather delegates to use as bargaining chips at the convention, and to keep their campaign momentum going. Franklin D. Roosevelt was trying to win the necessary two-thirds of the delegates required for the nomination before the convention, through primaries and state conventions, to achieve a first-ballot victory at the convention. Al Smith was trying to stop Roosevelt by winning at least one-third of the delegates in the primaries and state conventions. Neither succeeded in his goal.

As in 1912, the primary laws in 1932 were left up to the individual states, and the states varied on whether the voters chose only the convention delegates (uninstructed) or whether they used a presidential preference ballot to instruct the delegates for a particular candidate. Some states (Massachusetts and Pennsylvania) did both. There were other variations on the law as well: some states chose at-large delegates as well as delegates representing specific districts; some states decided every four years whether they would use a primary or convention to select the delegates (such as Alabama). In Florida, the party central committee made the decision about whether to have a primary. In most states, the primary results were only advisory, not binding on the delegates.

Very early in the 1932 race, Smith tried to take advantage of these differences in the laws. Three days after Smith entered the race, Jouett Shouse, the chairman of the executive committee of the Democratic National Committee, suggested that "it would be wiser not to instruct delegates to the Democratic convention in favor of any candidate save where such instructions are necessary under the law. The convention should be unfettered by instructions" (in Peel and Donnelly, 1973, p. 66). Shouse was a Smith supporter, and this proposal would have benefitted Smith, who wanted to keep the convention as open as possible to prevent Roosevelt from getting the nomination on an early ballot.

Roosevelt immediately saw through this proposal and attacked it, arguing that it violated "the principles of the party and intent and laws and party rules of almost every state." Furthermore, he saw the proposal as a threat to the primaries, which he said had been adopted to force the politicians to pay more attention to "the great body of Democratic voters throughout the forty-eight states" (Peel and Donnelly, 1973, p. 66). The primaries went forward without Smith's proposed change.

"LIGHT INSTRUCTIONS"

In the 1912–1968 period, the majority of presidential primaries were *advisory* only. Thus, even though a candidate won a state's primary, the delegates were chosen by state party "caucuses, conventions, or committees, which were . . . easily controlled by party officials" (Wayne, 1992, p. 87). In the 1952 Republican primaries, fewer than half of the delegates were legally bound to vote for a specific candidate (David, Moos, and Goldman, 1954, p. 45). In the Illinois Democratic primary in 1952, Senator Estes Kefauver won handily, yet he still emerged without any substantial delegate support because the Democratic state organization backed Stevenson (Richard J. H. Johnston, "Taft Takes Lead," *New York Times*, April 9, 1952). No wonder columnist Arthur Krock referred to many of the convention delegates as having "light instructions" (Krock, "Convention Patterns," *New York Times*, April 6, 1952).

While the delegates generally received "light instructions," this did not mean that they could ignore the primary results altogether. The system allowed them to have their cake and eat it too. They would often "go through the motions of fidelity to instructions, and this can be done by conformity on the first ballot," explained Krock. Then, if another candidate seemed to be getting a majority and they wanted to shift to him, they could make the shift "before the vote is counted without getting into trouble at home" (Krock, "Convention Patterns," *New York Times*, April 6, 1952).

Another factor that reduced the power of the "voice of the people" in the primaries was the fact that most of the primary ballots did not identify which presidential candidates the delegates represented. Although delegates in a state's congressional districts might publicly identify with a particular presidential candidate, only the party insiders were likely to know that. It took Herculean efforts for candidates to inform the voters that certain delegates were committed to them. The efforts of the Eisenhower campaign in the 1952 New Hampshire primary serve as an illustration. As campaign manager Henry Cabot Lodge II described it:

Sample ballots were printed for each of the more than 250 precincts in the state. Each had to be printed differently because the order of delegates changed with each precinct. The sample ballot was marked to show where to put a vote for Eisenhower and was handed to every single voter. It was grueling—but most effective. (Lodge, 1973, p. 100)

In this period, presidential candidates entered primaries selectively where they thought they had a good chance to win, or primaries that had particular importance in convincing the party leaders that their candidacy was viable. Primary voters often confronted a ballot lacking the names of major contenders. It therefore became common for voters to write in the name of their favorite candidate, and sometimes the write-in effort was a deliberate campaign strategy. In the 1952 Illinois Republican primary, though Taft won and Stassen came in second, Eisenhower received a heavy write-in vote. This was due at least in part to the campaigning of Governor John Lodge of Connecticut, encouraging an Eisenhower write-in (Johnston, *New York Times*, April 9, 1952). The write-in vote for Eisenhower in the Minnesota primary that year was so large (over 100,000) that Eisenhower came in only 20,000 votes behind winner Stassen, the former governor of that state.

State rules concerning filing dates for primaries posed a particular stumbling block for would-be candidates in the 1952 Democratic primaries, because incumbent President Harry Truman waited so long before announcing that he would not run for re-election on March 29. Several candidates entered the primaries before Truman's announcement (Senator Estes Kefauver of Tennessee, Senator Richard B. Russell of Georgia, and Senator Robert S. Kerr of Oklahoma), but most party leaders held back until Truman made his plans known. By the time Truman decided, the filing dates for most presidential primaries had already passed or were fast approaching, and only Kefauver had entered most of them. This early planning was a great help to Kefauver, who gained momentum by winning most of the primaries and entered the convention with a delegate lead of 257½ to Russell's 161½ and Harriman's 112½ (David, Moos, and Goldman, 1954, p. 65).

One of the most studied campaigns in history is the 1960 presidential race between Richard Nixon and John F. Kennedy. There are exciting stories about primaries that year, particularly about Kennedy's victories in Wisconsin and West Virginia (White, 1961; Silvestri, 1987). However, Kennedy campaigned in only seven of the 16 primary contests, using them to prove a point to the party leaders: that he could prevail over Senator Hubert Humphrey of Minnesota, and that he had the viability to appeal to American voters in different parts of the country. The West Virginia primary became especially important in proving that he could win in a state that was 95% Protestant, in spite of his Catholicism. His primary victories "produced just 18 percent of the delegates he needed for the nomination" (Wattenberg, 1991, p. 157). The controlling power still lay with the party leaders.

This weak primary system continued through 1968. The Democratic nominee that year, Vice President Humphrey, did not enter a single primary. President Johnson's April 1 announcement that he was not running for re-election came after several primaries had already been held, and long after the filing deadlines for many others.

There were many important elements to primaries in the 1912–1968 period, and they will be discussed in subsequent chapters. But as far as the rules go, these primaries were a hodgepodge of contests, few leading to slates of delegates pledged to specific candidates. State party leaders pulled the strings at party conventions and caucuses, and rank-and-file party members had little or no say in the selection of the nominee.

RETURN TO THE EARLY VISION: MODERN RULES REFORM, 1972

> It's a whole new ballgame in 1972. They've changed the rules.
> —Mayor John Lindsay, *Meet the Press*, NBC,
> February 13, 1972, Tape 5055, Nixon Project

> The new rules are so mixed up, no one understands them.
> —Theodore White, CBS News Special Report,
> May 16, 1972, Tape 5379, No. 5, Nixon Project

> Among the . . . states with presidential primaries, there were, in fact, 18 recognizably different primary plans. . . . no state needed to apologize for a lack of institutional creativity.
> —Lengle and Shafer, 1976, p. 26

The rules changed dramatically in 1972, and they have changed frequently since then. It was the 1968 Democratic Convention that brought things to a head. When President Johnson withdrew his candidacy on April 1, 1968, the majority of delegates to the convention had already been chosen, mainly by state party caucuses and conventions committed to the Johnson administration. Party members wanted to be actively involved in choosing a nominee, but only a few states had primaries left in which party members could vote. Furthermore, the majority of convention delegates were former Johnson supporters, who then became supporters of Vice President Humphrey; there was no mechanism other than the few remaining primaries by which other candidates could be considered for the nomination. There was widespread dissatisfaction with this state of affairs, resulting in a push to make the party's selection of delegates more open and timely.

At the convention, delegates created the Commission on Party Structure and Delegate Selection and charged it with establishing requirements for the state parties for the 1972 convention. The first chair was Senator George McGovern of South Dakota; the second was Representative Donald Fraser of Minnesota: thus, the McGovern–Fraser Commission.

Of the 17 guidelines drafted by the McGovern–Fraser Commission and accepted by the Democratic Party, four were especially important: (1) the nominating system must be open to participation (through voting and serving as delegates) by all Democrats; (2) delegates must be publicly identified with the candidates they support and must vote for them at the convention; (3) there must be an increased demographic representation in the delegate slates, with specific quotas set for delegates by age, race, and sex; and (4) the state parties had to carry out these procedures, publishing their rules for delegate selection by January 1 of the election year (Trent, 1986, p. 9; Polsby, 1983, p. 34).

It was the first of these four guidelines that had the effect of stimulating an increase in the number of presidential primaries. To open the selection process to all party members, state parties could no longer select delegates by party caucuses or conventions; they had to choose either primaries in which candidates' names appeared on the ballot, or open conventions or caucuses. In 1972, 23 states adopted primaries as a way to meet these guidelines, and the number steadily increased in the years that followed.

Another important provision of the new guidelines was to prohibit the unit rule, a winner-take-all practice by which the candidate who won a plurality of votes in a primary received all of the state's delegates. Instead, the Commission advocated a system by which delegates were chosen by congressional district, with the number determined by "past party vote, straight population, or half of each"; the "candidate with the plurality in each district receives [all] its delegates" (Lengle and Shafer, 1976, p. 27).

The Commission tried to discourage Independents and Republicans from voting in the Democratic primaries, although it gave the states leeway in their loose definition of Democrats as "people identifying them-selves as Democrats at the time of voting, or who requested Democratic ballots" (Wayne, 1992, p. 90). Thus, crossover voting was still permitted, in which registered voters declared their partisanship at the time of the primaries, even if they had been Independents or members of another party before that time. This definition precluded open primaries, how-ever, in which any registered voter could vote in the primary of any party.

In the past, the rules regarding delegate selection had been established wholly by the state legislatures, under the direct influence of the domi-nant political leaders in the state. But the new rules required that a state's delegate selection procedures conform to the national party rules. For the first time, the national party was stepping in to make the rules more uniform and to control the power of the state party "bosses." Although all of these changes were made by the Democratic Party, the Republican Party also was directly affected, because Democrats dominated most of the state legislatures. The creation of a presidential primary in a state meant that both parties would have a primary there.

While the Democrats in 1972 produced major changes in the system of presidential candidate selection, the primary rules were still far from uniform. Different states selected the winner-take-all, proportional, or congressional district delegate system, depending on their needs. The Republican Party, while forced to increase the number of primaries, did not follow the same course as the Democrats. It left much more of the decision making to the state parties, rather than instituting national guidelines. There is no minimum threshold of votes for candidates to receive delegate support (though many states have instituted these thresholds), and the party has not taken a position on winner-take-all primaries. In 1988, among Republicans, 14 states and the District of Co-lumbia had proportional primaries, and 19 had winner-take-all primaries within the district or the state. With more "winner-take-all" contests, the leading candidates can move more quickly to lock up the nomination.

There was a direct connection between the rules and the campaign communication of the candidates. Each type of primary "called for a different campaign strategy and, hence, a different strategy for using broadcasting" (Becker and Lower, 1979, p. 28). The best example is the way Senator George McGovern exploited his insider's knowledge of the new rules in 1972. By targeting his campaign in certain congressional districts where he had slates of delegates pledged to him, for example, he was able to win 65% of the primary delegates, while getting only 25% of the primary votes. He actually finished second to Humphrey in the popular vote (Busch, 1997). None of the other candidates knew how to use the new rules so skillfully. Wallace was particularly unprepared. In Pennsylvania, for example, where Wallace came in second and McGovern third, he had fielded only four delegates, while McGovern had fielded an entire slate. McGovern won 37 convention delegates there, Wallace only two (Mayer, 1996a, p. 145).

Gary Hart, McGovern's campaign manager, and Rick Stearns, the deputy campaign manager, spoke of other ways the McGovern campaign used their knowledge of the rules to improve their communication position. First, in choosing which state primaries to enter, they chose states with a long history of strong progressive movements, such as Wisconsin, Nebraska, and California, as McGovern identified closely with that wing of the party (Stearns, in May and Fraser, 1973). Second, they focused heavily on Wisconsin because all of the candidates were on the ballot. A victory there would therefore be a triumph, showing the ability to win over all of the opponents (Hart, 1973). Third, the McGovern campaign knew how difficult the reform rules were far in advance of the other candidates and could organize the necessary workers to go through the process successfully. For example, petitions had to be submitted for the California primary by March 7, with 15,000 signatures, "an immense task" (Stearns, in May and Fraser, 1973, p. 107).

Predicting a new reality, where candidates were chosen in the primaries, McGovern said, "I've felt from the very beginning that the nominee of our party will be the candidate who demonstrates the broadest and the greatest strength in the primary election." With a sweep of primary wins, he said, "the old line politicians" would have to accept the winner, like it or not (McGovern, CBS, April 27, 1972, Vanderbilt TV Archives).[4] McGovern's campaign organization excelled not only in the primaries, but also in the caucuses and party conventions (Busch, 1997). Governor Jimmy Carter of Georgia credited McGovern's success to "his intimate knowledge of the rules" as well as to his "extraordinary organization" (Carter, "Campaign '72, CBS, June 6, 1972, Nixon Project, 5459).

Carter followed the McGovern model and planned successfully for the 1976 primaries, and "by 1980, almost all candidates were doing the same things: announcing early; targeting Iowa and New Hampshire"; and realizing they had to enter and win *many* of the primaries and caucuses, not just a select few (Mayer, 1996b, p. 62).

The type of primary rules could well influence the way a candidate targeted campaign resources. For example, winning a state that has a winner-take-all system is much more profitable than winning a state with a proportional system. McGovern focused on Massachusetts, with its winner-take-all primary, and though he won only 51% of the vote there, he won all 102 delegates. Muskie, with 22% of the Massachusetts vote, won no delegates ("Political Polls," Public Affairs, PBS, April 26, 1972, Nixon Project, 5307). In 1988, the winner-take-all rules were a big help to Vice President George Bush's candidacy in the South; in nine Southern states with this system, he got 59% of the popular vote and 97% of the delegates (Wayne, 1992, pp. 97–99). In 1992, the Republican nomination was settled by the time of the March 17 Michigan primary; "the result had been speeded by the prevalence of winner-take-all rules in the Republican nominating process" (Ceaser and Busch, 1993, p. 41).

EFFECTS OF THE MCGOVERN–FRASER COMMISSION REFORMS

One of the effects of the new rules was that many more candidates entered the primaries than in the past. When the Commission set a low threshold of only 15% of the vote required to get delegates and encouraged a more proportional voting system rather than the winner take all, the effect was to encourage people to run for president who were not major figures in the party, such as Mayor John Lindsay of New York. Thirteen people ran for the Democratic nomination in 1972, eight considered major contenders, and thirteen again in 1976. Among Republicans, nine ran in 1980 and six in 1988. Before the Commission's reforms, in contrast, the mean number of candidates who entered more than one primary had been 3.2 for the 1952–1968 period, in both parties (Polsby, 1983, p. 62). This multiple candidacy resulted in a splintering of the primary vote among many candidates, so that "winners" prevailed on the basis of a few percentage points' plurality.

Because there were so many more candidates than in previous primaries, the intraparty battles were more numerous. As each of the many candidates developed and publicized his or her policy positions, all "under the spotlight of modern media," party disputes that in the past remained at least partially hidden from the public were laid bare in all of their ugliness (Shannon, in Rose, 1991, p. 257). Party leaders feared that this public divisiveness in the primaries would hurt the party's chances in the fall elections, both by providing "the enemy party with ammunition it can later use with blast effect against whichever primary contender emerges victorious" (White, 1961, p. 78), and by making it difficult to rally the party activists who supported losing candidates behind the eventual winner. Research findings indicate that their fears were well founded. Lengle (1980, p. 263) found that "a divisive presidential primary in the spring increased the likelihood of the party losing that state in the fall."

Another development in 1972 that was assumed to be due to the reforms was that the primaries and caucuses held *early* in the campaign had a disproportionate influence on the results. The New Hampshire and Florida primaries were good examples: the results there in the first two weeks of the primaries elevated McGovern, Wallace, and Humphrey and put Muskie into a defensive position from which he was never able to recover. The heavy influence of small states such as New Hampshire in determining which candidates were seen as viable was especially galling to the party leaders, as few delegates were at stake in New Hampshire.

One of the intentions of the reformers had been to open up the party to wider participation. But as author Theodore White commented, "They can't open up this political party *only* to the reformers; it has to be open for George Wallace to voice those sentiments for which he stands" (White, CBS News Special Report, May 16, 1972, Nixon Project, 5379, Tape 5). Wallace's great success in the primaries came as a shock to the party regulars.

Many of the lesser-known politicians entered the race early in 1972, hoping to establish national visibility and become known to the voters. This had the effect of lengthening the pre-campaign period: for example, McGovern entered in January 1971. Though the field quickly narrowed as candidates dropped out, the nomination was not firmly secured by anyone until June 1972, after the last primary in New York. The nominating campaign period was therefore very long, shortening the time for the party to build unity before the fall election. One study of contested primaries found that while in 1932 Democratic candidates formally entered the race on an average of 148.5 days before the nominating convention, by 1984 these announcements occurred 427.3 days before the convention. Republicans also have announced earlier in recent years; while in 1940 they announced 303.3 days before the convention, in 1976 this period had lengthened to 337.5 days (Reiter, 1984, p. 35, Table 2.5).

The year 1972 was the first in which a candidate (McGovern) won enough delegates from primary victories that by the time of the convention he was able to gain the necessary margin to become the predetermined nominee. Other candidates (such as Muskie and Humphrey) hoped that there would still be a great deal of negotiation at the convention. The party's credentials committee encouraged them by taking an action that placed McGovern's nomination in jeopardy, giving 39% of McGovern's California delegates to Humphrey because of a ban on the unit rule (Busch, 1997). On the first night of the convention, however, the delegates were restored to McGovern, and he went on to win the nomination.

While favorite-son candidacies were common in earlier primaries, an effect of the reform requiring delegates to publicize their candidate preference was that there were now few uncommitted delegates, thus there was little leeway to introduce favorite-son candidates. While in 1968 only nine primaries had the names of presidential candidates on the ballot, and in only three of those were convention delegates required to vote for the primary winner, by 1980, 35 of the primaries had the candidates' names on the ballot, and 33 were binding on the delegates (Kamarck, in Rose, 1991, p. 297). The McGovern–Fraser Commission ended the practice of giving delegate status to party leaders and elected officials automatically, and this too had the effect of removing any cushion of independent delegates who might bring in a new candidate at the last minute.

Although it was the Democratic National Committee that instituted the McGovern–Fraser Commission reforms imposing more uniformity on the state parties, in many respects the national committee lost much more power than it gained. While in earlier elections the national committee staff customarily ran the general election campaign, "since 1972, no general election campaign has been run by either the Republican or the Democrat national committee staffs" (Cigler, in Rose, 1991, p. 269). Once the nomination is secured, the campaign advisers and consultants who have masterminded the primary victory stay on to run the candidate's general election campaign.

The reform goal of involving party members more actively in the nominating process was a huge success in one respect, that of increasing voter turnout in the primaries. While in 1968 only 12 million people (11% of the voting age population) voted in the primaries, in 1972 that number climbed to 22 million, and it increased in every election after that until 1984. In 1988, when both parties had heavily contested nominations, 35 million people (24.4% of the voting age population) voted in the primaries. Turnout was highest in the early primary states. Though critics often bemoan the low voter turnout in the primaries compared to the general election, voters are actually much more interested in primaries than they used to be.

Who are the people who vote in the primaries? The states vary in their rules about who can vote. Geer (1986, p. 1017) has found four different degrees of flexibility. The first is the "open" primary, which "allows any registered voter to participate," as in the Wisconsin primaries,[5] and in most Southern primaries. In such a flexible situation, crossover votes from the opposite party can make a big difference in the primary outcome. This happened in 1972, when many Republicans voted for Wallace in open primaries, and in 1988, when white Southern Democrats voted in the Republican primaries, hurting Democratic moderates Gore and Gephardt and helping Democrat Jesse Jackson. The second type of primary, also very flexible, allows any registered voters to vote if they declare their partisanship at the time of the primary, as in the New Hampshire primary.

The third type, which Geer calls the "semi-closed," allows registered independents to vote in the primary of either party, but those registered in parties may only vote in the contest of their own party. The fourth and most restrictive type, called the "closed" primary, permits only party members to vote in that party's contest. In general, party leaders have actively discouraged participation in the primaries by members of other parties, fearing mischief and skewing of the results.

Demographically, the people who vote in the primaries are more likely to be "the better-educated, higher-income, older members of the society," according to Wayne (1992, p. 104). Bartels (1988) agrees, adding that primary voters are more likely to be interested in politics, to be better informed, and to use the media more frequently. There is no real proof that primary voters are more extreme in their views than other members of their parties (Wayne, 1992; Bartels, 1988).

Concurrent with the party rules changes and surge in the primaries in 1972 was the institution of the Federal Election Campaign Act. Congress passed the bill on January 19, President Nixon signed it on February 7, and it went into effect on April 7, 1972. By then the primaries were underway. The act limited the amount the candidates could spend on paid advertising, required that radio and television stations provide reasonable rates, placed limits on campaign contributions, and required disclosure of both contributions and expenditures (Becker and Lower, 1979, p. 26). These new finance rules affected the 1972 campaign immediately, not only in the newly required record keeping and public disclosure, but also in the dispute among Democratic candidates over who was most faithful in observing the rules. In 1976, campaign finance reform, which provided matched funding for primary candidates, began, enabling candidates to run who relied on small contributions at the grassroots level. Carter "raised enough in small contributions to receive more matching funds in the crucial period through mid-March than any of his competitors except Wallace and Jackson" (Busch, 1997, p. 142).

CONTINUED RULES CHANGES, 1973–1992

Dismayed with many of the unforeseen effects of the 1972 rules changes, the Democratic Convention "authorized the appointment of a commission to . . . study the rules on delegate selection" every four years through 1988 (Reinsch, 1988, pp. 251–252). Each commission proposed new changes, tending to reflect the specific dissatisfaction with the last election and trying to fix it. Starting with the 1976 primaries, the party required either a district or a proportional system, forbidding the winner-take-all system. The Wenograd Commission tried to shorten the 1980 primary campaign by establishing a "window" period of dates in which the primaries could be held. It tried to restrict participation in Democratic primaries to Democrats (many states asked for exceptions), and it moved some of the Southern primaries to earlier in the primary season in an attempt to offset the heavy influence of the Iowa caucuses and the New Hampshire primary. But the attempt to shorten the campaign failed; there were 37 primaries in 1980, and many of the candidates started campaigning two years early, following the successful example of Jimmy Carter.

Changes for the 1984 campaign shortened the period between the Iowa caucuses and the New Hampshire primary from five weeks to 15 days in an attempt to prevent Iowa from having such a large impact on the campaign. But suddenly Maine inserted itself into the early process, "holding a cosmetic presidential vote between the Iowa and New Hampshire elections," which got heavy media coverage (Reinsch, 1988, pp. 251–252).

Continuing their attempt to shorten the primary process, the Democrats in 1988 set the "window" period for the primaries from the second Tuesday in March to the second Tuesday in June. However, South Dakota and Vermont ignored the window and scheduled their primaries earlier; then Iowa and New Hampshire moved their caucuses and primary earlier still. The party finally granted them exceptions. In 1992, there was another effort, this time to set the window from the first Tuesday in March to the second Tuesday in June. Again, many states marched to their own drummers, with the Iowa caucuses, the New Hampshire primary, the Maine caucuses, and the South Dakota primary all held in February.

The Democrats made many adjustments in the minimum vote needed in a primary before a candidate could receive delegates. They had conflicting agendas: on the one hand, they wanted to broaden participation in the party, but on the other hand, they wanted to move rapidly toward a winning nominee rather than encourage minor candidates to battle on and on through all of the primaries. In 1984, the minimum vote required to gain delegates was raised to 25% in a state primary (and 20% in a caucus), but when lesser-known candidates complained that this left them out, it was lowered again to 15% in 1988 (Wayne, 1992, pp. 93–97).

Other important changes made in 1984 were: (1) to add 566 uncommitted delegates ("super delegates") drawn from state party leaders and Democrats in Congress; (2) to give states a "winner-take-more" option, in which candidates who won a district would not only gain delegates on the basis of the proportion of their vote, but also would win a bonus delegate (Geer, 1986, p. 1008); and (3) to remove the requirement that delegates were legally bound to support the candidate they were publicly identified with in the primary, though "their initial selection as delegates must still have the approval of the candidate to whom they are committed" (Wayne, 1992, pp. 93–97).

The reintroduction of party officials into the delegate pool was an attempt to restore some of the weight of the nomination decision to party leaders. The idea was that these delegates would not endorse anyone in the primaries and would represent an uncommitted bloc that could "play a compromising role at the convention" (Cigler, in Rose, 1991, p. 272). But the idea played out rather differently. Instead of withholding their commitment, the 1984 "superdelegates" committed themselves even before the primaries to Vice President Walter Mondale, in order to give him added momentum.

The winner-take-more option was seen as a way to aid the front-runner in securing a majority of delegates earlier, so that the outcome of the primaries would be known earlier and the party would thus have more time to unify itself to prepare for the fall campaign.

The lifting of the obligation to support the candidate with whom delegates were identified grew out of the 1980 convention, when Senator Edward Kennedy's supporters strenuously objected to this rule. Since the lifting of the obligation, there have not been any significant defections at the Democratic National Convention by people who have shifted their allegiances.

The total effect of the 1984 changes resulted in the campaign being pushed forward even further than it had been. As Judith Trent reports: "Candidates, in an effort to build the image of electability and to establish early momentum turned to the straw polls of the surfacing states," polls that "did not gather the votes of registered voters [or] . . . of a state party's rank and file" (Trent, 1986, p. 12).

An important change in 1988 was the creation of "Super Tuesday" on March 8, 1988, in which the Southern states and several others all had primaries on the same day. The intent was to give more weight to the Southern, more moderate wing of the Democratic Party in the hope of nominating a candidate who would be more acceptable to the voters. The effort failed in 1988, as Governor Michael Dukakis of Massachusetts gained significant momentum before Super Tuesday. Since Dukakis did well on Super Tuesday too, he was the person most benefitting from this new "regional" primary, rather than a Southerner. Nevertheless, Democrats continued with Super Tuesday in 1992, and this directly benefitted the candidacy of Governor Bill Clinton of Arkansas. He swept to victory in all of the Southern primaries, as well as winning early primaries in the important Northern industrial states of Illinois and Michigan.

The Democrats continued to add to the number of delegates from the party leadership. In 1988, there were 648 superdelegates. In 1992, these "superdelegates" grew to a total of 766, over one-third the number necessary for nomination (Ceaser and Busch, 1993); they included all Democratic governors, four-fifths of the Democrats in Congress, and party-elected officials. The superdelegates, however, instead of operating as an independent force, followed the lead of the primaries; by late May 1992, the majority had committed themselves to Clinton, the winner in the primaries.

Ron Brown, chairman of the Democratic National Committee, argued that the fights over the rules every four years were "very disruptive to focussing on winning elections." He was successful in preventing a fight over the rules for 1992, and declared, "I think it served us well" (in Royer, 1994, pp. 51–52).

After experiments with various systems of delegate allocation based on primary results, the Democrats in 1992 returned to the system of universal proportional representation, which awards all candidates a proportion of the delegates in each state based on the percentage that they have won. The danger of this system is that by dividing the vote into so many pieces, it is possible that no one will get a majority of the delegates. But as in other primary campaigns, the 1992 front-runners built up such momentum that the race narrowed quickly, and the proportional system produced little change.

MOTIVES OF THE RULES CHANGERS

The ideas of openness, of encouraging the voice of the people and relegating the party bosses to the scrap heap of history reverberate in Democratic Party reform language. Yet as the quadrennial reform commissions tackled the rules, it became increasingly apparent that the so-called party "reformers" had other agendas. Each generation of rules revisions directly benefitted a particular candidate or group. A good illustration of this process is the way in which the 1984 rules protected Mondale's front-runner advantage: by the rule requiring a 25% vote threshold in each state to secure delegates, by the addition of 594 unpledged delegates from Congress and party officials (most of whom announced their support for Mondale before the primaries began), and by the change in primary and caucus dates to an earlier period in the campaign. All of these rules revisions allowed Mondale to capitalize on his early advantage, building his momentum (Reinsch, 1988).

NATIONAL VERSUS STATE PARTY POWER

Since 1972, the Democratic Party has imposed certain structural rules on the state parties in an effort to control the delegate selection process. The party's right to do this has been upheld in a court case (*Cousins v. Wigoda*, 419 U.S. 477, 1975), in which the Supreme Court ruled that political parties are private organizations "with rights of association protected by the Constitution. . . . While states could establish their own primary laws, the party could determine the criteria for representation at its national convention" (Wayne, 1992, p. 100). Not only does the party determine criteria for delegate representation, it also allocates specific numbers of delegates to the states by a formula that "rewards both sheer (Electoral College) size and past Democratic support." This allocation system favors candidates who are popular in the "big, urban, industrialized, working class, ethnic-and-racial-minority-oriented states" (Lengle and Shafer, 1976, pp. 31–32). All of these party-imposed rules have the goal of creating a guaranteed-to-win system, the outcome of which will be the selection of a presidential nominee who will win the election in November.

But there are 50 states, and each state has its own internal political dynamics. Within the parameters of developing their own primary laws, the states have enormous powers separate from the national party. For example, the decision about when to hold the state primary remains the state's prerogative. Now that the party's presidential nomination is determined by the primaries, and not by the political conventions, the timing of the individual primaries has taken on enormous implications.

The importance of the first primary, held in New Hampshire, is legendary. Its presidential primary law was passed in 1913. In 1915, the legislature selected Town Meeting Day in early March as the primary date to save money and to have the vote before the roads turned muddy. The primary did not receive much attention in the 1916–1948 period, as the citizens voted for delegates, not candidates. But in 1949, Governor Sherman Adams got the legislature to adopt presidential preference primaries for Democrats and Republicans to help Eisenhower. Since 1952, the New Hampshire primary has been a dominant presence, gaining extensive publicity for the winners and losers. With only one exception since 1952 (Clinton in 1992), no one who lost the New Hampshire primary has been elected president. In 1975, the New Hampshire legislature mandated by law that their primary must be one week earlier than any other.

In most presidential years, one or more candidates drop out of the race after New Hampshire. Reputations are made and lost there. In the years this study focuses on, the 1952, 1972, and 1992 New Hampshire primaries were all watershed moments. In 1952, Eisenhower's New Hampshire win established that he could do well against Taft; Kefauver's win in the Democratic primary established that President Truman was vulnerable within his own party and gave Kefauver a national audience. In 1972, the Democratic front-runner, Muskie, won, but his somewhat stumbling campaign and less-than-majority vote raised questions about whether he was the *de facto* nominee after all. At the same time, McGovern's better-than-expected showing catapulted him into national attention. In 1992, New Hampshire's February 18 primary introduced a little-known politician to the nation, in Tsongas's victory there, and it established that Clinton could survive, despite scandal. In the Republican primary, although President Bush won, Buchanan's 37% vote raised questions about Bush's strength, especially as a national candidate. The 1988 New Hampshire primary had been very important for Bush too, in a positive way, establishing that he could win after all, in spite of his humiliating loss to Dole and Reverend Pat Robertson in the Iowa caucuses the week before.

The importance of the New Hampshire primary lies not only in the electoral results there but in the interpretation of those results by politicians and the media. The power of coming first in the sequence of primaries has given its voters the power of kingmaker and kingbreaker.

Other states also have capitalized on this power by position. The timing of the South Carolina primary, on the Saturday before the Super Tuesday primaries in the South, proved important to Republicans—Reagan in 1980, Bush in 1988, and Dole in 1996. In each of these years, careful planning to win over the South Carolina governor and enlist his help in the state paid off, and the candidates went on to win on Super Tuesday.

In 1992, "several smaller states with progressive Democratic traditions . . . grabbed a strategic position" between the New Hampshire primary and Super Tuesday: South Dakota, February 25, and Colorado, Georgia, and Maryland, March 3 (David Broder, "Democratic Dynamics," *Washington Post National Weekly Edition*, December 9–15, 1991, p. 4). Kerrey's victory over Harkin in the South Dakota primary was undoubtedly a factor in Harkin's withdrawal. The decision by Governor Zell Miller of Georgia to move that state's primary one week earlier also gave Clinton an early boost. In reflecting on important developments in the 1992 primaries, Paul Begala of the Clinton–Gore campaign spoke of Georgia's action to move its primary earlier as a significant help, while in contrast, Mary Matalin of the Bush–Quayle campaign said, "We saw that as a very pivotal advantage for Governor Clinton and one we desperately did not want to happen" (Royer, 1994, p. 52).

The clear pattern for both primaries and caucuses has been an increase in the "front-loading" of the schedule. Haskell (1996, p. 382) reports that while in 1980 only 19 states held their contests by March 31, by 1992, 30 states had voted by March 31. The trend escalated still further in 1996, when 38 had voted by March 31. Much of the criticism of the primaries has focused on the front-loading phenomenon. Rosenstiel (1993) believes that many of the weaknesses in media coverage are due to the increased front-loading, pointing out the impossible task of adequately covering 28 contests in 28 days in 1992.

There was talk during the 1992 Democratic primaries of throwing over the primary system altogether and going back to the powerful convention. "Appalled by the spectacle of the campaign and worried by Clinton's simultaneous weakness and continued ascent, some party leaders publicly called for a restoration of deliberative conventions as the mechanism for party nominations" (Ceaser and Busch, 1993, p. 79). But Clinton won the presidency, and all talk of going back to the convention system ended.

CONCLUSIONS

Both in 1912 and in 1972, those advocating change in the presidential selection rules wanted to remove decision-making power from the metaphorical "smoke-filled back room" of party leaders and bring it out into the open, where the "voice of the people" could speak. The reformers were disappointed with the results in 1912. Finally, in 1972, the number of presidential primaries surged, voter turnout in the primaries grew, and the revised rules assured that primary victories would bring delegate votes. The winner of the primaries actually secured the nomination.

What was not foreseen by these reformers, however, is that a major new actor, the party commission, would appear on the presidential nomination stage as a direct result of the rules changes, and that other actors would take on new roles, changing the process in a way no one could have imagined.

Many of the benefits that advocates of the rules changes foresaw have occurred. Party bosses and machines no longer have much influence in the presidential nomination process. Back room trading at conventions is over. One could even argue that there are closer democratic ties between voters and elected officials; at least the voters in states with early primaries have a chance to make a choice among candidates within their party, to select the party nominee.

The early reformers would undoubtedly find fault with some of the changes and try to repair and revise the rules, just as the parties have continued to do. There was no sign in 1912 that the reformers wanted or expected the kind of rushed and compressed primary process we have today, with the nominees already known just one month into the primaries, most of the candidates out of the race, and citizens in many states left only to rubber-stamp the results. The 1912 reformers also would be surprised at the enormous amounts of money candidates need to keep a primary campaign going, though they too could not think of entering the primaries without the assurance of support from wealthy backers.

But right from the start, reformers could see that the primaries promoted a candidate-based system rather than a party-based system, they knew that the primaries would weaken the party, and they actively sought this change. Where was party discipline when three prominent Republicans ran against each other? Where was party discipline when Roosevelt decided to run even though he knew it might split the party and give victory to the Democrats? It was the opponents of the primaries who feared the weakened party, not the reformers.

NOTES

1. Several works containing valuable exposition of the party rules are Busch (1997), Mayer (1996a), and Davis (1980, 1997).

2. Hereafter, the *New-York Daily Tribune* is referred to as the *Tribune*.

3. Much of the material on the 1912 primaries has appeared in Corcoran and Kendall (1989), or in Corcoran and Kendall (1992).

4. In reflecting back on his position on party reforms many years later, McGovern said that he never intended that the primaries would become the main form of nominating contest. He said that he much preferred caucuses to primaries (McGovern, Lecture at the National Archives, Washington, DC, February 6, 1996).

5. Although the Democratic Party went to court to force Wisconsin to give up its open primary, and the court upheld the party, the Wisconsin legislature refused to change the law. The party then gave exemptions to both Wisconsin and Montana (Wayne, 1992, p. 100).

Chapter 3

Speeches and Debates
for Dozens . . . and Millions

The primaries: "They tell whether a candidate can frame a message and present it effectively in both speeches and ads to a variety of constituencies."

—David Broder, *Washington Post*, April 27, 1992

During the 1952 presidential primaries, Senator Robert A. Taft spoke in Brookline, Massachusetts. The author and her father went to hear him. Though Taft's words are long forgotten, the event is not. It was exciting just to be in the presence of someone who might be the future president. Presidential candidates need to capture the attention of the voters, and speech making is one of the traditional ways they accomplish this. They also use the occasion to lay out their vision of the future under their presidency.

Ever since the Greek polis there has been a close relationship between democratic politics and public speaking. In a democracy, those who lead must continually communicate with the public, in a circular process of interaction, in order to govern successfully. Speeches are one of the main ways to do that. The great English historian Macaulay said that "Parliamentary government is government by speaking" (June 1859, *Harper's*, in Baker, June 8, 1996). Even in the age of television, the speeches of political leaders continue to occupy a major place in public life, though presented in truncated form through summaries by political reporters (Kendall, 1993). This chapter will explore the nature of public speaking and debate in the presidential primaries from 1912 to 1992, noting especially any qualities distinctive to primaries, and the changes over time.

The power of messages to influence public opinion in the early primaries has been verified by several modern researchers. The primary candidates are less familiar to the public than in the general election, and therefore the potential for learning is greater (Zhu, Milavsky, and Biswas, 1994). Audiences show substantial change in their evaluation of candidates' image and style after watching them debate. These factors are particularly important in the primaries, where candidates often have virtually indistinguishable positions on issues (Lanoue and Schrott, 1989). Debates early in the campaign also serve as an important source of information about issues, affirming the relationship between timing and political learning (Pfau, 1988). All of these indications of the power of primary messages have to be tempered by the fact that far fewer people are paying attention to the campaign at this stage.

Jamieson (1992) has analyzed the changing nature of speeches in the general election campaigns over the years, finding the following significant changes from the past: (1) that candidates used to take "clear stands on controversial policy issues," but that "increasingly campaigns have become narcotics that blur our awareness of problems" (p. 204); (2) that reasoned argument in campaign speeches has declined as the length of speeches has declined, with arguments now often stopping at the level of mere assertions; (3) that candidates today do not answer questions with the degree of specificity that they used in the past; and (4) that "candidates are learning to act, speak, and think in television's terms. . . . transforming speeches, debates, and their appearances in news into ads." In fact, Jamieson finds that "campaign speeches have now become soundbite-filled ads strung together with transitions" (p. 206). This study will look for these changes in the 80-year period of primaries studied to see if they have occurred in the primaries as in the general elections.

THE 1912 CAMPAIGN

Since few had any experience with presidential primaries before 1912, it is not surprising that the 1912 campaigners blended together their experiences from the pre-convention campaigns and the presidential general elections of the past. While past pre-convention campaigns had involved mainly a kind of interpersonal communication, with campaign managers and committees negotiating with state party leaders, in the primary states the audience was now broader, more like a general election, necessitating much more public speaking and mass communication. Yet the majority of states did not have primaries; they used the old methods of party caucuses and conventions. The candidates had to be agile to adapt to these new circumstances.

President William Howard Taft built his campaign committee of Congressmen from presidential primary states, including one to head the "literary bureau," through which campaign speakers were arranged. When Taft could not speak himself, personal representatives stood in for him. Eminent speakers were regular features of the 1912 primaries. In February, Louis D. Brandeis, the famous Boston lawyer, began a speaking tour in Nebraska on behalf of Senator Robert LaFollette, Sr. (New York *Tribune*, February 2, 1912; hereafter *Tribune*). Woodrow Wilson's campaign organization reported that a large corps of "star orators" and "spellbinders" would campaign in Nebraska for him, including U.S. senators from Mississippi and Oklahoma (*Tribune*, May 15, 1912). William Jennings Bryan, three-time Democratic presidential nominee, campaigned for Wilson in Ohio. In California, LaFollette was the only major candidate to appear personally, but the other candidates were represented by both national and local luminaries. Former Indiana Senator Albert J. Beveridge stood in for Theodore Roosevelt, and Taft was represented by Secretary of State Knox, ex-Governor James Gillett of California, former Congressman Ralph D. Cole of Ohio, and Joseph Scott, a prominent lawyer from Los Angeles (*San Francisco Chronicle*, April 21, May 7, May 12, 1912).

Special attention was given to the more populous states; whistle-stop tours carried the candidates through the hinterlands to rallies in major cities. The models for this behavior were the presidential campaigns of the recent past. Bryan had started the practice of the presidential candidates traveling and speaking; before him the candidates adopted a dignified pose, meeting delegations at their home while surrogate speakers traveled on their behalf. In the 1896 campaign, Bryan traveled "18,000 miles in three months, during which he gave as many as nineteen speeches in one day. In the end, he reached an audience of fewer than five million" (Reinsch, 1988, p. 162). The campaign of 1908 was the first in which both major party candidates stumped the country (Stebenne, 1993). In 1910, Roosevelt went on a major speaking tour, traveling 5,500 miles "delivering 14 prepared speeches and hundreds of impromptu speeches to often tumultuous crowds"; in effect, he was "previewing the platform on which he would campaign in 1912" (Friedenberg, 1990, pp. 81–82).

Gangs of newspaper reporters followed the candidates, wiring their dispatches to editors each evening. In many respects, the primary campaign in 1912 bore an uncanny resemblance to the primaries of today, with reporters following the candidates to their speeches and rallies, often attending a press conference or "press opportunity" afterwards and sending in their stories the same day.

In 1912, LaFollette set the pace, campaigning in person in the primary states well before the others. Taft's presidential responsibilities kept him in Washington more than his competitors. But he offset this disadvantage by using the incumbent strategies available to him with some skill, appearing as the powerful and benign leader. The press reported on him performing his duties of office: urging a food appropriation for those left homeless in a flood, recommending to Congress measures for economy and efficiency in government, and examining designs for the Lincoln Memorial (*Tribune*, April 4–5, pp. 11–12). When the *Titanic* sank in April 1912, in the midst of the primaries, President Taft gave expression to the nation's profound shock, becoming actively involved in the public inquiry into the disaster and giving a eulogy for his former aide, Major Archibald Butt, who was lost on the *Titanic* (*Tribune*, April 17, 19, 29, 1912; May 6, 12, 1912). In general, Taft spoke in a calm, deliberate voice (Murphy, 1955), never dramatic, but always the solid incumbent.

Roosevelt's image was already legendary. Even endorsements of Taft granted this (*San Francisco Chronicle*, May 14, 1912). Roosevelt considered his Columbus, Ohio, speech of February 21, 1912, and his Carnegie Hall speech of March 20, 1912, as the foundation of his platform during the primaries (Murphy, 1955). In these speeches he endorsed a wide variety of Progressive reforms, such as initiatives and referendums, and one that particularly alarmed the conservative Republicans: the recall. His advocacy of the recall, "even for judges . . . was especially disturbing . . . to the conservative monied interests that dominated the Republican party, as the judiciary had typically upheld their interests" (Friedenberg, personal correspondence, July 18, 1998).

While there was popular support for his goals, Roosevelt's own personality played a large role in attracting the crowds. As Vice President Thomas R. Marshall said in his memoirs, "It was Roosevelt, the man, that people followed" (in Murphy, 1955, p. 320). He was a fighter, who announced his entry in the primary race with the words, "My hat is in the ring and the fight is on!" (letter to Herbert Spencer Hadley, *Letters*, February 29, 1912, p. 519). Regularly adopting a hortatory tone, he was "like a preacher," speaking of good and evil, quoting Scripture, and preaching what Friedenberg (1990) has called "the rhetoric of militant decency." This "rather serious verbal style was relieved . . . by platform antics, grimaces, and humorous falsetto emphases in his voice" (Murphy, 1955, p. 350). He frequently ended his speeches with a slogan from the football field: "Don't flinch, don't foul, and hit the line hard!" (Murphy, 1955, p. 344). He gestured frequently, pointing with his full arm outstretched. And "most expressive was the face. The snapping, extended jaw, the flashing teeth, the full moustache gyrating . . . his whole manner was vigorous" (Murphy, 1955, p. 358). He did have some difficulty with his voice, which was rather high pitched and could become raspy; his throat "was a constant trouble" (Murphy, 1955, p. 357).

In late February, Taft was able to make a speaking tour through New York, Ohio, and parts of Pennsylvania. The trips of both Taft and Roosevelt grew longer as the campaign developed. Roosevelt made a six-day speaking tour in late March, going as far west as Iowa and Minnesota, then returning to New Hampshire, Maine, and Boston. Taft made a three-day speaking tour to Ohio and Pennsylvania. The candidates often gave 10 to 15 whistle-stop speeches each day.

Wilson spoke in Philadelphia, and soon after he set off on a speaking tour of Kentucky and Illinois. His speeches were described as "serious" and "intelligent" by the press, but the reports generally were consigned to the back pages. Wilson had been a popular lecturer and the president of Princeton, and his characteristic approach was to define issues "in terms of principles." He gave most of his speeches extemporaneously, working from an outline and delivering them "in a clear, tenor voice that carried to the edges of crowds" (Hogan and Andrews, 1995, p. 114). Wilson's agenda for progressive reform stressed the theme of change. The enemies were the "standpatters." Business was changing, he said, and securing unwarranted privileges. Congress was "half a generation behind" in dealing with these changes. Politics must be more active, in the manner of Andrew Jackson, and must catch up with the needs of the country (*Tribune*, February 8, 1912). Wilson especially attacked the trusts and the tariff. In a speech on "The Relationship of Business to Government" in Topeka, Kansas, in February 1912, he declared that he did not want to "hamper the great processes of our economic life." But the men who "are making use of our corporation laws for their own advantage," he said, must be restrained so that they do not "establish monopoly" (*Tribune*, February 23, 1912). Though he would be the eventual winner of the presidential election, Wilson barely pierced the veil of the Republican press in the primaries.

Despite the many resemblances of 1912 primary campaigning to modern times, one clear difference was that the 1912 candidates wrote their own speeches. Though travel was slower, speechwriting could still be a frenetic task. Roosevelt composed one speech in the smoking room of Penn Station in New York while waiting for a train to Louisville. The *Tribune* reported that the news of Roosevelt's presence spread rapidly, and a "curious crowd grew and grew" (April 3, 1912).

The last month of the primaries received the most attention from both candidates and the press. In Massachusetts, the headlines read "Taft and Roosevelt Rock Old Bay State. President and Ex-President Dash Through Massachusetts Towns in Final Appeals for Votes at Primary Today. Cheering Crowds Greet Them" (*Tribune*, April 30, 1912). Here the candidates participated in what the *New York Times* called "the most remarkable political joust that the United States has ever seen"; it was a kind of prefiguring of the modern "fax attack." The two men literally followed each other around the state, speaking in the same cities. Roosevelt received regular telegraphic reports of Taft's speeches and began "a long distance debate by retorting to Mr. Taft's statements" (*New York*

Times, April 30, 1912). Roosevelt made the "sleaze factor" one of the main issues, charging that Taft was backed by corrupt bosses and "the sinister special interests which stand behind the bosses," while Taft rather weakly defended his unpopular tariff reform and charged Roosevelt with fostering class hatred (*Tribune*, April 30, 1912).

After a divided result in Massachusetts, both candidates moved on to Maryland, which Roosevelt won handily. While Taft and Roosevelt did not travel to the West Coast, their Washington staffs coordinated the local committees there and provided personal "representatives" to stand in for the candidates. Taft campaigned nine full days in Ohio, his home state, speaking in every congressional district. Again he was closely followed by Roosevelt. The energy required to keep up this pace began to take its toll on Taft. On the day of the Ohio primary, the pro-Taft *Los Angeles Times* (May 21, 1912) painted a poignant picture of the candidate's fatigue: "It was a hard day for Mr. Taft. The sun was hot and he often spoke in its full glare. His voice showed the strain of the long tour." Taft lost the Ohio primary by a 16% margin.

In the New Jersey primary (May 26) campaign, Roosevelt and Taft again followed each other from city to city, using the telegraph to keep informed about each other's speeches. Each speech was surrounded with hoopla: parades, brass bands, mass rallies with thousands of noisy partisans, and festive banquets.

THE 1932 PRIMARIES

Governor Franklin D. Roosevelt did not whistle-stop and barnstorm in the 1932 primaries. He adopted a "rose garden" strategy, taking the public position that he needed to tend to his job as governor of New York. However, from January through June 1932, he gave 26 speeches; most of them were in New York and on New York issues. The three speeches he gave outside of New York were on April 18, a Jefferson Day Dinner Address in St. Paul, Minnesota; on April 27, an Address to the Governors' Conference in Richmond, Virginia; and on May 22, a Commencement Address at Oglethorpe University, Atlanta, Georgia (FDR Speech File, Roosevelt Library, Hyde Park, NY).

Roosevelt also used the radio to reach the public. The broadcasting of speeches in their entirety through the radio was a common practice of the times (Andersen and Thorson, 1989). Roosevelt gave eight radio addresses during this period (FDR Speech File, Roosevelt Library, Hyde Park, NY).

His radio address on April 7, though only 10 minutes long, was particularly important. It foreshadowed his 1933 inaugural speech and his new administration, and it introduced a philosophy directly contrary to the prevailing Republican theory of trickle-down economics. Instead of boosting the economy at the top, he said, attention should be paid to "the forgotten man" at the bottom. Hoover was neglecting people's needs. Prosperity depended upon plans "that rest upon the forgotten, the unorganized but the indispensable units of economic power . . . that build from the bottom up and not from the top down, that put their faith once more in the *forgotten man* at the bottom of the economic pyramid." He advocated a number of reforms to help farmers, ideas that he implemented when he was president. The Depression was "an emergency at least equal to that of war," he said. "Let us mobilize to meet it." The military metaphor emerged again in his first inaugural speech.

According to Samuel I. Rosenman, a close Roosevelt adviser and speechwriter, Raymond Moley had submitted an "excellent draft" of the speech, including the "forgotten man" phrase, which came from an essay by sociologist William Graham Sumner in 1883.[1] Rosenman described the speech's effect: it "threw down a challenge to all his conservative rivals for the nomination. It created a great deal of discussion at the time; in many quarters, it evoked the epithet 'demagogue'—but it kept him in the forefront as the outstanding liberal fighter" (Rosenman, 1952, p. 61).

On May 22, Roosevelt spoke at the graduation at Oglethorpe University in Georgia. Much of this speech was written by a group of newspaper men who had teased Roosevelt about his speeches; he responded by asking them to write one. The main author was Ernest K. Lindley of *Newsweek*, and according to Rosenman, "The Governor made very few changes in the language." He continued the attack on the Hoover administration made in the "Forgotten Man" speech, and he spoke of the need to redistribute income. As with the April 7 speech, Roosevelt portrayed the country as being in dire straits, and thus, he said, "the country needs . . . the country demands bold, persistent experimentation. . . . It is common sense to take a method and try it: If it fails, admit it frankly and try another. But above all, try something" (Rosenman, 1952, pp. 65–66).

There was a certain vagueness in these speeches, as Roosevelt, Howe, and Farley were working to build a national coalition and needed to play down differences with supporters in different parts of the country. Unlike Smith, who openly advocated a strong anti-Prohibition stand, Roosevelt took a moderate Wet-Dry position, more acceptable to the rural Protestant Democrats he needed to get nominated. In general, he wanted to focus on economic issues rather than on the divisive repeal issue.

Roosevelt has been a favorite subject of rhetorical analysts over the years.[2] They generally have found him to be a master of public speaking in every respect. His speech style was heavily influenced by his schooling at Groton, where there was much attention to Bible study and reading great literature aloud. At Harvard, he was trained in public address by

George P. Baker, the famous speech teacher of the time (Brandenburg and Braden, 1955, p. 460).

Roosevelt "was happiest when he could express himself in the homeliest, even the tritest phrases." He used slang, idioms, and colloquial language (Sherwood, 1949, pp. 212–213). He insisted on clarity, and a study of his First Inaugural and a radio address of October 22, 1933, found that "about 70 per cent of his words . . . [fell] within the limits of the 500 most commonly used words of the Thorndike Word List" (Brandenburg and Braden, 1955, p. 505). He wanted his speeches to have an oral quality, and he often read the speech aloud, "for every word was judged not by its appearance in print but by its effectiveness, over the radio" (Sherwood, 1949, p. 215).

Because of the paralysis of his lower body, Roosevelt's body movements and gestures were quite limited. When he spoke, "he had to use at least one arm constantly to grip some support." But his "vigorous head movements," "eloquent facial expressions," and "broad, friendly smile" created a dynamic, vigorous impression. His voice added to this effect and was widely admired; it was tenor, clear, vibrant, friendly, with lots of variety, and he was skilled at adjusting the rate to the needs of radio schedules (Brandenburg and Braden, 1955, pp. 516, 520).

Since Roosevelt himself seldom left New York during the primaries, the campaign made active use of surrogates. The Democratic National Committee also assisted the Democratic candidates. In an "unprecedented move, the Democrats had left open their 1928 National Headquarters for use as a publicity vehicle" to take advantage of the mistakes of the Republicans (Carcasson, 1998, p. 351). They sponsored a speaking tour, and radio speeches were broadcast coast to coast on NBC, denouncing the Hoover administration and proclaiming that the Democrats had a good chance for victory (Boxes 1190 and 1191, Democratic National Committee Files, Roosevelt Library, Hyde Park, NY).

Smith started campaigning considerably later than Roosevelt. He stressed the importance of being simple and sincere and the necessity to "amuse as well as instruct" (in Troy, 1991, p. 153). He preferred the narrative form in order to hold audience attention: "Keep your audience in suspense as a storyteller does," he said (in Winkler, 1925, p. 20). Smith had excelled in declamation in school, and he studied and memorized many model speeches, especially from the British Parliament. He considered himself more of a debater than an orator, explaining that a debater "takes what the other fellow says, tears it to pieces, and shows how impossible it is. Then he sets up his own house and shows you how easy it is to live in" (Smith, 1930, p. 5).

A background in theatre also influenced Smith's speaking. "Amateur theatricals helped me more than anything else in sizing up audiences and giving them what they want," he said (in Winkler, 1925, p. 20). Pringle (1927) reported that he had a voice that "bellows and roars and cracks and penetrates to the last row of seats." He used two characteristic gestures, a pointed finger and a fist crashing down (p. 29). He spoke in colloquial language, saying that speakers should "talk to the man on the street in language he can really understand, not in the Court of Appeals language" (in Warner, 1956, p. 306).

Smith believed that one could not be effective as a speaker unless one looked into the faces of the audience. Hence "he never read his speeches," but spoke extemporaneously from notes written on envelopes (Jones, 1968, p. 370). One account of his speech making reported that he was much more effective in extemporaneous, personal appearances than on the radio, because "his speaking style was too hot, too passionate, to be piped into the nation's living rooms." His voice was "raspy and accented," and it called up an image of the "urban bogeyman" (Troy, 1991, p. 155).

Smith gave few speeches during the primaries. Biographers and contemporary newspapers focus on four speeches in this period, two in January, one on March 31 in New York, and one on April 13 at the Jefferson Day Dinner in Washington, D.C. In the January speeches, he called on the party to work for the repeal of the Eighteenth amendment, and he proposed an economic program with "a vast program of public works to create employment" and reform of the tariff and government regulations (in Handlin, 1958, p. 158). His March 31 speech proposed a six-point program of reform to deal with the Depression and attacked the Hoover administration for its indifference to unemployment ("Al Smith Proposes," *Philadelphia Inquirer*, April 1, 1932, p. 16).

The most important Smith speech in the primary period was his response to Roosevelt's "Forgotten Man" speech. Speaking in Washington at the April 13 Jefferson Day Dinner six days after Roosevelt's speech, he accused Roosevelt of fostering the kind of "group hatred" advocated by Huey Long and Father Coughlin (Handlin, 1958, p. 160). Roosevelt had sided with the farmers and had ignored the industrial laborers, he believed. "I will take off my coat," he declared, "and fight to the end against any candidate who persists in any demagogic appeal to the masses of the working people of this country to destroy themselves by setting class against class and rich against poor" (in Handlin, 1958, pp. 160–161). The *New York Times* declared that "Smith ran away with the Democratic mobilization gathering." "Not only did his open fire on Roosevelt provide the dramatics," it said, describing his "eyes flashing and face red with anger" as he "hurled his denunciation at demagogic appeal." He ended his speech "in this striking phrase which brought the audience to its feet: 'If the United States is not going to win, what difference does it make which party wins?'" (*New York Times*, April 14, 1932, in Warner, 1956, p. 254).

President Hoover was assured of his party's nomination despite the gloomy economy, and the Republican primaries were of no importance to him. As the incumbent president and the object of the Democrats' attacks, however, Hoover was an important actor in the political scene. He opposed giving direct government payments to the unemployed, but he took actions in early 1932 to establish the Reconstruction Finance Corporation, "which initially lent money to shore up financial institutions and businesses" and supported construction of public works projects like dams. Despite such measures, "the public perceived him as a distant, uncaring leader, and his popularity plunged" (Burgchardt, 1995, p. 135).

Hoover's *Public Papers* show that the number of his speeches as president was fairly high. In the January–June 1932 period, he gave seven addresses (including two on the radio), made four "Remarks," and held 25 press conferences. Only two of the speeches focused on the economic situation, and most of the rest were ceremonial. It is clear that Hoover did not feel the need to use the bully pulpit of the presidency to defend his administration in early 1932. He had actually given more speeches and held more press conferences in a comparable period in 1931. He waited until very late, October 1932, to begin his major campaign addresses, under heavy fire from the Democrats, but it was too late.

Hoover's reluctance to give speeches is understandable. "For most of his life ... he was painfully shy and dreaded public speaking." He worked at his speeches methodically, however, first doing extensive research, then dictating or writing out a first draft, then showing copies to aides for suggestions, then correcting and editing further. Multiple versions were the rule, and "one of Hoover's 1931 speeches went through 14 drafts before he was satisfied" (Burgchardt, 1995, p. 136).

In spite of all of this work, he was a poor speaker. His style and delivery were the problems. As an engineer, he saw speeches as a way to report the facts, and his long sentences, extensive citing of statistics, use of the passive voice, and unfamiliar vocabulary made his messages dull and difficult to understand. Though he worked hard on the content of his speeches, he seldom practiced them out loud, and while delivering them he read them rapidly and without vocal variety or emphasis (Burgchardt, 1995; Carcasson, 1998; Short, 1991).

THE 1952 PRIMARIES

In two respects, the speeches of the 1952 primaries differed from those of earlier years. First, candidates were interviewed on nationally broadcast television and radio shows, where their answers took the form of short speeches, or pieces of speeches. Second, there were several debates in the 1952 presidential primaries (the first debate had occurred in the 1948 Oregon Republican primary campaign). In addition, the candidates and their surrogates traveled and spoke in the primary states, in much the same way candidates had done in 1912.

Two unique communication problems of the 1952 presidential primaries were captured by a cartoon by Fitzpatrick in the *St. Louis Post-Dispatch* in April 1952. Headed "The 'Thinkers,' " it showed an elephant and a donkey sitting musing to themselves, next to a shoreline. The elephant, looking out to sea, was thinking, "How to get Ike from Europe?" The donkey, facing inland, was thinking, "How to get Adlai from Illinois?" (reprinted in the *New York Times*, April 6, 1952, Section 4, p. 3). Neither candidate campaigned; Stevenson even refused to be a candidate. How could their backers overcome such obstacles?

The Republicans

Eisenhower was absent for most of the primaries period, as he was serving as commander of the North Atlantic Treaty Organization (NATO) in Europe and was constrained by a military order that prohibited officers from participating in political campaigns while on active duty. His campaign manager, Senator Henry Cabot Lodge II of Massachusetts, therefore spoke in his place, or he arranged for other surrogates to do so. Lodge said that he accepted all television and radio invitations, "never turned down a press conference, and never slept more than three nights in a row in the same bed" (Lodge, 1973, pp. 85–86). Others who frequently served as surrogates were Senator Frank Carlson of Kansas, Representative Hugh Scott of Pennsylvania, Senator Duff (Pennsylvania), Representative Judd (Minnesota), and Paul G. Hoffman, co-chairman of the Citizens' Committee for Eisenhower (Arthur Krock, "South Dakota Primary May Tell G.O.P. Story," *New York Times*, May 25, 1952).

When Eisenhower returned to the United States, his first speech was in his hometown of Abilene, Kansas, on June 4. It was not very successful. The *New York Times* reported that, "After mumbling through his first televised speech, Eisenhower threw his prepared talks 'out the window' " (June 15, 1952, p. 50). His difficulty with prepared speeches was confirmed by the Television Plans Board, which helped him with his campaign. Their research showed that he was at his best when he could face questioners, while "prepared speeches were deadly" (Barkin, 1983, p. 329).

According to Medhurst (1995), Eisenhower's rhetorical skills had been influenced by three military role models: Fox Connor, Douglas MacArthur, and George C. Marshall. For three years Eisenhower had to write a field order for Connor every day. "Connor insisted that the order be in the form of a five-paragraph statement in which everything essential for understanding and carrying out the order was covered." From this experience, Eisenhower became very skilled in expressing his ideas clearly and simply, without extra words. MacArthur, in contrast, was a negative role model; Eisenhower thought he spoke too often, with language that was too ornate, and in a manner that was "arrogant and condescending" to his subordinates. Marshall confirmed "that words should be used sparingly and simply, and that deeds were the most eloquent form of expression." In addition to these principles of communication, Eisenhower's own warm personality and ability to make people feel at ease contributed to his effectiveness (Medhurst, 1995, pp. 192–193).

Since Eisenhower did not campaign in the primaries, none of his speaking skills could be demonstrated. He was especially vulnerable to charges of having no position at all. As Taft told New Hampshire voters, "The truth is that my principal opponent has taken no definite position on any issue" ("Senator Taft Challenges Ike Forces on Taking Stand," *Union Leader*, March 8, 1952, p. 1). A book of quotations from Eisenhower speeches of the past appeared during the campaign, and from that his general principles regarding society and government could be discerned: his "strong belief in individualism and opposition to centralized government, [and] strong distaste for bureaucracy and warning against it" (Sullivan, 1952). However, such a philosophy was almost indistinguishable from Taft's.

Underneath this vague front, however, there was a bitter ideological battle going on between Eisenhower and Taft. Eisenhower represented the internationalist wing of the party, Taft the more isolationist wing. As Hart (1982) has pointed out, candidates *embody* issues. Their views on issues are part of them, part of their political *personae*. This was emphatically clear with Eisenhower, whose widely publicized role as NATO commander symbolized his internationalist views; the senators who carried on his campaign also were publicly identified with these views. Taft made his anti-internationalist views well known too, denouncing Truman's post-war programs, such as Point Four and funds for economic aid to Europe.

In sharp contrast to Eisenhower's absence from the campaign trail, Taft campaigned actively from September 1951 until the Republican Convention in July 1952. His schedule, remarked columnist Jay G. Hayden of the *Detroit News*, looked "almost beyond human endurance." Taft attributed his large 1950 Senate race victory to his extensive speech making in Ohio. He adopted the same strategy for the presidential nominating campaign (Hayden, "History Shows Campaigning Fails to Win Nominations," February 13, 1952, p. 24). From October 1951 through early May 1952, according to a *New York Times* reporter, he had "made some 550 speeches, traveled 50,000 miles, and been seen by approximately 2,000,000 people," visiting 35 of the 48 states (in Patterson, 1972, p. 517).

By 1952, 19 million homes had television sets, mostly in the East.[3] The new medium of television provided a new outlet for speech making, but it changed the act in the process. Interview programs such as *Meet the Press*, which was broadcast weekly on television and radio, gave candidates a chance to use what Trent and Friedenberg have called "speech modules," or single units of speech on different issues. Each module "is an independent unit that can be delivered as a two-to-seven minute speech" on a particular issue (Trent and Friedenberg, 1995, p. 157). In modern campaigns, candidates routinely respond to questions with these well-developed, articulate speech modules.

Taft appeared on *Meet the Press* on January 20 and March 9, 1952, but there is little evidence that he knew anything about speech modules. Perhaps because the broadcast interview format was relatively new, he seemed to draw a sharp line between answering questions and giving speeches. Thus, his answers were brief and to the point of the question, and he seldom linked his comments to his campaign themes or used the chance to further his argument. The reporters on *Meet the Press* set the agenda for the discussion, questioning Taft on statements he had made and votes he had taken and putting him on the defensive (January 20, 1952, Library of Congress Sound Division).

In another speaking situation, at the National Press Club on June 10, Taft opened with what he called a "very brief statement of the important issues," which lasted 24 minutes. He then took questions for 39 minutes, and his answers were much more like speech modules than on *Meet the Press*, averaging over two minutes each. In this format, he dominated the agenda with his opening message, and he then used the questions to drive home his campaign themes (National Press Club, June 10, 1952, Library of Congress Sound Division).

Many of Taft's speeches on his extensive speaking tours also were broadcast over local radio stations.

The Democrats

Few candidates entered the Democratic primaries because of President Harry Truman's long delay in deciding whether to run again. However, the Democratic primaries became important because of the unorthodox primary campaigning of Kefauver, particularly in the pattern he established in New Hampshire. Kefauver defeated Truman there in a novel campaign devoid of party support. He came into the state for one day on February 10 and gave a speech at the Nashua Chamber of Commerce, spent a week campaigning there from February 13 to 20, and another week from March 4 through Election Day, March 11. The person-to-person style he used was reminiscent of James Farley's style in 1932, except that Kefauver was meeting voters, not party leaders. He went to church events, tea parties, home visits with Democrats, factory tours, and door-to-door canvassing, saying that he "considered a group of five to be a 'good crowd' " (Gorman, 1971, p. 124).

Kefauver was not effective when speaking from a manuscript. In April 1952, for example, he spoke on the CBS-TV series *Presidential Timber*. His biographer reports that the "folksy, informal exchanges during the preliminaries were extremely effective in communicating the man-of-the-people image." But when he gave his prepared speech, he read it heavily, in a dull manner (Gorman, 1971, p. 132). Governor Adlai Stevenson reported that at a dinner in New York in honor of Averill Harriman, Kefauver's speech was not very good, and he "got a little tight afterward to boot" (Martin, 1976, p. 566). Kefauver was quite frank about his lack of speaking ability. In Nebraska, he told voters that he was "not an orator or a great speaker" and just wanted "to meet people, and discuss . . . issues with them" (Gorman, 1971, p. 136). He spoke with a dignified, dull Southern accent, in a dry, serious, steady manner, with little humor or color and with few interesting examples.

Yet people responded to him. By the end of the primaries, Kefauver reported that he had traveled 96,000 miles campaigning and had spoken with thousands of people. He especially liked to answer questions, he told the press; he thought that was important. The party needed to be "strong, clean, [and] politically responsive," to organize at the grassroots level, to attract young people, he said (National Press Club, June 1952, Library of Congress Sound Division). Energetic, campaigning long hours, and working with volunteers, Kefauver and his wife Nancy attracted heavy press coverage. His wife, a rare female presence in a time when electoral politics was overwhelmingly a male domain, spoke and answered questions on topics of special interest to women (Gorman, 1971). James Reston of the *New York Times* said that her ability to speak to audiences in French "helped [Kefauver] immeasurably with New Hampshire's large French–American population" ("Eisenhower Vote Held Blow to Taft's Hopes; Kefauver Seen Forcing Truman to Run," March 13, 1952, p. 20).

Kefauver stressed the issues of crime and corruption, foreign policy, and the importance of the presidential primary (Churgin, 1972, p. 91). Known to Americans as the chairman of the recently televised Kefauver hearings on organized crime, he had high credibility on the crime issue. Truman's dismissal of the primaries as "eyewash" gave Kefauver the opportunity to become their defender. He told New Hampshire voters that he did not consider the primary eyewash at all, "but rather take[s] it as a democratic method for you to express your choice for nominee for the highest office in your power to give" ("Kefauver Scores Crime in Politics," *Union Leader*, February 11, 1952, p. 1).

One Democrat who many people wanted to run was Governor Adlai Stevenson of Illinois. He was not a willing candidate, but an energetic, small group of university professors and others organized a kind of shadow campaign to promote his name.[4] While Stevenson took no part in this campaign, he did give several speeches and interviews of national interest during this period. On April 16, he issued a statement saying he "could not" accept the nomination because of his duties as Illinois governor. The next day, he spoke at a Democratic State Committee dinner honoring Governor Averill Harriman of New York, and he "stole the show." He praised the Democrats, spoke of the president's daunting tasks, and the importance of which ideas would win. The speech "excited" those present. An April 24 Gallup poll showed that he was the favorite of Democratic county chairmen two to one over Kefauver (Martin, 1976, pp. 563–564). In the last three months before the Democratic Convention, he gave major addresses to the Dallas Council on World Affairs, the Oregon Democratic State Committee's Jefferson–Jackson Day dinner, and the San Francisco Commonwealth Club.

Whereas Eisenhower was an absent candidate who ran in the primaries, Stevenson was a highly visible noncandidate who ignored the primary route. These two men with their unorthodox approaches became their parties' nominees at the 1952 conventions.

The Debates

There were three debates in the 1952 presidential primaries. The idea of debating was new; the first broadcast debate between presidential candidates had been held in 1948, when Republican presidential candidates Harold Stassen and Thomas Dewey debated each other in the Oregon Republican primary, broadcast nationwide on radio. In 1952, Taft expressed his unwillingness to endanger party harmony by debating. He would much rather debate President Truman, he said, than any of the Republican candidates (*Meet the Press*, January 20, 1952).

This reluctance to debate within the party was shown in the fact that two of the three debates during the 1952 primaries were *bipartisan*. In early April, Republican Stassen and Democrat Kefauver had a joint televised debate in Wisconsin. One of the issues they debated was McCarthyism—Stassen accused Kefauver of being soft on Communism, and Kefauver raised the issue of freedom of speech (*New York Times*, April 7, 1952, in Gorman, 1971, p. 141). On May 1, three Democrats and three Republicans took part in a forum televised by ABC at the League of Women Voters Convention in Cincinnati; the League and *Life* magazine were the sponsors. The Democrats were Harriman, Senator Robert Kerr of Oklahoma, and Kefauver; the Republicans were Stassen, Governor Earl Warren of California, and Paul Hoffman (representing Eisenhower). Two invitees, Senator Richard Russell of Georgia and Taft, did not participate. The two questions were determined by a poll of citizens before the debate: one focused on how to prevent government dishonesty and inefficiency, and the other asked whether the United States should increase or decrease foreign economic aid ("5 Candidates Call Foreign Aid Vital," *New York Times*, May 2, 1952, p. 13). The debate also was broadcast on radio by ABC and NBC, as well as Voice of America and Radio Free Europe (Swerdlow, 1987, p. 151).

The third debate was more typical of modern primary debates, in that it was between two members of the same party, Democrats Kefauver and Russell, the night before the Florida primary. According to the Associated Press (AP) reporter, it was a hot fight. The two candidates "slashed at each other with bitter sarcasm," he said, "often almost shouting," and they ignored others who were supposed to be participating in the panel discussion (*Nashville Tennessean*, May 6, 1952, in Fontenay, 1980, p. 203). One analyst of the nominating process has concluded that debates from the 1980s on have contained many more sharp exchanges than debates in the 1950s and 1960s (Wattenberg, 1991). The Kefauver–Russell debate, however, sounds like a match from recent times.

THE 1972 PRIMARIES

President Nixon had little opposition in the 1972 Republican primaries; after New Hampshire, he ran virtually unopposed. But he was quite active in speech making during this period. While Democratic candidates were getting heavy press attention for their primary battles, Nixon gave six televised speeches to the nation. On January 20, he presented his State of the Union message; on January 25, he gave a national address on the Vietnam Peace Plan; on March 16, he addressed the nation on busing; on April 26, he gave another national address on Vietnam; on May 8, he announced the mining of North Vietnamese ports; and on June 1, he addressed Congress and the nation, reporting on his trip to the Soviet Union. He also gave four other speeches, 44 remarks (mainly ceremonial), one interview, and held four press conferences (*Weekly Compilation, Public Papers of the President*).

There was nothing accidental about the timing of Nixon's messages. He and his staff followed the Democrats closely, entering into a virtual contest to dominate the news agenda. On February 2, for example, Muskie made a speech about Vietnam, attacking Nixon's policies and calling for unilateral American withdrawal. The speech enraged Nixon, and he determined to make Muskie a target, having surrogates attack him in the media. Muskie also became the main object of "dirty tricks" organized through the White House.

Nixon wanted to get the voters thinking about *his* issues rather than the Democratic issues. To do that, he suggested picking "three or four positive issues . . . [to] hammer home . . . rather than be constantly dragged into answering them on 'is the Administration pro big business?' " (Nixon to John D. Ehrlichman, April 9, 1972, in Oudes, 1989, p. 411). There was nothing positive about the issues he suggested, however; all were attacks on Democratic positions, on marijuana, welfare, and crime.

On April 28, Charles Colson wrote to H. R. Haldeman, reporting how much time each of the three networks had given to Nixon's speech of April 26, compared to other stories: ABC, 10 seconds; NBC, 40 seconds; CBS, 0 seconds. Colson complained that stories on the Apollo 16 splashdown, Muskie's withdrawal from the Democratic race, the Paris peace talks, Indochina, and an anti-busing march had all received much more time than Nixon's speech (in Oudes, 1989, p. 430).

Sometimes Nixon seemed to want to actively debate the Democratic primary candidates, who often gave speeches or interviews immediately after his addresses (Humphrey and McGovern, CBS, May 9, 1972, Nixon Project, 5351). Nixon's March 6, 1972, speech on busing came only 48 hours after the Florida primary, which Wallace, a strong opponent of busing, had won overwhelmingly. Nixon said that he had always opposed busing for racial balance. Blacks and whites were both committed to desegregation, he said, but "busing is a bad means to that end." He proposed a bill for a moratorium on busing and a $2.5 billion equal opportunity education act that would help upgrade inner-city schools (CBS Special Report, March 6, 1972, Nixon Project, 5204).

Though no Democrats were present to reply to Nixon on busing, the network commentators joined the debate with hostile questions and comments immediately after the speech. On CBS, the discussants were Dan Rather, Daniel Schorr, and Roger Mudd; on NBC, Edwin Newman. They raised the question of the constitutionality of Nixon's proposed bill, and they questioned whether the act of pumping money into schools could be called "equal opportunity" (CBS Special Report; NBC News, March 6, 1972, Nixon Project, 5204). In a real sense, Nixon and the media debated the busing issue, with the media having the last word that evening.

The media coverage of Nixon's trip to the Soviet Union was decidedly positive, including summaries of Nixon's speech to the Soviet people. NBC showed a 3½ minute excerpt and reported that 100,000,000 Russians had viewed the speech. Nixon sat at a white-and-gilt desk in the Kremlin, speaking of peace. He declared that the United States had no territorial goals, and he spoke of the similarities between the American and Soviet peoples. Using moving and appropriate stories and proverbs, he conveyed the image of a wise, benign leader. "No nation that does not threaten its neighbors has anything to fear from the United States," he said (NBC, June 1, 1972, Nixon Project, 5436, Tape 8).

The Democrats

Whereas most of Nixon's speeches were broadcast in their entirety on television and often on radio, the Democratic candidates' speeches reached American voters in abbreviated form, if at all—a few sentences from the speech and a quick summary by the television reporter. While this was longer coverage than in 1992, it was very short compared to Nixon's full speeches. For example, after the New Hampshire primary results, NBC showed two minutes of Muskie's victory remarks and two minutes of McGovern's speech to his supporters ("Decision '72," NBC, March 7, 1972, Nixon Project, 5169). Skimpy as the speech coverage was, it averaged two to seven times as long as the network news coverage of speeches in the 1992 primaries (Kendall, 1993).

Muskie was the Democratic front-runner in all of the polls when the primaries began, but the primary campaign proved to be his undoing, and on April 27, 1972, he withdrew from active campaigning. His public speaking and campaign organization and strategies played a role in this surprising decline.

While Muskie's Scheduling Files and Trip Books in 1971 and 1972 show that he made many campaign trips to Wisconsin, Illinois, and especially to Florida, New Hampshire seemed almost an afterthought (Edmund S. Muskie Papers). He failed to adjust to McGovern's intensive speech-making campaign there, as well as to other difficulties as the campaign unfolded.

Though it is impossible to measure the exact role of speech-making, some of the explanation for Muskie's surprising decline undoubtedly lay in his weak speech-making skills. He occasionally showed "flashes of fire" in his speeches, and he could be effective when he talked in a "straight-from-the shoulder" style with small groups (Miller, April 3, 1972). But he had two recurring problems: vagueness in language and dull delivery. In an interview on *Meet the Press* on January 16, 1972, Muskie was vague about almost everything. The following answer to a question about his record on the Vietnam War was characteristic of his style:

I said that I was wrong on the war. I haven't said that was the reason why people should support me. I hope that the considerations which voters will take into account are much broader than that and that they address themselves also to the future, the problems we face today across the board and what we need to do about them. (NBC, McGovern Papers, Mudd Library, Princeton, Box 4)

His strategy of "sitting on his lead" and not giving specific answers prevented him from effectively introducing himself to voters, from setting the agenda for the campaign, and from energizing his followers.

In Muskie's appearance on *Face the Nation* (March 26, 1972, Nixon Project, 5230), his speech delivery was weak in many respects, which tends to lower a speaker's credibility. Muskie sat in a slumped position, conveying low energy, and he did not use gestures to drive home his points. Rather than looking directly at the questioner or into the camera, conveying confidence, he often looked down or to the side, seeming to be searching for words. His hands lay crossed on the table; occasionally he would lift one hand for emphasis. The contrast was particularly sharp in joint appearances with candidates such as Humphrey and Wallace, who looked right into the camera and were dynamic, energetic, and fluent (*Face the Nation*, March 26, 1972, Nixon Project, 5230). Research on eye contact has shown that "avoidance of eye contact in televised encounters [is] universally interpreted as a sign of dishonesty, whereas a straight look into the eye and firm, unhesitating responses [are] interpreted as evidence of honesty" (Graber, 1984, p. 162).

Muskie began the campaign with a "Lincolnesque image," particularly based on the highly effective speech he had given replying to a Nixon speech on the eve of the 1970 elections (Bonafede, 1972, p. 462). He ran on the campaign slogan "Trust Muskie." But that image of honesty and wise maturity was undermined by his responses to two strategies of his rivals. He resisted their call for a debate, and he refused McGovern's repeated calls to reveal the names of his campaign donors. Ultimately, Muskie capitulated on both points, but it was too late to erase the impression that he had something to hide (McGovern, 1977).

The irony regarding Muskie's speeches is that from all appearances he had an excellent system of speech preparation. His main speechwriter was Robert M. Schrum, and there were over 30 task forces to research and develop policy proposals, directed by volunteer experts. His speech coordinator reported that Muskie insisted on thorough research and evidence for speeches and wanted them to be interesting to audiences. In the end, though, according to Milton S. Gwirtzman, a Washington lawyer who wrote for Truman and Robert Kennedy and traveled with Muskie, "85% of what he says in his total campaign is extemporaneous" (Cottin and Glass, 1972, pp. 350–353).

McGovern

Senator George McGovern of South Dakota was anything but fuzzy in image; he made the antiwar issue his central theme for much of the primary period. What he called the "centerpiece" of his campaign was the idea of returning to "the enduring ideals with which the nation began," a turning away from war and militarism, and a return to a society where people cared about each other and about the needy (McGovern, 1977, pp. 169–170). This thematic focus was in sharp contrast to Muskie's vague stance, and so was his approach to campaigning. According to his campaign manager Gary Hart, in New Hampshire, McGovern "went into almost every community in the state, into some towns and cities six times, carrying his message" (Hart, 1973, p. 140).

McGovern's announcement speech contained a pledge "to speak the truth about the hard questions fully and openly." To emphasize his candor, he decided to be open in his campaign. He published information on donors, filed a report on his income, assets, and liabilities, promised regular press conferences, asked for debates, and answered questions from audiences. Having taken these steps himself, he then made openness an issue, demanding that the other candidates open their records (McGovern, 1977, pp. 176–177). The strategy turned out to be especially effective against Muskie and Jackson, who strenuously resisted publishing information on donors. Though they had complied with campaign laws, McGovern made people wonder why they would not open their records.

McGovern was not an exceptionally able public speaker. He feared Humphrey's speaking ability, according to his campaign manager, saying that "he hated to share a platform with . . . Humphrey, whose voluble virtuosity, that sheer ability to produce a Niagara of words, left the more methodical McGovern . . . feeling virtually tongue-tied and speechless" (Hart, 1973, p. 179). He much preferred a question-and-answer format to speeches, saying, "I'd never give a speech if it wasn't for the fact that speeches are required. I'd just say, 'Let's hear your questions' " (Cottin and Glass, 1972, p. 357). He had a laconic delivery, with little vocal or facial expression, a somewhat slow speaking rate, an "occasionally whiney pitch . . . and [a] tendency toward nasalized speech" (Jamieson, 1984, p. 324).

McGovern said that about 90% of his campaign remarks were extemporaneous and that he found it difficult to deliver speeches written by others (Cottin and Glass, 1972, p. 356). He was accustomed to writing his own speeches from his years in the Senate. McGovern's speeches were workmanlike, with touches of emotional appeal revealed through moving stories and personal experiences, but they excelled in the clarity of their focus and theme. For example, at a rally in Miami on January 20, 1972, he laid out his goals for America in four parts: a nation with a truthful government, a just tax structure, compassion for the poor, sick, and old, and peace (Tape transcript, McGovern Papers, MC#181, Box 62, "Papers, Speeches," Seeley Mudd Library, Princeton University). His speeches followed a pattern of attacking the Nixon administration, particularly for its war policy and dishonesty, and then outlining his alternative in general terms (McGovern Papers, MC#181, Box 64, "Speeches," Mudd Library, Princeton).

When McGovern spoke of his opposition to the war, he had moments of real eloquence, using language and examples that appealed to the emotions and enhanced his credibility as he drew on his own experiences. These remarks rang with conviction and outrage. In a Milwaukee rally speech on March 30, 1972, he listed the things he was sick of, building up to the war and to the following vivid sentence, which received a standing ovation: "Finally, as I have said so many times: I'm sick and tired of old men dreaming up wars for young men to die in" (McGovern Papers, MC#181, Box 64, "Speeches," Mudd Library, Princeton). At times he would use poignant letters to buttress his positions, strengthening the emotional appeal of his messages by personalizing them and casting them in story form, a form that is easier for audiences to understand and retain (McGee and Nelson, 1985).

Starting with a "liberal, antiwar base," McGovern broadened his attention to other issues as the campaign went on, speaking about "the economy, tax reform, pollution, aid to the aged ... in an effort to broaden his appeal" (Douglas Kiker, NBC News, News Summary, March 3–9, 1972, Nixon Project, 5180). He also began to argue that the "antiwar idealists" and the "alienated blue-collar workers" had much in common. Their common enemy, he said, was the "alien world of power politics, militarism, deception, racism, and special privilege" (Address to the Jefferson–Jackson Day Dinner, Detroit, April 15, 1972; McGovern, 1977, p. 183).

In reflecting back on the nominating campaign, Hart said that "one of the few serious structural mistakes ... was the decision ... to separate issue development from the political-organizational backbone of the campaign structure, keeping the substantive research and writing apparatus in the Senate office, out of touch with day-to-day campaign operations." The political review of manuscripts often was neglected, and "McGovern did a lot of his own issue work without extensive staff backup." Hart said that he worried that the issue research was not getting checked adequately, and he feared that "sooner or later ... something was going to go out half-baked or wrong and it would do us irretrievable damage" (Hart, 1973, pp. 204–205). His fears were realized when Humphrey scrutinized McGovern's policies in the California debates, undermining McGovern's image of competence and providing damaging quotations for Nixon's advertisements in the fall.

Humphrey

Humphrey was the Democratic candidate Nixon feared the most (Jeb S. Magruder, in May and Fraser, 1973, p. 49). In his speeches and interviews during the primaries, Humphrey displayed a broad knowledge of political issues and a confident, articulate speaking style. When he spoke, his tenor voice was warm and understanding in tone as he discussed "people," as in phrases such as "the people in this country." He repeatedly set "the people" up against the Nixon administration. He tended to focus on the economic issues in his speeches and less on Vietnam than McGovern.

In an "Issues and Answers" appearance, he spoke in crisp, short sentences, communicating competence and firmness, though modifying the sentences with a prefatory "I think." For example: "I think that also should be destroyed." He used strong language against Nixon, saying: "The so-called anti-inflation program has not worked; it's actually been a hoax" (March 26, 1972, Nixon Project, 5230).

Humphrey spoke rapidly, varying his pitch and volume for emphasis, and he looked directly at his questioners, never down or to the side, nodding a lot for emphasis, and smiling. He conveyed energy and certainty in his delivery, in marked contrast to Senator Muskie's and Senator Jackson's rather dull manner. One reporter said that Humphrey "spoke at eighty miles an hour with gusts up to one hundred" (*Newsweek*, November 1971, in Solberg, 1984, p. 428), but every word could be heard.

In the 1968 presidential campaign, Humphrey had used prepared speech texts, and there had been much attention to editing and style; however, he seldom used prepared texts in 1972, though his speechwriters provided him with them. Humphrey thought that American politics were getting more like British politics, with their emphasis on the issues; wherever he spoke, people asked him about the issues. Thus his speeches were generally extemporaneous, talking about the issues and answering questions (Apple, "Humphrey Says . . . ," March 12, 1972, *New York Times*; Cottin and Glass, 1972, pp. 353–354).

The California primary in June was "do or die" for Humphrey because McGovern was so far ahead in delegates. In early May, Humphrey commissioned a private poll from Oliver A. Quayle III and Company Inc., which showed "that a substantial number of voters who favored McGovern were unaware of his position on certain key issues. Moreover, when those positions were brought to their attention, they disagreed with McGovern's stand" (Glass, June 10, 1972, p. 967). Humphrey made these McGovern positions the focus of his California campaign.

Low on funds and unable to pay for ads or a get-out-the-vote drive (Solberg, 1984), Humphrey's only hope was to reach the voters through the free media. He challenged McGovern to a series of debates (discussed later in this chapter), and he campaigned all over the state.

Wallace

Governor George Wallace of Alabama burst on the scene in the Florida primary. He was a strong opponent of busing and forced all of the candidates to confront the busing issue. Hart (1973) observed that the busing issue was effective because it served to capsulize several other issues, such as taxes, government waste, welfare abuse, favoring the rich, and "pointy-headed bureaucrats"—the efforts of "them" to interfere in our lives (p. 132).

Though Wallace never did the necessary organizing to secure many delegates, he clearly influenced the messages of the 1972 primaries. He expanded beyond the busing issue to discuss "tax reform, the remoteness of government from the people, and foreign aid giveaway" (Billy Joe Camp, Wallace press secretary, in May and Fraser, 1973, p. 102).

Wallace's campaign theme was "Send them a message." In a post-election analysis, the rival campaign managers agreed that this was a brilliant theme because it conveyed hostility ambiguously, allowing people to fill in their own meaning for both "them" and the "message." Camp explained that the theme had come directly from Wallace's speeches early in the campaign. The staff noticed that he used the phrase repeatedly, and thus selected it for their advertising (May and Fraser, 1973, p. 102).

Wallace rallies were colorful and entertaining, full of country-western music and religion, dancing, and Wallace's populist speech style of denunciation and humor. Wallace's speeches had standard components, chiefly, attacks on the status quo and ridicule. Little children should not be bused to school, "welfare loafers" should be put to work, and there should be tax breaks for the "little man." Wallace had standard lines about the "pointy-headed liberals" who "couldn't park a bicycle straight," and he mocked government officials with strong overtones of class resentment: "If you look good and comb your hair right, and have a good suit of clothes and have a melodious voice, you are an authority on Bangladesh" (*60 Minutes*, May 14, 1972, Nixon Project, 5370). In a hilarious takeoff on President Nixon's talk with Chairman Mao Tse-tung in China, Wallace said that the two men spent about half of their time discussing busing. Mao told Nixon that they do not ask anyone about busing in China; they just do it, "whether they like it or not." The president could have told Mao, said Wallace, that "We do the same thing in the United States" (CBS News Special Report, May 16, 1972, Nixon Project, 5379, Tape 5).

As Wallace gained large percentages of the popular vote in the primaries, the media gave him increasing prominence in their coverage and interview shows. Such exposure increased his credibility, especially as he spoke with confidence and energy, and he in no way took a back seat to his questioners. His language choices added to the impression of firmness: "I *shall*," "No, we do not," "In my judgment, the legislature *will* reduce them." His gestures, such as chopping the air with his right hand, were forceful. His rapid speech rate and quick responses conveyed confidence. His eye contact was very direct; he seldom looked down. His volume and pitch conveyed energy and involvement, and he did not pause until he finished his idea.

Despite Wallace's success with voters in many states, his credibility met with great resistance from people who remembered him as the Alabama governor who stood in the schoolhouse door in 1963, when the first black students integrated the University of Alabama. He encountered hecklers at many speeches, and he was pelted with food. He handled these incidents skillfully, such as when he said that some people do not believe in freedom of speech except for themselves (WTOP-TV, Washington, May 14, 1972, "Campaign '72, the Maryland Primary," Nixon Project, 5370). Ultimately, however, he was felled and permanently crippled by a gunman during the Maryland primary campaign.

Other Candidates

Though there were many other candidates running in the Democratic primaries, none did as well as the four discussed above. Jackson seemed to be a strong candidate before the primaries. He was a U.S. senator, well known for his hawkish position on Vietnam and his expertise on defense issues. His campaign was well funded and well organized. But Jackson was a dull, ponderous speaker who spoke slowly, said "uh" a lot, and looked down at his notes frequently. He did not excite the voters, nor did he carve out a distinctive niche in the large pack of candidates.

Lindsay too was a familiar political name, as a former New York Congressman and now Mayor of New York City. He recently had switched parties, from Republican to Democrat, which is generally a handicap because the process weakens the candidate's base of support. He poured his efforts into the Florida primary, standing out from the others because he argued strongly in favor of busing to achieve integration. Lindsay was dynamic and charismatic, advertised heavily, and drew much press attention. But he also did poorly in Florida and dropped out after the Wisconsin primary.

The Debates

In 1972, presidential primary debates were no more institutionalized than in 1952, and there were still laws that discouraged their being held. Nevertheless, there were five debates in 1972, one before the New Hampshire primary, one before the Florida primary (only two candidates participated), and three before the California primary. None of these "debates" met the requisites for a debate set in the landmark essay by Auer (1962), that a debate "is (1) a confrontation, (2) in equal and adequate time, (3) of matched contestants, (4) on a stated proposition, (5) to gain an audience decision" (p. 146). Still, as joint appearances, they gave viewers their only look at the candidates side by side, addressing the same issues, and in some respects they might be considered "joint job interviews."[5] Eric Severeid praised the California debates as "the best we've had in a long time," describing them as "dialogues," and "a series of arguments on television" (CBS News, May 30, 1972, Vanderbilt Television Archives).

McGovern kept pressing Muskie to debate in New Hampshire, and Muskie finally agreed (May and Fraser, 1973, p. 114). The five Democratic candidates who had entered the New Hampshire primary participated: Muskie, McGovern, Yorty, Hartke, and an antipoverty worker named Edward Coll of Connecticut. They met for a 90-minute debate televised on the 220 PBS stations on March 5, 1972, from 6:00–7:30 P.M., in Durham, New Hampshire, three days before the primary. McGovern and Muskie clashed over the question of disclosing campaign finances: McGovern had publicly disclosed his sources, but Muskie had not yet done so in 1972.

The most publicized moment of the New Hampshire debate involved candidate Edward Coll, who during his remarks waved a rubber rat, which he said symbolized the country's problems. This prop became the much-reported visual highlight of the debate. The debate was widely considered a failure: a "travesty," a "debacle," "lackluster," "foolishness." Apple gave four reasons for the failure: the two major candidates (Muskie and McGovern) did not really engage each other on the issues, the panel of newsmen avoided pointed questions and major issues, the inclusion of minor candidates cut down on the time that the major candidates could develop their ideas, and "Mr. Muskie and Mr. McGovern agree on too many issues to produce a striking contrast" (*New York Times*, March 7, 1972, p. 26).

There were efforts to organize a debate of the seven Democratic candidates in the Florida primary, but the candidates could not agree on a format. In the end, the debate was held the night before the primary, but only two of the candidates, Muskie and Lindsay, showed up. According to James M. Naughton of the *New York Times* (March 13, 1972), "Mr. Lindsay and Mr. Muskie agreed on most issues, but argued about Mr. Muskie's vote regarding the use of Federal funds for busing to desegregate schools."

The three debates in California were major events in the primaries. Held on May 28 (*Face the Nation*), May 30 (*Meet the Press*), and June 4 (*Issues and Answers*), they were originally intended to be limited to McGovern and Humphrey, and they were described as debates by everyone except the networks. Because of the equal time requirements of the Federal Communications Commission (FCC), the networks organized them much as they did their usual one-hour interview formats and scheduled them in prime time. They also renamed them, avoiding the word "debate." CBS called the first debate a "joint appearance," NBC called the second debate a "confrontation," and ABC called the third debate a "special edition." If the networks had called them "debates," they would have been obligated to invite all eight Democratic candidates on the ballot in California, or offer the others equal time.

Two of the excluded candidates, Mayor Sam Yorty of Los Angeles and Representative Shirley Chisholm of New York, sued to appear in the debates, and Chisholm got a favorable court ruling on June 2, after two of the debates had already been held. ABC therefore expanded its June 4 debate to include Yorty, Chisholm, and a representative of Wallace; CBS provided Chisholm with half an hour of prime time, and NBC gave Yorty and Chisholm 15 minutes of prime time each and invited them to appear on the June 5 *Today* show (Glass, 1972, pp. 966–967).

The debates proved very damaging to McGovern. Not only did he plummet in the California polls, but Humphrey's vivid characterizations of McGovern's weaknesses provided rich material for Nixon in the fall campaign. Humphrey attacked sharply and effectively, surprising McGovern with the "vehemence and the depth" of his attack (Hart, in May and Fraser, 1973, p. 134). McGovern reported that he felt constrained from responding in kind because he expected to get the nomination, and he needed Humphrey's supporters to win the election. Though he won in California, he said that "millions of voters had seen me, a new figure in American politics, being slashed and blasted by one of the most experienced, best-known figures in American politics" (McGovern, 1977, pp. 184–185).

In negotiating the terms of the debate, Hart insisted that the answers be monitored and timed, fearing that Humphrey, who was notoriously long-winded, would otherwise dominate. The transcript of the debate reveals that the candidates contributed about an equal percentage of the words (*Face the Nation*, May 28, 1972, CBS, McGovern Papers, tape transcripts, Box 6, Mudd Library, Princeton). But in the videotape of the debate, Humphrey dominated. Domination takes many forms besides number of words. Humphrey dominated by assaulting McGovern's position and forcing McGovern on the defensive. His charges were vivid and metaphorical: McGovern's defense policy, he said, would "cut into the muscle of our defense" and make us into a "second class power"; McGovern's policy was one of "unilateral disarmament." He backed up his claims with facts about McGovern's proposed defense cuts, responding quickly and with an aggressive, forceful manner, conveying more competence than McGovern.

McGovern answered the attacks on his defense policy by referring to his patriotism and war record ("I saw a good many of my friends die right in front of my eyes because we weren't adequately defended"), and by asserting that Humphrey's charges were not true (*Face the Nation*, May 28, 1972, CBS, McGovern Papers, Princeton, Box 6). What was needed, however, in the face of Humphrey's persistent and specific attacks, was a greater sense that McGovern knew something about the particular needs of the military. Humphrey raised serious doubts about his competence on this issue.

Humphrey also charged that McGovern had "concocted a fantastic welfare scheme which will give everybody, even Nelson Rockefeller, $1,000, and it will cost the taxpayers 60 or 70 billion dollars, mostly middle-income taxpayers" (*Face the Nation*, May 28, 1972, CBS, McGovern Papers, Princeton, Box 6). When a panelist asked McGovern how much the welfare plan would cost, he said, "I don't know," explaining that he would cover much of the cost by reducing administrative expenses and cutting the military. Those words resounded through the debate and long afterward. A major candidate was proposing sweeping changes in welfare and did not know how much it would cost. Hart (1973) said that, "The slapstick handling of the welfare issue brought cries of grief and outrage from advisors and contributors" (p. 204). The three journalists added weight to Humphrey's attack, asking tough questions and at times pointing out contradictions in McGovern's words and deeds, creating a lopsided, four-against-one impression (Debate in California, May 28, 1972, *Face the Nation*, CBS, Nixon Project, 5416, Tape 5).

The second debate was very different from the first one. This time it was the panelists who were on the attack, in effect "debating" the candidates. There were four journalists, and they proceeded through 60 questions (including follow-ups) as though they were in an intense, one-to-one press conference. Though both candidates were thrown on the defensive, the negative impact on McGovern seemed greater, because Humphrey had already raised so many of the hostile questions in the first debate, because McGovern answered some of the questions vaguely, and because one of the questioners, Robert Novak of the Chicago *Sun-Times*, played the role of the negative debater against McGovern so effectively.

The third debate, with five candidates plus reporters, was much more diffuse in its effect, pulled in many different directions by the larger group.

The California debates resulted in a close and critical scrutiny of McGovern's policies by Humphrey and the media. The debates also gave the candidates an opportunity to present their visions of the future, which they did in their opening and concluding statements. Both men were very hopeful. McGovern said that he wanted to be able to proclaim some day soon that, "Peace has come," and to proclaim that "there is a decent job for every American." Humphrey wanted to "lift the spirit of this country" and give people a "sense of vision for this country"; he laid out his record and urged that the voters choose "performance" over "promise." These themes, though drowned out in the volatile middle section of the debates, served to reinforce the campaign efforts and reach a huge audience.

Humphrey closed the gap in the polls by 15 points in five days, though McGovern won in California and three other states on the same day, going on to win the nomination.

THE 1992 PRIMARIES

Speeches played a vital role in the 1992 presidential primary in New Hampshire. The special circumstances of New Hampshire make speeches more important there than elsewhere in the nation. The population is small, only 1,110,801 in 1992 (*World Almanac*, 1994). Although the main way that New Hampshire voters learn about the candidates is through mass communication—the candidates' television ads, and newspapers and television news—"retail politics" remain vitally important. Because the bulk of the population is clustered in the southern part of the state, the candidates can easily travel around and be seen by thousands of voters personally. The candidates know that the speeches they give in New Hampshire will be attended by the media as well as by groups of voters and will help form the basis for news and commentary about the campaign. This discussion of the speeches and debates in the 1992 primaries draws heavily on the events of the New Hampshire primary, including material from the other primaries as well.

The author observed 16 speeches or speech-type events in New Hampshire, including debates, dinners, whistle-stop speeches, individual speeches, and rallies. Hundreds of voters a day heard each candidate personally. Some of the rallies attracted close to 1,000 people; Clinton's Nashua rally the last Saturday night before the primary drew 1,200 people (Joe Grandmaison, in Royer, 1994). New and personal information, even in small amounts, has been found to carry more weight with voters than abstract information (Popkin, 1991). In a primary in which approximately 170,000 people voted for Democrats and 178,000 for Republicans (Devlin, 1994), a few thousand votes made a difference. The margin between the candidates who finished third and fourth, Bob Kerrey and Tom Harkin, was only 1,518 votes (*New York Times*, February 20, 1992, p. A21). The thousands who attended speeches during the campaign, with their networks of friends and family, could well have affected the outcome.

More important in terms of the number of people reached, the media attended these speech events. The timing of the speeches was adapted to media needs: candidates usually gave "their most substantial speeches in the morning, so the press [had] the most time to digest them, and the second event around noon [offered] pictures or wallpaper, to illustrate the morning's message." That night there might be a rally around 6:00 P.M. to reach the local news (Rosenstiel, 1993, p. 114). In spite of all that planning, network television showed little of the actual speeches to the public (see Kendall, 1993). As Tom Rosenstiel of the *Los Angeles Times* reported, "The irony of television—especially in 1992—is that reporters demanded politicians deliver serious speeches if they wanted coverage, and then reduced them into soundbites so that is all the public ever heard" (Rosenstiel, 1993, p. 117).

Though the public never heard these speeches, the speeches were important to the reporters, who used them as a basis for forming personal impressions about the candidates and their abilities, and to see who came to hear the candidate, how audiences responded, and how the candidate dealt with their questions.

The speeches provided excellent opportunities for the candidates to "write the play" their own way. The candidates had complete control over the content of the speeches, unlike press conferences or interviews, in which the press led with the questions. They had a chance to show their priorities, such as when Buchanan explained his support of the voucher system for schools (Concord, February 11) and Kerrey spoke on health care (Manchester, February 12). In choosing their priorities, they had a chance to show how much they knew, backing up their proposals with evidence or telling the audience about their experience in solving the problem. And they could use the content of their speeches to reiterate the campaign themes found in their pamphlets, ads, and interviews.

The candidates used the speeches to introduce themselves to the press and to the voters as people with unique qualities and feelings. Tsongas joked about his lack of charisma, telling the story of Abraham Lincoln, who said, "If I had two faces, do you think I would use *this* one?" (Talk at Logicraft, Nashua, February 14, 1992). Harkin spoke of his family's strong pro-union views and resentment of scabs, and his father's belief that "The best social program's a job" (Rally, Alan's Restaurant, Boscawen, February 13, 1992).

An important way to define oneself as a unique human being is through speech style, the choice of words to express ideas. Speech style is highly personal, affecting the speaker's efforts to persuade through the clarity, vividness, appropriateness, and accuracy of language. Clinton, for example, expressed his ideas clearly but seldom vividly in the primaries. His occasional use of a folksy Southern idiom enlivened his style, such as when he reported that people came up to him and said, "I really appreciate the fact that you've taken some licks," but said that he hadn't taken any "licks that can compare to the people of New Hampshire" (Rally at Hesser College, Manchester, February 17, 1992).[6]

Perhaps the speaker with the most vivid language was Buchanan, who was consistently metaphorical and selected words that underlined his campaign themes. Buchanan's speech at Concord (February 11) attempted to convey personal characteristics and inspire and ridicule through language. He was tough: he would "play hardball" with countries that "give us a hard time"; we shouldn't be "trade wimps," he said. He was patriotic, calling for a "new patriotism": "Not only America first, but America second and third as well." He ridiculed the Democrats, especially Teddy Kennedy, who would sign a bill "if only he can find his pants." "How many 59-year-olds do you know," he asked, "who still go to Florida for spring break?" He appealed to deeply held values such as "shared sacrifice" (he would roll back the federal pay raise, turn in half of the president's pay, and call for a reduction in the salaries of the boards of directors of automobile companies). He reminded his audience of the principles of the American Revolution; the federal bureaucracy was like the British, he said, spending 25% of the GNP. As Klien (1994) has noted, Buchanan's speeches often constructed a narrative based on analogies to heroic times in American history.

Vivid words can touch an audience's emotions, making them laugh, applaud, nod, and go away full of enthusiasm or anger. Cliches, such as Buchanan's jokes about Senator Kennedy, a favorite butt of conservative humor, can give audiences a satisfying sense of participation. The candidates' words are at the heart of the campaign ritual, tapping and "intensifying deeply held values" (Nimmo and Combs, 1990, p. 69).

Of all the primary candidates, Clinton showed the most awareness of the important role his speeches could play in shaping media and public opinion. The first time the nation heard a Clinton speech it had been an unmitigated disaster. At the 1988 Democratic National Convention, his nominating speech for Michael Dukakis was too long, poorly adapted to the audience, and oblivious to the frantic negative signals of the convention planners. By late 1991, the failed nominating speech got little public mention, but helped explain Clinton's unusually well prepared speech strategy in the 1992 campaign.

Stan Greenberg, Clinton's pollster, reported that it was decided early in the campaign to make speeches a central part of Clinton's candidacy (Royer, 1994). He gave three major, thematic speeches at Georgetown University, his alma mater, on October 23, November 20, and December 12, 1991, introducing what he called his "New Covenant." The speeches laid out his agenda for change, the first on rebuilding America, the second on his economic plan, and the third on national defense. The idea was to define his candidacy early by tying together the speeches with a theme and giving them close together and in one place, an unusual strategy. He also used original language to define his partisanship, running explicitly as a "new Democrat," in no way identified with "the liberal core of the national party or its unsuccessful presidential nominees" (Burnham, in Pomper, 1997, p. 2).

Having a clear, fully developed message prepared distinguished Clinton from his rivals. At an important meeting of Democratic state party leaders in Chicago in November 1991, Clinton's speech stood out from the rest, and he received a standing ovation (Goldman et al., 1994).

Clinton sustained the major Georgetown themes in his primary campaign speeches, though the speeches this author heard were huge, sprawling affairs, often trying to cover the contents of all three Georgetown speeches plus a wealth of local references. Smith (1994) has provided a useful overview of Clinton's organizing agenda, showing that he used the "consistent logic" of a modern political jeremiad. Over and over he stressed the message that a chosen people, the forgotten middle class, had followed false prophets (Reagan, Bush), who had "led them away from the 'first principles' that have always made America great." These first principles, deep and traditional American beliefs, were that "tomorrow will be better than today" and that "each of us has a personal moral responsibility to make it so." Salvation lay in new leadership to bring change. Clinton's primary speeches stayed within this framework (Smith, 1994, p. 1).

Clinton established a pattern of communicative behavior in New Hampshire that he was to follow in subsequent primaries: when the attacks on him were strong, he fought back by escalating the number of speech-related events. Thus, when his standing in the polls was dropping in New Hampshire, he scheduled a rally every night, brought over 100 Arkansas friends to the state to meet and talk to voters, bought two half-hour television segments for town hall meetings with call-in questions, and distributed 20,000 videotapes to Independent voters. Campaign research during this embattled period showed that "the public responded positively to Clinton's lack of defensiveness" (Greenberg, 1997, personal correspondence).

In sharp contrast to Clinton's speaking was Bush's failure to use speeches to shape the campaign agenda or to define his character. David Schribman, political reporter for the *Wall Street Journal*, said that when the Buchanan campaign began early in 1992, "We saw President Bush reduced to kind of cryptic notions of message—'I care'—and I think it all began to fall apart" (Schribman, in Royer, 1994, p. 105). Charles Black, consultant for the Bush–Quayle campaign, summarized the situation by saying, "We had a hell of a hard time with speeches. . . . It was the process. . . . You know, we didn't have good speeches" (Black, in Royer, 1994, p. 153).

It did not help that Bush had "had little training in public speaking," and "when he spoke extemporaneously, he often mangled syntax and used incredibly cryptic phrases." He did not like to rehearse his speeches, and he did not like to speak from texts. The speeches for which he is best known—the 1988 Acceptance Speech at the Republican National Convention and the speech to Congress after the war in the Persian Gulf—were exceptions. Both were "delivered from texts and heavily rehearsed" (Smith, 1995, in Ryan, pp. 346, 349).

Bush worried many Republicans by choosing to wait until January 1992 to launch his campaign, using the State of the Union speech as a vehicle. He built up great anticipation about this speech in his press conferences. It is true that the State of the Union address commands heavy media attention (Kendall, 1993), but at a time when Bush's approval rating stood at 45% and public anxiety about the economy was high too much was riding on the success of one speech.

The first third of the State of the Union message dealt with foreign policy and the military; one critic described it as "an ode to America winning the Cold War and the war in the Gulf" (Kiewe, 1993). Then Bush turned to domestic proposals. He said that the unemployment level "will not stand," a phrase from his Persian Gulf speech, and he said that he would submit an economic plan to Congress the next day. If they had not acted upon it by March 20, Bush promised to go into a battle mode. He then outlined short- and long-term economic growth proposals. The speech drew wide criticism, especially for being "a laundry list with no main text" ("The Tinkerer," *New York Times*, January 30, 1992, p. A20). The *Washington Post* reported that the speech had not helped Bush's standing in the polls (Eric Pianin and Richard Morin, "Bush Pushes Plan as Criticism Rises," January 31, 1992, p. A1).

Not only were Bush's speeches ineffective in commanding attention or in shaping the campaign agenda, he often chose not to speak at all. In New Hampshire, Bush gave a few short speeches but adopted a largely nonverbal personal style. He passed through malls, shook hands, and waved and smiled, providing good pictures but avoiding the microphone. His ads and leaflets and surrogate speakers carried his message. During the Los Angeles riots, many people thought that the president should address the nation, but he chose not to speak.

With his strong front-runner status in the Republican primaries, Bush won the nomination without making speeches central to his campaign. However, in the larger picture, this neglect gave the Democrats the opportunity to portray him for many months as a deeply flawed president, and no one replied.

Speeches gave the candidates a chance to make distinctions between themselves and their opponents. As Jamieson (1992) has pointed out, "the longer the statement, the more likely it is to compare and contrast candidates' positions," providing useful information to voters (p. 259). The audience needs a basis for comparison, particularly in the confusion of a multicandidate party primary. Speeches also gave the candidates a chance to move quickly to meet campaign developments, immediately replying to charges of opponents or media claims. When Harkin criticized Tsongas on nuclear power on February 13 at Seabrook, New Hampshire for example, Tsongas responded the next day at Nashua, discussing his own support by environmental groups and proclaiming that if companies violated environmental standards he would "prosecute and prosecute hard."

Finally, speeches gave the candidates an opportunity to interact directly with the voters, showing their quickness and adaptability, their knowledge of issues, and, when there were hecklers (as there were with Clinton and Bush), their ability to react well under fire. For example, when Bush was heckled by an ACT-UP AIDS demonstrator shouting, "What about AIDS?" the heckler was quickly hustled out the door by the Secret Service. Bush then departed from his text to say, "Understandably, they're upset, but sometimes their tactics hurt their effort. We are going to whip that disease . . . we're doing everything we can." He then cited figures about AIDS research funding in his administration (Derry, New Hampshire, February 15, 1992).

Some of the candidates regularly engaged in long, substantive question periods with audiences, using the opportunity to develop their themes and further shaping impressions of their character. Reporters remarked on Clinton's ability to speak knowledgeably and at length on a wide variety of public policy issues, and to answer virtually any question asked; those who saw him day after day came to admire his competence. Rosenstiel reports that during the primaries Clinton's speechwriter, Paul Begala, designed the speeches to meet what he believed were the media's needs: first, "the press was mostly interested only in conflict, scandal, polls, process, and gaffes," so most speeches contained attack lines. Second, he included sound bites or summaries for television coverage. And third, "a speech had to be a full, coherent argument, since it had to please the high-brow columnists as well as the local news" (Rosenstiel, 1993, p. 117).

Speeches also can prove damaging to candidates. The emerging "book" on Kerrey among reporters in New Hampshire, for example, was that although he knew a lot about health care, his knowledge about other public policy issues was thin. Perhaps, they said among themselves, he was not ready to run for president. His speeches contributed to this impression. Once he stopped speaking about medical care or farm issues, his discussion of other matters was vague, brief, and unsatisfying.

The Debates

There were five primary debates in 1972, and four in 1976. That number increased to six in 1980 and then began to escalate rapidly. There were 14 in 1984 (Hellweg, Pfau, and Brydon, 1992). According to Ron Brown, chair of the Democratic National Committee, there were "something like 70 joint appearances" by the presidential candidates in 1988 (in Royer, 1994, p. 40). Having so many debates appeared to lessen their impact.

In 1992, Brown asked the candidates to pledge to take part only in party-sanctioned debates, and then he went to the television networks to ask them to broadcast the debates nationally. The Democrats hoped to limit the number of debates to between six and eight, said Brown, to give "national focus" to the candidates. His plan had the effect of reducing the number of debates sharply from 1988; the Democrats ended up with about "fifteen or so," by his count (in Royer, 1994, pp. 40–41). There were no Republican primary debates, as President Bush announced that he would not debate any of his primary opponents.

The primary debates in 1992 differed from those in 1952 and 1972 in five ways. First, they were much more numerous, totaling at least 15. Second, they were held at fairly regular intervals throughout the primary period, rather than sporadically as in 1952 or bunched together at the end as in 1972. Third, they experimented with format, and they favored the single moderator and flexible time allotments for speaking rather than the panel of reporters and the strict time limits of 1972. Fourth, they helped convey a sense of a Democratic "team" with common principles, uniting in their opposition to Bush and their advocacy of "change." And fifth, they helped set the rhetorical agenda for the primaries to follow, as in their consistent discussion of Bush's failings in handling the economy and in their advocacy of a new and better health care policy.

The 1992 debates resembled the earlier debates in five ways. First, with so many candidates debating, it was difficult for any candidate to stand out from the crowd, though each made frequent use of attacks to differentiate each from the other and from Bush. Second, the lesser-known candidates gained stature by appearing on the same platform with the better-known candidates and having an equal amount of time to speak, thus seeming equal. In the 1992 primaries, the debates enabled Jerry Brown to influence the questioning in the debates, as well as to advertise his 1–800 number for fund-raising. Third, the candidates tended to attack the front-runner as well as the candidate who posed the biggest threat to their own candidacy. Wattenberg (1991) believes that these attacks contribute to the fading of public enthusiasm for the front-runner.

Fourth, having numerous speakers and/or panelists reduced the quality and depth of the primary debates. As media critic Walter Goodman wrote in the *New York Times*, "Calling on six politicians to cover every imaginable subject . . . in one-minute slices guarantees sloganeering" (December 26, 1991, p. D18). And fifth, the debates helped introduce the candidates to the voters. There were many opportunities in the debates for the candidates to establish their personal characteristics and views on policy. This is especially important in the primaries, when some candidates are little known.

CONCLUSIONS

Unique Characteristics

Certain characteristics of speeches and debates have been unique to presidential primaries and consistent across the years. First, incumbent presidents, and to a lesser extent, other incumbent officeholders, have been able to use their power of position with great effectiveness through speeches in the primaries. The most skillful incumbent in the five primary years studied was President Richard Nixon, who in 1972 traveled to China and the Soviet Union during the Democratic primaries and gave historic speeches to the nation, stealing the attention away from the Democrats.

A second characteristic of primary campaign speeches is that they are given live to audiences in the presence of the media and that journalists use their observations to form judgments that they communicate to the public. While the public sees and hears little of these speeches on network news (Kendall, 1993), journalists regularly summarize them and convey their own impressions and opinions in campaign stories. The candidates' own language is almost wholly lost in this process; in effect, they become "dummies" to the journalist-ventriloquists, who speak for them. Most of the candidates' individuality and personal inventiveness displayed in language is therefore lost.

Third, the candidates in all of the primaries have demonstrated consistently by their actions that they believe speech making is an important activity. All but a few have traveled to the primary states (or to selected primary states) and given speeches, accompanied by a press entourage. This was true in 1912, 1952, 1972, and 1992. Most have also given numerous substantive speeches, with the exception of General Dwight D. Eisenhower, who in 1952 remained in Europe as head of NATO during the primaries.

Fourth, most primary speeches and debates target the audiences of the particular states where they occur. Thus when McGovern and Humphrey debated in California, they frequently mentioned California problems. These speeches are different from the national addresses an incumbent president gives, for their immediate goal is to persuade an audience of voters within a specific state to vote for the candidate. However, there are exceptions to this pattern. When the candidate announces plans to run for president, for example, he or she speaks in broad themes.

Fifth, though the direct importance of speeches to voters has declined since the early days of the primaries, candidate speeches still help to mobilize the campaign's organizers and party workers, to provide much of the substance of news releases, and to serve as a foundation of information for the media stories. The significance of the fact that many primary speeches appear on C-SPAN in their entirety and on PBS in long portions also should not be underestimated; this audience is composed of political insiders and news junkies who take their politics very seriously.

Sixth, when presidential primaries are contested, the candidates inevitably criticize each others' positions in their speeches. To emerge from the pack of candidates, each must show that he or she is distinctive. The first to be attacked by the out-party candidates is the incumbent president. Once all of the candidates have announced and the poll standings have emerged, the candidates begin their intraparty attacks.

Seventh, because the primary candidates are in the same party, their views on issues often are indistinguishable. This makes political image extremely important as a way of differentiating among the candidates. Candidates must use their messages as a way to call favorable attention to themselves, especially to their personal qualities.

Finally, the primary speeches in the early primaries help set the agenda for the later primaries and for the fall campaign. They serve to shape and crystallize the topics that will dominate the campaign. This was particularly evident in 1992, when the weakened state of the economy in the first primary state, New Hampshire, became the central focus of discussion.

Changes in the Nature and Role of Primary Speeches and Debates

What changes occurred in the 1912–1992 period in the role of speeches and debates in the primaries? Let us first consider the changes noted by Jamieson (1992) regarding the general election campaign to see if the same changes occurred in the primaries.

(1) Have the primary candidates become increasingly vague in their stands on controversial policy issues? No. There seems to be no steady progression of vagueness in the primaries. Franklin D. Roosevelt was vague on Prohibition in 1932, and Smith took a clear stand; Eisenhower was silent on controversial issues during the primaries in 1952, while Taft took clear stands; Muskie was vague on the issues in 1972. Candidates often "sit on their lead," speaking vaguely and trying not to offend anyone by taking clear stands; this is a characteristic that transcends time. The intraparty nature of the primaries also dictates against clearly differentiated stands, because most of the candidates generally agree on most of the key issues.

(2) Has reasoned argument in primary campaign speeches declined

with the decline in the length of speeches? Yes and no. It is clear that the length of speeches has declined over time, with hour-long addresses common in the primaries of 1912 and 1932, decreasing to an average stump speech of "under seventeen minutes" in 1988 (Jamieson, 1992). Speakers cannot develop as many arguments with adequate proof in 17 minutes as in an hour, but the primary speakers do argue and back up their points in their stump speeches, going far beyond assertion. In Kendall's (1993) examination of 1992 primary speeches shown on C-SPAN, she concluded

The actual speeches . . . contain the unique qualities of language, the variety of individual inventiveness in arguments, and the conspicuous strengths and weaknesses in use of evidence and ability to adapt to different situations and audiences that make speeches such a valuable source of information about candidates. (p. 250)

Where reasoned argument has fared quite poorly is in the network news coverage of the primary speeches. With their severe time constraints, the networks in 1992 talked about the primary speeches for an average of 18 seconds a night in February, 17 seconds in March, 27 seconds in April, and 27 seconds in May (Kendall, 1993). Needless to say, argument, statement, and proof lost out.

(3) Have the candidates in the primaries learned to "act, speak, and think in television's terms . . . transforming speeches . . . into ads"? (Jamieson, 1992, p. 206). The evidence from this historical study suggests that candidates have *always* adapted to the media of the times, shaping their speeches accordingly. In 1912, the newspapers wanted full transcripts of the speeches, and the candidates provided them. Large audiences wanted to be entertained as well as informed, and the candidates filled the speech occasions with hoopla, parades, and music to entertain. In 1932, Roosevelt practiced the sound of his speeches to ensure that they were ready for radio. He also gave shorter speeches on radio than in live speaker-audience situations; his "Forgotten Man" speech was only 10 minutes long. In 1952, radio and newspapers were still the main media, and candidates gave hundreds of speeches, satisfying the now ravenous appetite of radio news. In these very early days of television, the candidates seemed awkward and inexperienced in the television news programs studied; this is one case in which the candidates had not yet learned to adapt to the media. In 1972 and 1992, the candidates were comfortable with the medium of television.

NOTES

1. Though Roosevelt gathered materials for his speeches from many people, he took an active role in the speechwriting process himself. After reading through

material from others, he would generally dictate a first draft, and in the 1920s and 1930s it was common for his speeches to go through five or six drafts, with consultation; the number increased in the late 1930s and 1940s (Brandenburg and Braden, 1955, pp. 464–482).

2. See Brandenburg and Braden, 1955; Daughton, 1994.

3. Kramer, 1992, p. 27.

4. See Chapters 1 and 5 for more information on this campaign.

5. I am indebted to an unnamed source for the perceptive term "joint job interview." It captures the nature of the so-called debates better than any other term I have heard.

6. Clinton's ceremonial speeches during his presidency, especially at moments of national tragedy, have been eloquent and inspiring.

Chapter 4

Advertising in a Multi-Candidate Field

On the isomorphism of issue and image: "Politicians are indeed packaged. Contained in their 'packages' are a host of *embodied issues*, the only sorts of issues relevant to a human, communicative enterprise like political affairs."

—Roderick P. Hart, 1982, p. 367

Researchers of political advertising often ask the public what specific television spots they remember, if any (Roberts, 1995; West, 1993). The author's choice from the 1992 primaries would be the "Echoes" spot of Democratic candidate Senator Tom Harkin, made by Ken Swope and run in New Hampshire. In this spot, Harkin, in shirtsleeves and a tie, spoke to an audience of working people in an empty factory. He used the setting as a metaphor for George Bush's failed economic policies, pointing down the barren corridors. "All over America," he said, "I see empty factories, the dashed hopes and dreams of working people all over this country." "You can look down this hallway," he said, gesturing, and the camera swept over the vacant halls, the dangling light switch, the single chair, the bare floor. "You can hear the echoes," he said. The strings and chords provided slow, serious "memory music." With the sight of the empty building came plucking, harplike tones in the treble register, wistful, a cliche for an empty building and what might have been. "They were good citizens, they fought our wars and they paid their taxes," said Harkin. And they were challenging us not to forget that what made America great was "people at work." They were calling to us, saying, "Don't forget. Don't give up. Build it again. We can do it." As Harkin visualized a more positive future, the music ended with a tonic chord, and the factory audience applauded. In 30 seconds, the spot evoked a mood of sadness, drawing the audience into the lonely corridors, listening for the voices of the past. Harkin conveyed compassion and concern for the unemployed, then he ended with words of hope and confidence. "Build it again. We can do it." Applause sounded. This engaging, moving story has a happy ending: the appearance of a strong leader who would work with the people to make things right.

Others noticed this spot too; West (1993) found that among Massachusetts voters interviewed, it was the third best remembered Democratic spot of the primary period. The story structure drew viewers into the message, holding their attention and making them notice Harkin, cast as the kind and confident leader figure. It was a good ad by any standards. But Harkin did poorly in the primaries, finishing fourth in New Hampshire and dropping out in early March 1992. A single political spot does not make a campaign. It is useful to remember that the word "campaign" comes from the French term *campagne*, meaning "open country, suited to military maneuvers; hence, military expedition" (*Webster's New World Dictionary*, 1988). An expedition takes place over time, requiring repeated efforts. The primary candidate must continually maneuver for position on the field.

Not only did Harkin have to contend with his four main primary opponents, he also had to interact with the reporters who followed him around and wrote and spoke about him. In addition, the public that was receiving his messages imposed its own prior views on what it heard. While the problem of unemployment could be appreciated by almost anyone, only certain people would define this issue as the critical variable on which they would base their voting decision. There also was the practical question of how many people saw the spot. In the cacaphony of the primaries, getting the audience's attention and gaining name recognition was Harkin's first challenge. He was a U.S. senator from Iowa, unfamiliar to most Americans. The political spot was one way for him to introduce himself, his name, and the issues and images he wanted people to identify with him, a way he could control. Yet only a small percentage of people, seldom exceeding 20%, are highly attentive to political spots during the primaries (West, 1993, pp. 24–26).

RESEARCH ON POLITICAL ADVERTISING

Advertising in the primaries has the potential to be more influential than advertising in the general election, particularly in the early primaries, because of the relatively unformed views of the public, as well as the fact that many candidates are not well known. The compressed time period of the primaries and their serial nature requires the candidates to adapt quickly, to try new strategies and responses. Political spots are well suited to this need for quick strategic adaptation. Many researchers have found that television spots are quite influential in the primaries (Atkin, 1980; Orren and Polsby, 1987; Owen, 1991; Payne, Marlier and Baukus, 1989; Pfau et al., 1993; West, 1993).

Voters are far more interested in a candidate's personal characteristics than in party identification or specific issues, and they are more likely to vote on the basis of a candidate's image in presidential elections (Miller, Wattenberg, and Malanchuk, 1985). Candidates work to convey image traits effectively through their messages, but the task is complex and difficult. Images are not only multifaceted and to some extent affected by the particular campaign context, but they also are co-constructed among the candidates, the media, and the voters. According to Louden (1990), image is "an evaluation negotiated and constructed by candidates and voters in a cooperative venture" (p. 1). Certainly, that is true, but the media also play a role in this construction.

Voters have an ideal image of a candidate in their minds, and some of the traits in that profile—honesty, competence (including experience), empathy, and strength and decisiveness—have reappeared across campaigns (Nimmo and Savage, 1976; Hellweg and King, 1983; Hellweg, King, and Williams, 1988; Trent et al., 1993). Primary ads tend to emphasize the personal qualities of the candidates more than in the general election (West, 1993). One reason is that there is so much agreement on issues among candidates of the same party that in order to distinguish themselves from each other they turn to personal qualities. In addition, the candidates have to spend a good deal of time simply introducing themselves and gaining the public's trust and respect. Kendall and Yum (1984) found that in a real sense the voters evaluated candidates as they would judge a new acquaintance, looking for signs that the person agreed with them in their broad worldviews and was like them.

Pfau et al. (1993) found that voters developed perceptions of presidential candidates in two stages in the primaries, first forming "relational perceptions" about the candidate's personal qualities, such as honesty, sincerity, warmth, and caring, and later building on these initial perceptions to make assessments of the candidate's competence and how well he would handle the job of president.

Important early research by Patterson and McClure (1976) established that "political commercials contain substantial information," giving voters "solid reasons why they should support one candidate instead of the other" (p. 102). They found that 70% of the 1972 presidential campaign spots that were examined contained substantial information on issues, and 42% were mainly focused on issues. The amount of information in the spots far exceeded that provided in the network news programs.

Kern's (1989) research explored this question further. In her study of the 1984 campaign, she found that most presidential advertising mentioned issues; in fact, 89% of the spots contained issue references. However, these references were usually vague. She called them "slogan ads," ones in which "no prospective policy statement is made, nor is there a why statement or answer." In contrast were the "platform ads," which contained "either a commitment by a candidate to a position, or a rationale for taking a position or opposing that of the opponent" (p. 51). Only 16% of the spots met the criteria of platform ads. The clear majority of ads were skimpy on information and reasons. Kern's findings were much bleaker than Patterson's and McClure's (1976) concerning the substance of ads.

The concepts of issue and image in political advertising have been widely researched and are useful ones. However, in practice, the two concepts overlap and merge until they are almost indistinguishable. When candidates talk, they talk about something, frequently about contemporary issues such as what they will do about taxes, health care, or education. As Hart (1982) said, politicians come to *embody* issues, and it is foolish to speak of political issues as something separate from the people who embrace them. The voters hear their words, and though they may forget the details, the general substance of a candidate's views becomes part of the underpinning for voters' images of a candidate. Kern (1989) has recognized this principle and has given it a name—dovetailing—which refers to the way in which character and policy messages are combined in political advertising, through visual, linguistic, and sound components. Candidates use dovetailing as one of their main ways to make arguments in their spots.

A second way in which candidates' spots make arguments is through narrative. Kern (1995) analyzed the way in which Ross Perot used stories in his infomercials to reveal values and to appeal to the audience's individual and collective identities. In narratives of his life, he set the scene, developed the characters, introduced conflict, resolved the conflict, and drew a moral to the story, a statement of values. He thereby attempted to connect with the voters' beliefs and values, to move the voter closer to the candidate. Patterson and McClure (1976) made a similar point when they observed that, "Political advertising . . . [like product advertising], tries to associate the candidate on an emotional level" with people's problems, thereby attempting to "build an affective link between candidate and viewer" (pp. 101–102). The Harkin spot described earlier illustrates this concept.

Primary candidates make heavy use of biographical spots to build their image with voters (Kaid and Ballotti, 1991). Diamond and Bates (1984) call them "ID spots," in which candidates try to raise their name recognition and create a positive impression by presenting "commonly valued personal characteristics and compact narrative histories" (p. 307).

In 1912 and 1932, the candidates were already nationally known when they entered the primaries, but when a candidate entered who was not well known, such as Kefauver in 1952 or McGovern in 1972, advertisements became an important means to increase their name recognition.

Political portraiture goes back to ancient Greece, and it has been part of political campaigns throughout history. Biographical spots, a kind of political portraiture, have dominated the caucus and primary periods. They make use of myths, which are narratives containing specific characters who are larger than life, narratives that have a moral. The information is shaped to emphasize the candidate's positive image traits, viability, and electability, with some attention given to his or her general ideological outlook or worldview (Gronbeck, 1989, pp. 351–363). Because "overt self-promotion" is seen as unseemly in American culture (Shyles, 1984, p. 419), however, these spots generally use narrators and/or testimonials by others to praise the candidate, and they place the candidate in an indirect relation to the camera.

Another way political spots carry arguments is through the use of condensation symbols (Graber, 1976; Elder and Cobb, 1983). These are referential symbols such as the flag, crosses in a cemetery, or a bride and groom, which have important meaning to the voter, evoking an emotional response. Candidates use them in the hope of getting the audience to transfer its feeling for the symbol to the candidate. Or, if the condensation symbol has negative connotations, such as the vulture in one of President Bush's anti-Clinton spots, it may be used to transfer negative meaning to an opposing candidate.

The bulk of research on political advertising has focused on the medium of television. There is a growing body of knowledge about the visual aspects of television. As Jamieson and Campbell (1988) report, "The language of the television is the language of close-ups," and because of the relationship of nearness with intimacy, television "simulates intimate relationships" (p. 45). Television gives the candidate the chance to capitalize on this illusion of intimacy. According to Lanzetta et al. (1985), "Psychologists have long recognized the face as the primary channel for affective communication. . . . Moreover, the communicative effects of facial expressions involve the vicarious instigation of an emotion in the viewer" (p. 86). A candidate who communicates in what is perceived as a warm and friendly manner therefore has an advantage in evoking positive responses from viewers.

If the spot is intended to evoke anything more specific than a vague emotion or mood, the accompanying linguistic message is important, helping to guide the viewer's interpretation to the meaning intended. Thus, though we tend to think of political spots and political speeches as two different genres, it is common for political spots to contain large sections of public speaking by the candidates, shaping the meaning of the message. According to Jamieson, "the speech remains the staple of paid political broadcasting" (1992, p. 490).

Negative campaigning and its growth have been deplored widely, and negative advertising makes up a large portion of such campaigning. Kaid and Johnston (1991) found that in general elections about 30% of presidential campaign spots were negative. Despite almost universal complaining about negative spots, they continue to be used because of their power. As Jamieson (1992) reports, "Negative information seems better able than positive to alter existing impressions and is easier to recall" (p. 41); the ability to recall attacks is confirmed by Roberts (1995), and Kern (1997). The public also makes distinctions between the types of negative spots, displaying more tolerance for attacks on the candidate's positions or record than for attacks on character (Johnson-Cartee and Copeland, 1991; Shapiro and Rieger, 1992).

Several researchers have examined negative spots in presidential primaries and have found that they occur less frequently than in general elections. Kaid and Ballotti (1991) found that during the 1968–1988 period, 18% of the presidential primary spots were negative. Payne, Marlier, and Baukus (1989) found that in their study of the early 1988 presidential primary spots, 23% were negative: they appeared less frequently than argumentative and identification spots. One would expect that primary candidates would make ample use of comparative advertising to distinguish themselves from their same-party rivals, but the usual sequence is positive biographical spots first, to gain name recognition and to become familiar to the voters, followed by negative spots.

The agenda-setting power of ads has been established (Atkin and Heald, 1976; West, 1993). West examined surveys during the 1976–1992 presidential primaries and found that "many issues and traits were correlated with ad exposure for each candidate" (p. 83). And Jamieson (1992) has noted that for *uninvolved* viewers, ads often serve as their main source of political information. Just et al. (1996) found that the influence of ads seemed greater "when other information [was] scarce." In news-poor areas of the country, citizens relied more heavily on ads for information (pp. 186–187).

METHODS

This chapter compares the nature of political advertising in the presidential primaries of 1912, 1932, 1952, 1972, and 1992. The author sought representative examples of advertising in each of these campaigns, particularly in the week just before the key primaries. Most of the examples were drawn from local newspapers in the years 1912, 1932, and 1952, and from television in 1972 and 1992. The author did not have specific "ad buy" data. However, accounts by Devlin (1994), Jamieson (1984,

1992), Diamond and Bates (1984), Patterson and McClure (1976), and West (1993), as well as by contemporary journalists and biographers, helped establish that the television ads discussed here were actually shown and that they played a role in the campaigns.

Newspapers were selected from major population centers within the states.[1] Television spots from the 1952 and 1972 primaries were obtained from the University of Oklahoma Political Communication Center, the Edmund S. Muskie Archives at Bates College, and the Nixon Project, National Archives. Television spots from the 1992 primaries were obtained from L. Patrick Devlin, University of Rhode Island, and from the Purdue University Public Affairs Video Archives.

ADVERTISING IN THE 1912 PRIMARIES

Patterson and McClure (1976) have made the point that political imagery did not begin with the age of television, contrary to popular belief. Instead, "it began with politics" (p. 102). The 1912 campaign confirms their point. The candidates portrayed themselves as veritable giants, in fact. Compared to the "cool medium" blandness of recent presidential candidates, the images and rhetorical visions of the candidates in 1912 stand out in sharp, colorful, and bold relief. However, the main medium for this message was *not* their advertising, it was their speeches and news coverage. The advertising, in contrast, tended to be cluttered with so many different appeals that the candidate's image was almost lost in the shuffle.

The characteristics of the newspaper ads in the 1912 primaries were that they (1) were crowded with appeals, often compressing several stages of a political campaign into one; (2) adopted a uniformly deductive pattern of argument; (3) made strong party appeals, including frequent use of testimony by party officials; (4) placed heavy emphasis on the candidate's viability; (5) presented the candidate's qualifications in brief lists of traits; (6) gave detailed information on how to vote in the primary process; and (7) used printing devices to emphasize points.

The ads were relatively few by modern standards, although there was a marked increase in advertising between the March and May 1912 primaries studied. The New York primary was held on March 26, 1912. In the New York papers reviewed, the *New York Times* and the New York *Tribune*, only one ad appeared in each paper in the entire pre-primary period, both on the last two days of the campaign, and both for Roosevelt. In an account of campaign expenses required by the secretary of state, it was reported that the Roosevelt campaign had spent $2,500 for advertising in New York County, 3.5% of its total expenses there (*Tribune*, May 12, 1912). The Maryland primary was held on May 6. In the Maryland papers, during the week leading to the primary, the *Baltimore*

American had 22 ads, averaging 3 a day, and the *Sun* (Baltimore) had 17 ads, averaging 2.5 a day. The main explanation for this difference is that the New York primary was not binding on the party, unlike the Maryland primary.

A front-page ad for Democrat Champ Clark on May 3, 1912, in the *Baltimore American* is typical of the period. This large double-column ad served several purposes: it was an announcement for a rally, a promotion for Clark's persuasive appeals, and an educational message about the ballot and the delegates. According to the ad, the "eloquent speakers" at the rally would include Baltimore Mayor James H. Preston, and three former or present members of the U.S. Senate and Congress. The slogan read: "Vote for a Winner. Champ Clark, The People's Choice. Always a Democrat," thereby making appeals based on his viability as well as party loyalty. Simons (1986) has described the five stages of a persuasive campaign as: planning, mobilization, legitimation, promotion, and activation. This ad combined the last three stages, giving legitimacy by reference to prominent party leaders, promoting the candidate's positions, and providing information on the delegates and ballot to enable the voter to take action on Election Day.

The deductive nature of these ads is illustrated by another Clark ad in *The Evening Capital and Maryland Gazette* (Annapolis) on May 3 and May 4, 1912, p. 4. The headlines read: "Champ Clark for President. Democrats must nominate a winner. CLARK IS THE MAN." The identical appeal appeared in an ad for Woodrow Wilson in *The Salisbury Advertiser* (Salisbury, MD), May 4, 1912, p. 4: "FOR WOODROW WILSON AND DEMOCRATIC VICTORY." In each case, the principle being appealed to was the party's desire to win in November, though the election underway was in May and concerned an intraparty battle for the party's nomination.

Most of the ads used variety in print as visual devices to draw the reader's attention and to emphasize certain points through differences in type size, type boldness, spacing, borders, layout, and ad size. A few were constructed to look just like news stories, with only a tiny identification line at the bottom revealing that they were ads, saying "Published by Authority of ——, Political Agent." Others were indistinguishable from the commercial advertising surrounding them.

In 1912, the presidential primaries were new, and the process was rather complicated. Many of the ads tried to help the voter by printing the ballot and marking it both with the name of the preferred candidate and his delegates. Some even suggested, "Paste this in your hat!" and "Take into election booth with you."

One-fourth of the 44 ads studied from 1912 contained explicitly negative material, which is comparable to the 18% to 23% found in modern primaries. One of these was a classic comparative ad, arranging the entire message in two columns, one for Taft, the other against Roosevelt. "A Vote for President Taft," said the ad, "Is a Vote For . . ." and it listed eight good things, summing them up as "Republicanism," but the vote for Taft also was a vote "Against . . ." and it listed eight bad things, summed up as "Rooseveltism" (*Baltimore American*, May 5, 1912, p. 16). This ad dovetailed its character and policy messages through the language chosen. For example, the character of Taft and Roosevelt was contrasted, with Taft being the honest man who would keep party pledges and Roosevelt being the man of "broken personal faith." At the same time, several contemporary issues were woven into the message, such as statements that Taft favored Progressive causes and was independent of the judiciary.

Most of the negative ads, however, had to do with internal party skirmishes within the state. For example, the Roosevelt faction in the Republican Party accused the Taft faction of what would be called today "dirty tricks": "circulating fake ballots marked for Roosevelt, but marked for the Taft delegates" (*Baltimore American*, May 6, 1912, p. 16).

Though information about candidate image had to compete with many other goals in these ads, there was some attention to image traits, usually by listing them. It is apparent that the ad writers were attempting to appeal to deeply held values, thus Taft was portrayed as a man of "deeds—not words" ("A Vote for President Taft," *Baltimore American*, May 5, 1912, p. 1), who would "support the rights of the workingmen" as he would everyone who did his duty as "an American citizen" ("Why Taft?" *Baltimore American*, May 5, 1912, p. 16). Roosevelt, according to the New York *Tribune* ad (March 26, 1912), "is the leader in YOUR cause, not his own. He stands for the rule of the people." He had strength and could win: he would "thrill the Republican party with hope of success, with strong purpose."

Only two of the ads that were examined contained a full discussion of the candidate's strengths and the philosophical differences between the rivals (Baltimore *American*, May 3, 1912; *The Evening Capital and Maryland Gazette*, May 3, 4, 1912, p. 4).

The Democrats had been out of the White House for so long (since Cleveland) that it is not surprising that their ads emphasized, above all else, that they could win. The theme of the fighter for the people also kept recurring. The condensation symbol of "the people," or "the common people" appeared often, sometimes joined with the word "American," or "Democracy," as in "the rank and file of the Democracy." Though the messages no longer used the log cabin imagery of the nineteenth century, the echoes could be heard in their choice of language.

Personal traits were described very generally. A Clark ad linked his personal traits to his "harmonious" leadership of the Democrats in the House of Representatives. He was "a man of strong and consistent conviction," "a fair man," "a kind man." The ad reflected American culture's unease with higher education in its description of Clark's education: he was "the rarest combination . . . of the college bred man and the 'cornfield lawyer' " ("A Vote for Champ Clark," *The Sun*, Baltimore, May 1, 1912, p. 1).

Much of the audience's desire for information about the candidate's image and issues in 1912 was carried by the appeals to the party. The party labels served both as condensation symbols for particular values and as shorthand versions of the traits and issues identified with leaders of each of the parties. Thus, though the primaries were intraparty contests, the candidates presented themselves draped in the party mantle, almost as though this were a general election.

In addition to newspaper advertising, it was common in the 1900–1920 period for both parties to send out "enormous quantities of lithographed portraits of their presidential nominees" and to put their pictures on "billboards, fences, and other structures" (Dinkin, 1989, p. 100). In the 1912 fall campaign, the Republican National Committee made heavy use of magazines, billboards, and a movie about Taft, shown in 1,200 theatres.

ADVERTISING IN THE 1932 PRIMARIES

The year 1932 was a slow one for advertising because there was no real contest in the Republican Party, and neither of the main Democratic contenders, Roosevelt and Smith, actively campaigned. However, there was a unique use of direct mail correspondence in the Roosevelt campaign.

Though publicly Roosevelt was the statesman, tending to his constituents in New York, behind the scenes his campaign had been off and running for two years, under the direction of Roosevelt, James Farley, and Louis Howe. Their main audience was Democratic Convention delegates, whether in state primaries or party conventions and caucuses; the lines were blurred. Interpersonal communication was dominant, with Farley and other campaign organizers traveling to persuade leaders in person and later at the conventions, but they could not possibly maintain contact with the party leaders by travel and telephone alone. They therefore developed an extensive direct mail campaign within the party. By the spring of 1931, they had set up their headquarters at 331 Madison Avenue, New York, where Howe was in charge and created organizational divisions in publicity, addressograph, newspaper file, telephone, and the women's division (Peel and Donnelly, 1973).

The addressograph proved to be a vital piece of campaign technology. It enabled the Roosevelt organization to correspond with thousands of people, sending them wave after wave of letters. Farley (1938) described the first mailing as "the opening 'feeler' of the Roosevelt campaign," an effort to start a correspondence with interested party leaders. It was a booklet about the New York State Democratic Committee, which he sent to "active Democratic workers throughout the country, principally to state chairmen, vice-chairmen, national committeemen, and others" (pp. 69–70). Many responded, and Farley wrote them personal letters. The second wide mailing was a tabulation showing how well Roosevelt had done in the 1930 New York gubernatorial race compared to Democrats of the past, particularly in the rural upstate region that usually voted Republican. Farley said that many party activists reported to him later that this document had a real influence on their thinking, as they wanted a candidate who could win the general election.

From these mailings, the campaign built up a huge list of names of people interested in the Roosevelt candidacy, potential organizers in different states, helpful contacts for the campaign to come, and vital information. Eventually they had the names and addresses of every Democratic precinct representative in the country on plates. The work was augmented by Mary Dewson, head of the campaign's women's division, who corresponded with most of the female delegates (Farley, 1938). The letters were supplemented by telegrams and telephone calls. As Farley sent Howe lists of the names of party leaders expressing interest in Roosevelt, Howe would give them to Roosevelt, who would call each of them personally. Farley reported on their thinking about this massive direct mail effort:

We went on the theory . . . that people love the personal touch; they delight in believing there is a close link between them and the folk who run the show and, above all, they want the knowledge that their efforts are being appreciated by the "higher-ups" in the organization. That desire for recognition is very human. (Farley, 1938, p. 71)

An additional aspect of this correspondence was the production of pamphlets, under Howe's direction, "adorned with Governor Roosevelt's photograph, and bearing such titles as: "Franklin D. Roosevelt—Who He Is and What He Has Done," and "Roosevelt and Human Welfare." These pamphlets were sent around the country, making use of the addressograph plates to reach the appropriate party members (Stiles, 1954, p. 161).

In contrast to Roosevelt's strenuous behind-the-scene efforts to woo party activists, the Smith campaign was quiescent. He "refrained from taking any very active part in the furtherance of his own interests until shortly before the early selections of delegates" (*Tribune Star*, Terre Haute, Indiana, May 29, 1932). According to Troy (1991), Smith "had no use for advertising executives" (p. 153). It should not be a surprise, therefore, that in the week before the important Pennsylvania primary in 1932, there was only one Smith ad in the major Philadelphia newspapers, on the day before the primary. The same ad appeared in the *Inquirer* and the *Public Ledger*, both on page 6, April 25, 1932. As in the 1912 ads, this one had multiple goals; it was four ads in one. A picture of Smith in a tuxedo caught the reader's attention. To the right were the following words, large and generously spaced for easy reading: "If Anyone Has Any Doubts This Letter Removes Them. Al Smith is Set! Vote for Him Tomorrow in the Democratic Primaries." Smith's supporters were right to be worried. He had managed to appear so reluctant that the ad's main message was devoted to convincing the public that he really was a candidate.

Smith's letter assured his "friends in Philadelphia" that if the Democratic National Convention wanted him "to lead," he would "make the fight." The language constructed an image of Smith as a leader, a fighter, a patriotic American, a Democrat, and a loyal friend (he used the word "friend" four times). It is clear, however, that he wanted to avoid any words that would cast him as a political candidate, even resorting to awkward and evasive syntax: "I am the same [same *what*?] as when four years ago I was nominated." The difficulty of pretending *not* to be an active candidate while running a campaign ad is apparent in the contortions of this message.

The Smith ad provided information on the voting process, giving the polling hours and directing the reader to "Mark Your Ballot" for Smith and Smith delegates and alternates. The ad helped the voter by listing the names, districts, and wards of all of the Smith delegates.

According to Dinkin (1989), political advertising in the 1930s and 1940s also relied on radio spot announcements, though the main use of radio in politics was for formal speeches. Other forms of advertising were movies and sound trucks. It is unlikely that either Smith or Roosevelt used these forms of advertising in the 1932 primaries, as they were not actively campaigning. It is quite possible, however, that supporters in the few contested primaries used radio spots.

ADVERTISING IN THE 1952 PRIMARIES

Newspaper and radio advertising were the main forms used in the 1952 primaries. The perceived power of these media can be seen in New Hampshire newspaper ads, which made prominent use of quotations from radio commentators and newspaper columnists ("To the Friends," *Union Leader* [Manchester], March 10, 1952, p. 2; *Foster's Daily Democrat* [Dover], March 10, 1952, p. 2). Taft and Eisenhower placed so many radio ads in New Hampshire that station WLNH in Laconia reported that it did not have "another one-minute advertising spot available until after election day" ("White-Hot New Hampshire Politics," *New York Times*, March 8, 1952).

Eisenhower

In 1952, there were 43 million homes with radios (Sig Larmon to Eisenhower, Whitman File, Name Series, Box 20, July 18, 1952, Eisenhower Library). In May 1952, *New York Times* columnist Arthur Krock reported that, "The Eisenhower forces, charged with having vastly superior financial backing, have undoubtedly spent a great deal on radio and newspaper advertising" (Krock, May 25, 1952, p. 3). Sigurd Larmon, head of the Young and Rubicam ad agency in New York, joined the Eisenhower campaign in December 1951 and "worked without cease to help the state Ike organizations with billboards, newspaper ads, radio and television time" (Lodge, 1973, p. 87). Short radio spots were used by the Eisenhower campaign in several primaries, including New Hampshire, New Jersey, and Massachusetts (Harris, "Lodge Jibes Ike Foes," *Boston Globe*, April 28, 1952).

George Gallup remarked upon the skill of the Eisenhower advertising in the New Jersey primary in April, saying that he had reviewed the polling information and that the evidence showed "unmistakably the success of the advertising and publicity campaign." The Eisenhower margin had increased particularly, he reported, "when [radio] spot and television programs were put to work." These were "superb" efforts, he said, in contrast to those of "the old-line politicians," most of whom "haven't even discovered that there is such a thing as radio and television" (Gallup letter to Paul Hoffman, April 17, 1952, Pre-Presidential Name Series, Box 57, Eisenhower Library).

Between 1948 and 1952, the number of televisions in American homes had increased from 400,000 to 19 million (Kramer, 1992, p. 27). Eisenhower's campaign was the first to see the potential for television ads and prepared at least three in the primaries. They also regularly bought television time for speeches, which, though not ads in the usual sense, did represent candidate-controlled time. General Lucius D. Clay told Eisenhower that the campaign had "arranged for 15 minutes each Thursday night of national television time, and propose[d] to use this time with [their] speakers to take the offensive henceforth instead of being on the defensive" (Letter to Eisenhower, February 26, 1952, Pre-Presidential Papers, Box 24, Eisenhower Library). In June, when Eisenhower gave a speech in Detroit, it was broadcast nationwide on radio and television because the Michigan Eisenhower committee had raised $100,000 for this purpose. Not until the fall campaign, however, did the campaign make extensive use of televised political spots.

Of the three pre-convention Eisenhower television spots available from the University of Oklahoma Political Communication Center, the first shows Senator James Duff of Pennsylvania endorsing Eisenhower, the second is called "Ike and Problems and Issues," and the third is a biographical ad called "Ike the Man." The Duff ad, which was 4 minutes and 37 seconds long, was nothing more than a film of a speech. Duff, standing by a picture of Eisenhower, read a statement saying that Eisenhower would make the best president because of his knowledge of foreign policy.

"Ike and Problems and Issues" was 1 minute and 42 seconds long. A narrator presented the message and focused on Eisenhower's image traits. He was portrayed as an honest, patriotic leader with a deep commitment to the nation's principles and with leadership skills far better than the incumbent's. Each of the statements functioned on two levels, both boosting Eisenhower and containing an implicit claim that Eisenhower's opponents could not do nearly as well as he could. For example, he would "clean up the mess in Washington" (this implied both that there was a mess in Washington and that he would clean it up, while others would not).

"Ike the Man" was four minutes and 35 seconds long. In its presentation of Eisenhower's biography, it adopted the style of a newsreel. Even the immediacy of the specific date was conveyed, as the narrator told how "eight years ago tonight" Eisenhower had completed the planning for the invasion of Normandy. Thus we know that the ad was made to be shown on June 4, 1952, the anniversary of the night before Normandy, and the time of his return to the United States from NATO. "In those stirring days," the narrator continued breathlessly, describing Ike's life story, a rise from "humble origins" and the "house beside the tracks" through high school, West Point, and the Army, campaigns in North Africa and Normandy, the presidency of Columbia University, and the NATO command. Above all, the stress was on Eisenhower as an "American": he was "the ordinary American" who "loves America"; he was "all-American."

In a complete change from the ads of 1932, "Ike the Man" never mentioned political party. Though the primaries were not quite over, the ad was constructed to appeal to a national audience, not a partisan one, and the meaning of "American" was assumed to carry tremendous weight.

The themes found in these few television spots had been honed in the primary season starting on March 11 in New Hampshire against Taft, Stassen, and a write-in effort by supporters of General Douglas MacArthur. Senator Henry Cabot Lodge II, Eisenhower's campaign manager, reported that they "decided to sink every penny into the New Hampshire primary" (Lodge, 1973, pp. 99–100). A review of newspapers in Manchester, Concord, and Dover during the week before the primary found that the Republicans ran far more ads than the Democrats, with

Taft advertising the most heavily (34 ads), Eisenhower second (16 ads), MacArthur third (six ads), Democrats Kefauver and Truman fourth and fifth (with three ads and two ads, respectively), and Republican Stassen sixth (one ad).

A typical Eisenhower newspaper ad of March 4 contained most of the same themes found in the television ads, stating that he could "assure the peace," "unify America," and "clean up Washington" ("Eisenhower," *Union Leader*, March 4, 1952, p. 1). Through the selection of verbs and nouns, the ad dovetailed the character and policy issues of the campaign, with the verbs carrying the image traits and the nouns carrying the issue traits; thus Eisenhower could "assure the peace." The meaning of the word "assure" carries with it the connotation of trust; one who can "assure" is one who convinces, gives confidence to, and reassures (*Webster's New World Dictionary*, 1988). The meaning of the word "peace" referred to a specific issue in 1952, when the nation was at war in Korea. The expression "clean up Washington" also dovetailed image and issue with a verb and a noun. The verb "clean up" implies a vigorous action of cleaning, a rooting out. In politics, one cleans up corruption, which implies that the cleaner-upper is honest and moral. The word "Washington" is a synecdoche, standing for the federal government, but it had an even more specific meaning in 1952, standing for the Truman administration, which had had some highly publicized scandals. By these pairs of words, the ad managed to summarize key issue and image factors.

In addition, the ad placed heavy emphasis on Eisenhower's viability: he could "win the election" because he was supported "by the people, Republicans, Independents, and disgusted Democrats, in every section of the nation" ("Eisenhower," *Union Leader*, Manchester, March 4, 1952, p. 1). So important was this factor of "winnability," mentioned in most of the ads, that there is good reason to see it as both a major issue and a highly desired image trait, rather than to look at it merely as evidence of the horse race fixation of the press. The campaign chose the words, not the press, and a prominent word was "winner." Winnability was a summative quality combining the issue and image factors presumed to be most attractive to the voter. The word "winning" had special significance to Republicans in 1952, for they had been out of presidential office since 1933.

As in the ads of 1912 and 1932, many of the 1952 ads near primary day attempted to activate the voters, showing them sample ballots marked for the candidate, listing the names of delegates pledged to the candidate, giving the primary date and times, and even offering "transportation and adult babysitters" ("Ward 8," *Concord Daily Monitor*, March 10, 1952, p. 6).

In addition to advertising through the mass media, the Eisenhower campaign also spent heavily to print sample ballots for every New

Hampshire precinct, so voters would know which delegates were committed to Eisenhower. This unusual step had real practical value, since the real ballots did not contain this information. On Election Day, the campaign also made use of sound trucks to play a recording of an Eisenhower speech (NBC News Microfilm, AP, March 11, 1952, Library of Congress).

Taft

Taft used no television spots, but he advertised heavily in newspapers, in ads that frequently contained a head-and-shoulders shot of a smiling Taft in coat and tie. He also published a book and autographed it and gave it away as a campaign technique; the book was sold in bookstores as well (I. Jack Martin to Everett Somers, January 15, 1952, Taft Papers, Box 446, Library of Congress).

Taft's ads, like Eisenhower's, stressed winning. Only Taft, said one ad, "can and will make the aggressive sweeping attack on the Truman Administration we Republicans MUST make to win this year" ("Republicans!" *Union Leader*, March 10, 1952, p. 2). The image traits valued were the qualities of a fighter: strength, persistence, commitment. Repeatedly, the ads proclaimed the following Taftian trait: "Taft is a fighter" who would conduct a "forthright, fighting campaign." His behavior in New Hampshire proved that, stated one ad; he was "wading through the snow and slush to tell people the truth" ("Vote for Robert A. Taft," *Concord Daily Monitor*, March 7, 1952, p. 14). There is irony in the heavy use of images of fighting and attacking by a U.S. senator who had no military experience, now running against a five-star general most famous for the World War II invasion at Normandy.

Taft's ads made more of a partisan appeal than Eisenhower's through the use of the title "Mr. Republican." The name made a powerful claim, that he was the leader of the party, the leader of the opposition to the Democrats. In his person-to-person campaign with potential delegates and party leaders, he emphasized that he was not only an organization man but the favorite of Republican Congressmen who deserved to be the nominee (David, Moos, and Goldman, 1954, pp. 47–48).

Implicit in most of Taft's ads was an attack on Eisenhower for not having a "program for positive action" and for not bringing his program directly to the voters. An ad called "Thank You New Hampshire Republicans," run in both the *Concord Daily Monitor* (p. 2) and *Foster's Daily Democrat* (p. 3) on March 10, was typical of many others. "Other campaigns," it said, brought "paid entertainers from New York and Hollywood," and "some big brass out of state politicians" to the state. [Eisenhower's campaign had done so.] But they did not have "a program for America." In contrast, the ad said, Taft himself had come to New

Hampshire and "discussed the issues" with the people, answering their questions "with courage and confidence." He had "submitted his program" and "faced the issues."

When Taft ads opposed Eisenhower directly, the tone tended to be gentle. One strike at Eisenhower's campaign style urged, "Never Mind What Broadway Says. . . . Up Taft!" ("Up Taft!" *Union Leader*, March 10, 1952, p. 2; *Concord Daily Monitor*, March 5, 1952, p. 7, and March 10, 1952, p. 6). Another advised, "If—You Think 'If' About 'Ike,' Vote for 'Bob' " ("If," *Union Leader*, March 11, 1952, p. 1). The sense of discomfort with intraparty wrangles came through in ads stating, "We Like Ike But BOB CAN DO THE JOB" ("Bob Taft," *Union Leader*, March 6, 1952, p. 1; "9 Good Reasons," *The Rye Chronicle* [New York], May 29, 1952, p. 9, in Taft Papers, Library of Congress).

The Democrats

Kefauver

Kefauver won the New Hampshire primary, but he did it by meeting the voters personally and getting heavy news coverage, not through his advertising. Only one of his three newspaper ads contained information about him. The other two were strictly activation ads, one urging people to "Meet Senator Kefauver in Person" (*Concord Daily Monitor*, March 7, 1952, p. 8), the other telling Kefauver supporters how to get rides to the polls ("Kefauver Supporters," *Union Leader*, March 11, 1952, p. 1).

The day before the primary, the Manchester Committee for Kefauver published an ad that was three columns wide and ran from the top to the bottom of the page. It was the kind of all-purpose ad commonly found in 1932, urging a vote for Kefauver, giving the time and place of the primary, and summarizing his program. It appealed to a major Democratic constituency—labor—saying that Kefauver had a "100% Labor Record," and adapted to New Hampshirites by referring to "New Hampshire industries."

The tone of the Kefauver ad was positive, urging that we "go forward with the social and economic gains we have made and press for further gains for all our people." But the ad made implicit battle with the incumbent president. In suggesting that the government needed to "enforce a vigorous foreign policy," "take a realistic stand on Communism," and "build a clean government with honesty and integrity," for example, Kefauver seemed to suggest that the opposite conditions existed under the Truman administration ("Vote For Estes Kefauver," *Union Leader*, March 10, 1952, p. 7). The ad "reinforced his established image as the soft-spoken crusader for clean government, who was now taking on organized politics in the same way he had previously taken on organized crime" (Gorman, 1971, p. 132).

Truman

The Truman advertising was even skimpier than Kefauver's. The president made no effort to campaign in New Hampshire, declaring that "the present system of state primaries was just eyewash as everyone would find out when the national convention was held" (Lawrence, 1952). Surrogates campaigned for him, using methods such as a radio broadcast of a taped speech by Congressman John McCormack of Massachusetts, urging the support of Truman delegates (news and commentary, *Union Leader*, March 10, 1952, p. 10). Of the three Truman newspaper ads examined, one focused on activation, telling how "voters for Truman" could get transportation to the polls ("Transportation," *Union Leader*, March 11, 1952, p. 1); another was a "how to use the primary rules" ad, explaining to Independents that they too could vote in the primary: "Just Ask For a Democrat Ballot" ("Independents," *Foster's Daily Democrat*, Dover, March 10, 1952, p. 2); and the last made apparent the importance of labor to the Democratic cause. Truman had been endorsed by the United Labor Committee of New Hampshire, the ad stated. Some attention was given to Truman's image. He was described as "A Veteran of World War I, A Friend of the Veterans, and the Champion of the American People" ("Democrats," *Union Leader*, March 10, 1952, p. 1). These references to groups in American society—labor and veterans—represented efforts to create a kind of image by association. The referents the reader attached to labor and veterans—hard work, courage, sacrifice—would presumably be transferred to Truman.

ADVERTISING IN THE 1972 PRIMARIES

Patterson and McClure's (1976) research on the 1972 fall campaign found that television advertising provided substantial information about the candidates' stands on issues, and that the ads were long enough—five minutes was a common length—to develop ideas rather fully. Voters were able to recall these ads. According to Patterson and McClure, "the 30-second spot was not a significant factor in 1972, accounting for only 2% of all ads shown and less than 1% of the total advertising time" (1976, p. 107).

The author's examination of ads in the primaries that year confirmed the finding that the ads addressed issues that concerned voters, such as taxes, busing, welfare, and the economy, and focussed less on a candidate's persona. However, in contrast to Patterson and McClure's findings on the fall campaign, many of the ads were quite short. Most of the primary ads reviewed were only 30 seconds long, with 60-second spots also common. The full extent of the use of these ads is not known, however, contemporary newspaper accounts referred so frequently to these short spots that it seems likely that they were used more often in the primaries than in the fall campaign.

Except for the shorter length, the primary spots were much like those in the fall campaign. The style of advertising that was popular with the particular producers, rather than the nature of the primary, seemed to dictate the nature of the political ads. For example, Charles Guggenheim, who made McGovern's ads, was an award-winning documentary film-maker, and the McGovern primary ads had a distinctive documentary style not found in the ads of other candidates.

Two ways in which the primaries differed from the fall campaign—that they came early and that they were multi-candidate—led to contrasts with advertising in the fall. Name identification was a more common ad strategy in the primaries, and the candidates' ads dealt with the fact that there were many opponents, not just one.

A huge difference between advertising in the 1952 and 1972 primaries was the predominant use of television advertising. In the first two primaries of 1972, New Hampshire and Florida, "most of the candidates spent 70 cents of every campaign dollar on TV advertising" (Bonafede, 1972, p. 461). McGovern, who campaigned actively against Humphrey right up to the end of the primaries, spent a total of almost $6 million on radio and television advertising (Joslyn, 1984). Television costs more than the other media, as indicated by the following comparison: in the New Hampshire primary, $1,000 would buy "two newspaper ads for three weeks in a newspaper with statewide circulation," $325 would buy "50 local radio spots," and $150 would buy "one billboard" (Newsletter, "McGovern for President," No. 10, February 1972, MC#181, Box 63, Speeches, McGovern Papers, Mudd Library, Princeton). In contrast, to show a single prime-time 30-second spot in a small state might cost $300; "in the country's major markets, it can cost more than $3000" (Napolitan, 1976, p. 122).

When the 1972 primaries began, there were no campaign spending laws. Some of the Democratic candidates signed agreements among themselves. In the Florida primary, for example, they agreed to individual limits of $133,000 for television and radio, and $133,000 for print material, "plus having the option of dipping into a bonus fund of $94,000" (Bonafede, 1972, p. 466). On April 7, 1972, however, the Federal Election Campaign Act (FECA) took effect, limiting the amount that candidates could spend on advertising in certain media to $.10 × the primary voting population. The media covered were radio, television, newspapers, magazines, automated telephone systems, and billboards; a maximum of 60% of expenditures could be spent on broadcasting media. There were other limits on spending as well, including the rule that all contributions of over $100 must be reported to the FECA (Jamieson, 1984, p. 291).

In general, newspaper ads in 1972 resembled the 1952 ads, having multiple goals, stressing the candidate's viability, attempting to activate the voter, and striving to demystify the primary process, especially the process of voting for delegates pledged to the candidate. As in earlier ads, the word "people" appeared frequently. Humphrey called himself "The People's Democrat," and Wallace urged people to "Hear the Real Issues of the People." Most of the ads were short and said nothing specific about the candidate. In the few longer ones, the candidate's positions and deeds were emphasized, especially to show his competence. The one major way in which these newspaper ads differed from earlier periods was in the routine use of a picture of the smiling candidate.

The Republican Candidates

President Nixon had little opposition within his party, but he and his two opponents advertised in New Hampshire before it became evident that Nixon would clearly win the nomination. Ashbrook spent $6,000 on radio spots there, and had 11 billboards around the state, with the message, "Ashbrook—Responsible Republican" (Bonafede, 1972, p. 471). Mc-Closkey campaigned for 91 days in New Hampshire, spending $25,000 on television and radio (Bonafede, 1972). Neither Ashbrook nor McCloskey was well known in the Northeast, however, and both were short on money.

Nixon

Peter H. Dailey reports that he set up a "task-force agency" called The November Group, which was "a fully staffed advertising agency . . . for the sole purpose of working for the President" (May and Fraser, 1973). Robert Teeter, Vice President of Market Opinion Research in Detroit, was hired to direct polling. The polling was "the most extensive polling program ever undertaken for a Presidential candidate" (Magruder, 1974, p. 152).

The polling results showed that Vietnam, inflation, and general unrest were the only important issues, and the president was seen as handling the first two well and was even with his opponents on the third one. In general, "The polls showed that people saw Nixon as informed, experienced, competent, safe, trained, and honest. He was not seen, relatively speaking, as warm, open-minded, relaxed, or as having a sense of humor." Based on these findings, the campaign decided to emphasize the *need* to keep such a leader, rather than *liking* for the leader. The slogan selected was, "Nixon: Now More Than Ever" (Magruder, 1974, pp. 152–155).

To counter McCloskey's vigorous campaigning in New Hampshire, Nixon's campaign was prepared to make an all-out effort, using the full panoply of advertising. Noticing that McCloskey's campaign was not catching fire, however, Nixon instead adopted "a very, very limited effort in newspapers and radio" in which the strategy was to use the testimony of Republicans to tell New Hampshire Republicans how satisfied they were with Nixon (in May and Fraser, 1973, pp. 80–81). McCloskey dropped out after New Hampshire.

In the Florida primary, where Ashbrook was Nixon's only opponent, Nixon's media coordinator said that the campaign was "so low-keyed, that it [was] almost a non-campaign." He said that he used printed materials, but no paid television. Nixon was getting excellent media coverage from his trip to China on February 21–27, and the coordinator reported that, "More than what we are doing, the media is doing for us" (Roy Nielsen, in Bonafede, 1972, p. 470). Nixon's tour of Russia on May 22–28 brought more glowing media coverage. After he returned and addressed a joint session of Congress, his approval rating was up to 61%.

The Democrats

The main contest was among the Democrats. Never had there been so many candidates or so many primaries, and never had there been so many ads. In January 1972, the Gallup poll showed that Muskie led with 32%, Edward Kennedy (who was not a candidate) was second with 27%, Humphrey was third with 17%, and McGovern was fourth with 3%.

Congresswoman Shirley Chisholm of New York, Senator Vance Hartke of Indiana, Congressman Wilbur Mills of Arkansas, and Mayor Sam Yorty of Los Angeles were minor candidates who spent little on media and campaigned only sporadically. None of them were well known nationally, and they soon disappeared in the large field of Democrats.

The major Democratic candidates advertised through television, radio, and direct mail. The direct mail used the same technique as Nixon's, the personalized computer letter, both for soliciting votes and for raising money. Muskie, McGovern, and Mills all used this technique heavily in New Hampshire ("Five Democrats Agree," *New York Times*, March 1, 1972), and Humphrey and McGovern used it in Florida, in marked contrast to the 1952 primaries.

The most prominent candidates were Muskie, McGovern, Humphrey, Jackson, and Wallace. Their advertising campaigns will be discussed next.

Muskie

How did Muskie lose his overwhelming lead in the primaries? That is one of the most interesting questions of the 1972 presidential primaries. In January 1972, he led in the polls, with 32% of the support. Yet by late April, Muskie had suspended his campaign. What role did Muskie's ads play in this debacle?

Bob Squier was Muskie's television producer. He spent two years preparing for the primaries, portraying Muskie "as the one man who could beat Nixon" and "as a politician who could communicate easily with the man on the street" (Gardner, 1972). If the sheer amount of advertising could make a difference, Muskie had an advantage. He spent heavily in New Hampshire and Florida, the first two primaries. He and McGovern agreed to an expenditure limit of $68,000 for television and radio and $68,000 for print advertising in New Hampshire. Muskie advertised on Boston and Maine television stations. In Florida, he concentrated on the four media markets of Miami, Tampa/St. Petersburg, Orlando, and Jacksonville (Bonafede, 1972, p. 466).

The television spots in the Muskie Archives were targeted mainly to five primaries: New Hampshire, Florida, Illinois, Wisconsin, and Massachusetts. Though a few were made in 1971, the full-fledged advertising campaign began on February 14, 1972. There were 55 discrete spots in all, including many 30-second versions of 60-second ads, as well as five longer ads. There were 20 60-second spots, 30 30-second spots, and 5 longer spots (length: 30 minutes, 15 minutes, 13 minutes, 5 minutes, and 4½ minutes).

When the spots are viewed in their entirety, there is no clear indicator of why the campaign failed. Of the 30-second and 60-second spots, 29, or about 60%, targeted specific audiences and/or problems for discussion, also providing information on Muskie's character. There were 21, or 40%, which worked to convey a mood and impressions of the man as a person, without much reference to specific issues.

One polished spot focusing on Muskie the man was "Hometown USA," showing Muskie in Kennebunk, Maine, with two of his children. In 60-second and 30-second versions, it showed him driving down the street in Kennebunk with his children, talking with a shopkeeper, getting a haircut, and walking with his children in the snow. Everyone was very friendly. The camera lingered on the faces of the residents in a natural, relaxed way. Muskie introduced his children to the shopkeeper ("Honey, this is Mr. ——"). Guitar music and a narrator provided commentary: "He's been liked and trusted . . . a sense of community." (#3, CMT10, February 14, 1972, Muskie Archives). The mood was comfortable and upbeat, giving a glimpse of Muskie as a neighbor. The spot stressed important image traits, particularly trust. The Kennebunk scene looked much like New Hampshire, and Muskie was well cast as the friendly neighbor. The slogan at the end of his ads was "Muskie—For the Country."

His long ads all discussed campaign issues, including the Vietnam War, jobs, taxes, farm problems, the environment, defense, and food prices (#5, VT39, PB, April 3, 1972; #6, VT57, PB 329, April 3, 1972; "Mass 5," MA, April 13, 1972; #6, VT62, 238, April 17, 1972).

The one apparent weakness in the Muskie ads was their vagueness. The slogan "Muskie—For the Country" was about as vague as one could get, and except for the longer ads, it was difficult to know what he stood for, as illustrated by the following ad based on a Muskie speech:

What our country needs at this time is to bring together in one fold a solid majority of Americans who understand, not withstanding their differences, what they share together is more important. And that if they will pursue what they share together, their different interests will be served as well, and indeed better than if they divide themselves. ("God Bless America," #4, VT 21, CMT 35, March 2, 1972, Muskie Archives)

While no one could possibly disagree with these sentiments, the idea of "sharing together" conveyed no clearer meaning than the slogan "Muskie—For the Country."

It is understandable that Muskie and his advertisers did not want to do anything to hurt his lead in the polls, and vagueness offends no one. But in the context of the primaries, in which other candidates were defining themselves vividly and sharply, both as individuals and as advocates for particular positions, Muskie's vagueness may have contributed to his eclipse.

There are other reasons why the ads may have hurt his campaign. Savage (1986) has pointed out that if a candidate is especially good at projecting certain desired image traits, this success "may ultimately prove to be an Achillean heel." For example, in the 1970–1972 period, Muskie developed a public persona as a stable and mature, Lincolnesque figure, from the time of his Election Eve speech of November 1970. Thus when he cried in front of the *Union Leader* building, his "presidential fortunes" plummeted (Savage, 1986, pp. 46, 51). In this analysis, the success of Muskie's campaign, especially through televised speeches and political spots, built him up as an ideal leader figure, making the revelation of his clay feet all the more incongruous.

The fact that Muskie hired a number of different producers and directors for his television spots and that he changed his campaign strategy in a major way in the Wisconsin primary also may have contributed to the campaign's difficulties. His campaign lacked the programmatic unity of the McGovern campaign. Muskie's ads were variously credited to eight different producers (Muskie Archives, Bates College).

McGovern

McGovern's first communication problem was name recognition. He and Muskie were the only major candidates to enter the New Hampshire primary—the others waited for the Florida primary—and Muskie was far ahead in the polls. According to Joseph Grandmaison, the McGovern campaign distributed campaign literature to 230,000 people (the state's population was only about 750,000) and also worked hard at person-to-person communication (Bonafede, 1972, p. 466).

Whereas Muskie had been endorsed by many party leaders and had developed a large war chest from sizable private gifts, McGovern had no such advantages. The question of where the money for advertising would come from was a serious one. Direct mail advertising proved to be the answer. According to Clifton Daniel, by May 1972, McGovern "collected more campaign contributions by direct mail than any candidate in history" ("Insight," May 31, 1972, Reel 76, Box 6, Tape Transcripts, p. 7, McGovern Papers, Mudd Library, Princeton). Assisted by Morris Dees of Alabama, a direct mail consultant, he obtained lists of names of donors to liberal causes and "sent out a lengthy letter to those on the lists." The response was much heavier than expected, and he went back to these donors again and again; he collected $3,000,000 before the convention and $12,000,000 by the general campaign (Dinkin, 1989, p. 176).

McGovern's media adviser, Charles Guggenheim, did all of the television and radio production (with few exceptions) from the beginning of the campaign (Hart, 1973, p. 125). Guggenheim had worked on McGovern's successful 1962 and 1968 Senate campaigns. He exercised an unusual degree of control, not only making the ads but making decisions about their distribution. Patrick Caddell, the McGovern pollster, advised Guggenheim, providing "broad background for the concepts surrounding the media buy" (Glass, 1972, p. 974). Other firms assisted in the individual states, doing newspaper advertising, producing local radio spots, and so on (Hart, 1973).

The unity and coherence of the advertising campaign was striking. Guggenheim made 14 spots for McGovern in January 1972. Ten ran in all of the primary states in which McGovern campaigned. Nine more spots were made in late April to supplement the originals as well as a half-hour campaign biography, "McGovern." The style was cinema verité, with "dramatic camera angles, flat lighting, revealing close-ups, and sudden shifts of scene" (Glass, 1972, p. 974). In all of the televised spots, Guggenheim showed McGovern talking with citizens about their problems in an informal setting. Much of the attention was focused on the citizens, their faces, and their words. A citizen would mention a problem, such as Social Security payments, McGovern would listen to the person, and then he would state what should be done to solve the problem. In all of the spots, McGovern was shown listening, conveying a sense of compassion and concern for voters.

The ads reviewed for this analysis included the campaign biography, two spots that were four minutes and 20 seconds long, six 60-second spots, and five 30-second spots. Contemporary sources established that the three longer spots (the campaign "Bio," in both long and short versions, and the spot "Vets") as well as the 60-second and 30-second versions of "Right to Know" and the 30-second spot "Wages" were used frequently in the campaign.

McGovern's "Bio" received high praise in an internal memo from Pat Buchanan and Ken Khachigian in the Nixon campaign, describing it as "an excellent piece of work—designed to portray him as the antithesis of the 'radical,' indeed, as the bomber pilot who won the war against Nazi Germany" ("Assault Strategy," June 8, 1972, Haldeman files, in Oudes, 1989, p. 464). This ad, like the rest, ended with the slogan "Mc-Govern . . . Right From the Start."

The spot "Vets," which was 4 minutes and 20 seconds long, was "one of Guggenheim's first and best-remembered spots." It was "used through the primary season and on into the fall campaign" (Diamond and Bates, 1984, p. 191). If this were the only ad seen from the 1972 campaign, it would be easy to form the impression that the 1972 primary ads were highly emotional and moving, appealing to basic American values. But Kern (1989) has indicated that the regular use of this kind of ad came later, and that in 1972 the emphasis was still heavily on specific issues. The evidence from the other 11 McGovern ads proves her correct: each dealt with a specific issue or concern. The "Vets" ad, however, was a progenitor of the moving, emotional ads of a later period. McGovern shook the hands of the veterans in wheelchairs, as the narrator reported that, "Most of them were still safe in grade school when this man first spoke out against the war, risking political suicide in the hope they might be spared." The veterans spoke frankly, even crudely, about their loss of bodily functions and their sterility; the camera showed McGovern's stricken face. The human tragedy of the veterans' plight and the horror and finality of the war came through in this ad, as did McGovern's compassion and his stated determination to "help raise the vision and the faith and the hope of the American people" as president.

Guggenheim's documentary style often closed in on faces. Gary Hart, McGovern's campaign manager, used the word "archetypal" to describe these people: they were "your neighbor, your friend, your co-worker." The same term could be used to describe McGovern's language in the spots. McGovern spoke in colloquial English, the comfortable, familiar language people understood, never really vivid and striking, but familiar, using phrases like "behind closed doors," "wouldn't stand the light of day," and "treat the people of this country like children." This candidate was far from the Titans of earlier campaigns; he was one of the people. Jamieson (1984) has noted another characteristic of the language in the ads: McGovern spoke with a tentative tone, saying things such as,

"The President can help set a new tone . . . raise a vision . . . and that's what I'd like to *try* to do." The overall impression in the ads was that of a nice, compassionate, honest, plain-speaking public figure, concerned about the people's problems.

McGovern made a wise decision not to focus on the Florida primary, which, with its plethora of candidates, proved to be the undoing of other campaigns. According to Bonafede (1972, p. 466), "McGovern spent less on the media in Florida than any of the leading candidates." Later in the primaries, as his victories grew in number, his funds and advertising grew too. In the Wisconsin primary, McGovern blanketed the state "with locally filmed television spots, adhering strictly to a media plan drawn up months ago and specifically tailored for Wisconsin" (Weaver, April 3, 1972). By the time of the Ohio primary, Hart reported that "the television and radio spots, running every day for 20 days . . . made a tremendous impact, telling hundreds of thousands of Ohio voters who McGovern was and what he stood for" (Hart, 1973, p. 163).

The McGovern campaign was able to advertise heavily in California, putting its televised commercials on the air five weeks before the primary; "they increased in tempo as the election approached and finally culminated in 2 half-hour productions that together were shown 85 times in all 12 media markets" (Glass, 1972, p. 972). His television spots outnumbered Humphrey's "in the Los Angeles area by a factor of three-to-one; in San Francisco, the ratio was closer to four-to-one" (Glass, 1972, p. 966).

The McGovern Papers at Princeton contain many hours of McGovern's speeches and interview excerpts on audiotape; they provided a rich source of "actualities" for news and radio ads. Jamieson (1984) has noted that McGovern was much more specific in the policy proposals he made in the primary radio ads than in general election ads later on.

The newspaper ads followed the persuasive patterns of an earlier time. There was the endorsement ad, as in one signed by about 40 Maryland clergymen, saying that they based their support on McGovern's positions on four issues ("George McGovern," *The Evening Sun*, May 12, 1972, p. A11). There was the viability ad, proclaiming 10 times that "McGovern Can Win!" ("McGovern Can Win!" *Baltimore Jewish Times*, May 12, 1972, p. 37). There was the all-purpose ad, showing McGovern's picture, commanding people to vote for him, presenting information on his positions, giving the primary day and date, and listing the names of the six McGovern delegates ("Vote for Senator George McGovern," *Evening Capitol* [Annapolis, MD], May 12, 1972, p. 10). There also were the fighting ads, fending off attacks and buttressing the candidate (McGovern generally limited his attacks to President Nixon rather than to candidates in his own party).

Humphrey

According to Jeb S. Magruder, Deputy Campaign Director of the Committee for the Re-election of the President, the Nixon campaign concluded from its polling that Humphrey was the only Democrat the public perceived to have "the characteristics to be President" (in May and Fraser, 1973, p. 49). Humphrey had the highest name recognition of the Democrats, having run for president in 1968, and there was no doubt that he had a large reservoir of Democratic support. However, he began his campaign late, and he did not have the money to advertise as heavily as Muskie or McGovern.

Humphrey's first primary was in Florida, where he came in second in a field of 11. There, according to his Florida campaign director, he expected to spend $266,000, the agreed-upon limit for media. His ads were filmed in Florida settings (Bonafede, 1972). His media consultant, D. J. Leary, said that they planned to stress Humphrey's unique strengths: his "record of service, his legislative accomplishments, and his record as a traditional Democrat" (in Gardner, 1972).

It was in Florida that Humphrey began using a form of advertising well suited to the underfinanced campaign, the half-hour telethon. He had tried telethons in the West Virginia primary in 1960, but according to White (1961), they were not successful. His national media director, Leary, observed that they were cheap and easy to produce. Humphrey usually was joined by a celebrity host such as Lorne Greene, star of the television show *Bonanza* (Glass, 1972). The telethons were advertised in the newspapers, as in the following Maryland ad: "Tonight, 9:00 P.M.–9: 30 P.M., WBAL-TV-Channel 11. Talk with Hubert Humphrey. Call this number: 900–777–8778, and discuss the issues with the People's Democrat" (*Evening Sun* [Baltimore], May 15, 1972, p. A6). This was his main form of advertising in Florida and Wisconsin (Weaver, April 3, 1972). The night before the California primary, Humphrey's telethon "appeared on nine independent . . . stations from 8 to 9 P.M. The program also was seen on 32 cable outlets at an overall cost of about $20,000" (Glass, 1972, p. 972).

Gardner (1972) judged Humphrey's television spots as "a little dull and heavy handed," and he thought that the advertising strategy was "very diffuse." *NBC News* described the spots as "hard sell, direct, unadorned" (May 30, 1972, Vanderbilt Television Archives). The spots in the Oklahoma Political Communication Center fit these descriptions. There are 13 spots in the collection, all 30 seconds long. Five were made on February 10, some specifically targeted to Florida, and eight were made on May 22 for California. The author has established from contemporary sources that "Score Card" and three of the California ads were actually used ("Welfare #2," "Disarmament," "Property Tax"), and the analysis focuses on these.

Unlike McGovern's remarkably integrated ad campaign, there was no "Humphrey look" to his ads. Leary's plan to emphasize Humphrey's specific accomplishments was followed in the early ads. "Score Card" showed a list of the candidates running in Florida, and a hand checked off Humphrey's name for legislative accomplishments (Gardner, 1972). This ad underlined Humphrey's experience and competence as an effective leader and provided new information for the voters.

"Prices," "Busing," "Welfare," and "Taxes," which also were made in February, used another format. This time Humphrey appeared in person, speaking to an audience. In each ad, someone from the audience asked him a question, and he answered the question in the form of a mini-speech.

Humphrey's California spots were all done in a studio, and they showed him speaking directly into the camera, attacking McGovern's policies. Each ad focused on a different issue, using strong, negative language to attack McGovern's position; no information was provided about Humphrey's own record.

Humphrey was able to afford using radio much more than television. In California, he used small radio stations heavily and ran spots as short as 10 seconds. These spots were mainly attacks on McGovern's positions. He also emphasized radio advertising in Spanish in Southern California (Glass, 1972). Humphrey's assault on McGovern had begun in earnest during the Nebraska primary (May 9). According to Hart (1973), the Humphrey campaign relied mainly on brochures and newspaper ads to attack McGovern's positions on the "three a's": abortion, amnesty, and acid, portraying him as a radical on these social issues. McGovern launched a "campaign of retaliation," running ads accusing Humphrey of distortion, appearing on statewide television with Frank Morrison, a popular former governor, and redirecting his campaign into areas where these rumors hurt him most (p. 170).

Humphrey's newspaper ads were much like those of earlier years, commanding the reader to vote for Humphrey, giving information on the primary date and the names of the Humphrey delegates, and using large, dark type and capital letters to attract attention. Pictures were used in three of the four ads examined, including a picture of Humphrey with his six delegates ("Humphrey," *The Times* [Ellicott City, MD], May 11, 1972, p. 13). The arguments in the newspaper ads focused mainly on Humphrey's image of competence and experience.

Jackson

Jackson was a prominent U.S. senator from Washington, an expert on defense, and much was expected of him when he entered the primaries.

He skipped New Hampshire and launched an impressive advertising campaign in Florida. For two weeks he was the only candidate on television, and his campaign proved skillful in placing spots on top-rated television programs. He ran many spots reflecting his position on Israel on radio station WKAT in Miami Beach and a newspaper ad in the weekly *Jewish Floridian*. By the last week before the primary, he had spent $145,000 on television and $25,000 on radio (Bonafede, 1972). He broadcast three half-hour telecasts in Florida, "two more than any competitor" (Weaver, March 13, 1972, p. 28). In Wisconsin, too, where he was little known, he began his television advertising before his opponents (Gardner, 1972), and he planned to spend over $100,000 on a schedule of spots. His main one there was a half-hour political documentary (Weaver, April 3, 1972), but Jackson did poorly in the primaries and dropped out after Wisconsin.

It is not evident from Jackson's ads why he failed to impress the voters. He came across to the author as a knowledgeable, sensible, friendly candidate, well informed about important problems of the day. Each spot was about a different issue: "Drugs," "Busing," Crime," "Wisconsin Farm," "Youth Conservation," and conserving the Everglades. Jackson appeared in five of the six spots, in a variety of settings; in four spots he was shown speaking to audiences in both conversational and public speaking settings.

Alan Gardner, an advertising consultant who analyzed the candidates' television spots in 1972, praised Gerry Hecht, Jackson's advertiser, for capturing "the Senator's straight-talking, no-nonsense manner so that it [came] across on television as good old American common sense." He thought that this was a real accomplishment, because Jackson was "a somewhat stolid, uncharismatic candidate" (Gardner, 1972). One of the spots, "Crime," pictured him speaking dynamically and the audience applauding. In another, "Wisconsin Farm," the dullness crept into his voice-over, a slow, nasal drawl broken up by "uhs."

According to a Jackson political adviser, the audience for his commercials was "unyoung, unpoor, unblack, middle aged, middle class, and middle minded" (Gardner, 1972). The positions he espoused in the spots seemed well suited for this audience, as did his image as a serious, thoughtful, kind leader. He opposed busing for integration, advocated getting France and Turkey to help in the control of drugs, and favored strong support for farmers. However, this kind of targeting excluded many Democrats, appealing to the more conservative wing of the party as well as to Republicans; to win the primaries, he had to win over the Democrats. The job was made harder by the fact that several of his opponents, notably Humphrey, Muskie, and Wallace, were competing vigorously to win support from the same voters.

Wallace

Wallace used less television advertising than the other major candidates, running a low-budget campaign and relying more on rallies and attention by the news media. In three days of continuous viewing, just before the Florida primary, one reporter saw only one Wallace ad, a "half-hour ... documentary, a sort of illustrated version of the basic speech he has been delivering all over the state for weeks" (Weaver, March 13, 1972, p. 28). In Wisconsin, too, Wallace relied mainly on this half-hour film of his rally. Bonafede (1972) described it as "very professional and political," showing "a field of outstretched hands reaching up to clutch Wallace" and scenes of the candidate with people of varied ages and races (p. 465).

In addition to the documentary, Wallace used "studio declaration" ads (Weaver, April 3, 1972). Each of the 10 "studio declaration" ads viewed by the author focused on a particular issue, such as "Tax Structure," "Busing," and "Welfare." The spots had strong thematic unity. Visually they were immediately recognizable, as Wallace sat in front of a blue backdrop in every one. The message was an "us against them" refrain, "us" being "the people" and "them" being "Washington." By our vote we could "send a message to Washington," said Wallace. The wrongs perpetuated in Washington were described in colorful, colloquial expressions: the tax structure was "out of kilter," we were "paying through the nose," we should take money from "welfare loafers" and use it for worthier causes. But Washington was not just a distant enemy; in four of the 10 spots, Wallace linked his primary opponents to the sins of Washington.

Wallace's image in these ads was of a fighter, taking on the big guys from Washington, fighting for "the people," siding with "the average working man." Strength is one of the qualities that people associate with their ideal political leader. By establishing a common enemy, Wallace used a powerful form of identification; as Kenneth Burke argues, we feel closer to people who are against the same things we are against (Burke, 1972). There was nothing about Wallace's own record in these spots; he did not develop his image of competence as a political leader.

Wallace used an unusually broad variety of types of advertising. Joe Azbell, Wallace's director of communication, was responsible for the publication of five papers and magazines, three books, a coloring book, records of Wallace speeches, and campaign paraphernalia, as well as for television and radio spots. He reported that one periodical, *Wallace Stand*, had a circulation of over 300,000. The advertising often had a Nashville influence (in Bonafede, 1972, p. 464).

The Wallace newspaper advertising reiterated the themes and language developed in the televised spots ("Campaign '72, The Maryland

Primary," May 14, 1972, WTOP-TV, Washington, Nixon Project, 5370; "Send Them a Message," *Evening Capitol* [Annapolis, MD], May 13, 1972, p. 19, May 15, 1972, p. 5).

ADVERTISING IN THE 1992 PRIMARIES

The author reviewed 91 different presidential primary spots from the 1992 primaries: 21 Clinton spots, 15 Bush, 14 Tsongas, 10 Kerrey, 8 each for Buchanan, Brown, and Harkin, 5 for Andre Marrou, and 1 each for Larry Agran and Jim Leynane.[2] The most striking differences in the spots compared to 1972 were the greater variety of production techniques and the increased use of narrative. In 1992, the shots changed frequently, the colors, sounds, settings, print, and pictures changed, and the angles, lighting, music, and voices changed. Wooden candidates were no longer staring into the camera. A spot was more likely to tell a story than in 1972, a story appealing to deeply held American values, such as in the "Echoes" spot of Tom Harkin, described at the beginning of this chapter.

In addition, the 1992 spots generally made no reference to political party, a trend already emerging in 1972, and shifted more frequently in response to campaign developments (Arterton, in Pomper, 1993).

One of the stable factors in campaigns over time is the percentage of a candidate's funds spent on advertising. In 1992, as in 1952 and 1972, candidates spent about two-thirds of their campaign budgets on political advertising (West, 1993).

Jamieson (1992) has observed that "the speech remains the staple of paid political advertising" (p. 490). In 1992, speeches played a significant role in almost half of the 91 presidential primary spots viewed; 45% were based mainly or partly on an organized speechlike message spoken personally by the candidate.[3]

In 1992, the media paid much more attention to the candidates' ads than in the earlier campaigns studied. Ad watches, which had begun in the 1990 elections, were now used in great numbers. Newspapers and television news regularly printed or showed political spots and evaluated them, based on their accuracy. Perhaps the most intensive examination occurred in the New Hampshire primary; according to West (1993), the *Boston Globe* ran ad watches on 48 of the 53 spots shown in New Hampshire. He also noted that the *New York Times* published 15 ad watches in the primary period, and the *Washington Post* published 21.

CNN, ABC, NBC, and CBS did ad watches as well. CNN's *Inside Politics* had senior correspondent Brooks Jackson working full time on the analysis of ads. The network ad watches were of two types: either they evaluated the ad, showing in what way it was misleading in its claims, or they presented the ad simply as news, without evaluating its accuracy. The second type had the effect of providing free advertising for the candidates. The networks were particularly interested in negative spots, using them to support their claim that the campaign was getting meaner and more personal. This was the main emphasis when spots were discussed on the NBC, CBS, and ABC nightly news programs during the period February 14–March 14, 1992.

In contrast to the network vision of the campaign as a bloody battlefield, an examination of the primary spots themselves found that the majority were positive, developing reasons why voters should admire a candidate's character and position. Of the 91 spots viewed, 63, or 69% were positive, and 28, or 31%, were negative. The comparative spots, which attacked the opponent's flaws and praised the candidate's strengths, were counted as negative. The percentage of negative spots was higher than that found in earlier studies (Payne, Marlier, and Baukus, 1989; Kaid and Ballotti, 1991), reaching the level that Kaid and Johnston (1991) found in general election spots. Without information on time-buys for these spots, it is impossible to know what types of spots were seen most frequently. Nevertheless, a major thrust of primary advertising in 1992 seemed positive, not negative. Yet network news coverage created exactly the opposite impression.

The voters in the 1992 presidential primary period were especially concerned about the condition of the economy. Several researchers have examined the political spots in this campaign to see how they addressed the economic issue. Marsh (1995) found that "jobs and economic growth had the highest frequencies respectively, and were the most highly connected issues with each other and with all other issues" (abstract). Just et al. (1996) found that in the primary spots, Clinton devoted 17% of his individual messages to economic matters, often discussing his "plan" for the economy. Bush stressed the economy in 24% of the primary spots.

How informative were the 1992 spots on these issues? While issues concerning the voters were frequently mentioned in the spots, most of the references were vague and general, conforming to Kern's (1989) description of "slogan ads." Only about one-third of the spots were platform ads (32 out of 91), which contained "either a commitment by a candidate to a position, or a rationale for taking a position or opposing that of the opponent" (Kern, 1989, p. 16). Two-thirds were slogan ads (59 out of 91). The political spots in general provided little substantive information on specific policy positions.

INNOVATIONS IN THE 1992 PRIMARY ADS

The nature of the political advertising of individual candidates in 1992 has been extensively analyzed by scholars and journalists.[4] Rather than repeat their findings, this analysis will focus on the innovations in the advertising. Brown was the leading innovator. He was the first to use a

1–800 telephone number in his spots, to attract donations and volunteers. He also was the first to use the 30-minute infomercial, which Renee Loth of the *Boston Globe* described as "revolutionary" because of its length (*McNeil-Lehrer Report*, PBS, February 1992). He did not have money to run the infomercial on commercial television, so he used cable; according to Dan Butler, Northeast Field Coordinator of Brown for President, this was the sole method of advertising in the early phases of the campaign (Royer, 1994). With cable, Brown could buy time for a 30-second spot on CNN for the whole state of New Hampshire (195,000 subscribers) for $200. An ad targeted just to Nashua, New Hampshire was $25, or to Manchester, $50 (Hoefler, 1991, pp. 46–47). This "narrowcasting" of advertising made it much more efficient to reach an audience within a geographically defined area. The audiences are smaller for cable, but the advantages of cost and targeting are significant.

Brown's infomercial told a dramatic story about General George Washington and the enlistees in the American Revolution, narrated by Brown. The soldiers wanted to go home when their service ended, he said. At first, none would re-enlist, and Washington feared that the cause was lost. He begged them to stay. At last one stepped forward, and then in twos and threes the others re-enlisted too. Brown urged his audience to "enlist as winter soldiers in the cause of America." "We the people," he said, must reclaim America. The story of Washington and the troops served as a vivid metaphor for courage and moral commitment in the face of great obstacles. But Brown did little in the spot to establish the enormous personal credibility necessary to engender such trust himself. The spot failed to dovetail the candidate's personal image and the issue of saving the country.

Other innovations in advertising were adopted by Tsongas, who was the first to provide a long booklet, *A Call to Economic Arms*, spelling out his economic positions, and by Clinton, the first to purchase time for a half-hour combined call-in and town meeting.

Customized campaign videos had been new in 1988, used by primary candidates such as Bruce Babbitt and Pat Robertson; in 1992, Brown, Clinton, and Kerrey had such videos in New Hampshire. During the last weekend before the New Hampshire primary, the beleaguered Clinton distributed 20,000 free copies of a 12-minute videotape to undecided households in New Hampshire. The Clinton campaign called recipients and reported that 60% to 70% had watched the tape (James Carville, comments to press, Manchester, New Hampshire, February 16, 1992, author's notes). Half of those who watched it reported that they had voted for Clinton (Ceaser and Busch, 1993).

The Clinton tape portrayed him as a person of strong and admirable image traits. The main theme was a vision of hope, as he spoke constantly of "change," of "making life better," and of "the future." There was a tremendous emphasis on winning as a people; he managed to equate *his* winning with *their* winning, taking over the game metaphor that so dominates media coverage and changing it from the victory of an individual candidate into the victory of a group—the middle class.

Of all the primary spots, the best remembered were Buchanan's "Read My Lips" ads, attacking Bush for breaking his promise that he would not raise taxes (West, 1993). Bush was shown making the fateful promise at the 1988 Republican Convention ("Read my lips. No new taxes."). The spots skillfully dovetailed the important image of trust with the issue of taxes. Bush came to embody the issue of raising taxes.

CONCLUSIONS

Unique Characteristics

There are few unique characteristics in primary campaign advertising when compared to advertising in the general election. Those that exist are directly traceable to the demands of the primary context. First, the candidates must design a series of "mini campaigns" to meet the needs of the different states, because the primaries are in serial order rather than all on one date, as in the fall. Thus, in 1992, the Bush campaign tailored a spot directly to the autoworkers in Michigan, telling them that Buchanan owned a foreign car. The Clinton campaign in New York attacked Brown's flat tax proposal, using quotations from a New York newspaper and from a U.S. senator from New York. In earlier years, the candidates also adapted their advertising to the states in which the primary took place.

Second, because there are multiple candidates in the primaries, it is more difficult for a candidate to stand out and be noticed, or even to achieve name recognition, than in the fall. This phenomenon first occurred in 1972, with the surge in the number of candidates. Until then, there usually were only two or three candidates competing actively within a given state. Today, all of the major candidates generally compete and advertise in the primaries.

A third unique characteristic of primary advertising found by earlier researchers is that it is less overtly negative than in the fall campaign. However this finding may be distorted by the method used: researchers have looked at the total number of primary ads and found what percentage were positive and negative. This treatment of all of the ads as one pool of data ignores the fact that many candidates drop out along the way, never going much beyond their early, positive biographical spots. Blatant attacks are seldom found in the early primary period, but once the campaign comes down to a fight among a few candidates, the number of negative ads rises, as shown in the contests between Clinton and Tsongas and Clinton and Brown in 1992, and between McGovern and Humphrey in 1972. By counting all of these ads together, the researchers may be overlooking the fact that the primaries tend to become very negative indeed, like the general election, when a tight, two-person or three-person contest develops.

Changes in Political Advertising

Some striking changes have occurred in political advertising in the presidential primaries. First, reference to party has all but disappeared in primary advertising. In 1912, 1932, and 1952, candidates were closely identified with their parties. By 1972, party references had declined. By 1992, it was unusual for an ad to mention party. One can infer that the candidates do not believe that the party label will help them in their persuasive effort.

Second, a huge change occurred when advertising moved from print to television. There were only a few television ads in the 1952 primaries, but after that the number rapidly escalated. Suddenly the candidate was "embodied" in a moving picture rather than presented through printed words and perhaps a photograph. The candidate changed from two-dimensional flatness to three-dimensional roundness, and from being distant to being close. As Jamieson and Campbell (1988) have said, television "simulates intimate relationships" (p. 45). Suddenly the candidate was right there in the living room. Personal qualities have always been important in primaries, because there is so little difference in issue positions among same-party candidates. Television ads made the candidates and those personal qualities far more immediate and interesting.

Voters were interested in personal characteristics in earlier elections; the newspaper ads of 1912 and 1952 listed the candidates' traits in a deductive arrangement, often equating their party strength with the ideal political image of the time, but with television another form was possible. Rather than listing traits, the television producers could develop a narrative, a mini-play, stressing the candidate's traits but arranging them much more inductively, using the conventions of storytelling. The first use of this kind of spot was by Eisenhower in the 1952 Republican primary; now it is de rigueur.

With television, the sense of distance was reduced and the candidates came down to earth. Whereas they were Titans in 1912, larger-than-life heroic figures, the candidates of the 1972 and 1992 primary ads were professional men, managerial, skilled and competent, friendly and decisive, but *not* larger than life. The spots made sure of that, removing all distance with their conversational tone and friendly manner: "I'm Bob Kerrey." "I'm Bill Clinton." Still on a pedestal, perhaps, but a *low* pedestal.

Third, the advertising changed as the advertising industry changed. New ideas tried in commercial advertising found their way into political advertising, often being tried first by the candidate with the least to lose, as diffusion of innovation research would predict (Savage, 1981). Those lagging behind look for new ideas to work miracles for their campaign. Thus, in 1992, last-place Brown tried the 1–800 number and the half-hour infomercial on cable television. Clinton, besieged by charges about his character, bought half-hour blocks on New Hampshire television stations for call-in shows. In 1952, the experimenter was Eisenhower, the first presidential primary candidate ever to use television advertising; though he was not an underdog, the contest with Taft was fierce, and nothing about the nomination was certain.

Fourth, there has been a sharpening in the focus of the ads. Early primary ads tended to be crowded in content and tried to accomplish multiple goals within one fixed frame. But television allows information to be presented serially rather than all at once, thus the viewer can consider one subject at a time, making for less confusion.

Finally, media attention to political advertising has intensified greatly. The 1992 presidential primaries were the first in which the ads were regularly scrutinized by the media for inaccuracies. This scrutiny affected the ads themselves; candidates increasingly cited their sources of information right on the screen, lest they be charged with fabricating information. While the educational goal of these ad watches is admirable, showing the ads provides a kind of "free advertising" for the candidates.

Advertising Constants in the Primaries

Much about primary advertising has remained the same in the 1912–1992 period. First, in all of the advertising candidate viability was stressed. The candidates were always portrayed as "winners." The second constant in advertising is the idea of fighting, which bears a close relationship to candidate viability and winning. These concepts of fighting and winning are deeply ingrained in American culture. While the press has been criticized for its obsession with the "horse race" to the exclusion of other, more substantive issues, a survey of the ads in this 80-year period suggests that it is the candidates, not the press, who are most responsible for the horse race metaphor. They clamor to capture the characterization of fighter and winner. Perhaps they simply reflect American culture in its fascination with the individual's struggle to win.

Third, the ads have consistently been what Kern (1989) calls "slogan ads." They have rarely presented much information on what the candidate's plans are or why he favors one policy or another. There were exceptions in every primary year, but the tendency in both print and television advertising has been to present scanty information. The biographical spots have provided more information than the other types.

Fourth, though Kern (1989) has described "dovetailing" as occurring in television advertising, the concept could easily be expanded to include print advertising in campaigns throughout history. In the ads from 1912–1992, candidates routinely blended personal information with information on political issues. Dovetailing transcended time.

Fifth, from the first primaries, the ads drew conspicuously from the speeches. Even with the increasing use of the narrative form, almost half of the 1992 ads still relied on speechlike messages by the candidates for much of their content.

Sixth, the primary ads were addressed to "the people." Throughout the 80 years studied, this phrase was central to the advertising. In 1912, it often was couched as "the American people," or "the Democracy." In 1992, "the people" were still frequently mentioned, as well as a term characterizing the majority of the people—"the middle class."

NOTES

1. In 1912, ads were examined in the following papers. New York primary: *New York Times, New York Tribune.* Maryland primary: *Baltimore American, Montgomery County Sentinel, Salisbury Advertiser, Evening Capital and Maryland Gazette* (Annapolis), and *The Sun* (Baltimore). In 1932, the clipping file from the Democratic National Committee, Roosevelt Library, Hyde Park, New York provided information from many newspapers. Ads also were examined in the following papers: Pennsylvania Democratic primary: Philadelphia papers with the largest circulation (*Inquirer, Public Ledger,* and *Evening Bulletin*). Massachusetts Democratic primary: *Boston Globe* and *Boston Herald.* Maryland Republican primary: *Evening Sun* (Baltimore). Some 1952 newspaper ads were found in the Robert A. Taft Papers, Library of Congress. Ads also were examined from the following New Hampshire papers: Manchester *Union-Leader, Concord Daily Monitor,* and *Foster's Daily Democrat* (Dover). For 1972, occasional examples of newspaper ads were found in Senator George McGovern's Papers, Mudd Library, Princeton University. Ads also were examined from the following Maryland newspapers: *Columbia Flier, Prince George's Post, Evening Capital* (Annapolis), *Evening Sun* (Baltimore), *Baltimore Jewish Times,* and *The Howard County Times.*

2. These spots came from tapes compiled by the Purdue University Public Affairs Video Archives (April 30, 1992), and by Devlin (1992).

3. Short chats of candidates with voters and monologues by professional narrators were not counted as speeches.

4. See West, Kern, and Alger, 1992; West, 1993; Devlin, 1994; Rosenstiel, 1993; Whillock, 1994; Marsh, 1995.

Chapter 5

Through Media Eyes in the Pre-Television Era: News Media Shaping of the Primaries, 1912–1952

Newspapers are unable, seemingly, to discriminate between a bicycle accident and the collapse of civilization.

—George Bernard Shaw

INTRODUCTION TO CHAPTERS 5 AND 6

Republican presidential candidate and commentator Pat Buchanan reflected on the New Hampshire Democratic primary and the media in 1992. "I felt if Cuomo [Governor Mario Cuomo of New York] got in, it'd be very exciting," he said. "Cuomo vs. the six-pack." But when Cuomo did not enter, he continued, "I thought *we'd* get the free media. Then the Clinton news broke, and the free media went wild" (comments on the Buchanan press bus, February 17, 1992, author's notes). Buchanan's remarks depict a powerful media, drawn to conflict and scandal and well-known candidates, unpredictable in their choices, ready to seize upon excitement wherever it might appear. Candidates hope for their attention ("I thought *we'd* get the free media"), but they never know when the media will dash off after stories of sex or corruption. Democratic candidate Bob Kerrey's campaign manager, discussing this same period, lamented that the media gave so much attention to the Clinton stories of infidelity and the draft that they pushed Kerrey's candidacy out of the picture (Tad Devine, in Royer, 1994).

REVIEW OF THE LITERATURE

The Power of Deciding Who to Cover

Candidates are concerned about the media's role in the primaries, with good reason. The primaries are about *starting*; they come first, early in the campaign. Of the four phases of a presidential campaign (pre-primary, primary, convention, and general election), it is the primary phase that gets the most prominent and frequent coverage on television news, an average of 36% of the news stories (Woodard, 1994). Many of the candidates are unknown to national audiences, and they must have publicity to become known. Voter perceptions are less developed in this early period, there is much "volatility and unpredictability," and "most voters make up their minds at the last minute when the primary campaign finally reaches their state" (Popkin, 1991, p. 115). In such a formative period, the media become the main channels through which the candidates communicate with the voters.

Research by Lenart (1994) found that in the "early, introductory stages of a political campaign . . . candidate exposure elicits more positive evaluations than nonexposure" (p. 104). But newspapers do not have endless space, nor television endless time. Reporters and editors serve as gatekeepers for the candidates' messages, making the choices about which ones get attention. Political columnist David Broder (1976) describes reporters as "talent scouts" who observe the candidates and decide which ones deserve serious consideration; their news accounts reflect these opinions. The devastating effects of the media's noncoverage of Democratic candidate Larry Agran in 1992, resulting in his remaining invisible to the public, have been described by Meyrowitz (1995). Meyrowitz concluded that the present national news system of deciding which candidates to cover is "relatively closed," and "one could certainly argue that a true democracy deserves—and requires—something better" (p. 60).

The Power of Interpretation

In addition to the power of deciding who to cover, the media also have the power to translate and interpret what they see. Iyengar and Kinder (1987) and Iyengar (1991) have described the way in which the media introduce an evaluative component to their coverage, through priming, in which they reveal their positive or negative view of public figures through cues such as story placement, length of story, and so on. This power goes beyond the setting of the news agenda, or agenda setting, described by McCombs and Shaw (1972). Page, Shapiro, and Dempsey (1994), in a study of television news coverage and public opinion over a period of decades, found that certain factors in television news have demonstrable power to change opinion, especially the comments of individual news commentators and the testimony of experts or accounts of research studies.

In observations more directly focused on the primaries, Asher (1992) has noted that because the primaries are decided by pluralities rather than majorities, the media have a broader scope for defining winners and losers. Usually the winner gets the most attention, but occasionally the press will give its heaviest coverage to a candidate who did better than expected, such as Buchanan in the 1992 New Hampshire primary. Some of the media's interpretations have become heavily stylized and patterned. Kendall (1993), in a study of network news coverage of candidate speeches in the 1992 primaries, found that the networks regularly reduced the candidates to gesturing, voiceless figures, the power of their language and ideas lost in reporters' summaries.

The nature of this media power in the primaries, as well as the efforts of candidates to influence the media, is the focus of Chapters 5 and 6. In addition to the media's power to decide what to cover, and their power to interpret what they see, there are other issues. To what extent, for example, do the media describe, and to what extent do they prescribe? Sabato (1992) reports that there has been a shift in approach by the media from 1941 to the present, going from a period of (1) "lapdog journalism" (1941–1966), in which reporters "served and reinforced the political establishment," to a period of (2) "watchdog journalism" (1966–1974), in which they "scrutinized the behavior of political elites by undertaking independent investigations of their statements," to a post–Watergate period of (3) "junkyard dog journalism" (1974 to the present), characterized by "reporting that is often harsh, aggressive, and intrusive" (pp. 132–142). In the face of Watergate, the media have increasingly questioned the character of presidential candidates, he says, making the character issue a much greater focus than in the past.

In a study of media coverage of campaigns from 1898 to 1984, Andersen and Thorson (1989) found evidence that seems consistent with Sabato's (1992) "lapdog" analysis. In the *New York Times* stories examined from 1898 to 1960, the paper concentrated on the candidates' arguments. Many campaign stories, "approximately a fifth to a third" (p. 270) were devoted to transcripts or reports of candidates' speeches. Though Sabato calls this "lapdog" journalism, Andersen and Thorson cast it in a much more positive light, particularly in contrast to the kind of coverage that followed. From 1960 to 1984, they found *New York Times'* news coverage shifting from a focus on political discourse to a heavy emphasis on candidate strategy and image. The authors lament this change. In marked contrast to coverage in an earlier day, they say, the 1984 press presented "a campaign of assertions, slogans, and punch lines rather than one of sustained arguments" (Andersen and Thorson, 1989, p. 277).

Stebenne (1993) suggests an explanation for this change in reporting, noting the powerful effect of Theodore White's four books, entitled *The Making of the President*, from 1960 through 1972. White's best-selling reports of these campaigns focused on the process of campaigning, shifting attention to the question, "How is this candidate running his campaign, and what does that say about his likelihood of winning?" (p. 87).

The Horse Race

Many researchers have commented on the prevalence of horse race journalism in coverage of campaigns, with the media focusing on the question "who can win" and discussing the campaigns' strategies to win (Arterton, 1984; Jamieson, 1992). While the focus of campaign news coverage should be on "who is offering a compelling understanding of the state of the nation, the challenges it faces, and the directions it should take" (p. 164), Jamieson notes that the language of campaign reporting talks of candidates in terms of "win," "place," or "show," and of "winners" and "leaders" (1992, pp. 164, 175).

An integral part of this horse race coverage is the media's heavy reliance on opinion polls to report who is ahead and who is behind. The media favor polls because the numbers "suggest a measure of objectivity and precision," and the poll results help them structure their coverage (Traugott, 1985, p. 109). Front-runners in the polls receive the heaviest coverage. Exit polls are reported extensively for primaries and help the press make interpretations of the results.

Which Primaries Receive the Most Coverage?

Some primaries receive much more news coverage than others. Those with the heaviest coverage are: (1) those in which the first votes are cast; (2) those primaries being held on a day when no other primaries are held; (3) primaries in which the results are clear; (4) primaries that many candidates have considered important enough to enter; and (5) primaries that are highly competitive (Joslyn, 1984). Woodard (1994) compared television news coverage of primaries and caucuses from 1972 through 1988 and found that the focus on Iowa and New Hampshire grew heavier and heavier, by 1988 virtually crowding out coverage of many other states.

The time sequence of the primaries also affects coverage. Leubsdorf (1976) summarized the patterns of coverage by campaign period, finding that in the period before the first primaries, only the major national papers gave much coverage. In the early primary period, television and print reporters followed the campaign closely and stressed the viability of the candidates. As primary results mounted, the vote outcomes influenced the proportion and tone of the coverage. Coverage changed in the late primary period, from early April on, he reported. As candidates were seen as potential presidents, the press became more critical and scrutinized candidate policy positions more closely (in Traugott, 1985).

The sequence of the primaries before 1972 provided a neat framework for press coverage as they "unfolded in a nice, temporal and geographic sequence starting in New Hampshire, moving to Wisconsin, and concluding in Oregon and California" (Asher, 1992, p. 269). Reporters moved west with the candidates. Generally there were only one or two primaries on the same day, but that ended with the resurgence of primaries in 1972. It is hard to focus on one primary when there are five on the same day.

Media Handling of Ambiguity

Asher (1992) has noted a tendency of the media to avoid complexity and ambiguity in primary coverage. For example, in 1976, the press chose to emphasize Democrat Jimmy Carter's win in the Ohio primary rather than his surprise loss in New Jersey. New Jersey was ignored, he said, because the primary there was more complicated to cover, with *separate* votes for delegate selection and for the candidates. Smith (1992) has a somewhat different interpretation of the reasons for media choices, believing that journalists decide on a story line and ignore evidence that fails to contribute to the drama. The dramatic logic dominates over the empirical logic of coverage, with journalists focusing on the quest of hero figures for the nomination and ignoring contradictions. A recent example of this pattern was the media focus on Bill Clinton and their much slighter attention to Paul Tsongas in the 1992 Democratic primary in New Hampshire, in spite of Tsongas's strong poll standing and eventual victory in New Hampshire.

Negative Coverage

Another finding about media coverage of the primaries is that it tends to be quite negative (Joslyn, 1984; Hallin, 1992; Patterson, 1993). Stories of candidates' deceptiveness and peccadillos far outweigh positive ones. The recent development of ad watches, in which candidate advertising is dissected and lies and distortions are exposed, contributes to this negative aura. Joslyn (1984) claims that several factors influence the media's decisions to give positive or negative emphasis to their stories. They tend to scrutinize front-runners more closely than those not likely to win, exposing their clay feet for the voters, and they generally conform to the horse race scenario, questioning the viability of those running behind in the polls. Kendall (1995) found that the one candidate characteristic likely to draw positive media coverage was the image of "the fighter against the odds," who exerts superhuman efforts to overcome obstacles. Thus, media coverage of Buchanan and Clinton in the 1992 New Hampshire primary often had an admiring tone.

Conflict among candidates often is portrayed in a very negative light. Paletz and Elson (1976, p. 123), in their study of television coverage of the 1972 Democratic National Convention, noted that intraparty disagreements and competition *could* have been interpreted as signs that the party was "active and vital," proof of "democracy at work," but instead "commentators tended to portray divisiveness in terms of bitterness, hard feelings, bickering, arguing for the sake of arguing, and a severe impediment to victory" in the fall campaign.

When there is an incumbent president who is unchallenged within his own party, and the other party has presidential primary contests, the heavily negative portrayal of the primaries can be dangerous to the out party. Reinsch (1988) reported that in the 1984 primaries, for example, the Democratic candidates "appeared on every television news program in a self-destruct mode," while President Reagan "took the high road" (pp. 255–256). Another illustration of the advantage of not having to face the media in contested primaries was the emerging independent candidacy of Ross Perot in the spring of 1992. Perot entered no primaries. By May, he had risen to the top in the opinion polls, while President Bush and Governor Clinton, battered and bruised under the close scrutiny of the press during the primaries, limped along behind. The May 16, 1992 *Time* poll showed Perot leading with 33%, Bush with 28%, and Clinton with 24% (*ABC World News Tonight*, May 16, 1992).

Candidates' Influence on the Media

While the candidates tend to view the media as powerful and fickle, some researchers have argued that it is the candidates who dominate the media, or at least have equal power. Wolfsfeld and Gamson (1992), writing about the relationship between social and political movements and the media, have called the relationship one of "competitive symbiosis," in which "each side is dependent on the other for needed services but each tries to obtain those services while incurring the least amount of cost" (p. 2). Strong organization and ample resources are particularly valuable in securing media attention, because with these tools movements are better able to control the flow of information and "to carry out actions which will be considered newsworthy" (p. 9). Similar principles apply in the interaction of primary campaign organizations and the media. In the media's focus on the campaign as a process, they "are at the mercy of the campaign for the information and pictures they need," says Kerbel (1994). In his study of ABC and CNN coverage of the 1992 campaign, he found that the campaign itself was "the strongest external influence" on the election story, except for "breaking nonelection news" (p. 142).

There is no question that the candidates strive to gain positive media attention, employing incumbent and challenger strategies. The incumbent has the built-in advantage that the media cover the president continuously. Trent and Trent (1995, p. 72) reported that President Bush "made use of each of the traditional symbolic strategies [of the incumbent]." For example, he "attempted to use 'the trappings of the office' to remind voters that they were seeing 'the President' as opposed to just another politician," appearing on the CBS program *This Morning* while sitting in the White House Rose Garden, answering questions from tourists (p. 73). In the 1980 primaries, President Carter commanded the media agenda when he called a press conference early on the morning of the Wisconsin primary to announce a possible break in the Iranian hostage crisis, a break that failed to materialize.

Meyrowitz (1995) found the media more influenced by political party professionals than by the campaigns themselves in their decisions about which primary candidates to cover. Wanting to cover "winners," the reporters in the national press sought the advice of party professionals to sort out the major and minor candidates, and then they restricted most of their coverage to a "narrow set of largely predetermined 'major' candidates" (p. 45). They also were influenced by their colleagues in the press, looking at each others' work "to see who is being taken as a 'serious' candidate" (p. 49), and then engaging in what Meyrowitz calls "protective coverage," trying to cover what the other news media were covering as well as their own choices. This kind of decision making sounds much like the pack journalism described so vividly in Crouse's account of the 1972 presidential campaign *Boys on the Bus* (1972).

Ceaser and Busch (1993) and Busch (1997) identify a preoccupation of the media with "outsiders." They find that "outsiderism" has been a long-time theme in American politics, a populist perspective regularly encouraged by the media. George Wallace and Jimmy Carter were two such outsiders. Outsider appeals, according to Ceaser and Busch (1993), have been inflated by "a communication system that favors new and outside appeals" (p. 9).

Citizens' Use of Media for Campaign News

Any discussion of the media and the primaries must examine the question, "Which media do citizens use for campaign information?" One would expect to find that television is the most important medium in modern campaigns, and indeed, that is what people say when they are asked. Asher (1992) states that in citizen self-reports, reliance on television news as the most important campaign source grew from 32% in 1952 to 65% in 1960 and has remained approximately at the 1960 level ever since. In 1988, about 66% said they relied most on television, 25% on newspapers, and the rest were divided between magazines and radio. However, it would be a mistake to look only at television, for the majority of citizens report using two or more sources of campaign information. One study found that 50% of the public used three or four sources and that 50% used two or less sources, with television and newspapers being the most commonly mentioned (Yum and Kendall, 1988). The use of media for campaign information changed in the 1952–1988 period: in 1952, 79% of the respondents reported using newspapers, 70% radio, 51% television, and 40% magazines. By 1988, newspaper use had dropped to 64%, radio use to 31%, and magazine use to 25%, while television use had risen to 95% (Asher, 1992).

Little research has been done specifically on media use in the primaries. Yum and Kendall (1988), in a study focusing on what media were used for news of the 1984 New York presidential primary, found that people reported using an average of 2.6 news sources, particularly television and newspapers—86% reported using television, 82% newspapers; 30% mentioned magazines, 21% radio, and 18% friends and family. Research comparing news usage on the national, state, and local levels suggests a much heavier use of television for international and national news and newspapers for local and state news (Witt, 1983; Reagan and Ducey, 1983); however, this research was done in the 1980s, and the situation may have changed. It also is the case that a presidential primary cannot be neatly categorized as national, state, or local, but contains elements of all three.

Candidates give much attention to the local press when they are campaigning in the primaries, "making themselves available to reporters and editors" and "timing speeches and announcements to receive maximum press coverage" (Wayne, 1992, p. 121). The local press has a somewhat different logic of journalistic coverage; even candidates who are being ignored by the national press may get local coverage, merely by coming to the community (Meyrowitz, 1995).

Visual Factors in Television

The growth of television as the dominant news medium has led to research on the role of visual messages in the news. While this research has not focused on the primaries, the findings are valuable as a guide to our consideration of media in the primary setting. Jamieson (1988), in a study of presidential speeches in the modern era, has found that television encourages an interpersonal style of address epitomized in the speeches of President Ronald Reagan, a far more self-disclosive and intimate style than the one used in classical oratory. Speakers attuned to the visual aspects of the medium are more likely to use visual examples and stories that appeal to the emotions rather than the logical arguments and evidence valued in classical oratory. Pfau and Kang (1991) note all of the ways in which television is an interpersonal medium: we see the speaker's face up close; we usually are viewing the television at home, either by ourselves or in a small group; and the unique qualities of television, the visual and nonverbal, are ones valued in interpersonal communication. Meyrowitz (1995) describes television as a medium of "aura," in which "the gestures and expressions of candidates are often as important as, if not more important than, the words and ideas expressed" (p. 56).

MEDIA IN THE 1912 PRIMARIES

In 1912, the newspapers were the dominant medium, and journalists were courted by the candidates and their staff.[1] The newspapers were remarkably pliant to President Taft and his campaign spokesmen, often publishing their news releases unedited. Roosevelt was available to reporters on a daily basis, and his warm relations with the press were apparent in his regularly addressing them as "Boys," while they called him "Colonel." As president, he had "established a press room in the White House and began the custom of regular presidential press conferences" (Murphy, 1955, p. 338). Press attention focused on these two Republicans; other candidates were nearly invisible.

This study of media in 1912 focuses on newspapers.[2] Technological developments in communication also should be mentioned. Telegraphic wire facilities for the national reporting of news played a critical role and also were used by the candidates to monitor their rivals' speeches and to respond immediately with counterattacks throughout the day's speaking itinerary. One candidate exploited the medium of the telephone. When 700 newspapermen from all parts of the country met at the Waldorf Hotel in New York, Taft addressed them by telephone from Washington. A telephone receiver had been installed for each guest. He told them he was glad to give his testimony to the "concentrated power" they represented. "The safety of the country," he said, lay in the fact that they neutralized each other, "and in the great conviction of the citizens of the country that the truth lies not in you but between you" (New York *Tribune*, April 26, 1912; hereafter *Tribune*).

When the Republican National Committee met in June 1912 to decide on disputed delegate contests, the meetings were, in an unprecedented fashion, open to the press. The change had been suggested by Roosevelt and his manager, undoubtedly in the hope that the presence of journalists would strengthen his position for the nomination. It did not—Taft got the Republican nomination—but it ingratiated Roosevelt with the press (*Tribune*, June 2, 1912).

In 1912, the major newspapers presented the presidential primaries as important events. Significantly, however, there was very little emphasis on the novelty of the series of presidential preference primaries. Perhaps this was because primaries at the state and local levels were not uncommon. In effect, the reporting was simply an adaptation, covering the presidential election as it was traditionally treated, as a story of top priority newsworthiness. The largest coverage was given to the most populous states. With only two exceptions, for Oregon and Nebraska, the results of primaries were reported on the front page. Little else appeared on the front pages of all newspapers except news of the sinking of the *Titanic* for a week after April 15. The *New York Times* (March 20, 1912) recognized the uniqueness of the earliest primary, held in North Dakota, calling it "the first State-wide Presidential primary ever held in the United States," and placing the story on the front page in the right-hand column. The primary results in New York, New Jersey, and Ohio received front-page, three-column coverage in this paper.

The saliency of the cross-continental primaries in the press in 1912 stands in marked contrast to the press perception of the isolated presidential primary in Wisconsin in 1908. When Senator Robert LaFollette's new primary law took effect in 1908, Wisconsin newspapers focused chiefly on the local primary elections for mayor, aldermen, and state Supreme Court judge. The reporting conveyed no sense that something unusual was about to take place, and no emphasis was given to the fact that Wisconsin was a pioneer in presidential primaries.[3] Only in the "how to do it" notice explaining the voting procedures on primary election day was there a hint that the voters were about to have a new experience. Paid political advertisements appeared in the newspapers for local candidates but *not* for the presidential candidates: LaFollette and Taft for the Republicans and William Jennings Bryan for the Democrats. On primary election day the delegates at large who pledged to LaFollette won the Wisconsin Republican primary, and the delegates who pledged to Bryan won the Democratic primary.

The 1912 primary campaigns were pursued in much the same way as full-scale presidential general elections, with gangs of newspaper reporters following the candidates on speaking tours, wiring their dispatches to editors each evening. In many respects the campaign in 1912 bore an uncanny resemblance to the primaries today. The candidates created media events just as they do today, for example. Schoolchildren could no more vote in 1912 than in 1996, but candidates took the campaign—the press entourage—to them anyway. Roosevelt addressed a schoolhouse filled with children in Huntington, New York. The meeting began with Roosevelt joining the children in singing "America." Everyone recited the Pledge of Allegiance and then sang "Columbia, the Gem of the Ocean." It was reported to the nation that the children "waved their little flags and cheered lustily." He talked with them about the salute to the flag and the meaning of "liberty" and "justice." "I want you to insist on liberty and justice for others, not alone for yourselves," he said, "and don't put this off until you are grown up." Roosevelt promised to return and talk about his African safari and then left the children with his favorite football maxim: "Don't flinch, don't fall, and hit the line hard" (*Tribune*, March 19, 1912).

There was never any doubt nor any attempt to hide the fact that Taft was given favorable treatment and the most extensive coverage by the newspapers in this study. The one exception was Clark's endorsement by the *San Francisco Examiner*. The massive coverage of the Taft campaign, the constant vilification of Roosevelt, the token coverage of La-Follette, and the only brief, casual references to Democrats gave the impression that no Democratic primary campaign existed. In California, extensive and respectful coverage was given to the absent candidates' support groups, local and national managers, and financial backers, as well as information about itineraries, special speakers, where rallies were to be or had been held, and the size of audiences. Often in the headlines was the appropriately named skating rink in San Francisco, used by several candidates for huge rallies, "Dreamland."

The campaign managers' access to the press was remarkable. In the *San Francisco Chronicle* (April 23, 1912), after Taft's poor showing in the Oregon and Nebraska primaries, a front-page headline, "Taft Managers Score Roosevelt's Tactics," introduced the text of a press release, quoted verbatim except for a candid introductory paragraph. It began:

The Taft national headquarters at Washington has sent to the headquarters of the Taft Republicans in this city a statement indicating its belief that President Taft will be nominated at Chicago on the first ballot, with votes to spare.

With newspapers in the singular position of being both the only mass medium reporting campaign news and the target of the candidates' publicity efforts, the reader was regularly confronted with interviews, press releases, and telegrams, printed verbatim, from persons routinely identified as "managers" and "handlers" (*San Francisco Examiner*, May 7, 1912). This reflected, of course, the extremely partisan stance of the newspapers. Roosevelt's manager complained about the anti-Roosevelt bias, writing in a letter of March 7 published in the *Tribune* that the New York newspapers were "moving heaven and earth to avoid the nomination of Roosevelt."

Managers also knew how to put a favorable "spin" on bad news in 1912. When LaFollette won the first primary, held in North Dakota, "the

Taft people called it a victory, because every vote taken from Roosevelt mean[t] a gain for them, and the Roosevelt followers called it a victory because Taft ran third, and a bad third at that" (*New York Times*, March 21, 1912). When Taft lost the Illinois primary, his campaign manager explained that "the issues which occupied the attention of the people of the state were so peculiarly local as to cause the Presidential issue to be lost sight of" (*Tribune*, April 11, 1912). They made the same excuse after defeat in Pennsylvania. The *Tribune*, staunchly for Taft, reported that "astute Pennsylvania politicians" were almost unanimous in declaring that the sweeping Roosevelt victory "was not a victory for Roosevelt, but was a victory in a fight against machine politics" in the state. According to the paper's pro-Taft interpretation, voters were simply using Roosevelt as a way to overthrow the present state Republican machine, and he had won only "because of his ability to appeal to the passions of the multitude" (*Tribune*, April 15, 1912).

The press gave some coverage to the personal lives of the candidates, though there was none of the feeding frenzy often found today. For example, the wives of the candidates played prominent roles. A much publicized event was the Dolly Madison Breakfast in Washington, attended by 450 women, including Mrs. Clark (wife of Democratic candidate Champ Clark), serving as toastmistress, Mrs. Bryan, Mrs. Harmon, and many wives of Congressmen. The press noted that the breakfast cost $5.00, and each woman took home a reproduction of Dolly Madison's snuffbox. Mrs. Clark toasted the women of the White House: "Be to her virtues very kind, and to her faults a little blind" (*Tribune*, May 21, 1912).

The attention given to the candidates' family members during the campaign had clear political overtones. When Mrs. Taft visited the Woman's Industrial Exhibition in New York but did not stop at the Woman Suffrage Association booth, a suffragist commented that this was "very bad policy on the part of the wife of a man who may want the votes of the women out West to elect him" (*Tribune*, March 2, 1912). A story associated Taft with the wealthy when his daughter was reported to have ridden "with fifty hounds and forty of the best riders in Washington society" in a "drag chase" of the Riding and Hunt Club of Washington (*Tribune*, March 31, 1912). When Mrs. Roosevelt and her daughter Ethel returned to New York after three weeks in Panama, Roosevelt was pictured as a loyal husband and father, hurrying to meet them "as soon as they land" (*Tribune*, March 18, 1912). Another story cast the Roosevelts as a close, strong family, not to mention physically fit, taking "a long cross-country walk over to the north shores of Green Bay," returning hours later in the "raw and foggy" evening (*Tribune*, April 15, 1912).

Polling

A professional polling and survey industry did not exist in 1912. Nevertheless, with election outcomes purely speculative, campaign staffs and newspapers estimated candidate popularity, voter support, and delegate strength freely and frequently. Competing claims and counterclaims about likely voting results were always in the headlines, and elaborate estimates were made of the size and relative enthusiasm of each candidate's crowds. These often were frankly propagandistic exercises in wishful thinking. In a front-page article on the Ohio primary in the *Los Angeles Times* (May 17, 1912), under the headline "Roosevelt is Doomed," was the subhead "Close observers in Washington see end of Colonel in day's work." Despite these predictions, Roosevelt won the primary.

Opinion polls did exist in rudimentary form, and one type was used by the parties. The *Tribune* (April 21, 1912) reported that the Progressive Democrats sent ballots to 2,500 enrolled members of the party and to other "prominent" Democrats in New Jersey, asking them to mark their preference for a Democratic candidate and to indicate which issue they thought was the most important one for the country. They received 649 replies, a one-in-four response rate, with Wilson receiving the most votes, and the reduction of the tariff was reported as the leading issue. Newspapers also conducted polls. A Roosevelt communique claimed that "literally hundreds of test votes of political sentiment in both the great parties have recently been made by reputable newspapers and other agencies," with Roosevelt leading Taft by more than five to one (*Tribune*, March 1, 1912).

Looking back to 1912, one is struck by the paradox of how presidential preference primaries immediately focused and intensified pre-convention candidacy to the narrow confines of a four-month period, while at the same time they opened up and diffused the campaign in its scale of appeal, its demand for resources, and the enlarging of the scope of competition beyond party organizations. The newspapers played a major role in this process, publicizing what the candidates were doing and saying and relying heavily on the campaigns themselves for the messages.

Perhaps because of the undoubted qualifications of both the leading Republicans, their primary campaigns became embittered and, to put it mildly, "negative." As Taft and Roosevelt hurled charges at one another, growing more and more personal, the press laid it out for all to see, usually on the front page. As Pfau and Kenski (1990) have observed, "campaigns were certainly rougher during the era when print was the dominant channel of communication and there was a strong tradition of a partisan press compared to more objective, professional media" (p. 5). The attacks on Taft began when Roosevelt lost the New York primary on March 26, and Roosevelt charged Taft's managers with fraud and trickery, resorting to practices "worse than Tweed's." The primary process in New York had been "a criminal farce," he said. Furthermore, he accused Taft of "political chicanery" and of "cooking" the Southern primaries (*Tribune*, April 9, 1912). He released a letter accusing Taft of using federal officeholders in acts of vote fraud in Kentucky (*New York Times*, April 9, 1912). By late April, in Massachusetts, his attacks were described as a "torrent of hot denunciation," charging that Taft had used "deliberate misrepresentation" and was disloyal not only to their past friendship but "disloyal to every canon of ordinary decency and fair dealing" (*Tribune*, April 27, 1912). The next day, he backed away from such a bitter charge and avowed in the future to refer to Taft as little as possible (*Tribune*, April 28, 1912).

As the Taft campaign met successive defeats in the primaries, it attacked Roosevelt more aggressively, charging him with demagoguery and "Caesarism" for violating the unwritten law against a third presidential term, as well as breaking his own pledge not to accept another nomination (*New York Times*, March 20, 1912). Taft's personal secretary, Charles D. Hilles, held a press conference and released an elaborate report alleging that in 1907 Roosevelt had improperly intervened in an investigation of the International Harvester Company to delay a prosecution (*Los Angeles Times*, May 18, 1912). A charge circulated in the Midwest that Roosevelt was an alcoholic, which he denied (*New York Times*, May 21, 1912).

The Taft campaign's aim of projecting an image of competence, stability, and assured victory was at odds with its increasingly harsh attacks upon the obviously popular Roosevelt (*Los Angeles Times*, May 21, 1912). An article entitled "Nation's Executive Scores Colonel's Vanity and Egotism," described Taft's speeches in Ohio as "marked by the most pronounced verbal assaults upon Colonel Roosevelt to which Taft has so far given public utterance," in "speeches that were filled with indignant attack that bubbled over with uncomplimentary adjectives" (*San Francisco Chronicle*, May 14, 1912).

Many Americans were appalled at the level of negative campaigning in the primaries. This "spectacle . . . should bring a blush of shame to the cheek of every American," wrote one *New York Times* author, longing for the more "seemly procedure" of the convention process (April 28, 1912, p. 16, in Troy, 1991, p. 126).

The results of the first prominent use of presidential primaries were not anticipated by the reformers. It seems unlikely that the experience of 1912 contributed substantially to the aims of progressive reform or "people's power," unless the eventual weakening of both state and national party structures was to be taken as implicit in those aims.

The 1912 presidential primaries served as an effective means for popular, charismatic, and already well-established national figures such as

Roosevelt and LaFollette to mobilize national campaigns. Primaries therefore enhanced the appeal of personality, both to the electorate at large and to powerful backers, as a rival force to the established national parties. Winning the primaries required an ever-expanding popular focus on the personalities of aspirants. As a consequence, the primaries engendered an inherent conflict between the power of personality and the power of party organizations.

Such campaigns shifted the emphasis to mass-mediated perceptions of candidates: their "experience," image, and symbolic contexts. In reply to Sabato's question (Sabato, in McCubbins, 1992), "Is the emphasis on character in political reporting a recent development?" the answer is no, not in the primaries. Character and image in 1912 were pivotal concerns, in the context of intraparty competition. The primary process became a struggle to generate popular recognition in the mass media, the polls, the primary elections, and the parties in descending order of importance. Inevitably, this process distanced itself from party ideology and gave priority to personal factors and the ability of the candidate and his own organization to interact effectively with the media and the voters. Finally, this first major primary experience illustrated the importance of promoting the candidate's image and led quickly to the awareness by both candidates and media that an essential part of that promotion was the attack and destruction of the image of one's opponents.

MEDIA IN THE 1932 PRIMARIES

Compared to the news coverage in 1912, the presidential primaries of 1932 were practically invisible. The main reason for this was that the candidates and the voters had lost faith in the primaries, as it had become obvious that the state party leaders and conventions still retained an iron grip on the selection of the nominee. Thus, the 1932 presidential primary campaign in the Democratic Party followed the earlier model of campaigns before 1912, shifting attention back to the state conventions and caucuses. In contrast to the all-out primary campaigning of 1912, it now was customary for candidates to enter only a few primaries and to adopt a public posture of being above the battle, not campaigning in person. All of these conditions served to reduce news coverage of the 1932 primaries.

Nevertheless, there were news messages about the primaries. Even silence carries a message. The author examined the following works to determine how the press covered the primaries: the texts of President Hoover's press conferences, January–June 1932; coverage by the Philadelphia newspapers of the Pennsylvania Democratic primary, the Boston papers of the Massachusetts Democratic primary, and the Baltimore papers of the Maryland Republican primary, each during the week before the primary; the Roosevelt campaign's newspaper clipping file, January–June 1932, Louis Howe Papers, Franklin D. Roosevelt Library, Hyde Park, NY (featuring especially the *New York Times* and the New York *Herald Tribune*); coverage by the Universal Newspaper Newsreels, January 1–June 30, 1932 (National Archives); and the schedule of candidate appearances on NBC radio.

Press Conferences

President Hoover held 35 press conferences during the primary period in 1932. There is no evidence that he deliberately increased his contact with the press. In fact, he had held 33 press conferences the year before in a comparable period. Press conferences were not broadcast and were presented to be used as "background" for the journalists, not quoted. There were few questions (*Public Papers of the President*, 1931, 1932).

Newsreels

There were no stories about the presidential primaries in the Universal Newspaper Newsreels, January–June, 1932, nor would one have known that the nation was in the midst of a serious economic depression. The stories emphasized visual action: fatal explosions, floods, the Japanese invasion of China, sports stories, the Lindbergh kidnapping. The entire coverage of May 9, 1932, contained the following stories: a $2,000,000 Cunard pier fire, an accident at an auto racetrack, an Indian pageant, a new visual education plan to teach geography, a couple being married in a lion's den, an architects' poll of the countries' finest structures, and the results of the Kentucky Derby (Vol. IV, No. 39, National Archives).

Movie attendance was high in the 1930s. A 1936 survey revealed that 37% of the respondents attended movies once a week or more; another 25% attended once a month or more. In all, 80% said yes to the question, "Do you go to the movies?" (April and November 1936 polls, in Cantril, 1951, p. 485). The feature film was preceded by a newsreel, a visual and auditory form of news that had the potential to shape public opinion about the presidential primaries, but the primaries were never mentioned in the newsreels.

However, the president of the United States often was mentioned in the newsreels, always favorably. In spite of the Depression, Hoover's flattering portrayal displayed the benefits of the incumbency. From January 1 through June 20, there were six stories about President Hoover and no stories about the Democratic candidates. Hoover appeared at his Annual Open House ("Hundreds wait[ed] in line all night" to shake hands with him and his wife); at the bicentennial of George Washington's birth, placing a wreath on the tomb; attending Easter sunrise memorial services with his wife at the Tomb of the Unknown Soldier, bareheaded in the rain, where they were "hailed by the thousands"; tossing out the ball to start the baseball season; being nominated at the Republican Convention; and entertaining war veterans at a "brilliant White House lawn festival." Only when the Democratic Convention began did the newsreels pay any attention to the Democrats, with three stories in the June 23–30 period.

Radio

In 1932, newspapers remained the main source of political information. Nevertheless, by this time, about 61% of American households had radios, a huge increase from 5% in 1924 and 27% in 1928 (Barone, 1990, p. 53). When asked what their favorite radio programs were, respondents in a 1937 survey listed entertainment programs first, such as Jack Benny and Eddie Cantor; news broadcasts and specific news programs such as *March of Time* were farther down the list (January 9, 1937, survey, in Cantril, 1951, p. 716). Still, radio provided an opportunity to learn about the candidates. It was heavily used in the 1928 general election, with short speeches by "Minute Men" for the Republicans, vaudeville speeches lasting about an hour, and a radio play about Governor Al Smith's life, written by Fulton Oursler (Clark, 1962). Radio news in the 1920s and most of the 1930s, however, "consisted largely of the reading of news bulletins taken off the tickers of the wire services" (William Paley, in Ryan, 1963, p. v), like an oral newspaper.

The leading candidates gave radio speeches during the 1932 primary campaign period, although none of the speeches dealt specifically with the primaries. Roosevelt gave five addresses and Smith gave 10. Roosevelt had mastered the medium of radio while governor of New York. As one author described it: "After over seventy-five talks during four years as a governor, Roosevelt delivered textbook examples of how to combine a genial tone and familiar language for familiar effect" (Troy, 1991, p. 163). Despite his skill and advantage with the medium, there is no sign from the numbers, topics, or timing of his radio addresses that Roosevelt was attempting to use radio especially for the primaries.

Newspapers

Sabato's (1992) image of "lapdog" journalism is one way to describe newspaper coverage of the 1932 primaries, but it does not exactly do it justice. True, reporters drew heavily on the politicians and their campaigns, and they reported what they were told. Articles combined the summary and quotation of the words and actions of political figures; it was not unusual to find two or three paragraphs of direct quotation in an article. In coverage of Roosevelt's speech in St. Paul, Minnesota, on April 18, for example, the papers devoted most of their account to Roosevelt's own words (Ernest K. Lindley, "Roosevelt Informs Critics," *Tribune*, April 19, 1932; Louis Ruppel, "Roosevelt Pleads For Low and High," *New York Daily News*, April 19, 1932). Reporters made their own contributions to the reports by attempting to be the "eyes and ears" of the reader, describing scenes and settings surrounding political events, but these descriptions had no real critical content.

On the whole, though, the candidates must have found many of the news articles disquieting, for in a primary campaign there are many candidates, and the press, merely by serving as a channel for different candidates, communicates conflicting positions. They also selected the most vivid quotations and the horse race news in preference to news of the candidates' policy positions. There was no guarantee of coverage either. Is "lapdog journalism" the right term if the press ignores the candidates? In the news context of the Lindbergh baby's kidnapping, which dominated the front pages in early 1932, the nomination process struggled to be noticed. Contemporary humorist Will Rogers' observation seemed to reflect the press philosophy that "You can take a sob story and a stick of candy and lead America right off into the Dead Sea" (December 2, 1933, in Collins, 1993, p. 2).

As in the contemporary newsreels, which were based on the newspapers, the press had a bias—for action, for the famous, and for the bizarre. It used the neutral model of reporting politics, presenting both good and bad statements about the candidates, but the dramatic story was its obvious preference.

One story that met the press criteria for excitement in the 1932 prenomination period was the clash between Roosevelt and Smith in April over the issue of class warfare. Roosevelt addressed the nation by radio on April 7, giving a speech under the auspices of the Democratic National Committee. The title of the address was "Objectives of a National Program of Restoration." He said that there was a national economic emergency, and he focused especially on the farmers, who had lost their purchasing power. The most controversial section of the speech called for economic reforms that built from the bottom up instead of the top down, concentrating on "the forgotten man at the bottom of the economic pyramid." Smith responded by attacking Roosevelt at the Jefferson Day dinner on April 13, saying that Roosevelt had made a "demagogic appeal . . . setting class against class and rich against poor."

The press reported this intraparty fight with relish, casting it in battle metaphors. For two weeks the Democratic contest received coverage as good as the stories of blasts, wrecks, and prison escapes. The headlines read: "Smith Opens War Upon Roosevelt's Candidacy 'To End'," "Smith Speech Stirs Praise and Attacks By Party Members," "Smith, Roosevelt

May Clash Openly," "Smith Will Quit President Race If Roosevelt Retires," "Roosevelt To Meet Challenge of Smith in St. Paul Speech," "Roosevelt Pleads for Low and High," "Roosevelt Informs Critics He Pleads, Not for Class, But for the Entire People," and "Roosevelt Used Good Strategy, Capital Holds" (from the *Philadelphia Inquirer*, *New York Times*, *New York Daily News*, and *Tribune*, April 8–21, 1932).

Another press source of opinion and interpretation was the columnists. Smith "had the support of liberal columnists like Heywood Broun, of the Scripps–Howard chain, and of the metropolitan and Eastern press"; they were particularly critical of Roosevelt, calling him a "master of evasion" (Handlin, 1958, p. 163).

The press approach to the first primaries in 1912, portraying them as unique and special tests of popular opinion, had virtually disappeared in 1932. Instead, reporters tended to merge discussion of the primaries with discussion of the party conventions and caucuses and insider stories: they were all part of the same "campaign," what one paper called a "free-for-all contest" (*Philadelphia Inquirer*, May 2, 1932, p. 1). Most of the coverage focused on the horse race: who was winning and losing, and who *could* win the nomination?

Key Primaries Covered

Several of the 1932 primaries received fairly heavy attention, though this was not the general rule. New Hampshire then, as now, was seen as distinctive because it was first. Until Roosevelt defeated Smith there, said the *Philadelphia Inquirer*, "the 'Stop Roosevelt' movement . . . [had] been confined to paper" ("Disturbing News for the Smith Candidacy, March 10, 1932, p. 8). Now, in a "real contest," Roosevelt had won an "overwhelming victory." Smith was cast as the spoiler, a candidate who had little chance of winning the nomination but could prevent Roosevelt's nomination and throw it to someone else. Inner-party battles and campaign organization were discussed.

The press noted the disadvantage to the Democrats of publicly "grappling with their factional problems" in primaries and conventions, while the Republicans sailed ahead "with few worries." If this had been the extent of the coverage, one could rightly have charged that the reporter was a "lapdog," in fact, a Republican lapdog. But he went on to report that there was some discomfort among Republicans about Hoover, evidenced by the fact that Harold L. Ickes, a Chicago lawyer, was trying to revive interest in the candidacy of Governor Gifford Pinchot of Pennsylvania. Ickes claimed that the "rank and file" of the Republican Party opposed Hoover. "Why not replace a man who is certain to lose by a man who is certain to win?" he asked (John M. Cummings, " 'Stop Roosevelt' Drive Proves Dud," *Philadelphia Inquirer*, March 20, 1932, p. 6).

The Pennsylvania Democratic primary of April 26 received little coverage in the *Philadelphia Inquirer*—only four stories in April, three of them in the last four days of the campaign. In Maryland, there were no stories on the Hoover–France contest by the Baltimore papers, probably due to Hoover's huge lead in convention votes and the fact that the primary was not binding on the party.

Smith's victory in the Massachusetts primary, in which he gained 36 delegates, reenergized his campaign and led to more talk about the "stop-Roosevelt" movement. On May 3, the last major contested Democratic primary was held in California. The press heralded it as a way for Roosevelt to regain his momentum for the nomination, or for Smith to gain traction in his efforts to stop the Roosevelt bandwagon. Instead, Speaker John N. Garner of Texas won. This was "the worst setback to his [Roosevelt's] candidacy," said the *Philadelphia Inquirer*, explaining that there were now enough holdout votes to block Roosevelt's nomination on the first ballot ("Victory of Garner Foreseen as Block To Gov. Roosevelt," May 5, 1932, p. 1).

Most newspapers were Republican on their editorial pages. But on June 11, the Scripps–Howard chain of 25 newspapers announced that they were endorsing Al Smith for president. They declared that both Roosevelt and Hoover were poor choices because they possessed a weakness in character: "Faced in a pinch with political consequences, they yield." Smith, on the other hand, was a bold man of action, just what the country needed ("Chain of 25 Papers Declares for Smith," *New York Times*, June 11, 1932).

Coverage of Policy Issues

While the bulk of press coverage focused on the candidates' activities and the winning and losing of delegates, many of the same articles contained short discussions of the parties' and candidates' positions on policy issues. The issue of Prohibition was mentioned more than others: the "wets" and "drys" argued over the issue within the Republican Party, and the Democrats favored repeal of Prohibition. The Stop Roosevelt movement was said to be driven by another issue, Roosevelt's advocacy of "government ownership in some phases of the utility field," which was opposed by wealthy Democratic contributors (Cummings, 1932, p. 6). "Old Man Tariff" was presented as an issue of likely importance in the fall campaign, with Republicans defending and Democrats opposing the Hawley–Smoot Tariff Act.

Coverage of Individual Characteristics of Candidates

The press clearly differentiated between Smith and Roosevelt by the energy levels of their campaigns. Smith's supporters longed for him to become "an aggressive, rather than a receptive candidate." In contrast, the Roosevelt supporters were "pushing ahead with energy and enthusiasm," buoyed by Roosevelt's wins and Smith's losses (Cummings, 1932, p. 6). Roosevelt's supporters actively sought out the press to report how well the campaign was faring ("Wheeler Predicts Solid Support of Roosevelt in West," *Philadelphia Inquirer*, March 21, 1932, p. 1).

As in 1912, though there were no professional polling firms, there were polls. In citing the results of a nationwide straw poll conducted by *The Pathfinder*, a magazine for farmers, the *Philadelphia Inquirer* failed to mention that the sample was undoubtedly biased. Instead, it reported the poll's results as significant, because not only was Hoover the preferred Republican, but he led his nearest Democratic rival, Roosevelt by two to one.

In summary, the concept of the primary as a unique kind of campaign was buried by the press in 1932, following the lead of the parties. While newspaper stories of delegate counts appeared frequently, they were as likely to focus on party conventions and caucuses as on primaries. However, press fascination with the personal clashes of the primary candidates continued to be a staple of coverage.

MEDIA IN THE 1952 PRIMARIES

By 1952, the number of news media had proliferated to include television, as well as radio, newspapers, newsreels, and newsmagazines; all of these media covered the 1952 primaries. The most famous quotation about the primaries that year was from President Harry Truman, who "said the present system of state primaries was just eyewash as everyone would find out when the national convention was held" (W. H. Lawrence, "Truman Bars Test in New Hampshire," *New York Times*, February 1, 1952, pp. A1, A10). Truman was right . . . and wrong. He was right in predicting that the Democratic primaries would not select the nominee, nor did the Republican primaries settle the nomination.

In 1952, the convention was king, not the primaries, as Truman said. But Truman was wrong too. In a world in which political figures lead through their use of language (Hart, 1987), primaries are only "eyewash" if they are perceived as eyewash. Truman lost control over the perception of the primaries soon after he derided them with his pithy remark. In a major upset, he, the incumbent president, lost the New Hampshire primary to Kefauver. Polls of newspaper editors had predicted that Truman would defeat Kefauver by a three-to-one margin. Instead, Kefauver won 19,800 to 15,927 for Truman (Fontenay, 1980). According to Gorman (1971, p. 129), "The nation's press . . . viewed the vote as a tremendous blow to the prestige and political future of the President." New Hampshire stunned the Republicans and the press too, with Eisenhower, a total newcomer to electoral politics and still in Europe, defeating "Mr. Republican" Taft in a landslide. From then on, the news media treated the primaries as something very important, as did the candidates, thus they became important in the process of the campaign.[4]

Just as in 1932, there was huge latitude for the press and the candidates to interpret the results of the primaries, because (1) so many primaries had unpledged slates of delegates, such as New York and Pennsylvania, (2) the candidates selected a few primaries to run in, so they often ran virtually unopposed, and (3) the majority of delegates were still chosen by state and district conventions. In addition, President Truman announced very late (March 29) that he would not be a candidate, thus deterring many potential Democrats from entering the race until the primary filing dates were past.

Television

The Eisenhower campaign led the way in the use of television. Only 39% of American homes had television sets in 1952, and most of the stations were east of the Mississippi. But the number of viewers was impressive. That summer "an estimated 60 million viewers watched the 1952 conventions on black-and-white television screens" (Reinsch, 1988, p. 63). Eisenhower's managers saw the potential, both for advertising and for news. A group of nine men with broadcast industry connections, five from NBC, organized to help with the television campaign. They called themselves the Television Plans Board, and they met regularly under the direction of Senator Henry Cabot Lodge II, the campaign manager. In early January 1952, they laid plans to arrange for promotional slides and copy for Eisenhower events, to kinescope shows that might be accepted by television stations without time charges, and to persuade Camel News Caravan and CBS News to cover a particular event (Barkin, 1983). In February, the campaign sponsored a dramatic staged event, an Eisenhower rally in Madison Square Garden, organized by Tex McCrary, a New York radio and television figure; 30,000 people attended. This was very early in the campaign for such an impressive showing and attracted wide media coverage (Ambrose, 1983). In contrast, there is no such evidence in the Taft Papers that his campaign developed any television strategies (Library of Congress).

The Eisenhower campaign was most unusual in that the candidate was in Europe, but he had an exceptionally prominent group of campaign supporters who commanded press attention through their own stature as well as through their connection to the campaign. Thus, in news releases from the Eisenhower campaign during the week of February 21–28, 1952, the spokesmen quoted were Senator Frank Carlson of Kansas and Senator Lodge of Massachusetts (Taft Papers, Library of Congress).

As the time of Eisenhower's return from Europe approached, there was high interest in the press. Herblock, the *Washington Post* cartoonist, showed him contemplating his return, staring in amazement at an army of microphones, as a man with an "I Like Ike" button asked him, "All ready for D-Day?" (*New York Times*, May 25, 1952). There was so much attention from radio and television stations to his first speech in Abilene, Kansas, that Taft "made an issue of demanding equal time from the Federal Communications Commission" (Patterson, 1972, p. 536).

A dominant presence in television news in 1952 was the weekly program *Meet the Press*, which was broadcast on both radio and television. Lawrence E. Spivack, who had begun his journalistic career working for H. L. Mencken, was the founder and moderator of the program. He said that his approach was "Learn as much as you can about your guests and their position on the issues and take the other side. If you do that each and every week . . . you'll create a little bit of tension and you'll make a lot of news" (in Nolan, *Boston Globe*, November 8, 1997).

Taft, Stevenson, Kefauver, and Governor Averill Harriman of New York (who entered the race in April) appeared on *Meet the Press* during the primary period in 1952. The live, televised interview format was new, and it took its form from radio and newspaper interviews. The questioners were mainly from newspapers, and they exercised great freedom in pressing the candidates for answers. An example was the January 20, 1952, interview of Taft. The reporters set the agenda for the discussion, questioning Taft aggressively and putting him on the defensive (*Meet the Press*, January 20, 1952, Library of Congress Sound Division). Stevenson was more agile in his interview in March, joking a bit and making distinctions, but often hesitating before he answered, which made him look uncertain or evasive (*Meet the Press*, March 30, 1952, Seeley Mudd Library, Princeton University). There had been press interviews before, but never had viewers been able to *see* the candidates. Compared to modern candidates who have grown up with television, the 1952 candidates looked stiff and uncertain.

The fact that Senator Kefauver was known at all to Democratic voters in early 1952 was due to television. He had chaired the recently completed Kefauver Senate committee hearings on organized crime, events receiving wide media attention, including television. Paramount News reported that one of the top three stories of 1951 was the activities of the Kefauver committee (January 2, 1952, National Archives). Kefauver's face was well known to the voters from these televised hearings, and he was associated with honesty and ethics at a time when the Truman administration was under fire for corruption and scandal. His biographer reports, "The televising of the New York hearings . . . transformed Kefauver into a genuine national hero and vastly heightened his availability for the Presidency" (Gorman, 1971). There also was a symbolic dimension to his candidacy, emphasized by the *Concord Monitor*, which called on Democrats to support Kefauver to encourage other candidates to enter the race against President Truman (Gorman, 1971, p. 123).

Newspapers

Newspapers still dominated the news business in 1952. Their typical style of primary coverage was much like that of 1912 and 1932. They began by setting the scene of which candidate was speaking where, to whom, and about what. They then reported what the candidate had said, quoting directly and at length from the candidate's speech. Andersen and Thorson (1989) found this pattern of coverage in their study of newspapers in 1896, 1928, and 1960. It is clear, as Patterson (1993) says, that "The press gave the candidates regular opportunities to present their issues, as they wished them to be seen" (p. 69). But in no sense should this be taken to mean that the press was a conduit for the candidates' messages, communicating them directly to the voters without interpretation. Political news in the print media included not only reports of candidate messages, but also strongly partisan editorial pages and opinionated political columnists. A 1945 poll of a national cross section of newspaper readers revealed that 41% said they read political columns regularly. Their top five favorites were Drew Pearson (28%), Westbrook Pegler (17%), Ernie Pyle (15%), Walter Winchell (15%), and Walter Lippman (12%) (May 1945, in Cantril, 1951, p. 518).

From many accounts it is clear that the elite press favored Eisenhower. The *New York Times* and *Tribune* endorsed Eisenhower early, and the large news magazines were pro-Eisenhower. *Newsweek, Life,* and *Time* featured him on their covers when he returned to the country (although they also gave Taft generous coverage: he appeared on the cover of *Newsweek* in April and *Time* in early June). Magazines such as the *New Republic, Christian Century, Atlantic,* and *Harper's* wrote sharply critical pieces about Taft, especially attacking his foreign policy views and his "ability to grasp [the] modern world"; on May 17, the *Nation* said that he was "the leader of an aggressive neo-fascist coalition" (Patterson, 1972, pp. 531–533, 536–538). A repeated theme found even in the New Hampshire newspapers early in the campaign was that Taft could not win. Taft lamented, "My greatest handicap in this whole campaign . . . has been the solid backing of General Eisenhower by many of the eastern papers and others throughout the country as well as a majority of the national magazines and syndicated columnists and commentators" (Patterson, 1972, p. 531).

Taft's personality did not endear him to the press or public. He was reluctant to smile or give autographs or to take time to mix with the crowds; he was "stiff, partisan, and fiercely loyal and competitive in public." It was not difficult for the press to cast him in an unflattering light (Patterson, 1972, p. 533). The press picture was not entirely bleak, however. Major papers such as the *Chicago Tribune* and the *New York Daily News* endorsed him. In his correspondence are friendly letters from newspaper publishers and owners in states he planned to visit, offering their help in meeting informally with the media, publishing his views, and so on (Robert A. Taft Papers, Library of Congress).

Taft had built a large reservoir of support within the party and became well known to Americans in the 1948–1952 period through radio and newspaper coverage, as a point man attacking the Truman administration. For example, on May 16, 1950, he gave a speech sponsored by the Republican National Committee attacking the Truman program, broadcast over combined ABC, CBS, NBC, and MBS networks (Taft Papers, Library of Congress). Known as "Mr. Republican," he was popular within the party for his conservative views and party loyalty, and he campaigned strenuously. By the time of the national convention, he had more delegates than Eisenhower, 530 to 427, the majority won in state conventions rather than in primaries. Yet in both parties the vote in the convention, and not in the primaries, prevailed.

Governor Adlai E. Stevenson of Illinois was not a candidate in the Democratic presidential primaries; he insisted that he was a candidate only for re-election as governor. However, the "Operation Wintergreen" campaign (see Chapter 3) worked to get the media to write about Stevenson. There was heavy coverage in the national newsmagazines and elite papers as well as in city papers all over the country. In January, he appeared on the cover of *Time*. Arthur Krock, prominent *New York Times* columnist, devoted a column to him. The *New Republic* wrote an editorial about him, and on February 18 it had a cover drawing of him and a story, with a collection of his statements. *Newsweek* devoted a story to him on February 4. On March 11 there was a *Wall Street Journal* editorial, on March 22 a story by Richard H. Rovere in the *New Yorker*, and on March 24 a *Life* article; on April 10 *Newsweek* discussed Stevenson's stands on nine issues. The "Wintergreen" file also contains dozens of press clippings of Stevenson stories from papers across the country (George A. Ball Papers, Seeley Mudd Library, Princeton University). Stevenson himself added to this publicity, giving speeches and appearing on television interview programs.

It is amazing to see how far the Wintergreen campaign got without the cooperation of the candidate. It had little money and relied chiefly on winning over prominent journalists and securing press attention. At the same time, of course, Stevenson's reluctance added an air of suspense to the campaign, something like Governor Mario Cuomo's effect in 1991. "Will he or won't he?" was the question. However, the general public knew little about Stevenson. An April 1952 poll indicated that "barely one-third of those surveyed identified him as the Governor of Illinois" (Troy, 1991, p. 197, citing George H. Gallup, *The Gallup Poll*, Vol. 2, pp. 1054–1056).

Newsreels

Millions of Americans attended the movies in 1952. A survey in 1946 revealed that 69% of the respondents went to the movies at least once a month (November 27, 1946, in Cantril, 1951). While there, they watched newsreels of the week's events preceding the main feature. These newsreels were changed two or three times a week. Apparently no one has ever looked at the newsreels and their coverage of the presidential primaries. This research is based on viewing newsreels and reading catalogues of the Universal Newsreels and Paramount News newsreels in the National Archives, Washington, from the January 1–June 15, 1952, period.

The newsreels were heavily influenced by the newspapers. In the print "releases" of the newsreels, which give details on their preparation, including the research and script, sources such as the *New York Times* and the *Tribune* are much in evidence. Even the camera shots show the newspapers' influence. For example, a Universal newsreel of March 13 used the same camera shot of Truman's storefront headquarters in New Hampshire as the one shown in the *New York Times* story of March 4.

The professional narrator and the musical score provided unity to the newsreel and influenced the mood. All of the 1952 Universal newsreels were narrated by Ed Herlihy, who had an upbeat, clear, warm voice, with much variety in pitch. He made every story sound important. Band music dominated the medium, starting loud at the beginning of each story and then fading, with much use of cheerful Sousa marches, though the music could grow grim for reports of shipwrecks and other disasters. The overall mood created was fast moving and bright; no one's fun at the movies would be spoiled by the newsreels.

In this context, the stories of the primaries and of President Truman's activities were given a kind of equality among stories of ice skaters, the Dionne quintuplets, and movie stars. All stories were announced in dramatic tones, whether in sports, entertainment, or politics. The quick shifting of shots to show different people and scenes characterized all of the stories.

Universal Newsreels had five primary-related stories in the January–June 1952 period, headed as follows: "Ike's Hat in Ring," "Kefauver Hat in Ring," "Eisenhower–Kefauver Win in New Hampshire Primaries," "Truman Won't Run," and "Ike's Home-Coming; Nomination Campaign Launched in Abilene." They ranged in length from about 10 seconds (the Kefauver announcement) to about 1 minute and 45 seconds for the New

Hampshire primary story. Paramount News had 10 primary-related stories, covering the announcement speeches of four candidates, and primaries not only in New Hampshire but also Wisconsin, Nebraska, New Jersey, and Massachusetts.

Based on their choice of coverage, the newsreels told the viewers that announcing candidacy and winning primaries were important events. In addition, they set other important agendas for the primaries. They gave President Truman and General Eisenhower far more coverage than any other political figures. The advantage of the incumbent in securing news coverage was apparent in the eight stories Universal focused on Truman and his actions. Even more evident, however, was the appeal of Eisenhower, not only as a presidential candidate and general but also as a person providing pictures well suited to the visual medium: reviewing troops, meeting with royalty and heads of state in Europe, entering and leaving planes, and waving to crowds. Universal devoted a total of eight stories to him during this period, all flattering, with only one devoted to Taft; Paramount had 17 stories on Eisenhower, compared to only six on Taft. The power of this image of the smiling, take-charge military leader in influencing primary voters can only be guessed at. Eisenhower dominated this visual medium; none of the other candidates came close.

The content of the newsreel stories, like those in the newspapers, focused on the contest, on who could win and who was winning. There also were brief glimpses of the candidate as a person, glimpses not available elsewhere for most Americans. In the coverage of Kefauver's announcement, for example, in a mere 10 seconds, viewers could learn: what he looked like, that he had a wife and children, that he was famous because he had chaired the Senate Crime Committee, that a large audience of reporters had come to see him speak, and that he sounded determined (saying he was "in the race for keeps"). As skimpy as this information was, it could be used by the viewer to begin to construct an image of this candidate's characteristics, information that voters generally care more about than policy positions.

Little of the candidates' own language appeared in the newsreels; as with modern television, the narrator briefly summarized the words spoken and showed the speech scene (Kendall, 1993). One could learn little about the candidate's priorities or vision of the future. There was one major exception, in a Paramount newsreel of January 5, 1952. Harold E. Stassen, former Minnesota governor, announced that he was a Republican candidate. The newsreel identified him and then showed him talking about his program, speaking to the camera. The narrator said that this was an "exclusive interview with NBC." It was a remarkable aberration in its fullness and unedited presentation of the candidate.

A final impression from examining these newsreels is that they conveyed the sense that presidential primaries were part of "our great

American way." The March 13 Universal coverage of the New Hampshire primary was the most extended example of this theme, with smiling candidates, spirited music, waving flags, scenes of candidates shaking hands with small groups of voters, and campaign workers putting up posters ("Everyone is in there pitching"). In this portrayal, voters gathered to hear Taft and Stassen speak ("Citizens of the Granite State are not easily won"), and they traipsed through "bitter snow and sleet" to stand in long lines to vote, exercising their rights in our "free country," said the announcer. The New Hampshire primary was constructed as a triumph of American values, in a pleasing, reassuring, and even stirring patriotic image.

Radio

Primary candidates in 1952 made fairly heavy use of radio news to convey their messages. The listings of radio appearances on just one network, NBC, show that the Democratic candidates spoke on the radio 24 times in the primary period; Republican candidates spoke 15 times (Library of Congress Sound Division). In addition, candidates who traveled around the country spoke on regional radio networks.

These radio appearances took the form of personal interviews, such as on the *Kate Smith Show, On the Line with Bob Considine,* and *Meet the Press;* question-and-answer sessions for groups of candidates, such as the League of Women Voters' sponsored program "A Citizen's Views of 1952"; broadcast speeches at special events, such as the testimonial dinner for W. Averill Harriman, the West Point U.S. Military Academy Founders Day, and the Russell for President Dinner; discussions of issues, such as the American Forum of the Air discussion on the topic "Has the Administration's Foreign Policy Failed?"; press conferences, such as Eisenhower's in Abilene, Kansas; and special reports, such as Eisenhower's April 1 one on the work of NATO. These occasions provided the candidates with some opportunities to develop their ideas in an extended and a substantive way, in their own words, and to outline their plans for the presidency. They added significant breadth and depth to the news about the primary period and the candidates.

A popular source of radio news in 1952 was the news commentary programs, generally 15 minutes long, either weekly or nightly. An earlier survey had asked people, "Do you listen regularly to any commentator on the radio?" and 63% said yes (May 2, 1945, in Cantril, 1951, p. 708). According to the A. C. Nielsen ratings for 1951–1952, the most popular news commentators were: (1) Walter Winchell, ABC; (2) Drew Pearson, ABC; (3) Lowell Thomas, CBS; (4) Gabriel Heatter, Mutual; and (5) Edward R. Murrow, CBS (Summers, 1971). The author read the *NBC Radio Masterbook* edited scripts of radio commentary by H. V. Kaltenborn on

Pure Oil News Time, Richard Harkness on *Pure Oil News Time*, and Robert Montgomery on *A Citizen Views the News* just before and after key 1952 primaries in New Hampshire, Wisconsin, Nebraska, Ohio, Florida, and South Dakota (Library of Congress).[5]

The commentators added one important factor not present in the regular news bulletins: they gave their opinions. Thus, H. V. Kaltenborn said that the "Democratic pols" could no longer ignore Kefauver's vote-getting appeal, and that he had definite strengths, particularly that he was "smart" and "indefatigable" in shaking hands and meeting voters. The same evening, he discussed Eisenhower's NATO report at length and praised him for having the "ability to say what needs to be said without giving offense." Eisenhower had shown by this report that he was "much more than a military commander," said Kaltenborn (April 2, 1952, *NBC News*, MR 1305, Library of Congress). Richard Harkness expressed a skeptical view of the primaries in his May 6 broadcast, describing the Florida Democratic primary campaign between Kefauver and Russell as a ridiculous "war of the hats" in which Russell's supporters wore a three-cornered colonial hat and the Kefauver backers wore coonskin hats. Robert Montgomery, who would later become President Eisenhower's television adviser, expressed his opinion about the Ohio and Florida primaries by *not* talking about them on his program on May 6 and 7. Instead, his theme was "the forgotten men of Korea."

These popular commentators, like the political columnists, provided interpretation of the news, creating a far more varied array of perspectives than those available in news broadcasts.

The primaries provided excellent news filler for the voracious radio news programs of 1952. Every half hour there was another news bulletin, and in the course of the day, the story kept changing slightly, so that the news was "new." Radio news treated the primaries as an important event. As NBC declared, "This is probably the most important election year in history. . . . For this reason, WNBC will keep at your fingertips all the latest facts . . . trends . . . and developments on the political scene" (*NBC News*, April 5, 1952, 6:15 P.M.). The frequency of coverage and the use of on-the-scene reports also added to the impression that the primaries were important. The excited, "sportscasting" language of Bill Sprague's March 12 *World News Roundup* report (at 8:00 A.M.) was typical of the coverage:

This New Hampshire thing isn't at all what they've been expecting. [On the Republican side] it looks as if the fight for the nomination will go on more furiously than ever right up to and into convention time. The outlook is for some very rough infighting. [On the Democratic side,] Kefauver's "sweep" is bound to make party leaders stop looking to the White House for their cues and set them to thinking of other men for the nomination.

It looks as if nobody's got 1952 in the bag. (Library of Congress Sound Division)

But the primary's moment in the sun was fleeting. For example, by the night after the Wisconsin and Nebraska primaries, the story had slipped from first to third place; by the night after the Ohio and Florida primaries, the story had been pushed out of the top five (*Pure Oil News*, April 2, 1952; *News of the World*, Morgan Beatty, May 7, 1952, *NBC News*, Library of Congress).

News coverage of the 1952 primaries was affected by the changing needs of the media. On the face of it, little had changed since 1932, when the nominees were chosen at the conventions and the primaries played only a small role. But in 1952, the news media treated the primaries as though they were important, and they became important. In part, the surprising New Hampshire primary results provoked this change in attitude. But it also seems that the primaries met the news needs of radio and increasingly of television, providing a stream of stories of contests with many parts and details to fill the available news time.

Other factors contributing to this symbiosis between the primaries and the media were the needs of the Eisenhower and Stevenson campaigns. Eisenhower was out of the country, and his organizers saw the need to keep him in the public eye. They were the first to explore the powers of television news and advertising, and they developed successful strategies for their use. Eisenhower also met the needs of the newsreel medium for live and moving pictures exceptionally well, and he appeared in the newsreels far more often than the other candidates. On the Democratic side, Kefauver had risen to prominence on television in 1951, chairing the crime hearings in the U.S. Senate. Adopting an indefatigable campaign style of meeting voters face to face in New Hampshire, he began to win primaries and to gain heavy news coverage. In the meantime, Stevenson's supporters worked feverishly to keep their reluctant candidate in the news by running a kind of shadow campaign paralleling the primaries, using every connection with the elite media they could think of.

The media did not replace the parties in 1952, nor did the primaries establish who the nominee would be. Truman was right: the party conventions were more important than the primaries. But the increase in media interest in the primaries between 1932 and 1952 was enormous. The story of the ongoing primaries fight was perfectly suited to the media's needs, especially for radio, with its multiple daily news broadcasts. And the candidates whose supporters built the strongest connections with the media, Eisenhower and Stevenson, gained tangible benefits and eventually secured the nomination of their parties.

CONCLUSIONS

An examination of the media coverage of three presidential primary years at 20-year intervals, 1912, 1932, and 1952, reveals several distinct patterns. First, the primaries are ideally suited to the news media's needs for a colorful story. Primaries provide a wide scope for interpretation, a varied cast of characters, continual conflict between candidates, and a series of dramatic conclusions. They also last a long time, providing a ready supply of news. In the presence of these conditions in 1912 and 1952, the primaries were top stories in the news. In 1932, there was much less coverage, as President Hoover faced no serious challenge in the primaries, and the leading Democratic candidates did not campaign publicly. Still, as soon as Roosevelt and Smith clashed over Roosevelt's "Forgotten Man" speech, the press gave the story front-page attention.

Second, negative campaigning occurred in all of these primaries because of its pragmatic value to both candidates and the media. Candidates use negative campaigning to define a personal image and to distinguish themselves from their intraparty rivals. Journalists focus on negative campaigning as a means of identifying the best fighter, whose supposed attributes—tough, strong, willing to take on the odds—are much revered in the primaries. While the primary candidates declare in effusive pledges and denials that they will not engage in negative campaigning, there is no escape. The primary situation of multiple candidates makes differentiation mandatory, and whether the candidates define their differences implicitly or explicitly they must show that they are better than the rest of the pack. The opposite of "better" is "worse"— every assertion of one's goodness contains the opposite term as part of the meaning (Saussure, 1959). If the nomination is contested, there *will* be negative campaigning, and because of the number of contenders, the number of attacks are likely to be greater than in the general election. In all of the primaries studied, with the exception of the unchallenged Republican incumbent situations in 1932 and 1972, primary candidates engaged in sharp clashes.

Negative campaigning not only meets press needs for exciting stories but also helps the press identify the best fighter. The bitter exchanges between Roosevelt and Taft in 1912, the "Forgotten Man" dispute between Roosevelt and Smith in 1932, and Kefauver's surprising victory over President Truman in the 1952 New Hampshire primary were given coverage as top stories, often in admiring tones, bringing rewards in attention and free media exposure to the assailants.

Third, news coverage of the primaries has never met Jamieson's (1992) ideal standard for news coverage of presidential campaigns: that the media should tell "who is offering a compelling understanding of the state of the nation, the challenges it faces, and the directions it should take"

(p. 164). The coverage has focused more on the horse race, the polls, the bizarre, the conflicts, and the visually dynamic. The nature of the candidate's vision of the future has been hard to discern from news stories of the primaries over the years.

NOTES

1. See Corcoran and Kendall (1989, 1992) for further discussion of the media and the 1912 primaries.

2. Magazines were not studied for this book, and the topic deserves further research.

3. The author is indebted to Bonnie Donzella for her assistance in reviewing the March and April 1908 editions of the *Milwaukee Journal*, the *Wisconsin State Journal*, and the *Milwaukee Sentinel*.

4. The research on the media in the 1952 primaries included reading candidates' biographies; examining the Robert A. Taft Papers at the Library of Congress, the George Ball Papers at the Seeley Mudd Library, Princeton University, and the Henry Cabot Lodge Papers at the Massachusetts Historical Society; viewing Universal newsreels and reading the catalogue of Paramount Newsreels, January–June 1952 in the National Archives; listening to tapes of radio speeches and reading the radio scripts of NBC news broadcasts before and after key primaries in the Library of Congress Sound Division; reading prominent news columnists in the *New York Times* and *New York Herald Tribune* in the primary period; and reviewing the programming schedule and several tapes of *Meet the Press* interviews.

5. These are the final program records of the *WNBC Master Programs*. They are available only on microfilm, and many of the scripts are so pale that they are almost impossible to read. According to the librarian at the Recorded Sound Division, Library of Congress, they are the only copies extant.

Chapter 6

Through Media Eyes in the Age of Television: News Media Shaping of the Primaries, 1972–1992

The screen brings into view those imponderables of character and personality which make us decide, not whether we agree or disagree with somebody, but whether we can trust him.

—Hannah Arendt, 1960

Television ownership grew by quantum leaps in the 1950s, going from 4.6 million households in 1950 to 60.1 million households by 1970 (A. C. Nielsen Company, in Hiebert, Ungurait, and Bohn, 1985). By 1972, television and newspapers were the dominant news media, followed by radio and newsmagazines.[1] This research focuses on television and newspapers.[2] The definition of which medium was "dominant" varied with the beholder. President Nixon arranged to have the nightly network television news videotaped in a weekly summary for his viewing, so convinced was he of the power of television (Nixon Project, National Archives). Millions of Americans sat down each night to watch the national news, and the names of anchors and commentators such as Chet Huntley, David Brinkley, Eric Severeid, John Chancellor, and Howard K. Smith were household words.

Among journalists, however, the print reporters were at the top of the hierarchy. According to Timothy Crouse (1972), who traveled with the media and interviewed them, it was hard for the print reporters to take anyone seriously "whose daily output lasted two minutes on the air" (p. 151). "There were only a handful of reporters who everyone in the business agreed were exceptional," he said, and they all worked for newspapers, particularly for the *New York Times* and *Washington Post* (pp. 73–74). So influential was the *New York Times* in the press, said Crouse, that "once a story hits page one of the *Times*, it is certified news and can't be ignored" (Crouse, 1972, p. 78).

Television used film to cover the campaigns; the breakthrough to videotape and electronic news gathering did not occur until the 1976 campaign (Becker and Lower, 1979). Film required developing and editing, and it placed strict limitations on television reporters, who had to "go everywhere chained to a human ball and chain, which consisted of a cameraman, a sound man, a lighting man, and sometimes a producer as well" (Crouse, 1972, p. 153). After they got their story, they had to find a nearby town with a large television studio so they could edit the film and transmit it to New York. Rick G. Stearns, deputy campaign manager for George McGovern, believed that the expense and the cumbersome process of moving media equipment directly influenced the nature of media coverage in 1972. "The press prefers to start in the East and move slowly across the country to the West," he said, "and then fly it all back to New York from Los Angeles. So the natural progression of primaries would run from New Hampshire out to Wisconsin to Nebraska to Oregon and finally down to California and back to New York" (May and Fraser, 1973, p. 97).

A quotation by a prominent television news commentator of the time helps capsulize key aspects of media coverage of the 1972 presidential primary period. CBS news commentator Eric Severeid interpreted the status of the Democratic primaries after the Florida primary: "In New Hampshire, Muskie won but lost, while McGovern lost but won; in Florida, Muskie lost but lost, McGovern lost but lost, Humphrey lost but won, and Wallace won but won" (March 15, 1972, Vanderbilt Television Archives). Severeid's clever tongue twister illustrates the liberties the media took in interpreting the 1972 primaries. They were not content merely to report the voting results in each primary. Asher (1992) has pointed out the media's heavy interpretive role in the early primaries, noting that though Muskie and Wallace won the first three primaries, the media portrayed Muskie's candidacy as collapsing and McGovern's candidacy as building.

Gary Hart (1973), McGovern's campaign manager, reflected on several specific instances of media coverage that helped McGovern and hurt Muskie in New Hampshire. All were in the elite Eastern newspapers. First, Robert Healey of the *Boston Globe* on February 18 wrote about a "McGovern surge," reporting that people in a factory had jumped up in excitement to meet McGovern. Second, Muskie's February 26 appearance on the steps of the Manchester *Union Leader* building, in which he defended his wife against the paper's attack and seemed to be crying, was followed by stories of trouble in the Muskie campaign and of wavering support; on February 28, political reporter David Broder of the *Washing-*

ton Post reported, "Support for Muskie Wavers in New Hampshire." Third, a story in the March 1 *New York Times* by political reporter R. W. Apple sounded the theme "For Muskie, Mild Support; for McGovern, Intensity" (Hart, 1973, p. 127).

Theodore White's books on *The Making of the President*, 1960–1972, had provided a stimulus to this interpretive bent, changing the perception of political campaigns. In 1972, the *Washington Post* covered all 12 Democratic primary candidates, as did the *New York Times*. The White model affected everyday news reporting, placing heavy emphasis on the "inside story." Two colorful stories in the April 4, 1972, *New York Times* illustrate this point. In one, Walter Rugaber tells of a determined and energetic Humphrey in Wisconsin, rushing to get on a small plane and taking off in the midst of a heavy snowstorm, as nervous reporters on the plane sang "Onward Christian Soldiers" ("An Old Campaigner Says Viable Means Humphrey," *New York Times*, p. 36). Jon Nordheimer's story, "Wallace's Traveling Show Pulls Crowds in Wisconsin," on the same date is rich in Wallace anecdotes (p. 36). Rosenstiel (1993) suggests that Joe McGinniss's book on the 1968 campaign, *The Selling of the President*, also was influential, encouraging journalists to be more cynical and critical.

Paletz and Elson (1976), in their study of the 1972 Democratic Convention, found television reporting highly interpretive. They identified specific techniques used by television reporters to heighten the impression "that conflict, division, confusion, and disorder were rampant" at the convention (p. 126). Some key factors contributing to this impression were: (1) the thematic approach used by anchors and reporters; (2) the technique of juxtaposing opposing views; (3) interviewing techniques that emphasized divisiveness; and (4) visual techniques that emphasized brief scenes and rapid switching of pictures.

As the amount of journalist interpretation (and talk) increased, the length of a candidate's sound bites dropped sharply. A sound bite is "a film or tape segment, within a news story, showing someone speaking" (Hallin, 1992, p. 5). Hallin (1992) has traced the decline of average sound bite length in the fall campaigns from 43 seconds in 1968 to 9 seconds in 1988, with the largest decline coming in 1972. The reason for this precipitous drop in sound bite time in 1972 could well be related to the growing tendency of reporters to replace the candidate's words with their own. But it could also be due to the great increase in the number of candidates. Television has a limited "window" for coverage, and dividing the time among many candidates inevitably affects length.

The overall picture of 1972 primary coverage is of an active, opinionated media. This finding is at odds with Hallin's (1992) research on the fall campaign of 1972, which maintained that the journalist's role in this period "was relatively passive," with heavy use of quotations from the candidates (p. 9). But in the primaries, the television and newspaper media showed a readiness to set the agenda by declaring which primaries were important, which candidates were important, what the image traits of the candidates were, and what policy matters were important to voters, as well as passing judgment on the success or failure of the candidates (Joslyn, 1984, has also noted this trend). They set the agenda not only in decisions about what topics to cover, the classic finding about media agenda setting (McCombs and Shaw, 1972), but also in their choice of language about each of these matters.

WHICH PRIMARIES ARE IMPORTANT?

In early 1972 media coverage, the March 15 Florida primary was described as the first important primary, as it was the first one in which the majority of the Democrats would participate. But as polls showed the gap closing between Muskie and McGovern in New Hampshire, the portrayal of that primary suddenly changed. Now New Hampshire was described as "a crucial test for the front-running Mr. Muskie" (Kovach, *New York Times*, March 5, 1972).

After the Florida primary, which was won handily by Wallace, Apple (*New York Times*, March 15, 1972) declared that "a new contest" had started. Florida was important because Muskie had been vanquished, he said. With the benefit of hindsight, however, one could make quite a different interpretation: the significance of Florida was that Wallace drew the most conservative votes, and the rest of the Democratic votes were fragmented among a large group of more centrist candidates.

The Illinois primary of March 21 was treated almost as a nonevent. Miller of the *Wall Street Journal* (April 3, 1972), said that "Politicians generally discount [Muskie's] victory in the Illinois primary . . . because he faced only light competition." But he did win delegates; following that primary, he was leading all of the other candidates with 96.5 delegates. In contrast, the Wisconsin primary of April 4 was portrayed as enormously significant, a potential watershed, and certainly a winnower of candidates. Wisconsin had only 2.8 million eligible voters (Kneeland, *New York Times*, April 4, 1972), yet the *New York Times* devoted 20 articles to its primary in a six-day period (March 30–April 4). It stressed the closeness of the battle between McGovern and Humphrey, though Wallace ultimately came in second to McGovern.

Why did the media give so much attention to Wisconsin? One answer lay in recent history. The Wisconsin primary had been important in 1960, when John F. Kennedy defeated Hubert Humphrey, and in 1968 the media had given heavy daily attention to the primary there. In 1972, the McGovern campaign helped attract attention to the state by pouring in staff and other resources. The sheer number of candidates entering the contest brought press coverage. And finally, there was Wisconsin history going all the way back to Fighting Bob LaFollette, the father of the primaries. The state had a reputation as "a peculiar place ... with an eye for the maverick," and as an "issue-oriented place" (Kneeland, *New York Times*, March 30, 1972).

WHICH CANDIDATES ARE IMPORTANT?

The journalists were not passive about directing the citizens' attention to certain candidates rather than to others. In coverage of the New Hampshire primary, for example, Harry Reasoner of ABC described the contest between Muskie and McGovern as "the race of interest," showing their two campaign buttons on the screen, thus ignoring and excluding all of the other Democrats (Vanderbilt Television Archives, March 8, 1972). In early April, Eric Severeid of CBS and others reported that there was a "triangle of candidates" remaining in the race: Muskie, McGovern, and Humphrey (Vanderbilt Television Archives, April 5, 1972), leaving Wallace out of the "triangle," though Wallace had the second largest number of delegates.

WHAT IMAGES OF THE CANDIDATES DID THE MEDIA CONVEY?

Richard M. Scammon, Director of the Elections Research Center of the Governmental Affairs Institute, identified image as one of the "big issues" of the 1972 campaign. Voters were concerned about "personality, that is, trust and confidence in the person you're going to vote for," he said (*Meet the Press*, NBC, May 14, 1972, Nixon Project, 5369). "The key factor," said Apple (*New York Times*, March 3, 1972), after interviewing 120 New Hampshirites, "is the image of the candidate, built up over the last two or three years." As a group, the Democrats were portrayed on one program as a "vast horde," who were out there "cutting each other up" (*Today*, NBC, March 14, 1972, Nixon Project, 5192). Never had so many candidates run in the primaries, which made the task of covering them all especially difficult for the media.

Reporters labeled the candidates, based on personal observations, interviews with voters, talks with party leaders, the language of the candidates, and polls. Muskie's characterization as the "front-runner" was an obvious description of his early poll standings. Many labels, however, took the form of ridicule. Lindsay was "the charisma candidate" and the "media candidate" (*60 Minutes*, CBS, January 16, 1972, Nixon Project, 4974), Humphrey was "used goods" (Hal Walker, *60 Minutes*, CBS, January 16, 1972, Nixon Project, 4974). McCloskey was "the anti-war maverick" (Apple, *New York Times*, March 3, 1972). McGovern, said Howard K. Smith, was a bland man with an unimpressive record (CBS "Campaign '72," June 6, 1972, Tape 5459, Nixon Project).

Humphrey

Humphrey had a serious image deficit with the press because of his failed 1968 campaign; many viewed him as a "has-been." Recognizing the problem, he changed his physical appearance before the 1972 campaign, losing weight, dyeing his hair and wearing it longer, and dressing in a more modern style. Reporters varied in their early presentation of him, ranging from ridicule to a somewhat patronizing kindness, and frequently discussing his physical appearance (Reston, *New York Times*, March 5, 1972; *60 Minutes*, CBS, January 16, 1972, Nixon Project, 4974; Roger Mudd, *CBS News*, March 2, 1972, McGovern Papers, Princeton, Box 5, Tape TS). As the primaries evolved, the Humphrey image in the media grew more positive. His second-place finish in Florida led to more media emphasis on his popularity (Waldron, *New York Times* March 12, 1972; Apple, *New York Times*, March 15, 1972). As the Florida primary faded from view and Muskie won in Illinois on March 21, the Humphrey image became more mixed, suggesting that candidate image is closely linked to election results. Shannon (*New York Times*, April 3, 1972) warned that Humphrey "badly needs a first-place finish to erase his loser image."

By late May, the dominant media characterization of Humphrey had changed again. Now he was an "attacker" who had torn into McGovern's positions. When Humphrey lost in a remarkably close California primary, the media returned to their benign, almost patronizing portrayal (Nixon Project, Tape 5459).

Jackson

Senator Jackson's image in the media was as a "hawk" on defense, a friend of Boeing Aircraft in his home state of Washington, a strong supporter of Israel, and an opponent of busing for racial balance, and in general, as more conservative than his fellow candidates. He was treated as a serious candidate from the beginning, but Jackson never succeeded in emerging from "the pack" in a way that commanded media attention. In Florida, he came in third after Wallace and Humphrey, and his adviser, Ben J. Wattenberg, complained that the media coverage was so poor that "it was enough to make a grown man cry" (May and Fraser, 1973, p. 106). In none of the campaign stories reviewed for this book were there strong, enthusiastic reports about Jackson.

Lindsay

New York Mayor John Lindsay's image in the media was closely linked to his pictures: he was a handsome, smiling man, boyish and athletic, often shown in shirtsleeves shaking hands or playing tennis. The emphasis was on his youth, his vigor, his friendliness; he was "the charisma candidate" (*60 Minutes*, CBS, January 16, 1972, Nixon Project, 4974). The press treated him as a major candidate, but when he did poorly in Florida, after extensive personal campaigning and huge expenditures, the *New York Times* constructed a weaker image of the former fighter reduced to talk. Though he "talk[ed] bravely of going all the way and of waging stiff battles" in other states, it was quite possible he would run a weak sixth in Wisconsin, they said (Kneeland, *New York Times*, April 2, 3, 1972).

McGovern

Press coverage of McGovern from New Hampshire on was generally positive. Crouse (1972) says that the early reporters covering McGovern soon began "to identify with the candidate" (p. 68). Apple cited evidence from citizen interviews to show that McGovern's image was growing stronger among New Hampshirites who found him frank and courageous in his early opposition to the war (*New York Times*, March 3, 1972); interviews in Wisconsin also found that he was seen as trustworthy, sincere, and honest (Apple, *New York Times*, March 31, 1972). Other reporters noted that though he lacked charisma, he was seen as a compassionate man of convictions; commentator Jack Anderson compared him to the tortoise in Aesop's fable of the tortoise and the hare (Master Tape, Pennsylvania Primary, April 21, 1972, McGovern Papers, Princeton).

A more negative portrayal began to appear in early April. Shannon (*New York Times*, April 3, 1972) wrote an Op-Ed piece reminding people that McGovern had "been defeated in the first three primaries" and sought to minimize the significance of McGovern's success in Wisconsin "with its liberal and antiwar tradition." McGovern's image as a steady, decent man was threatened by accusations raised in April that he was for amnesty, abortion, and the legalization of marijuana. A CBS News report on a McGovern fund-raiser at which Barbra Streisand simulated marijuana smoking and quipped that, "It may be illegal now . . . but it won't be much longer," called more attention to the issue (Rona Barrett, April 1972, Tape TS, Reel 36, Box 5, McGovern Papers, Princeton). Evans and Novak, in their April 27 column, reported that Democratic politicians feared that McGovern's nomination would be as devastating to the

Democrats as Barry Goldwater's had been to the Republicans (Crouse, 1972, p. 124).

The intense examination of McGovern's positions by both Humphrey and the press during the California primary called public attention to problems and inconsistencies, raising questions about his competency and honesty. At a California press conference, a reporter cited a Brookings economic study that suggested that McGovern's tax change proposal "would not be feasible." Reporters pressed him about the cost of his welfare proposal; McGovern's answer seemed evasive and uninformed (Southern California Press Conference, May 25, 1972, McGovern Papers, Box 6, Tape TS, Princeton). In the three Humphrey–McGovern debates in California, reporters and Humphrey continued to press him about the welfare proposal, as well as about his proposal to cut the defense budget by $30 billion in a three-year period. The cumulative impact of this barrage of well-researched questions was harmful to McGovern, whose hesitant answers further weakened his public image.

Muskie

Muskie's wide lead in the polls throughout 1971 and early 1972, as well as his endorsement by major Democratic leaders, gave him the unassailed position of "front-runner." Entering the 1972 primaries, he had the image of "a cool and controlled exponent of New England reserve and restraint" (Jules Witcover and Don Irwin, "Muskie Wins 48% to McGovern's 35," Los Angeles Times, March 8, 1972, p. 1).

But the front-runner faces close press scrutiny. When Muskie stood on the steps of the Union-Leader in Manchester, New Hampshire, and angrily denounced the paper for attacking his wife, weeping with emotion, the media interpreted the event as a sign of weakness in character. As Kovach wrote in the New York Times, the incident was "used to cast doubt on his image as a calm, controlled leader of men" (March 5, 1972). Mike Wallace of CBS reported that the New Hampshire factory workers saw "Muskie's emotional performance as evidence of mental instability" (News Summary, March 3–9, 1972, Nixon Project, 5180).

Behind the scenes, according to Crouse (1972), the press had seen Muskie lash out at people in bursts of emotion on a number of occasions; the Union Leader occasion was not the first. "Publicly and privately," wrote Kovach (New York Times, March 5, 1972), "the Senator's ability to withstand the pressures of a long campaign was being questioned." But McGovern (1977) argued that the press blew this incident all out of proportion: "The notion that this event ended Muskie's presidential drive was a myth concocted in the fertile minds of a few journalists looking for an easy story" (p. 180). McGovern's own polls showed that Muskie's weeping attack evoked a sympathetic reaction and actually improved his position with New Hampshire voters, by about 3 or 4 percentage points.

Muskie's comments on the New Hampshire results were described as "defensive" and "bitter," as he denounced "Monday morning quarterbacks and sideline coaches," apparently meaning the media (Apple, *New York Times*, March 8, 1972). Just before the Florida primary, Waldron (*New York Times*, March 12, 1972) reported that voters "had only a vague impression" of Muskie, aside from his good character. Headlines on the Florida results dramatized his loss: "Muskie Far Behind in Wallace Sweep" (Jules Witcover, *Los Angeles Times*, March 15, 1972, pp. 1, 14). Muskie took on the image of a loser, though he had won two of the first three primaries and led in delegate count (Sullivan, *New York Times*, April 3, 1972; Kovach, *New York Times*, April 3, 1972; Apple, *New York Times*, April 3, 1972; Kneeland, *New York Times*, April 2, 1972). Apple's Election Day story in Wisconsin virtually sounded his death knell, describing "signs of trouble all around him" (*New York Times*, April 4, 1972).

Muskie's language was identified as being one of his problems. Apple (*New York Times*, April 4, 1972) said, "For too long Mr. Muskie ran too bland a compaign [*sic*]—a campaign described by a Washington operative as 'a determined effort not to offend anyone anywhere.' Few people were offended, but few were very excited, either."

After his fourth-place finish in Florida, Muskie made a major change in campaign strategy, dropping his "Trust Muskie" slogan and portraying himself as a fighter who was "tough" and "tells it like it is" (Miller, *Wall Street Journal*, April 3, 1972). The media reported that politicians were skeptical that Muskie could make such a change successfully, as the new image contradicted his personality and record. He was a reserved person, with a cautious approach to issues, known in the Senate as a "skillful reconciler of clashing viewpoints," not a fighter.

As Muskie's campaign limped from one disappointing finish to another, he tried to analyze what mistakes had been made. According to Frankel (*New York Times*, April 5, 1972), he "brood[ed] about his predicament" and blamed others, "notably the press, for raising expectations of a runaway that he says he knew he could not fulfill."

Wallace

One image trait all candidates want to have is to be considered a "serious candidate." In Wallace's case, much of the media discussion of his image had to do with whether he *was* a serious candidate, and, if he was, what the Democrats should do about it. The portrayal of Wallace was intertwined with the portrayal of the Democrats; he was seen as a problem for them. Thus, in February 1972, Steve Bell of ABC News focused on Wallace's claims that the Democratic officials were treating him better than before, because he was doing so well on the campaign trail (News summary, February 18–24, 1972, Nixon Project, 5124). This theme of the outlier, of Wallace as the threat to party unity, continued throughout the primaries, until Wallace was shot in mid-May (Apple, *New York Times*, March 5 and March 15, 1972; Harry Reasoner and Howard K. Smith, ABC News Special Report, March 14, 1972, Nixon Project, 5195; Sander Vanocur, *New York Times*, March 15, 1972).

Wallace's image in the media was tightly bound to the issue of busing. The NBC News coverage in late February was typical, saying: "Wallace is using the busing issue very effectively in Florida" (News summary, February 18–24, 1972, Nixon Project, 5124).

Nordheimer (*New York Times*, April 4, 1972) followed Wallace around from rally to rally in Wisconsin. His account of this trip constructed a Wallace with several positive traits—not a great man, but a likable, energetic man, effective among farmers and workingmen. There was the sympathetic, kindly Wallace, hurrying to thank the people who had stood in the cold for so long waiting for him. There was the vigorous Wallace, "typically jaunty," who "bounded up on the stage" to speak. There was the rustic, country figure who loved country music and found audiences who warmed to his "countrified argot and his titanic battles with syntax." But not all audiences responded so well, said Nordheimer. With a hostile audience at Lawrence College, he tried to use more sophisticated language and stumbled over words and phrases, looking foolish when he pronounced "carte blanche" as "car-tay blank."

Apple's *New York Times* article about Wallace on April 2, 1972, attempted to settle the question about whether he was a national or regional candidate, concluding that he was a regional candidate. Wallace was unpersuaded. When he came in second in Wisconsin, "he said that the results ... would convince the press of what he had known all along—that he was 'a serious candidate' " (Apple, *New York Times*, April 5, 1972).

Nixon

There are marked differences in the ways in which the incumbent president's image was portrayed in the media compared to the Democratic candidates. In 1972, President Nixon had one television interview in January, a "Conversation with Nixon," with Dan Rather on CBS (January 2, 1972, Nixon Project, 4933); this was the only television interview Nixon gave during the period of the primaries. He announced in the interview that he would not "engage in partisan politics" until after the Republican Convention, and from that point on, all of his campaigning efforts were carried out behind the scenes, through his actions as president, or through surrogates.

Through the nature of his questions, Rather challenged Nixon's performance as an administrator, as a military leader, and as a popular leader. But Nixon had the freedom to make his answers as long and full as he liked, and he discussed the Vietnam War at length, explaining his decisions and citing figures on how many troops he had withdrawn. He seemed well informed, loyal to his subordinates, and direct and vigorous in his answers, conveying a positive, assured image. Still, he and his staff were angry at Rather's aggressive questioning, and after the interview, they "generated approximately fifty telegrams" to Rather complaining about the way he had treated the president, as well as programming telephone calls to Rather's office (Magruder to Colson, January 3, 1972, Oudes, 1989, p. 353).

The I.T.T. case was a serious threat to Nixon's image as an honest, ethical leader. The acting Attorney General and former Attorney General were accused of arranging to drop three antitrust suits against I.T.T. because the company had guaranteed a $400,000 donation to the Republican National Committee. In the period March 1–March 15, the *New York Times* published front-page stories every day about this case, and network news commentators discussed its suspicious circumstances (Howard K. Smith, ABC News; Eric Severeid, CBS News, News Summary, March 3–March 9, 1972, Nixon Project, 5180, 5182).

Another cloud hovering over the White House was the press coverage of the war in Vietnam. Ambrose (1989) discussed Nixon's reaction when viewing the news summary of the March 30 North Vietnamese offensive, with scenes of South Vietnamese in retreat. It looked like a scene of impending catastrophe. The possibility that the North Vietnamese might win the war would repudiate Nixon's policy there, raising serious questions about his competence and strength, and he thought that he would thereby lose the election, so he counterattacked in Vietnam with B-52s, aircraft carriers, and naval attacks up the North Vietnamese coast. At the same time, he withdrew another 20,000 American troops. His actions, his speeches to the nation defending them, and the press coverage of these events contributed to the public's perception of his character during the primaries.

Much of the anti-Nixon imagery was constructed by the other presidential candidates, both Republicans and Democrats. Republican Congressman Paul McCloskey, for example, focused most of his efforts on attacking Nixon's performance in Vietnam. As long as there was a contested primary, McCloskey's criticisms received wide coverage. In a post–election analysis, Jeb Magruder of Nixon's campaign remarked that McCloskey was a minor candidate who received "tremendous media exposure" in New Hampshire (May and Fraser, 1973, pp. 81–82). John

Ashbrook, Nixon's other Republican opponent, received much less coverage than McCloskey, but that too was chiefly composed of attacks on Nixon (for example, the January 9, 1972, Ashbrook interview on *Issues and Answers* with Sam Donaldson and Bill Lawrence, ABC News, Nixon Project, 4954).

There is no doubt that the primary system with its multiple candidates brings out a regular fusillade of attacks on incumbents who symbolize the status quo. The Democrats did not attack Nixon for his trips to China and the Soviet Union, however, although Senator Jackson, who had by then withdrawn from the race, opposed the arms treaty with the USSR (CBS News, June 1, 1972, Nixon Project, 5436, Tape 8). The media coverage of these trips was overwhelmingly favorable. The reporters seemed to be caught up in the excitement themselves. Both trips were like magnificent travelogues, with the Nixons as the stars.

In the Soviet Union, Nixon visited the huge Leningrad War Memorial, and Marvin Kalb's report for CBS reflected his own awe; he was visibly moved at the huge expanse of unmarked graves and the sheer number of people who died in the 900-day siege of Leningrad. There were many pictures of Nixon, of graves, of inscriptions, and of wreaths. The experience gave "a new and intensely human meaning to the nuclear missile agreement," said Kalb (June 1, 1972, Nixon Project, 5436).

The timing of the Russian trip, in the midst of the California primary, showcased Nixon as a statesman, in contrast to the warring Democrats. George Herman of CBS, in asking an opening question at the California Democratic debate of May 28, 1972, on *Face the Nation*, delivered a virtual encomium to Nixon. "Gentlemen," he said to McGovern and Humphrey, "President Nixon is about to return from Moscow with an arms agreement. . . . The economy has rapidly expanded. Food prices have fallen. . . . Vietnam is deteriorating. Do either of you . . . believe you can beat President Nixon?" (Tape TS, Box 6, McGovern Papers).

MEDIA CHARACTERIZATION OF THE IDEA OF THE PRIMARY

In 1952, newspapers and radio had treated the primaries as major events. By 1968, television news also covered the primaries heavily (Rubin, 1981), creating the impression that winning primaries was the key factor in the nomination process, though of course it was not. In a 14-day period in March 1972, the *New York Times* averaged eight primary-related stories a day. From the sheer attention paid to them, the primaries appeared to be important events in the media.

The cumulative impression of the media presentation was that the primaries were *not* a good way to pick a nominee. Positive statements about the primaries came chiefly from the candidates and a few columnists. The primaries, they argued, were: (1) a way to test the strengths and weaknesses of the candidates (Lindsay); (2) a way to discover what the "pattern" of voter preferences was in several states (Muskie); (3) a way to increase voter participation (Wicker, March 14, 1972); (4) a way for voters to see the candidates up close (McGovern); (5) a way to introduce "potential national leaders" to the nation (Reston, *New York Times*, March 5, 1972); and (6) a valuable education for the candidates (McGovern). One candidate, George Wallace, waxed eloquent about the primaries as the voice of the people (Vanocur, March 15, 1972).

Negative remarks about the primaries were more common, however, like the cartoon appearing on May 15, 1972, equating the primaries with a "Demolition Derby" (Jim Berry, NEA, reprinted in *Evening Capital* [Annapolis, MD], p. 5). Senator Mike Mansfield called the primaries "useless and worthless" ("Mansfield Assails Primaries," UPI, March 9, 1972, *New York Times*, p. 32), and with Senator George D. Aiken of Vermont, he proposed a Constitutional amendment to establish a single national primary ("Key Senators Seek a National Primary," AP, *New York Times*, March 13, 1972, p. 29). Harry Reasoner of ABC News thought the New Hampshire primary was "a bad and expensive idea" (News coverage, March 3–9, 1972, Nixon Project, 5181); Tom Wicker, *New York Times* columnist, lamented over the high cost and the "unforeseen factors" that gave some primaries so much more impact than others (March 14, 1972).

The press displayed low tolerance for the prospect of a long primary process without quick and decisive results, as shown in a conversation on the *CBS Morning News* on April 5, 1972, among John Hart, Bruce Morton, David Schumacher, and Walter DeVries (Nixon Project, 5259). Though only *four* of the 23 primaries had yet occurred, they agreed among themselves that there would not be any decisive primaries in 1972, and they anticipated that there would be a brokered convention. DeVries sounded exasperated as he asked, "We've gone through all these primaries—and what does it mean? It still has to be clarified to me."

The candidates themselves had some sour and bitter words to say about the way the media interpreted primary results. After the Florida primary, Muskie said, "I won in Iowa, and the press said I lost. I won in Arizona, and the press said I lost. I won in New Hampshire, and the press said I lost. And now that I've lost in Florida, maybe they'll say I won" (Apple, *New York Times*, March 15, 1972).

HORSE RACE/CAMPAIGN ACTIVITY COVERAGE

The horse race, rich in numbers, and stories about campaign activity regularly characterized media coverage of the 1972 primaries, as in earlier primaries. Hallin (1992) reports that there has been greater emphasis on the horse race in recent campaigns than in earlier times, with 82% of correspondents' "wrap-ups" focusing on the horse race in 1988.[3] Though "wrap-ups" were less common in 1972, the present study found that correspondents interlaced their reports with horse race reports and language just the same. For example, Walter Cronkite used classic horse race speak about the California primary, saying it had "long been recognized as the big ball of wax, the winner-take-all race for 271 delegates that could well mean the nomination at Miami Beach" (CBS, June 2–4, 1972, McGovern Papers, Tape TS, Reel 78, Box 6, Princeton). Blankenship (1976) found that in the images of the 1972 primaries in eight daily newspapers and four weekly magazines, "the nomination process is one in which violence is the norm rather than the exception." Sports metaphors abounded, particularly "gladiatorial" sports (p. 258).

The extraordinary number of Democrats competing for the nomination affected media coverage. In 1952, there had been five major Democrats and four major Republicans running. In 1972, there were 11 Democrats and three Republicans (though the Republican race quickly fizzled). How does a reporter decide who to cover when there are so many candidates? At first the media covered the clear front-runner, Muskie, and others who held high national office or governed major cities. Soon, though, the coverage focused on those running highest in the polls.

USE OF POLLS

In the 1972 primaries, the media made heavy use of polls and other numbers.[4] The *New York Times* cited polls almost daily. For the Florida primary, they did "in-depth interviews, 60 people, up to three hours each, in seven cities . . . to illuminate voter attitudes" (Waldron, March 12, 1972). They also hired Daniel Yankelovich, Inc., to do exit polls in five key primary locations in Florida, noting that such "systematic postvote studies" were unusual ("Survey at Polls to Seek Voters' Views on Issues," March 14, 1972, p. 30). Polls by Oliver Quayle Associates of New York also were cited, one for NBC in early March (Robinson, *New York Times*, March 11, 1972) and one for the Wisconsin American Federation of Labor and Congress of Industrial Organizations in late March (Fox, *New York Times*, March 30, 1972). The Gallup poll figures on Nixon's approval ratings were regularly reported (*New York Times*, March 9, 1972).

Reporters spoke of the influence of polls on the candidates, and they used poll numbers as a basis for questioning the candidates. Roger Mudd of CBS cited the *Boston Globe* poll, reporting that Muskie had slipped "in a poll taken just after Muskie's emotional outburst" (News summary, March 3–9, Nixon Project, 5180). Reporters made evaluative remarks about polls and raised cautions about the use of polls.

Pollsters informed the media and the public about which issues were important in the campaign. For example, Richard M. Scammon, Director of the Elections Research Center of Governmental Affairs, and Louis Harris, of Louis Harris Polls, were interviewed on *Meet the Press*. Scammon listed the five "big issues" of the 1972 primaries: (1) personality or trust; (2) the economy; (3) "a feeling . . . of lack of confidence in the establishment"; (4) busing; and (5) the Vietnam War (May 14, 1972, NBC, Nixon Project, 5369).

INTERVIEWS WITH VOTERS

Another way in which the media can "spin" or interpret campaign news is in their selection of sources of information. In 1972, the main sources on television news were the candidates and the public. Over 20% of the sound bites in the 1972 fall campaign were devoted to statements by voters, a marked increase from earlier years (Hallin, 1992). This focus on the voter also emerged in the primaries. Crouse (1972) reports that "the 'mood-of-the-country' piece . . . had suddenly come into vogue" (p. 129), that "almost every sizeable news organization in America made an attempt . . . to canvass precincts, interview families, check out local issues, and find out what the voters were thinking" (p. 131).

CANDIDATE EFFORTS TO CONTROL THE MESSAGE THROUGH IMAGE CONSTRUCTION AND HANDLING THE PRESS

The media did not have complete control over communication in the 1972 primaries, however. The candidates worked actively to shape the agenda. Humphrey's appearance on *Meet the Press* on March 12 (NBC, Nixon Project, 5185) is a good example of the jousting between candidates and media for definition of image. Lawrence Spivak asked Humphrey two questions at the start of the program: Why should he be nominated again? And was he not linked to the people and politics of the past? Humphrey answered skillfully, in a confident, clear, articulate manner. To the first question he replied that 1968 was a close election, and that he had gained momentum at the end. He said that he had not "the slightest doubt" that he could win in 1972. To the second question he replied that people wanted experience: "I offer the people of the United States experience—a Mayor, a Senator, a Majority Whip, a Vice President." Throughout the interview, he sounded knowledgeable about past events and well informed about current legislation, at ease in discussing facts and figures.

Humphrey's language characteristics helped build a positive image and hold the viewer's attention. He used the pronouns "I" and "we" frequently, and he mentioned names, dates, and numbers, creating the impression that he had been directly involved in important government decisions. He often used confident tag lines at the end of his statements, such as "I haven't the slightest doubt that that is very possible," creating an image of a firm, confident person (*Meet the Press*, NBC, March 12, 1972, Nixon Project, 5185). Vivid phrases and colloquialisms made him interesting to listen to and helped to hold attention: "By the way, I am not a candidate on the Sainthood ticket, I am running on the Democratic ticket" (CBS News, March 2, 1972, Box 5, Tape TS, McGovern Papers, Princeton).

The dynamic, knowledgeable image constructed by Humphrey in his television interviews was in sharp contrast to Muskie's television image. Political image is an evaluation jointly constructed by the candidate, media, and voter in a kind of "Rashomon," multiperspectival process (see Kruse and Kendall, 1995). In the context of the 1972 Democratic primaries, Muskie's image could not have been strengthened by his performances on the television news programs examined here. Compared to his opponents, he was evasive, vague, and dull. His interview on *Meet the Press* on January 16 was particularly poor (NBC, McGovern Papers, Box 4, Tape TS, Princeton). Again and again, he evaded the tough questions, often conspicuously. His slow speech, vague language, and low-key, almost tired delivery made him far less impressive and interesting to listen to than other candidates.

McGovern campaigned hard with the argument that the candidates should disclose the sources of their campaign finances, and this issue helped cast Muskie in an unfavorable light on the important image trait of trust. The media followed up on the issue, as when Broder of the *Washington Post* and Apple of the *New York Times* both pressed Muskie regarding his source of funding on *Meet the Press* (NBC, January 16, 1972, McGovern Papers, Box 4, Tape TS, Princeton).

On January 9, 1972, David Broder of the *Washington Post* wrote, "As the acknowledged front-runner and a resident of the neighboring state, Muskie will have to win the support of at least half of the New Hampshire Democrats in order to claim a victory" (in Crouse, 1972, p. 47). He thus set up a hurdle for Muskie, which Muskie called the "phantom candidate." Unfortunately, his own staff had done much to emphasize his need to get at least 50% of the votes. Muskie won decisively in New Hampshire, but the "phantom candidate" haunted him.

There were a few moments when Muskie came across in the news as a firm, principled candidate, even vivid and eloquent. Fox (*New York Times*, March 30, 1972) reported that in a speech to 900 people in Kimberly, Wisconsin, Muskie spoke movingly about Vietnam, saying it "will remain an issue for me as long as a single human being dies, not for a cause but for a mistake." Muskie also was one of the first candidates to attack an opponent, and he did so strongly and bluntly, saying that

George Wallace had built his whole career on "people's fears" (News summary, February 18–24, 1972, CBS, Nixon Project, 5124).

Behind the scenes, Muskie was handling the press poorly, according to Crouse (1972): "He whipsawed between begging the press and bullying them" (p. 52). He also treated his staff badly, so disgruntled staff members were all too willing to talk with reporters. In a post-election conference, Richard H. Stewart, Muskie's press secretary, said that the intense press scrutiny had been very harmful to the campaign, that it was hard to hold up under such scrutiny (May and Fraser, 1973, p. 51).

A consistent communication strategy of the McGovern campaign was to attack Nixon. He did this in speeches, news releases, and letters issued from his campaign office. Between February 3 and February 16, 1972, for example, his papers list seven different statements he made attacking Nixon and his administration on the topics of farm income, Vietnam peace negotiations, Nixon's trip to China, the Kleindienst nomination for Attorney General, and Haldeman's "impugning other people's motives and patriotism" (February, 1972, McGovern Papers, MC #181, Box 63, Princeton). Each time Nixon addressed the nation, McGovern gave a speech attacking his policy.

McGovern's success in communicating a positive image was borne out by the reluctant testimony of two Nixon staff members. McGovern was seen as an honest man, they said, an anti-Establishment figure, someone "outside the power elite," an "underdog," and "the newest, freshest face on the national scene" (Buchanan/Khachigian, "Assault Strategy," June 8, 1972, H. R. Haldeman's files, in Oudes, 1989, pp. 463–464).

However, there were negative aspects to his image as well. Charles Colson, another Nixon staff member (May 23, 1972, in Oudes, 1989, p. 453), reported that McGovern was getting an increasingly radical image, in part due to the extreme positions of his supporters on the issues of amnesty, marijuana, and abortion. McGovern was questioned on these topics in the media. He defused the charge of extremism with a skillful, understated reference to South Dakota, where he had been elected four times, and where Republicans outnumber Democrats by two to one. "Ordinarily," said McGovern, "we don't send wild-eyed radicals to the United States Senate from South Dakota." His ideas were not radical, he said; they were simply new solutions that looked to the future.

McGovern used celebrities to command media attention; Lydon said that McGovern was "the only candidate with an entourage" (New York Times, April 2, 1972). There were actors, football players, and former Kennedy advisers. The attention did not always help the candidate, however. In one story, movie star Shirley MacLaine's malapropisms and peculiar ideas were ridiculed, particularly her discussion of "the bamboo theory" about the "inherent flexibility of Asians" (Lydon, New York Times, April 2, 1972).

Incumbents typically have symbolic and practical strategies available to them that enable them to convey an image of a powerful, wise leader (Trent and Trent, 1995). President Nixon's trips to China on February 17–28, and to the Soviet Union on May 20–June 1 were especially successful. Haldeman reported that Nixon was "extremely pleased" with the media coverage of the China trip: "While they responsibly reported the low-key arrival ceremonies yesterday, they're shifting to almost euphoric reporting of the banquet and the Mao meeting" (Haldeman, 1994, p. 416).

Nixon took a remarkably active role in attempting to secure favorable media coverage for his presidency. Ehrlichman (1982) reported that Nixon "was a talented media manipulator" who "could think like an editor." On January 25, for example, Nixon addressed the nation, reporting that he had made a secret offer in Paris but that it had been rejected by the North Vietnamese. James Reston of the *New York Times* (Ambrose, 1989, p. 510) wrote that by this announcement Nixon had "temporarily stunned the Democratic opposition, dominated the news, and thus changed the politics of the issue."

Unfriendly reporters and news media were a constant source of worry to Nixon. He and his staff kept watch on the news coverage and took steps to "punish" the unfriendly and reward the friendly with interviews. Another Nixon strategy was to try to influence the press to give negative coverage to leading Democrats. Jeb Magruder (1974) reported that in late 1971, the Nixon campaign was able to hire a driver for Muskie, who passed on several Muskie documents to columnist Robert Novak; Novak used them to write columns that were embarrassing to Muskie. In early February, after a Muskie speech calling for American withdrawal from Vietnam, Nixon attacked Muskie directly. First, Haldeman appeared on NBC's *Today Show* in an interview with Barbara Walters, saying that the critics of the war "now are consciously aiding and abetting the enemy of the United States." This interview became the lead story on all three networks that night, and it continued as an issue for several days (Haldeman, 1994). Three days later, Nixon held a press conference and told reporters that Muskie's statement could well undermine American foreign policy, causing the North Vietnamese to wait until after the election to negotiate (Ambrose, 1989, p. 511). These statements as much as accused Muskie of treason.

CONCLUSIONS: 1972 PRIMARIES

The media coverage of the 1972 primaries had much in common with that of previous years. First, the coverage was heavy, particularly in hard-fought contests, such as between Muskie and McGovern in New Hampshire and Humphrey and McGovern in California. Second, there was extensive focus on the horse race story, especially on polls, and on the campaign process. Third, the personal characteristics of the candidates received more attention than their policy positions. Fourth, the media stressed stories of fighters against the odds, such as Wallace, Mc-Govern (early in the primaries), and Humphrey (late in the primaries). Fifth, individual candidates displayed particular skill in influencing media coverage, particularly President Nixon, with his carefully timed trips and speeches.

There also were some unique characteristics in the media coverage of 1972. Most important was the shift to the medium of television. Voters could now see the candidates and make judgments based on their appearance. As Hannah Arendt wrote of the power of television, "The screen brings into view those imponderables of character and personality which make us decide, not whether we agree or disagree with somebody, but whether we can trust him" (Arendt, 1960).

A second change was that the media were more heavily interpretive in their coverage, a trend that had begun in the early 1960s with Theodore White's *Making of a President* books and continued with Joe Mc-Ginniss's book *Selling of the President* on the 1968 campaign. This tendency to interpret affected both the media's language and their agenda-setting role.

Accompanying the increase in interpretation was a sharp decrease in the length of sound bites, from 43 seconds to 25 seconds between 1968 and 1972. Viewers heard less of the candidates' own words and more of the journalists' words.

The portrayal of the primary as a symbol took on more negative tones in 1972: newscasters, columnists, and editorialists criticized primaries and found them tiring and confusing. This may have been a result of the huge increase in the number of primaries. Positive portrayals of the primaries were most likely to come from the candidates themselves.

Finally, 1972 marked a new interest by the media in the voters themselves. Voters were interviewed, quoted, polled, and shown on the news to a far greater extent than in earlier times.

MEDIA IN THE 1992 PRIMARIES

Television and newspapers remained the dominant news media in 1992. When asked during the 1992 primaries where they got most of their news about the presidential campaign, respondents said television (83%), newspapers (48%), radio (14%), magazines (4%), and other (3%) (*Times Mirror* poll, March 26, 1992, in FitzSimon, 1992). However, the medium of television had changed dramatically, particularly with the growing role of cable television and the frequent use of the talk show format.[5] The tendency for journalists to be heavily interpretive in their reporting of the primaries continued; by 1992, these interpretations had effectively replaced the words of the candidates, whose language was seldom heard, except as translated by reporters (Kendall, 1993). In newspapers, too, "the length of the candidate's quoted statements . . . [had] shrunk by half since 1960" (Patterson, 1993, p. 160).

The tone of the interpretation also had changed. Hallin (1992) found that while television news stories about the general election from 1968 to 1988 were predominantly neutral in tone, there was an increasing negativity: in 1972, only about 2% of the coverage was negative, but by 1988, almost 26% of the coverage was negative (p. 15).

The amount of research on the media's role in the primaries expanded exponentially between 1972 and 1992. One factor in this expansion was the recognition of the importance of the primaries. The McGovern lesson was not lost on candidates and the media after 1972. The creation of Super Tuesday in 1984 broadened the opportunities for media interpretation, as there were so many primaries on the same day that the explanation of results was of necessity more complex. In the *New York Times*, the amount of interpretive front-page election reports increased 10 times from 1960 to 1992, going from 8% to 80% (Patterson, 1993).

Several new centers for the study of media and politics emerged at major universities, such as the Gannett Center at Columbia University and the Shorenstein Center on Press, Politics, and Public Policy at Harvard University. Academics, journalists, and political practitioners met in these centers and examined the interaction of media and politics, and much more research became available.

In January 1990, David Broder, the influential political columnist from the *Washington Post*, wrote a column chastising the press for its coverage of the 1988 presidential campaign, particularly for neglecting real issues and for giving Bush ads free coverage ("Five Ways to Put Some Sanity Back in Elections," January 14, 1990). Broder and others, such as Kathleen Hall Jamieson, in her book *Dirty Politics* (1992), spurred a reformist effort in the press. One result was the ad watch, an "attempt to cover political advertising in an analytical fashion" (Kern and Wicks, in Denton, 1994, p. 204). The 1992 election was the first year in which the networks and major newspapers examined the presidential primary campaign ads critically, showing the ads and pointing out their strategies and distortions.[6]

In 1992, "most insiders claimed that their [news] organizations had done more issue-oriented coverage than in the past" (Freedom Forum, 1992, p. 27). There were many examples, such as *Newsweek's* "Straight Talk," in which candidates answered "direct, issue-oriented questions" (Freedom Forum, 1992, pp. 27–32). This media focus on issues characterized the period of late fall 1991 through late January 1992, but much of the effort dissipated in the feeding frenzy surrounding the Gennifer

Flowers case in January 1992. Kendall (1995) found that little attention was paid to the candidates' positions on the nightly news from January 23–June 6, 1992; on only 11 nights of the 134—8%—were there lead stories devoted to policy issues (also see Rosenstiel, 1993, p. 153). The easiest explanation for the media's return to their regular pattern of horse race coverage is that the scandal stories were more exciting and sold more newspapers and advertising. Other attempts to explain this shift suggest that (1) the press prefers clear, sharply drawn issues that are "rooted in controversy and sharply define the candidates" (Patterson, 1993, p. 136); and (2) the press finds "detailed policy discussion" much harder to cover than the horse race (Rosenstiel, 1993, p. 55; Kerbel, 1994).

The attention to polls was, if anything, greater in 1992 than in earlier primaries; Kerbel (1994) called it a "poll orgy" (p. 81). On the face of it, poll stories need not be superficial. Reporters could examine the various groups of supporters that make up a candidate's poll support, for example, or the policy positions of the candidate that contribute to his or her strengths or weaknesses in the polls. However, most horse race/polling coverage, while providing information on candidate viability, is otherwise not of much value to the voters; it provokes little discussion and increases the level of cynicism (Just et al., 1996; Cappella and Jamieson, 1996).

THE NEW MEDIA

Many new media technologies and changes in existing technologies affected primary coverage in the 1972–1992 period. In 1976, satellite technology allowed network crews to send live or taped coverage back to the networks via their portable video cameras and satellite trucks. This broke the tie to film, which had required studio time for editing and sending; news could now be broadcast instantly.

With satellite technology, many local stations were able to send reporters to primaries. According to Pavlik and Thalhimer (1992), the percentage of local television stations using satellite technologies to interview the presidential candidates grew from 20% in 1988 to 43% in 1992, averaging four interviews each. "In effect," said Swanson (1997), "many local stations were offered greater access to the candidates for live interviews than the network news programs were able to get" (p. 1271).

Satellite technology facilitated the use of the video news release (VNR), which candidates supplied to local television. The VNR was a flattering, news-style version of the radio "actualities" used by candidates in 1972.[7] Candidates sent them to local stations by satellite or distributed them on cassette. In a nationwide survey of television news directors, Pavlik and

Thalhimer (1992) found that one-tenth of the stations had used a VNR sent by a candidate, especially stations in small markets with small staffs.

The fax machine speeded up communication between candidates and the press. In the 1992 New Hampshire primary, for example, the Tsongas campaign provided the author with daily early morning faxes of the candidate's latest schedule.

New machines such as graphics generators and electronic editing units speeded up editing. Hallin (1992, pp. 11–12) noted that the new equipment made it possible to use a faster-moving format in the news stories, with cutting every few seconds; in contrast, the television news stories of the early 1970s were "dull, disorganized, and difficult to follow," in Hallin's view (p. 12). Between 1988 and 1992, video equipment became significantly more portable and sensitive to light, reducing the staffing needs for video coverage. Computer chips made large lights unnecessary. The total weight of the camera and recorder dropped from about 70 pounds in 1988 to 28 pounds in 1992, and the "umbilical cord" that formerly connected the camera and recorder was no longer needed, as the camera and recorder were in one self-contained unit (Bill Loucks, Washington News Editor of the Canadian Broadcasting Company, personal interview, February 14, 1992).

The number of television channels increased from four in 1980 to 50 in 1992 (Rosenstiel, 1993). This change led to an explosion of news sources. Ratings for the network evening news shows dropped steadily during this same period, though a majority of viewers—56%—still chose these shows (Nimmo, in Denton, 1994). One of the rivals to the network news was their local affiliates, many of which had expanded their news to an hour or more in length. Another rival was cable television, which by 1992 reached 60% of American households (Nimmo, in Denton, 1994).

C-SPAN, a nonprofit public affairs network subsidized by the cable industry, began in 1979. C-SPAN used a straightforward, "point and shoot" style, without commentary. It covered the presidential primaries intensively, beginning in 1988. In 1991, C-SPAN began its weekly 90-minute program *Road To the White House*, showing all of the primary candidates in speeches, interviews, rallies, handshaking tours, and so on. Voters could see and hear the candidates for themselves, without editing or interpretation.[8]

The CNN cable network also offered continuous public affairs programming. Public use of cable television rose to a record high on January 17, 1991, when the Allies bombed Baghdad and "about 12.9 million households" tuned in to CNN ("Coming Into Their Own," *New York Times*, July 14, 1997). During the 1992 primaries, CNN's *Larry King Live* provided a forum for the primary candidates, in a kind of "soft interview" format with call-ins. It also was on this show that Ross Perot first confessed that he would be willing to run for president in February 1992.

Richard Threlkeld of CBS said that 1992 was "the year of the talk show," citing as highlights the *60 Minutes* interview with Bill and Hillary Clinton, Perot on *Larry King*, and Brown and Clinton on Don Imus's radio show and the *Donahue* show (CBS, April 17, 1992).[9] While radio and television talk shows and call-in programs had existed for many years, the number increased in the 1990s, and the shows "more regularly feature[d] political guests and topics" (Dooley and Grosswiler, 1997, p. 35). From 1982 to 1991, radio stations "devoted entirely to talk, much of it political," tripled in number (National Association of Radio Talk Show Hosts, in Rosenstiel, 1993, p. 168).

There is evidence that the talk shows had some salutary effects. Chaffee et al. (1994) found that "attention to appearances of the candidates on talk shows seems to have improved people's knowledge of the issue positions of those candidates" (p. 317), and Just et al. (1996) found that focus groups watching candidate interviews were stimulated to "grapple with ideas, rather than images, strategies, or personality" (p. 241). Ridout (1993) found that talk shows provided a more substantive discussion of the candidates' policy views than network news.

Most candidates clearly preferred "interactive" formats to seeing their words interpreted by reporters. As Clinton said, "Anyone who lets himself be interpreted to the American people through these intermediaries alone is nuts" (Golson and Range, 1992). Clinton, Brown, and Perot held electronic town halls during the primaries. They appeared before television studio audiences, often with satellite hookups with other audiences, taking questions both from the audience that was present and from others by telephone (Muir, 1994a).

Except for the fact that satellite technology allowed large and geographically scattered audiences to watch them simultaneously, the 1992 electronic town halls differed little from the televised telephone marathons used by Hubert Humphrey in 1972. In both cases, the candidate found a relatively inexpensive way to bypass the press and to reach the voters.

One computer source that proved very valuable to the press was Campaign HOTLINE, a daily electronic news service of the American Political Network, which provided candidates' travel schedules, news releases, and speech manuscripts to its subscribers. Access to this information made it possible for people to follow and study the campaign from a distance, reducing the overwhelming advantage held by the traveling press corps.

Candidate Jerry Brown was the first to introduce the 1–800 telephone number in his primary campaign. Kevin Connor, assistant campaign manager of the Brown Campaign, reported that by mid-February, the campaign had already received 50,000 calls to the 1–800 number (author's notes, Manchester, NH, February 16, 1992). Other candidates copied Brown. On March 13, Perot established his 1–800 number; in a 24-hour period, the number was dialed 500,000 times (Loevy, 1995).

The dramatic changes in the candidates' abilities to reach the voter directly, over the heads of the media, have provoked much research and discussion. The "interactivity" has been heralded as a major improvement, a way to stir voter interest and to aid understanding of issues (Muir, 1994a; Just et al., 1996; Chaffee et al., 1994). But there are dissenting voices. Nimmo (in Denton, 1994) and others are critical of the town halls as well as of the talk shows, saying that they are really not interactive and that they allow the candidate to avoid tough questions. The candidate tends to give long "recitative" answers on standard campaign themes, and the moderator often asks more questions than the audience. Dooley and Grosswiler (1997) report that print journalists see this bypassing of journalists as a potentially dangerous development, whereby politicians will try to control journalists.

The candidate-media clash on this issue is easy to understand. Not only is there a natural rivalry between these agents, both struggling to shape the news agenda, but the research by Hallin (1992) and Kendall (1993, 1997) clearly shows that television news gives scanty attention to the candidates' words and ideas. It is true that in these new forums the candidates avoid tough questions and get away with long recitative answers on standard campaign themes, but one could argue that the candidates are simply trying to get their words and ideas across to the voters who are not receiving these messages from the traditional news media.

FOCUS ON PRESS CONDITIONS, 1992

In 1973, 15% of the public had "hardly any confidence" in the press, and by 1993, this critical audience had grown to 39% (Cappella and Jamieson, 1996, p. 83). One particular complaint that emerged during the 1992 primaries was that the media paid "too much attention to a candidate's personal life." Voters were disgusted with the scandal stories (Alger, 1994, p. R-14, quoting *National Journal*, February 22, 1992, p. 474). In the last week of the 1992 election, the public gave the press a grade of C on its coverage (*Times-Mirror* poll, cited by Patterson, 1993).

When journalists judged primary coverage, print was still the most respected medium. The author observed this in New Hampshire, as journalists avidly read and discussed coverage in the *Boston Globe* and the *New York Times*, as well as in the local press. Rosenstiel (1993) also noted the dominance of print and the Sunday talk shows. But other forces competed to set the news agenda. As Kolbert (1992) said, "The newspapers and the networks often seemed to be responding to supermarket tabloids and television talk shows." The Gennifer Flowers story was a vivid illustration of this process: "The story squirted from the bottom-feeding *Star* onto Fox TV's evening newscasts that night and from there to the raunchier big-city tabloid dailies the next day. In turn, their interest attracted the attention of the respectable media" (Goldman et al., 1994, p. 89).

While print reporters have always had the luxury of being able to use more words than television, this advantage was reduced somewhat by the "televisionization" of newspapers. According to Chris Black of the *Boston Globe*, in 1980 "a reporter could write a 1,200-word article on a candidate going nowhere, but now [in 1992] 200 words would be a lot." For major primary candidates, he said, stories were rarely over 500 words (in Meyrowitz, 1995, p. 63, note 13).

Because of the poor state of the economy in 1992, the news media reduced coverage of the campaign to save money. On ABC, previous presidential candidates had been assigned "a correspondent, crew, and producer . . . and sometimes double that," but in 1992, "ABC would assign to each candidate a single off-air producer who filed a daily memo to New York" (Rosenstiel, 1993, pp. 36–37). The other networks also reduced coverage. In addition, they tried money-saving experiments, such as pooling coverage of the candidates, but ABC News Political Director Hal Bruno reported that the experiment failed: "We were inundated with tape, and we had to bring on more people to sort the tape out," he said (Freedom Forum, 1992, p. 26).

DEFINITION OF "THE PRIMARY" BY THE MEDIA

The media characterized the primary in 1992 in much the same way they had done in past years. They gave it great salience: during the period of late January through early June, 35% of the network lead stories were on the primaries, far exceeding any other event (Kendall, 1993). Reporters spoke of the primaries in varied metaphors, most of them related to a contest or a battle: a baseball game, a horse race, a fight, a matter of high stakes. They also portrayed the primaries as constituting a season, though literally the primaries extended over two seasons, winter and spring. After the early season rush, some reporters quickly tired of the primaries, though citizens in most states had not yet voted.

Media criticism of the primaries took two forms: the primary process was flawed, and the candidates were mean and negative. One flaw was that the primary process was too expensive. A second flaw was that the primary results were unclear. As Tom Brokaw said, "It's a muddle. A muddle at a time when the country is hungry for answers and direction" (NBC, March 4, 1992). Millions of people were dissatisfied with the primary process, said Jeff Greenfield: they found it "irrelevant, distasteful, even corrupt" (ABC, June 2, 1992).

Not only was the process flawed but the candidates were portrayed as quarrelling children, hardly the desirable image of a president. "The campaign's turned sour," said Bob Schieffer, describing how Bush "lit into" Congress, Buchanan "lit into" Bush, and the Democrats "lit into" each other on the campaign trail (CBS, February 29, 1992). The campaign "has turned mean," said Andrea Mitchell (NBC, March 1, 1992). In spite of the consistent focus of the networks on candidate clashes, none of the reporters gave the slightest hint that the media could be shaping the public's negative perception of the campaign.

THE STRUGGLE FOR DOMINANCE

The image of the campaign as "a struggle between politicians and a more or less independent media establishment over who shall control the agendas" (Swanson and Mancini, 1996, p. 252) certainly rang true in the 1992 primaries. The image of the *struggle* seems more apt than the image of the reigning media portrayed by Patterson (1993). While there was much evidence of media power, the candidates exerted every effort to resist such media dominance, and in certain circumstances, the candidates prevailed.

AGENDA SETTING BY THE MEDIA

What role did the media play in setting the agenda in 1992 as to: (1) which primaries were important? (2) which policy issues were important? and (3) which candidates were important? Kenneth Burke has pointed out the power of naming. "Naming . . . [is an] interpretive act," he said, and thus has the power not only to describe but also to shape events (1972, pp. 176–191). The media, by their headlines, choice of stories, and pictures, exercise this power.

WHICH PRIMARIES WERE IMPORTANT?

The "front-loading" of the primaries schedule by the states was a new development in the 1972–1992 period, which affected campaign coverage. By the end of March 1972, there had been only three Democratic primaries; by the end of March 1992, there had been 17. The Republicans had a similar schedule (Buell, 1996).

The Earlier Contests Tended to Receive the Most Coverage

The tendency for the media to focus on a few states, particularly those with early contests, and to give little or no attention to others, was shown in research on the 1980, 1984, and 1988 primaries (Marshall, 1983; Adams, 1987; Lichter, Amundson, and Noyes, 1988). In 1992, eight of the 10 primaries mentioned most frequently in leads on the network news took place in February or March (Kendall, 1993). In the January 23–June 6 period, 27 states were mentioned in the leads, with New York, California,[10] and New Hampshire leading the way. About half (23) of the state primaries and caucuses were never mentioned in the lead stories. The typical pattern of heavy news coverage of the New Hampshire primary occurred again in 1992: "In the February 11–19, 1992 period, 60 percent (15 out of 25) of the lead stories on ABC, CBS, and NBC [early evening news] were about the New Hampshire primary" (Kendall, 1995, p. 15).

Individual states tended to lose their identity in the story of Super Tuesday. Though 10 states held primaries that day, "candidate and press interest . . . very quickly settled on Florida," where Tsongas tried to prove that he could defeat Clinton in the South (Loevy, 1995, pp. 86, 88), but Clinton won in Florida by 51% to Tsongas's 34% and Brown's 13%.

The 1992 primary receiving the most lead stories on the network news was New York's, held on April 7, approximately halfway through the primary schedule. The stories and pictures from New York focused heavily on the chilly, rude, and even assaultive treatment given to Clinton (Andrea Mitchell, NBC, March 25; Chris Bury, ABC, April 2; Peter Jennings and Jeff Greenfield, ABC, April 6, 1992). This tone of coverage both reflected and perpetuated a negative stereotype of New York and may well have evoked voter sympathies for Clinton. The fixation upon New York also effectively removed other primaries from the news; although Minnesota, Wisconsin, and Kansas had primaries the same day, they received comparatively little media attention (Loevy, 1995). After New York, media interest in the primaries dropped sharply: there were only four lead stories on the primaries in May 1992 (Kendall, 1993).

WHICH POLICY ISSUES WERE TREATED AS IMPORTANT?

In every election from 1976 on, Gallup has found Americans most concerned about economic problems (Myers, 1996, p. 435). In 1992, the economy received the highest number of lead stories on network news (Kendall, 1995). Foreign policy matters, which are seldom of interest to Americans, except in times of crisis (Graber, 1988; Sobel, 1998), faded even farther from view than usual, with the end of the Cold War and the absence of any obvious threat to American defense.

WHICH CANDIDATES WERE PRESENTED AS IMPORTANT?

Alger (1989) has found that the media heap coverage on the winners of early races and on candidates who do better than expected. This finding was borne out in the 1992 primary coverage. In February 1992, for example, Republican Bush, who won all of the Republican primaries, and Republican Buchanan, who mounted a stronger challenge to Bush than was expected, led the list of speakers shown on network television, and Tsongas and Clinton appeared more than the other Democrats. This pattern of front-runner coverage characterized the January–June period of the 1992 primaries (Kendall, 1995).

The main reason for this order of attention seems to be related to candidate viability or electability. Others receiving heavy coverage are incumbents, those who are leading in the polls and those designated as strong contenders by party leaders (Buell, 1996; Meyrowitz, 1995). Once the candidates secure enough delegates to assure their nomination, the news coverage drops off precipitously, as it did with Bush and Clinton in 1992. In the eyes of the media, the story is basically over, even though the primaries are not over. In 1992, however, Ross Perot broke the mold. He was not an early winner or an incumbent; he was not even a candidate in the primaries. Yet he received heavy coverage. Any model of media coverage of the primaries must include the possibility that a wealthy public figure might choose to campaign outside of the primary system, making a competitive claim on the media's attention.

HOW WERE THE CANDIDATES COVERED BY THE MEDIA?

On network news in 1992, the presidential primary candidates rarely were allowed to speak for themselves; instead, they were presented through the filter of the journalists' language (Kendall, 1993). The significance of this removal of the candidate's language is underscored by the finding of Just et al. (1996), that "in general, the more candidates were given a chance to speak, the better the story was for them" (p. 111), while the reporters' words were much more likely to be critical.

Both television and newspapers emphasized the personal qualities of the candidates, evident in numerous examples (Freedom Forum, 1992). For those viewers just tuning in to the campaign, information on the candidates' character is valuable in forming judgments, and it "plays a more decisive role than issues" (Hellweg, Pfau, and Brydon, 1992, p. 109). Those seeking more specific information about the candidates' positions, however, will not find it easily on network news or on the front pages of newspapers.

MEDIA PORTRAYALS OF CANDIDATES' PERSONAL TRAITS

Buchanan

In her study of media coverage of the leading candidates in New Hampshire, Kendall (1995) found that the networks portrayed Buchanan as a strong, aggressive candidate, exuding confidence and attacking Bush. The question was raised, however, about whether Buchanan had real power or whether he was just a vehicle for the voters to send a message to Bush. Buchanan was portrayed in the newspapers as the "antibush"; he was defined by what he said against Bush. Though stories often reported that voters were using him as a messenger rather than as a serious candidate, the frequency of Buchanan stories established him as a major character in the New Hampshire primary; he was "the challenger," "the rival."

The dominant qualities emphasized in the Buchanan stories were his energy and strength—energy in fighting against Bush and strength in driving Bush down in the polls. This image was in direct contrast to the weak image of Bush. Words such as "pugnacious" and "aggressive" contributed to a clear image of Buchanan as a fighter. There was little suggestion in this coverage that Buchanan was competent to be president. In fact, the *Boston Herald* endorsed Buchanan in a front-page editorial, at the same time confessing that it did not know much about his leadership abilities, but urging a protest vote (February 12, 1992).

Bush

The network image of President Bush before the New Hampshire primary was decidedly mixed, both positive and negative. The networks showed him as an out-of-touch elitist, worried and fearful about a Buchanan protest vote and lacking in charisma. On the other hand, they showed Bush in his presidential role, actively and aggressively working for re-election and more statesmanlike than Buchanan. There was no doubt that he would win in New Hampshire, they said.

One thing that stands out in the Bush coverage is the pummeling he took from other candidates who were quoted in the media. There was only one incumbent, but many attackers. Buchanan used every opportunity to criticize Bush's record, Perot made attacks on the status quo under Bush a staple of his speeches, and the Democrats routinely attacked the Bush administration in their messages.

If the New Hampshire primary established the characterizations of the candidates for the campaign to follow, the image drawn in New Hampshire may well have tarred Bush for the rest of the year. The newspapers stressed Bush's weak campaign, his weak response to Buchanan's attacks, and the weak public response to Bush's appearances. One would hardly have known that Bush had won the New Hampshire primary. The beaming Republican "winner" on the front pages was Buchanan, not Bush.

Saussure (1916/1959) has argued that pairs of words (such as open/closed) get their meaning from each other, that one term in the pair becomes meaningful because we associate the other term with it. It is in the antithesis of the terms that meaning arises (Corcoran, 1990). The words used to describe the state of the Bush campaign after the New Hampshire primary gained power from just such antithetical meaning. The newspapers called the results a "wake-up call" (Judy Keen, USA Today, February 19, 1992), implying that Bush had been asleep. Although Saussure never talked about antithesis in relation to pictures, there is such a striking difference in the Bush and Buchanan pictures that the idea of such opposites comes to mind. In pictures, Bush looked worried, puzzled, and angry more than any of the other candidates. He also looked older. Pictures are much more ambiguous in meaning than words, and they leave much for the viewer to fill in. However, it would be understandable if voters had doubts about this old, tired, worried-looking president.

Clinton

The network coverage of Clinton's character was so heavy in the early primaries that other candidates had trouble getting through to the voters. While polls in the October 1991–January 1992 period had shown that "less than half of the public was following the campaign closely" (Smillie, 1992, p. 47), and 70% of those polled had not heard enough about Clinton to form an opinion (Frankovic, in Pomper, 1993), this all changed with the Gennifer Flowers and draft stories in late January and early February. By the third week of February, all but 19% of those polled said that they had heard enough to form an opinion of Clinton, a "phenomenal" change. In contrast, Michael Dukakis had not reached this level of public awareness until after the Democratic Convention in 1988 (Frankovic, 1993, p. 115).

The networks constructed an ambivalent characterization of Clinton in New Hampshire, questioning his electability in light of scandal, yet showing his fight to save himself as a mighty effort, displaying great energy and inventiveness. As late as February 17, Dan Rather wondered if Clinton might be politically dead. Members of the public were shown coming to his defense, however, lamenting that there was so much "looking for dirt" (CBS, February 11) and casting him as a kind of sympathy-evoking underdog figure.

In the post–New Hampshire coverage, the networks focused on two aspects of Clinton's character: (1) his tarnished image as a man of integrity, and (2) his competence as a leader. Most of the attention was devoted to the question of his integrity and whether he was so damaged by this issue that he could not win. Rival candidates and party officials raised the issue, and the networks made frequent use of polls to show that the question of Clinton's integrity was foremost on voters' minds (NBC, March 4; NBC, March 11; CBS, March 12; ABC, April 7).

The second major question of character concerned Clinton's competence. When the networks spoke about Clinton's ability as a campaigner, their tone was generally positive. Just et al. (1996) found that "the significant boosts to Clinton in all three media centered on the process of the campaign" (p. 110).

Newspaper coverage of Clinton during the New Hampshire primary was decidedly mixed too. Clinton was slipping in the polls during the February 11–19 period, and the words used to describe his status made him sound desperate and his campaign hopeless. On the other hand, he was fighting to save himself, and the press expressed its admiration for a tough, energetic fighter. The national press gave Clinton more front-page coverage than all of the other candidates, while the regional and local press focused on the Bush–Buchanan struggle.

Clinton's image took a sudden positive turn after he finished second to Tsongas in New Hampshire. He had demonstrated his "resilience," said the *Boston Globe* (Curtis Wilkie, February 19). More dramatically he had been resurrected, as though from the dead (Kevin Landrigan, "Clinton claims...," *Telegraph*, February 19). Clinton's own words were, "New Hampshire tonight has made Bill Clinton the comeback kid" (Richard Benedetto, *USA Today*, February 19).

Tsongas

Tsongas received major attention from the networks in New Hampshire, as he became the front-runner in the polls. But the networks seemed puzzled by Tsongas, trying out one description and then another. The only characteristic they discussed consistently was his lack of electability, expressing doubts that his success in New Hampshire would carry over to the rest of the country.

In spite of their doubts, they had to explain him to the voters, all the more so when he won the New Hampshire Democratic primary. They showed him as having the following traits: he was witty, he was a nice guy, he was knowledgeable and competent about economic issues, he was courageous, and clearly, as a front-runner, he was powerful.

None of the candidates fit the image of the ideal presidential candidate, as they were portrayed by the media. But Tsongas, who had not held a major elective office for eight years, had not been a dominant figure when he was in the U.S. Senate, and had rejected the idea of the popular middle-class tax break, deviated from the ideal image enough that the networks portrayed him as an unconventional, unlikely candidate. Tsongas fostered this idea himself the day before the election, saying in an astonished tone of voice, "This is so bizarre. This is so bizarre. I am such an unlikely candidate" (author's notes and NBC News, February 17, 1992).

When he won in New Hampshire, the networks suggested that Tsongas had simply been lucky, benefiting from Clinton's character problems, from a kind of protest vote against the economic situation, and from the advantage of his early entry and proximity to New Hampshire. They noted that he had little money or backing from leading Democrats, and both are usually necessary for a successful campaign. And lurking in the background was the question of his health: would his cancer recur? The question was not discussed openly but suggested obliquely, as when Richard Threlkeld asked whether the Tsongas campaign had the "stamina" to last through the primaries (CBS News, February 19).

The coverage of Tsongas by newspapers during the New Hampshire primary was more positive than by the networks, though the question of his electability was raised occasionally. *New York Times* and *Boston Globe* reporters gave Tsongas stature as a serious, substantive, knowledgeable candidate in several front-page stories, and the *Boston Herald* did it with an editorial.

FIGHTER IMAGE

On one image trait the media were in agreement: they admired "fighters." Demonstrations of fighting against the odds by Clinton and Buchanan received heavy coverage. Bush and the status quo were the main objects of this fighting. On the Republican side, the press portrayed Buchanan as strong, a fighter; Bush was weak, slipping in the polls, afraid.

On the Democratic side, the question of whether Clinton could survive the scandals, raised frequently by the media and Democratic leaders, gave a special definition to the concept of strength. Here the issue was whether a campaign would be strong enough to survive or would prove to be politically dead (Dan Rather, CBS News, February 17; Tom Brokaw, NBC News, February 18). The word "survive" suggests that one has remained alive in spite of a dangerous event, such as a wreck; the dangerous events were the stories of Clinton's infidelity and draft evasion. In the context of a multi-candidate campaign, a survivor is stronger than those who have not survived; the word takes its meaning combined with its opposite, the dead. The result is hardly the image of a winner. But Clinton's burst of energy to save himself won admiration and positive coverage in the media, more coverage than all of the other candidates in the national press. With their coverage of his strength and energy, they created an intriguing mosaic rather than the predictable, moralistic, negative images projected during the controversies over infidelity and the draft.

AGENDA SETTING BY THE CANDIDATES

As in past elections, the primary candidates in 1992 worked actively to influence the public message, both through the process by which they dealt with the media and through their self-presentation. The most direct opportunity they had to influence the media was through scheduling decisions. Reporters were dependent on the candidates for this information in order to plan their own schedules. Candidates produced "editors' advisories" or "press advisories" to inform the press about what they would be doing. The schedule was strictly factual, reporting on the events that the candidate would be attending each day. But the selection of groups and subjects addressed and the scope of the campaign effort provided clues to the visions and character traits of the candidates. High numbers of appearances, for example, created an impression of high motivation to win, and of vigor and energy.

Candidates also had important power to influence the media through their self-presentation. The media depended upon them for the raw material of the campaign, for the daily words and activities that would be turned into the story and pictures of the day. One factor in candidates' self-presentation was the effort to explain their vision for the future of the nation, their plans and priorities. Their emphasis on particular topics helped reveal that vision. A second factor in self-presentation was the personal qualities candidates chose to project. A third factor was their decision about which rival to focus on.[11]

In their efforts to explain their vision for the future, the candidates had to rely chiefly on themselves. The media gave little prominent attention to their goals or to the language they used to express them. The following analysis focuses on the efforts of the 1992 primary candidates to communicate with the public through the news media.

Brown

Dan Butler, the Northeast Field Coordinator of Brown for President, described Brown's campaign as "a lean, mean, low-to-the-ground campaign," which had to find cheap ways to reach the public (Royer, 1994, p. 21). Brown was an innovator in his use of several news channels, such as talk radio, where he made frequent appearances starting in September 1991 (Royer, 1994), local public access television channels, where he used a form of town meeting (Nimmo, in Denton, 1994), and satellite interviews and video news releases for local stations (Pavlik and Thalhimer,

1992). He also agreed to a series of nightly debates with Clinton in New York. Though the national media gave him little coverage in the early primary period, he used these local and regional news sources to get out his message. He also gained much free media attention by announcing his 1–800 toll-free telephone number at the end of speeches and debates.

Brown received his heaviest news coverage in the New York primary, where he chose to emphasize the issue of the flat tax. The topic was new to the public and somewhat complex. People did not know whether it was a good or a bad idea. There was much criticism of the idea from Clinton, from the popular Senator Daniel Patrick Moynihan of New York, and from newspaper columnists; they charged that, far from helping the middle class, the flat tax would only help the rich. Increasingly, the flat tax came to be seen as a radical, ill-thought-out idea, contributing to Brown's image as an incompetent "flake." Brown also named a vice presidential choice in New York, Reverend Jesse Jackson, bringing down the wrath of Jewish leaders who remembered Jackson's "Hymietown" remark, and in general hurting the campaign (Dan Butler, in Royer, 1994). While he gained heavy media coverage, Brown's self-presentation met with resounding failure among the voters.

Harkin

Harkin spent heavily on the Iowa caucuses, because that was his home state and he did not want to look bad. When he won with 73% of the vote, the victory was treated as "a non-event," because it was virtually uncontested (in Royer, 1994, p. 76). He also drew constant criticism for his negativity. Harkin trailed most of the other candidates in the early primaries (winning only the Iowa and Minnesota caucuses), until he dropped out on March 9, 1992.

Kerrey

When Kerrey announced his candidacy in the fall of 1991, he received heavy coverage. A U.S. senator, a former governor of Nebraska, and a successful businessman and Congressional Medal of Honor winner, he had many traits that people hold of the ideal image of president. When the Clinton scandal stories emerged, Kerrey had much more difficulty getting on the media agenda. There also was some disarray and indecision in his campaign over what themes to emphasize, as discussed in Chapter 4.

While the Clinton draft issue seemed well suited to Kerrey, he at first resisted going on the attack. However, when this issue developed into the broader one of Clinton's honesty, he attacked Clinton in the South and received immediate press attention. But Clinton won decisively, first in Georgia and then on Super Tuesday. Kerrey dropped out on March 5, 1992.

Tsongas

Tsongas was the first Democrat to announce his candidacy, on March 10, 1991. As a former U.S. senator from Massachusetts, he did not receive much press coverage for many months. Even so, he was able to reach thousands of New Hampshire voters by his extensive schedule of giving speeches and meeting people, and by distributing his booklet *A Call to Economic Arms*. However, in the last week before the primary, when media coverage is most intense, Tsongas made the fewest public appearances each day of all of the Democrats. Such evidence of low activity was not at all in Tsongas's interest. Questions about his health constantly circulated among the press, as he had had cancer and claimed to be fully recovered, but nevertheless, doubts lingered.

One of Tsongas's regularly scheduled events was his daily swimming practice. He allowed the press to come to these practices, which helped him build an image of strength to counter the questions about his health. News pictures of him swimming the difficult butterfly stroke reinforced his advertising campaign, which also featured pictures of him swimming.

Tsongas's decisions about scheduling and self-presentation generally proved successful in New Hampshire, where he won the primary. But his planning for the post–New Hampshire primaries was inadequate. He was not able to break out of the image of the regional candidate, and on March 14, he suspended his campaign.

Clinton

Of all the primary candidates, Clinton displayed the best understanding of how to secure favorable media attention and how to adapt to changing circumstances. His speeches at Georgetown University in late 1991 introduced him to many reporters and party leaders as a serious, substantive figure. In New Hampshire, he established a pattern of behavior that he was to follow in subsequent primaries: when the attacks against him were strong, he escalated his number of campaign activities, which exerted pressure on the media to give him more extensive coverage (see Chapter 3).

Clinton, like Brown, was quick to try new methods to reach the voters. Next to Brown, Clinton had the second highest number of satellite interviews by local television stations (Pavlik and Thalhimer, 1992). He made skillful use of local radio (Rosenstiel, 1993, pp. 315–316). Looking back on his use of the talk show in the primaries, Clinton expressed the view that these interactive shows made the campaign less artificial and remote from the voters. In the past, he said, "people haven't been able to relate. Being able to talk to candidates alleviates that" (June 9, 1992, *Today Show*, Bernstein, 1996, p. 49). There is no doubt that appearing on popular television talk shows increased his audience size, particularly in the context of scandalous stories about him in the news. In addition, Davis (1993) has noted that Clinton went up in the polls when he used these interactive media.

Clinton was quick to harness the credibility of news reports to serve his own goals, such as when he turned articles in *Time* and *Newsday* (a Long Island daily) into new ads. When the story about Clinton's letter to his draft board became public in February 1992, his decision to publish the entire letter as an ad in New Hampshire newspapers and to have Ted Koppel read the entire letter on the *Nightline* interview served to redefine the news agenda, almost like a rival news business.

There were moments in the campaign when Clinton seemed to treat the media like another candidate. This was particularly evident in the New York primary, when the tabloid newspapers attacked him every day. He created an ad identifying the tabloids as enemies of the people, and his press assistants "began suggesting that it was a real candidate plus that Clinton could take such heavy hitting in the media and still come back for more" (Loevy, 1995, p. 119). This approach is consistent with Kenneth Burke's notion that antithesis is an effective form of identification. By portraying the tabloids as the people's enemy, a view many already held, he showed his unity with people against a common foe.

Buchanan

Though Buchanan had a small campaign team, he had enough money from direct-mail solicitations and federal matching funds to make an energetic campaign in New Hampshire and Georgia. As a skilled communicator experienced in the news business, he and his staff always returned media calls and accepted "as much free media" as they could (Bay Buchanan, in Royer, 1994, p. 138). They also recognized that Buchanan's vivid language would appeal to the media, as would his underdog campaign against the president. As Bay Buchanan said, "Nobody likes a fight better than the press" (Royer, 1994, p. 25).

Another factor that helped Buchanan was the campaign's awareness of the power of the visual, particularly of facial expressions. When the New Hampshire primary results came in, Bush won, but a beaming Buchanan graced the front pages. Bay Buchanan said she believed that for people watching television, "Whoever was smiling the most won." So the Buchanan campaign representatives beamed and smiled, conveying the message, "This is a great victory for us" (Bay Buchanan, in Royer,

1994, p. 122). The wisdom of this strategy has been confirmed in research by Lanzetta et al. (1985), who report that the face is "the primary channel for affective communication."

Buchanan knew the national reporters personally from his many years at the White House and in the media, and they had a friendly rapport. He also proved helpful to the media in getting the stories and pictures they needed, as the author saw firsthand in her New Hampshire observations. Winning the media's attention was no problem for this candidate.

Bush

Bush's interactions with the media in the early 1992 primaries were awkward and unsuccessful. Rosenstiel (1993) described interviews that Bush and his wife granted to New Hampshire television station WMUR in December 1991, in which the Bush campaign "tried to control every aspect of the interview" (p. 86). Bush's answers to questions about New Hampshire and the economy were stiff and jumbled. Instead of following the usual "go to New Hampshire" model, Bush relied heavily on television ads, leaflets, surrogate speakers, and interviews from Washington. He gave extensive interviews from a special television studio in Washington, campaigning from a distance. These decisions tightly limited media access to Bush, while the other candidates of both parties were courting the media and competing for their attention.

Bush was slow to spell out his reasons for running for a second term. The contrast was stark between Bush's late focus on an agenda, and the behavior of his rivals. Some have speculated that he was simply confident that the highly favorable image he enjoyed as president after the Persian Gulf War would carry him through. Insiders reported that there were sharp differences between the campaign staff and the White House staff over the need to focus on the campaign (Matalin and Carville, 1994).

Though he won in New Hampshire, Bush's percentage of the vote was far smaller than his campaign had predicted, and smaller than most incumbent presidents had received. The image of Bush's weakness and ineptitude constructed by Buchanan, the Democrats, and the media haunted him for the next nine months.

CONCLUSIONS: THE MEDIA IN THE 1992 PRIMARIES

The media in 1992 treated the primaries as a major event, devoting many lead and front-page stories to them. They also adopted the expected horse race theme, replete with polls. The media agenda of candidates and issues adhered closely to those polls, focusing most on the front-runners and on their nearest opponents. The early contested primaries once again received the heaviest coverage, as well as the New York primary in early April.

Candidate image received much attention, particularly the issues of trust and of competence to handle the nation's economic problems. The character question dogged Clinton, yet was regularly offset by his steady stream of primary victories and resulting image as a winner. The competence issue, especially regarding the economy, was Bush's *bête noire*.

Both Clinton and Buchanan enjoyed favorable media attention for fighting against the odds. Though most of the candidates adopted the mantra of "fighter," these two, perhaps because they were surprisingly successful in the face of imposing obstacles, won the media's admiration.

Competition between candidates and the media for control over the campaign agenda characterized the 1992 primaries. Two primary candidates, Brown and Clinton, excelled in communication inventiveness. Brown, the conspicuous underdog in money and power, kept his campaign afloat by trying many forms of new media. Clinton's secret weapon was his expansive, articulate speaking ability, which he displayed daily, combined with long, impressive question periods. His decision to escalate the pace of these events each time he was under attack succeeded in commanding media attention and winning over the voters.

There also were unique developments affecting the 1992 primaries. The medium of television had undergone major changes in the 1972–1992 period, enabling candidates to make instant adjustments in their strategies, responding to events as they developed. News coverage changed just as rapidly, particularly in the growth of interactive news programs on radio and television. The effects were higher viewer interest and a demonstrable increase in learning. Another change in the 1972–1992 period was the expansion in research on the primaries, both through traditional academic organizations and journals and through new centers specializing in media and politics.

Finally, as in 1972, journalists were heavily interpretive, and much of that was negative in tone. Both in video and print, there was more emphasis on brevity. The irony is that not only did the candidates have important things to say, which the public never heard, but also that the reporters who traveled with the candidates were seldom given time or space to present a fraction of what they knew.

TAKING STOCK OF PRIOR RESEARCH ON MEDIA AND THE PRIMARIES: THE FINDINGS OF CHAPTERS 5 AND 6

This study of media coverage in the primaries over an 80-year period finds both confirmation and contradiction of prior research. The main findings are: (1) that the guiding principles of media coverage have changed little over time; (2) that candidates who have understood these principles of media coverage have increased their chances of success; and (3) that the technological changes of the visual medium of television and the increased speed of communication have dramatically heightened and underlined previously existing media tendencies. These three findings are summarized below.

1. *The guiding principles of media coverage have changed little over time.* From 1912 through 1992, the media covered conflict heavily, reporting on the primaries as contests between "fighters" in a horse race or battle. In contrast, uncontested primaries received little coverage. Throughout the 80 years, the candidates' image received major attention, though in 1912 and 1932 one of the desirable personal qualities was strong party identification, a trait relatively ignored in later primaries.

The media have always used their agenda-setting power to decide *which* candidates, primaries, and messages to pay attention to, as well as *how much attention* to give to each of these factors. The rationale behind these choices differed somewhat in 1912 and 1932 compared to later periods, as partisan newspapers spotlighted their favorite candidates and ignored others. The tendencies to cover the *first* races, the *best-known* and *front-runner* candidates, and the *conflictual* messages developed early and continued throughout this period.

Through factors such as story placement and length and pictures, the media have consistently added an evaluative dimension to their coverage of the primaries, giving "priming" cues for their audiences (Iyengar and Kinder, 1987). In viewing media coverage throughout this period, one is struck by (1) the huge advantage of incumbent presidents in the amount of coverage, (2) the demonstration that the primaries are always in competition for news coverage with other conflicts, contests, and disasters, and (3) the scope for media interpretation offered by the fact that pluralities rather than majorities often decide primary votes.

In earlier years, the media let the candidates speak in their own words more often than today. Sabato (1992) sees this as a kind of "lapdog" journalism, indicating a compliant, passive press. Andersen and Thorson (1989), in contrast, praise such coverage for making available to the public the sustained arguments of the candidates. In reviewing media coverage of the primaries throughout history, however, what stands out is the extent to which the media have consistently shaped messages, rather than letting the candidates speak unedited. Andersen and Thorson found that one-fifth to one-third of press coverage in the 1898–1960 period was made up of transcripts or reports of candidate speeches. This means that even in the 1898–1960 period, two-thirds to four-fifths of the coverage was composed by journalists, not candidates.

In light of the overwhelming dominance of media language by journalists in the past, the 1992 proliferation of talk show interviews with candidates was truly a "revolutionary" development (Kalb, 1992, A-25), making available large quantities of the candidates' own, unedited words.

2. *Candidates who have understood these guiding principles of media coverage have increased their chances of success.*

While the media have the power to set the agenda, they are dependent on the candidates for the information and pictures to present the story. In every one of the primary years studied, there were instances of brilliant candidate strategies to shape the media agenda and/or to reach the public more directly through the adoption of new technologies and through the construction of effective rhetorical messages.

3. *The technological changes of the visual medium of television and the increased speed of communication have dramatically heightened and underlined previously existing media tendencies.*

Did television and other new technologies change media coverage of the primaries? Yes. What they made possible was a dramatically expanded opportunity to portray the candidate's image. Campaign coverage has always devoted substantial attention to image. While this interest is not new, television brought the candidate right into the living room for a close look by the voter.

In the days of newspapers, primary candidate conflicts were reported from week to week, or at most from day to day. In the age of modern technology, these disputes have been covered 24 hours a day. Conflict as a newsworthy principle has remained the same, but the technology has enabled the candidates to speed up the rate of their exchanges, often creating a climate of unrelenting rancor.

In 1912, voters thronged to hear candidates speak on the campaign trail. Local media covered these visits extensively. Media interest in the "local angle" has been a constant. But with the new technologies of satellite dishes and cable television, local media have been able to play a more active role in relating the presidential primary campaign to the audiences in their specific geographic areas.

The speeding up of the message process may have contributed to the front-loading of primary coverage. In the primaries of 1912 through 1972, the media paid attention to contests as late as June. By 1992, however, the media declared the nominees in April; in 1996, it was March; after that, coverage diminished sharply. In the meantime, more and more states scheduled their primaries early. These front-loading decisions by state parties and media coverage seem to be closely related.

NOTES

1. For the study of the 1972 primaries, the author reviewed network television news programs from the Nixon Project, National Archives, and from the Vanderbilt Television Archives, particularly those just before and after primaries

in New Hampshire, Florida, Wisconsin, and California. She read the *New York Times*'s coverage in the weeks before and after the same primaries. Another excellent source of information was the George McGovern Papers at the Seeley Mudd Library, Princeton University.

2. Newsmagazines were clearly important as well. *Time* had 4,250,000 subscribers, and *Newsweek* had 2,625,091 subscribers in 1972 (Crouse, p. 139).

3. The mere introduction of closing lines may have contributed to the horse race emphasis. In 1968, only 12% of the nightly television news programs during the fall campaign had closing lines; by 1976, all had closing lines (Hallin, 1992, pp. 10–11). The journalist faced with the necessity to make a final, summary statement often uses that occasion to assess the state of the contest. Of course, the need to make a concise summary statement predates television. Before television, there were headlines.

4. This finding is in direct conflict with research by Fitzgerald (1996) on the fall campaign, in which he found little use of polls by the networks.

5. For the study of the media in the 1992 primaries, the author viewed 132 nights of network news coverage from late January to early June 1992, selecting one network at random each evening; the programs were ABC's *World News Tonight*, NBC's *Nightly News*, and CBS's *Evening News*. The New Hampshire primary was a particular focus; the author traveled around New Hampshire on a press pass for 10 days before the primary, observing the candidates and press, and examined major New Hampshire, Boston, and national newspapers in this period. She also examined press coverage by the *New York Times* in the periods just before and after key primaries.

6. See Chapter 4.

7. McGovern distributed a VNR in the 1972 California primary.

8. Though of course C-SPAN controlled decisions about who to cover, how many cameras to use, camera placement, and so on.

9. It was *after* the primaries that these talk show interviews really escalated in number.

10. The stories about California mainly dealt with the Rodney King verdict and subsequent riots, not the primary.

11. Many of these decisions about self-presentation are discussed in Chapters 3 and 4 on the speeches and debates and advertisements of the primary candidates.

Chapter 7

Communication Patterns in Presidential Primaries, 1912–2000: Knowing the Rules of the Game

This book has examined the distinctive patterns of communication in presidential primaries, focusing especially on 1912, the first year of numerous primaries, and then on primaries at 20-year intervals after 1912: 1932, 1952, 1972, and 1992. In Part I of Chapter 7, the author will report on the consistent patterns of communication found in primaries from their earliest days through 1992. Part II turns to communication in the 1996 primaries and the future, examining (1) the extent to which the communication patterns or rules used by candidates and the media in the past illuminate the 1996 primaries and those of 2000, and (2) proposals for change.

PART I: CONSISTENT COMMUNICATION PATTERNS

The conventional wisdom about the presidential primaries contains the following premises: (1) Before 1972, the primaries were not routinely important, as the political parties controlled the nomination process and selected the nominee at the national nominating conventions. As columnist Jules Witcover said, it was "rare when [the primaries] were critical" (1997); Asher (1992) mentions the primaries of 1960 and 1964 as two such rare occasions. "Importance" in this reasoning has meant attaining the requisite number of delegates to achieve nomination at the convention; (2) Primaries first became important in 1972, when the rules reforms of the McGovern–Fraser Commission adopted by the Democratic Party shifted power away from the party leaders and to the candidates and voters (Bartels, 1988)[1]; (3) Media coverage of the primaries changed with the advent of television, leading to a new focus on the campaign as a drama (Aldrich, 1980; Gronbeck, 1989; Bennett, 1996); (4) Another big change produced by television was that the candidates' personal traits rather than their ideas became the focus of media attention (Bennett, 1996; Gronbeck, 1989).

The results of this study suggest that prior research on the primaries has underplayed the power of language to create perceptions. Throughout the 1912–1992 period, the candidates and the media constructed a verbal context in which the primaries were of great importance. Those who ignore the public environment in which these events took place, the active efforts of candidates to inform and persuade through speeches and debates and political advertisements, and the media's coverage of the primaries miss a major part of the story. An examination of candidates' messages and news coverage of the primaries has given a new perspective.

It is certainly true that the rules changes that took effect in 1972 increased the power of the primaries, particularly because there were so many primaries, because the results bound the delegates rather than being advisory, and because most states now listed the names of the candidates on the ballot. The sheer number of primaries (23 in 1972, 31 in 1976, etc.) stimulated the development of a "professional consulting cadre," because with so many more primaries, "the candidates needed more help" (Witcover, 1997). But this book has shown:

- that there is evidence of the primaries' importance at many points in the 1912–1972 period, long before the McGovern–Fraser Commission reforms took effect in 1972;
- that the tendencies of the media to cover the primaries as a dramatic conflict or horse race and to focus on the personal traits of the candidate were present consistently throughout the period studied; they were not new in the Age of Television; and
- that a "powerful candidate" model, based on candidate innovations, often supplanted a "powerful media" model in the primaries.

IMPORTANCE OF THE PRIMARIES, 1912–1972

The presidential primaries were very "important" nationally in four of the five periods studied: 1912, 1952, 1972, and 1992, and of regional importance in 1932. They mattered to the candidates and to the media in all of these years, and by extension, to the voters, in ways not found in delegate counts alone. Candidates used the primaries to differentiate themselves from their opponents, to prove their vote-getting power to the party leaders, to build popular support, and to shape the way in which the media constructed the news agenda. Some candidates disappeared in the primaries, knocked out by an early defeat. Others were so bruised by the process that though nominated, they entered the fall election season at a distinct disadvantage. Patterson (1980) and others have found that among people who pay attention to the primaries, the views formed at that time remain consistent in the fall.

When primaries were contested, the media found them well suited to their need for stories about famous people and conflict and covered them heavily. The way in which they portrayed the candidates, parties, and issues during the long primary period could well have influenced the way in which the public viewed these matters in the fall. A party's image might be harmed, for example, if the primary coverage revealed its "serious rifts and associations with extremism" (Ceaser and Busch, 1997, p. 83).

The voters were told from the start that the primaries were a chance for "the voice of the people" to be heard. When parties ignored the primary outcomes, another power of the primaries became evident: they aroused and built expectations in the voters which, if ignored, might cause problems in party unity. In 1912 and 1952, for example, the primary winners and front-runners Theodore Roosevelt and Estes Kefauver[2] were cast aside by the party conventions, and other nominees were selected instead. The parties lost resoundingly in the fall elections in both cases. Though other factors played a role in these outcomes, it is clear that the enthusiasm and commitment to one candidate developed in the primary period did not automatically transfer to a rival candidate.

PART II: 1996 AND BEYOND

To what extent did the communication patterns of the candidates and media in the past foretell those of 1996? The 1996 primaries bore close resemblance to those of earlier years, in that (1) they were treated as important by candidates and the media; (2) the media covered them as a dramatic conflict and focused upon the personal traits of the candidates; and (3) several candidates showed remarkable inventiveness in shaping the media agenda and reaching the voters. One unique development in state laws clearly modified the communication patterns in the 1996 primaries: the front-loading of the primary schedule. Two other developments also deserve mention—the evolution of computer technology and the growing role of talk radio—although they affected a limited number of voters.

More Republicans entered the Republican primaries in 1996 than in any previous year: a total of 11 announced in 1995, dropping to 9 by 1996. Republican turnout was at an all-time high, especially in the early primaries, with almost 14,000,000 people voting in 40 states and the District of Columbia (*Congressional Quarterly Weekly Report*, August 3, 1996, p. 63). On the Democratic side, President Clinton as the incumbent started with a natural advantage in securing renomination. He also managed to discourage any possible opposition by raising a war chest of $26.8 million by the end of 1995, as well as having $11 million in campaign matching funds (Mayer, in Pomper, 1997). Though he ran unopposed, his name appeared on the ballot in 32 states and the District of Columbia, he campaigned in many of those states, and over 10 million Democrats voted in the primaries (*Congressional Quarterly Weekly Report*, August 17, 1996, p. 79).

The media in 1996 also gave the primaries much attention. Although the proportion of people who said they watched television news declined from 74% in 1994 to 59% in 1996 (Pew Center for the People and the Press, 1996), television still remained the predominant news source and will be the main emphasis here. Coverage of the primaries on network evening newscasts was actually 20% higher than in 1992 during the January 1–March 26 primary period, even though there was no contest in the Democratic primary (*Media Monitor*, March/April 1996). In the January 24–March 13 period, 30% of the lead stories on network television focused on the primaries, far more than on any other topic during that period.[3]

Some state legislatures acted to move their 1996 primary and caucus dates earlier. Louisiana chose to hold its caucuses on February 6, before Iowa's; Delaware chose to hold its primary on February 24, only four days after New Hampshire's; New York moved its primary from April to March 7, five days before Super Tuesday; and California moved up its primary by more than two months, to March 26, "aiming to give the state a more decisive role in Presidential campaigns" ("Bill for Earlier Primary," *New York Times*, September 10, 1993). This front-loading resulted in the greatest compression of the primary schedule to date and forced candidates to announce their candidacies earlier, to raise money earlier, and to use pre-primary contests to prove their viability and to attract media attention. Governor Lamar Alexander remarked that "the combination of federal limits on fund-raising and the bunching of primaries . . . pushed the real presidential race backwards into 1995"; he reported that he had attended 250 fund-raisers in 1995 (Alexander, 1997, p. 33).

The media coverage of the 1996 primaries reflected this change. As in previous years, the early Iowa caucuses (February 12) and the New Hampshire primary (February 20) received the greatest coverage, with the three television networks devoting 92 stories to Iowa and 98 stories to New Hampshire on their evening news in the January 1–March 26 period (*Media Monitor*, March/April 1996, p. 2). But Pat Buchanan's earlier wins in the Alaska "straw poll" caucus against Steve Forbes on January 30, and the Louisiana caucuses of February 6 against Phil Gramm also were treated as significant milestones. Buchanan rose rapidly in the polls, closing in on Dole and Forbes. By February 11, NBC anchor Tom Brokaw remarked: "There's a media frenzy in Iowa this year, the likes of which I have never seen in all the years that these caucuses have been going on (NBC, February 11, 1996).

With Dole's decisive victory in the South Carolina primary on March 2, in which he defeated Buchanan, Alexander, and Forbes, his opponents began to abandon ship. Gramm had withdrawn earlier, Senator Richard Lugar and Alexander dropped out on March 6, and Forbes dropped out on March 14. On March 9, only 18 days after the New Hampshire primary, the networks began to speak as though the primary contest was over. Media coverage dropped off precipitously from March on, true to the pattern found in primaries throughout history: no contest = no coverage. Primaries in some of the biggest, most important states—Illinois, Michigan, Ohio, and Wisconsin—"scarcely merited mention in the evening news" (Ceaser and Busch, 1997, p. 60). When coverage during the entire January–July 1996 period is considered, "the networks' 1996 election coverage was down 43% compared with 1992 and down a whopping 51% compared with 1988" (Tyndall, 1996, p. 4).

The media's treatment of the primaries as a dramatic conflict or horse race continued in 1996, with 47% of the network evening news stories in the January 1–March 26 period focused on the horse race, "up almost 50% from Campaign '92." Less than 30% of the coverage featured the policy debate, with the top stories being (1) taxes (especially the flat tax), (2) the economy, (3) jobs, (4) international trade, and (5) the federal budget (*Media Monitor*, March/April 1996, p. 2).

The personal traits of candidates again drew heavy media attention. Candidate issues, such as "controversies over the campaign trail conduct of the candidates or their staffs," received 29% of the network news coverage in the January 1–March 26, 1996 period (*Media Monitor*, March/April 1996, p. 2). As Goldman et al. have pointed out, "the media tend . . . to see a campaign as a mirror of the candidate" (1994, p. 84). Thus the media saw Dole's "inability to generate enthusiasm, . . . lack of a clear 'message,' and disorder in his campaign organization" as serious problems that were causally related (Just, in Pomper, 1997, p. 94).

In contrast to their critical attention to Dole's tactics, the media's coverage of Clinton dwelt much more on his ethics, particularly on stories of the Whitewater hearings during the primaries (lead stories on early evening network television on January 25, 26, and 30, and February 5, 1996). But more than any other characterization, Clinton appeared in his official capacity as president, offsetting the Whitewater portrayal of a dishonest and an unethical man with his image as a leader of the nation, competent, compassionate, firm in standing up to Congress and Cuba, signer of important bills, taking the lead in cooling tensions between Taiwan and China, and working hard to counter international terrorism.

The tendency of candidates to use the term *fighter* was less conspicuous and central in 1996 than in past primaries, not the stuff of big type or advertising themes. In glossy campaign pamphlets distributed in New Hampshire, for example, occasional references could be found to Dole, Buchanan, and Alexander as fighters for desired policies ("Bob Dole's Agenda for New Hampshire's Future," "Pat Buchanan: Reclaiming The American Dream," "Lamar Alexander for President"). A few television ads promoted a fighter image: Dole was "fighting for our conservative agenda" (C-SPAN tape), Buchanan was in "a fight for America" in Louisiana (Devlin tape), and Gramm "fought" against "big government-run health care" (Devlin tape). But the network news coverage identified one clear fighter: Pat Buchanan. In the January 24–March 13 period, candidates were labeled as fighters 17 times: Buchanan, 11; Dole, 3; Forbes, 2; and Alexander, 1 (see footnote 3). The heavy coverage of the fighter against the odds had been characteristic of the media's depiction of both Clinton and Buchanan in 1992. Though national reporters do not tend to agree with Buchanan's views, their 1996 portrayal of his tremendously energetic, defiant campaign and his vivid fighting language was far from negative. It is true that he met the criterion for the "fighter" label because he had such dramatic changes in fortune, both in winning and losing, but that also was true of Dole and Forbes. The journalists liked Buchanan—he was one of them.

In the 1996 primaries, Forbes and Clinton displayed remarkable inventiveness in shaping the media agenda and reaching the voters through unique rhetorical strategies. Rather than beginning his campaign with the usual biographical ads, Forbes went immediately to ads that "emphasized a single issue position: replacing the graduated income tax with a 15 percent flat tax. With this issue he seized control of the discourse," expanding the influence of his ads with January 1996 cover stories in *Time* and *Newsweek* (Just, in Pomper, 1997, p. 79). He "had almost unlimited resources [and] spent over $40 million . . . in only about five months" (Reed, Institute of Politics, 1997, p. 11). Other candidates found in their research that "Steve Forbes and flat tax were synonymous" (Reed, Institute of Politics, 1997, p. 75), and a January 1996 *New York Times*/CBS poll reported that "58% of voters had heard or read about the flat tax, up from 34% the previous year" (Just, in Pomper, 1997, p. 79). While eventually Forbes lost momentum under a barrage of public criticism for trying to "buy the election," and under attack by Dole for his "risky ideas" and "untested leadership" (Fabrizio, Institute of Politics, 1997, p. 75), his single-issue strategy took him farther than anyone had expected.

Clinton had been successful in getting his message across in the 1992 primaries, and he continued this pattern in 1996. Two highly effective rhetorical strategies used were (1) running early and continuous issue advertising through the Democratic National Committee (DNC), and (2) shaping the State of the Union Address to highlight his major campaign themes. The two strategies shared the same goals, devised for all of his messages by his advertising firm, his advisers, and himself. The campaign set out to "infuse everything the president did with a sense of optimism," "talk about values as opposed to programs," and "talk in terms of unity, not class," as well as emphasizing the good economy (Knapp, in Devlin, 1997, p. 1059). The president would "act Presidential," modeling his approach on that of President Reagan in 1984 (Scott, 1996).

The DNC advertising, which was attacked by the Republican Party (Black, 1997) and by the organization Common Cause for violating campaign spending laws, ran from late June 1995 until the Democratic Convention, August 1996. Democrats defended the ads as "issue advocacy ads in support of a legislative agenda of the President and the Congress" (Knight, Institute of Politics, 1997, p. 119). In December 1998, the Federal Election Commission finally decided not to order the parties to repay their spending for party ads. Of the 40 ads produced by the DNC, Devlin (1997) reports that about 10 ran in the pre-primary period, 20 in the primary period, and 10 more after the primaries. As Richard Morris, a major Clinton adviser, reported, "Week after week, month after month, from early July 1995 more or less continually . . . we bombarded the public with ads," running them in the key swing states and seeing Clinton go up in the polls where the ads ran (Morris, 1997, pp. 138–139). Clinton, in videotaped remarks to donors on December 7, 1995, told of the effects of these ads: "I cannot overstate to you the impact that these paid ads have had in the areas where they run . . . we are basically doing 10 to 15 points better than in the areas where we are not showing them" (Common Cause news release, October 28, 1997).

The DNC ads were mainly comparative, attacking Republican policy and praising President Clinton's policies on issues such as assault weapons, Medicare, and the "Gingrich–Dole Budget Plan." In one ad, for example, the Republicans were accused of wanting "double premiums and deductibles," "no coverage under [age] 67," and $270 billion in cuts on Medicare, while the president (shown working at a desk) wanted to "cut waste, control costs, save Medicare, balance the budget." In one strong ad warning of Republican designs on Medicare, Dole and Gingrich were each shown speaking out firmly against Medicare, a convincing use of their own words as evidence against them. In at least two of the DNC ads aired, Dole and Gingrich were shown together in a black-and-white visual in which "Dole appeared to slide from left to right behind Gingrich as a kind of *éminence grise*, while the voice-over accused the pair of threatening Medicare" (Just, in Pomper, 1997, p. 83).

The Republicans also ran anti-Clinton and pro-Dole ads in the pre-primary and primary periods. One anti-Clinton ad, starting in November 1995, made him look foolish and indecisive, as he was shown in many different speeches saying that he would balance the budget . . . in "five years," "seven years," "nine years," "ten years," "eight years," and so on, but this was one of only two party ads in the pre-primary period. Most of the Republican National Committee (RNC) spending occurred when the real primary race had ended, in May and June 1996, when Dole had run out of money. Sheila Burke, senior adviser in the Dole–Kemp '96 campaign, acknowledged that the Dole campaign had failed to realize the significance of the Democratic attacks on Medicare and were not prepared to respond adequately (Institute of Politics, 1997).

Clinton's handling of the State of the Union Address in 1996 was a second significant rhetorical decision in the campaign. The State of the Union Address is a speech the media cover heavily.[4] The Clinton campaign decided to use this speech and the Clinton acceptance speech at the convention "to bookend the issues" which they wanted to emphasize, laying out the campaign outline (Knight, Institute of Politics, 1997, p. 16). The speech stressed Clinton's accomplishments, emphasized the good economic news, and moved to the middle politically, proclaiming that, "The age of big government is over." He introduced a series of proposals to help the American family: expanding family leave, the V-chip, the Internet in the schools, college tuition tax breaks, portable health care, and school uniforms. The speech was upbeat in its style and content. According to Clinton's pollster, Mark Penn, the speech effects "began a repositioning in terms of what Democrats were saying about the economy and the President. . . . By the time we got into the spring, everybody was beginning to agree that the economy itself was moving in the right direction. And the President began to get a lot of credit for that" (Institute of Politics, 1997, p. 122).

There is no doubt that this speech was a resounding success as portrayed in the media. As Gwen Ifill said, "Bill Clinton was generally praised for his upbeat, polished address" (NBC, January 24, 1996). The success seemed all the greater because of the negative portrayal of Dole's "Republican Response to the President's State of the Union Address."

> Because of equal time laws, Pat Buchanan can no longer host *Cross-fire*, and Bob Dole can no longer host *Tales from the Crypt*.
>   —David Letterman

Dole's Response to the State of the Union Address was discussed often on the news in the next three weeks, criticized by Republican leaders and rival candidates as too "confrontational" (Gwen Ifill, NBC, January

24, 1996) and as "a shaky performance" (Phil Jones, CBS, February 12, 1996). According to Scott Reed, campaign manager for Dole–Kemp '96, the Dole campaign, feeling hard pressed by Forbes and others in the primaries, had decided to design a speech "that was ideological in nature to play toward the primary and caucus voters, not to play generally" (Institute of Politics, 1997, p. 73). The contrast with the Clinton speech was sharp, both in the delivery and content. Dole spoke to the camera, in a silent room, whereas Clinton spoke to a demonstrative joint session of Congress; Dole's voice was somewhat flat and lacking in feeling, whereas Clinton's resonated with energy and confidence; Dole gave a clearly partisan address, attacking President Clinton by name and linking him with "our country's elites," "meddlesome government," and "a discredited status quo." In his harshest sentence, he charged, "It is as though our government and our institutions and our culture have been hijacked by liberals and are careening dangerously off course." The managers of the Forbes and Alexander campaigns reported that the State of the Union Address had an electric effect on their campaigns. With Forbes, "It was almost like Dole collapsed with the State of the Union. Then all of a sudden, we filled the vacuum" (McLaughlin, Institute of Politics, 1997, p. 78). With Alexander, "We started the 'Alexander beats Clinton' [message] at that point. It was largely focused around one single thing—Clinton's extraordinary State of the Union Address and the weak Dole performance" (Griffith, Institute of Politics, 1997, p. 76). Gramm said after the speech, "it was clear to anybody who watched . . . that "Bob Dole cannot and will not beat Bill Clinton" ("Rivals Pile On," January 25, 1996, *The Hotline*).

One of the obvious changes in campaigning in the modern era is the compression of the news cycle. As James Carville remarked, "Now thirty seconds after the event, it goes on over CNN News. There's no time to reflect" (Carville, 1997). In an attempt to deal with this pressure to get and distribute information fast, candidates have used new computer technologies. In 1992, the Clinton general election campaign had made use of e-mail, and the expectation was that the Internet would be a major factor in the 1996 primaries. By the end of 1995, all major presidential candidates had web sites (Freedom Forum, April 1996). But there is little evidence that these pages had any particular impact on the primaries. A Media Studies Center/Roper survey in early 1996 "found that less than 5% of the public has ever visited a governmental or politically oriented World Wide Web site, and, of these, most are 'news junkies' who . . . are high consumers of several news media" (Swanson, 1997, pp. 1276–1277).

Although the new computer technologies did not have much direct influence on voters, they helped speed up the exchange of information within the press corps and the campaign staffs, where modem-equipped laptop computers were much in evidence and subscription news lines for journalists enabled them to get fast-breaking news. Clearinghouse sites, such as Campaign '96 Online, AllPolitics, B/CS Presidential Campaign Tour & Opinion Page, NetVote, PoliticsUSA, ElectionLine, and Vote Smart Web helped people find information fast (Freedom Forum, April 1996).

Talk radio, another new trend away from the traditional media, continued to grow, more than tripling in the number of programs from the late 1980s (Herbst, 1995; Jones, 1994). Rush Limbaugh alone had 20 million listeners on 650 stations (St. George, 1994). During the pre-primary and primary periods in 1996, large numbers of conservative Republicans participated actively in talk radio, discussing the Republican primary candidates, with a particular focus on arguments about Pat Buchanan (Jones, 1997). Pfau et al. (1998) found that among registered Republicans who used political talk radio just before the primaries began, this medium influenced their perception of candidates more than any other communication source.

EXPECTATIONS FOR 2000

In many respects the 2000 primaries are likely to resemble those of 1996, with numerous candidates, a heavily front-loaded primary schedule, and an early decision on the nominees. After observing the effects of front-loading in 1996, the Republican National Convention established a task force to change party rules to prevent such extreme crowding of the early primary schedule. They adopted a system of incentives, giving states bonus convention delegates if they would hold their primaries later (Republican National Convention, 1996). But most states decided to do just the opposite: instead they moved their primaries to an earlier date. Why hold a primary late, they reasoned, after most of the candidates have dropped out and there is little choice or chance for influence?

The 2000 primary schedule is so compressed that the presidential nominees are likely to be known by mid-March at the latest, perhaps even by March 7. The majority of primaries are concentrated in a single month. After the Iowa caucuses on January 31 and the New Hampshire primary on February 1, several other states will hold primaries in February, such as the South Carolina Republican Party on February 19, Michigan and the Arizona Republican Party on February 22, and Washington on February 29. (States were still changing dates as this book went to press.) As many as 16 states are scheduled to hold primaries on March 7; because of the presence of both California and New York in this group, some are referring to it as a "bicoastal primary." Four days later, on Saturday, March 11, many Western states will have primaries, and March 14 will be "Super Tuesday," including the large states of Florida, Texas, Michigan, and Illinois, and most of the Southern states.

As in 1996, the Republicans are trying to take back the White House, and this time there is no incumbent president to run against. At first there were 12 candidates: Elizabeth Dole, Gary Bauer (head of the Family Research Council), Steve Forbes, Lamar Alexander, Senator Robert Smith of New Hampshire, former Vice President Dan Quayle, Rep. John R. Kasich of Ohio, Senator John McCain of Arizona, Governor George W. Bush of Texas, Senator Orrin Hatch of Utah, Pat Buchanan, and Alan Keyes (radio talk show host and former diplomat). By mid-August 1999, Kasich, Smith, and Alexander had dropped out, leaving nine Republicans. Among the Democrats, Vice President Al Gore operated from a position of strength with eight years of vice-presidential experience, support from President Clinton, and an ample war chest; these formidable advantages discouraged other candidates from running. In January 1999, Gore gained one prominent Democratic rival when former New Jersey Senator and NBA player Bill Bradley officially became a candidate.

Candidates entered the race earlier and raised money faster than in previous years. Twelve Republicans and two Democrats had already entered by summer 1999. Bush's announcement on June 30, 1999 that he had already raised $36.3 million in campaign donations and would not accept federal matching funds was a stunning event, confirming his clear front-runner status. By July 14, he had been endorsed by more than half of the Republican governors, senators, and members of the House of Representatives. Gore, too, had a strong lead among Democratic elected officials who would automatically be convention delegates.

For a time in the summer of 1999 it seemed as though the 2000 primaries would be superfluous, that the nominees had already been chosen. Without adopting any systematic rules changes, the party leaders seemed to have seized control, selected the candidates, and pre-empted the primaries. Yet no one had voted. As in past elections, most people were not even paying attention during the pre-primary period. According to a CBS News poll conducted early in August 1999, "only nine percent of registered voters" claimed to be "paying much attention to the Presidential race" (Richard L. Berke, "For Lamar Alexander, the End of the Line," *New York Times*, August 17, 1999, p. A14).

The August 14, 1999 Republican straw poll in Iowa helped to open up the campaign again. Though the straw poll chooses no delegates and is merely a "beauty contest" with a poor record of predicting party nominees, it is widely seen as a measure of the candidates' organizational skill. By that measure, Alexander, who had been campaigning ever since the end of the 1996 campaign, ran only sixth and dropped out, and Quayle appeared to be in a much weakened condition when he only secured 916 of the almost 24,000 votes cast. The top four finishers, Bush, Forbes, Dole, and Bauer, received more attention from the press, as did McCain, who had ridiculed and refused to enter the straw poll. Bush seemed less invincible; though he had received 31% of the votes, other candidates had received 69%.

Speeches

The candidates travelled extensively in 1999, speaking with audiences as the media looked on. In this section the author looks for clues as to how the candidates might perform during the primaries, based on the pre-primary period of 1999.

Both Democratic candidates have been portrayed as dull speakers. Gore was the subject of a series of "Doonesbury" cartoons about his speaking in August 1999, with Clinton trying to give him advice on how to enliven his speech style. Journalists teased him about trying to change his delivery to sound more exciting, and noted how stiff he looked in appearances with Clinton. However, they credited Gore for his intensive focus on issues, covering more issues and in more detail than any of the other candidates. He clearly recognized the importance of the image trait of *competence* in politics. In his announcement speech he proposed helping to make pre-school available to all children, prescription drugs for seniors, expanding community policing, a patient's bill of rights, and other specific proposals for government action (Adam Clymer, "In Words, Gore and Bush Stake Out Middle," *New York Times*, June 20, 1999, p. 24).

Gore's reputation for being dull lowers audience expectations, which may have its advantages. The author has seen him delight a large audience of students with his vigorous, humorous, and well-adapted speech, and move New Hampshire audiences with his discussion of smoking and lung cancer. He has also demonstrated his effectiveness in debates, not only the vice-presidential debates, but also the NAFTA debate with Ross Perot.

Bradley, too, was portrayed as a dull speaker. Stephanie Salter of the *San Francisco Examiner* reported, "The man is a sound-bite disaster, about as pithy as a rice cake, about as witty as Janet Reno" ("Bradley Refuses to Play Political Ball," in Albany *Times Union*, June 19, 1999, p. A7). More sympathetic coverage noted that he was conducting a remarkable one-on-one campaign with voters; Bradley called it a "person-to-person" campaign (Todd S. Purdum, "Bradley Takes on California, One on One," *New York Times*, June 17, 1999, p. A27). Criticized by Gore supporters for vagueness, Bradley became increasingly specific as the campaign progressed, advocating strong gun control measures, universal health care, ending child poverty, improving race relations, and other clear positions on issues.

Among the Republicans, Pat Buchanan retained his reputation as a dynamic speaker, delivering "a typical stemwinder that had the crowd cheering repeatedly" at the Iowa straw poll (Dan Balz and David S. Broder, "Bush Notches Victory in Iowa," *Washington Post*, in Albany *Times Union*, August 15, 1999, pp. A1, A10). He was the only Republican opposed to NAFTA, and took a strong antiwar position on the nation's policy in Kosovo. Low on funds and low in the polls, he did not seem to have the power to threaten the front-runners, but his past record suggests he could surprise everyone again. As of fall 1999, he was actively exploring the possibility of a third-party candidacy.

Bush, the clear front-runner among the Republicans, "delivered a lackluster speech" at the Iowa straw poll, and "has a lot of work to do on his platform style" ("The New Republican Landscape," *New York Times*, August 17, 1999, p. A16; R. W. Apple Jr., "A Gregarious Bush Warms to Politicking," *New York Times*, August 21, 1999, p. A8). But in private talks and meeting people individually, he was exceptionally good, "a personable and charismatic campaigner" who was compared to Bill Clinton (Adam Nagourney, "As Bush Begins Campaigning in Earnest, Details Take Back Seat to Packaging," *New York Times*, June 15, 1999, p. A20). Fluent in Spanish, he usually includes several Spanish sentences in his speeches, targeting the growing bloc of Hispanic voters. He focuses on broad themes rather than specifics, and opponents and the media have called on him to be more specific. Vagueness has been a characteristic of primary front-runners in the past as well. In a move reminiscent of Clinton's unique presentation of three Georgetown speeches in 1991, Bush planned to give "a series of policy speeches" in the fall of 1999.

Bush has used one expression consistently in all his speeches: "compassionate conservatism." The phrase enables him to underline his conservative credentials and appeal to a large bloc of Republicans who consider themselves conservative, while at the same time decrying mean-spirited policies and strategies, appealing to more moderate Republicans and especially to women.

McCain brought extraordinary personal credibility to his speeches, based on his five-and-a-half year ordeal as a prisoner of war in Vietnam. In addition, his strong stands on issues such as the need for campaign finance reform and for federal anti-smoking legislation have constructed an image of the maverick, the man who stands up for what he believes. He is not a particularly dynamic speaker, but audiences respond well. As Alison Mitchell reported, "He read his speech fast. . . . He forgot to pause for applause lines. But in an odd way his delivery gave him almost more authenticity to an audience . . . that seemed to be yearning for an antidote to the political slickness of the Clinton years" ("The Mantle of the Maverick Suits McCain," *New York Times*, July 7, 1999, p. 1).

McCain seems most likely to capture the mantle of "the fighter" of the 2000 campaign. He is a fighter against the front-runner, an admired war veteran, and a maverick (or fighter) in his stands on issues. On the issue of campaign finance reform, he can portray himself as a "David" fighting against the "Goliath" of unchecked spending. McCain's own language encourages this image. Branding campaign donations as "an elaborate influence peddling scheme in which both parties conspire to stay in office by selling the country to the highest bidder," he says that he will "not give up this fight" to pass a reform bill in the Senate (in Alison Mitchell, "McCain Exhorts His Party to Reject Campaign System," *New York Times*, July 1, 1999, p. A17).

Bauer built his speaking experience as head of the Family Research Council, which has 400,000 members. In his campaign speeches he has appealed to religious conservatives, and identified closely with President Reagan, for whom he worked as Under Secretary of Education and senior policy adviser, making extensive use of Reagan quotations and anecdotes. Reagan is his "running mate," he says. Reporter Frank Bruni described him as "a confident, articulate speaker with a sharp mind and quick wit" ("Casting Himself as Reagan's Heir, Bauer Strikes Conservative Chord," *New York Times*, August 17, 1999, p. A14).

Forbes has repositioned himself since the 1996 primaries. He has "crisscrossed the country building political support," stressing his newly vigorous anti-abortion position and appealing to social conservatives. "With the help of voice coaches, Mr. Forbes has also loosened up a bit on the stump" (Richard L. Berke, "Fitting Forbes for Oval Office Is Advertising Man's Assignment," *New York Times*, May 30, 1999, p. 17). He no longer focuses so narrowly on the flat tax issue, as he did in 1996. His opponents take him "much more seriously than four years ago," recognizing that he has an early start and a private fortune, and remembering how damaging his negative advertisements were to Dole in 1996 (Richard L. Berke, "Forbes Declares Candidacy on Internet and the Stump," *New York Times*, March 17, 1999, p. A19).

When Elizabeth Dole campaigned with her husband during his presidential campaigns, she often gave speeches on his behalf. All agreed she was much the better speaker: articulate, informed, vigorous, and well-organized. She gained national recognition for her confident performance at the 1996 Republican National Convention, at which she strolled through the audience with her wireless microphone, free of notes, addressing people in a friendly, interpersonal style. In her own entry into the 2000 presidential race, she has maintained this effective style, though meeting with some criticism that she is too practiced and programmed.

In Dole's pre-primary campaign she stressed that she was not a politician, trying to turn to advantage what might be seen as a shortcoming, that she has never held elective office (though she served on the Reagan and Bush cabinets). She advocated reducing taxes, increasing defense spending, and returning more federal money to localities for education. One distinctive position which won her much media coverage was her strong support of gun control measures, especially her widely quoted statement that "you don't need an AK-47 to defend your family." She also distanced herself from the abortion issue, saying that "she would not be drawn into 'dead end debates' over a constitutional amendment to ban abortion" (Todd S. Purdum, "Elizabeth Dole Is Shunning 'Dead End' Abortion Fight," *New York Times*, April 10, 1999, p. A10).

Women have proved a supportive audience for Dole. While in all federal elections women account for only 25% of campaign donations, close to half of Dole's contributions have come from women. And "large number[s] of women, especially young women not much involved in politics . . . turn out whenever she makes a campaign stop" (B. Drummond Ayres, Jr., "Women to the Rescue of Elizabeth Dole," *New York Times*, July 22, 1999, p. A16).

Media Coverage

In past campaigns, when a presidential candidate gave an announcement speech, there was certain to be good press coverage. In fact, for many candidates, their *only* major coverage came when they announced and when they withdrew from the primaries. That changed in 1999, with the press becoming more parsimonious in their coverage, because the candidates broke their announcements into so many separate events: "announcing an intention to form an exploratory committee, announcing the committee, announcing the plan to announce and the announcement itself" (Adam Clymer, "In Words, Gore and Bush Stake Out Middle," *New York Times*, June 20, 1999, p. 24).

What did command enormous press coverage was George Bush's candidacy. NBC showed two segments on his campaign on June 14, and he appeared on the covers of both *Time* and *Newsweek* on June 21, coverage usually reserved for much later in the campaign. Factors influencing this attention were his huge lead in fund-raising, his first place in the polls, and the media's own observation of enthusiastic public response to his first national campaigning effort.

The media began to raise questions about Bush's character in August 1999. Felicity Barringer of the *New York Times* ("When an Old Drug Question Becomes New News," August 22, 1999, p. 28) traced the evolution of the question of his cocaine use, which was dismissed for lack of proof in a May 1999 *Wall Street Journal* article, and surfaced again on August 5 when the New York *Daily News* reported having asked the 12 presidential candidates whether they had ever used cocaine (11 denied using it, Bush avoided a direct answer). The story was then covered by Fox News and several large newspapers, emerging in the *Washington Post* on August 11. Another precipitant of anti-Bush discussion was Tucker Carlson's interview with Bush in the first issue of *Talk* magazine. Columnist

George Will described the interview as suggesting "an atmosphere of adolescence, a lack of gravitas . . . a seriousness deficit" ("Bush Is Taking Republicans for a Ride," Albany *Times Union*, August 12, 1999, p. A13).

The story subsided briefly during the coverage of the Iowa straw poll of August 14, in which Bush emerged the winner. But the cocaine story came to the fore immediately afterward, covered by CBS, ABC, and NBC News, the *Los Angeles Times*, the *Washington Post*, and the *New York Times*. Bush's defensive statements only increased the focus, as he went from a refusal to discuss the question to implications that he had not used drugs for 25 years. The treatment of this issue is a vivid example of the inevitable focus on candidate image in the primaries, when same-party candidates generally disagree little on major policy issues. It also shows the close link between images and issues. Republicans in this campaign were comparing their own "good" character to Clinton's moral failings, which left them open to the charge of hypocrisy. Bush was vulnerable because he had advocated strong anti-drug use policies as governor of Texas.

In the short term, at least, the drug controversy did not seem to undermine Bush's position. In an ABC News poll and a CNN/Time survey, respondents said that if he confessed to cocaine use as a young man, their opinions would not change (B. Drummond Ayres, Jr., "Voters Seem Inclined to Forgive and Forget," *New York Times*, August 25, 1999, p. A20). The subject did provoke the first sharp attack on Bush by a Republican rival; Bauer told reporters that Bush should answer the question about his cocaine use, saying, "I don't believe a question about a felony should be brushed aside" (Judy Holland, "GOP Says Bush's Silence Golden," Albany *Times Union*, August 30, 1999, p. A6).

New Technologies

The proliferation and speeding up of news coverage has continued since the 1996 primaries, resulting in heavy early coverage of the 2000 pre-primary period. Bill Kovach and Tom Rosenstiel have called this escalation of the pace of news "warp speed" (1999), and point to the difficulties in knowing the accuracy of this torrent of news. CNN, MSNBC, and Fox News Channel have 24-hour news cycles, television newsmagazines such as NBC's *Dateline*, ABC's *20/20*, and CBS's *60 Minutes* have added more nights to their schedules, and the Internet has grown by leaps and bounds. The news media have their own Web sites (such as abcnews.com, cnn.com, usatoday.com, nytimes.com), and increasingly they update their stories as they develop. Just as with radio news in the 1952 primaries, so in 1999 there was a voracious demand for something new to fill the frequent news broadcasts, and the multi-candidate, multi-state presidential primaries and caucuses helped to meet that demand.

The presidential candidates in 1999 were much more advanced in their understanding of the Internet than in 1996. All had Web sites, sometimes several of them, and they were updated daily. They could distribute any messages they wished through their Web pages, in their own words, without media intervention. Davis (1999) has identified six functions which candidate Web pages can serve: (1) to symbolize that the candidate is "current with the times, even futuristic in approach" (p. 98), (2) to disseminate information, (3) as an opinion gauge, (4) to reinforce vote choice and the get-out-the-vote campaign, (5) to identify volunteers and raise funds, and (6) to spur interactivity. The Forbes and McCain Web pages illustrate these functions in action, and show how far the craft has come since 1996, when Web sites were relatively static, serving more like bulletin boards.

Forbes officially launched his 2000 presidential campaign on his new Web site on March 16, 1999 (www.Forbes.2000.com). Making heavy use of photos, speeches, and links to news media and to state and national party organizations, the site also tried innovations such as an e-mail newsletter and a "Lead an E-Precinct" section, which recruited online precinct leaders for Forbes.

McCain's Web site has audio and video clips of his speeches and interviews, provided live by INTERVU, the Internet service provider. These can be downloaded from www.mccain2000.com. People can also arrange to view them at their convenience. Not only does the site provide information, but it is also used "to recruit campaign volunteers, attract small donations, organize supporters across the country through e-mail and daily Web updates about the candidate's appearances, and do it all in a cost-effective way" (PRNewswire, "John McCain Pioneers Creative Internet Strategy for His Presidential Campaign," San Diego, CA, June 9, 1999).

The most practical political use of the Internet may be as a place to organize groups of like-minded people to discuss political issues and causes, similar to the role of talk radio (Bentivegna, 1998). Candidates such as Forbes have ventured into this area with their use of e-mail newsletters and efforts to recruit and encourage online precinct leaders.

Claims abound that the Internet will "revolutionize" the political process, and there certainly has been a broadening of political communication through the Internet since 1996, on the local, state, and national level. But it is still true that there are many more people in America with access to television sets (100 million households) than to the Internet (37 million households) (Stuart Elliott, "Advertising," *New York Times*, July 23, 1999, p. C6). Presidential primary candidates in 2000 will use traditional means to reach the habitual users of television, newspapers, and magazines, as well as advertising their Internet sites through these media.

Advertising

It is too early to analyze the advertising campaigns of the primary candidates. The parties will be spending "soft money" for issue advertisements, as in 1996; the Republican National Committee made heavy use of such ads in the 1998 elections. Forbes has already begun major advertising, focussing not on the flat tax, but on the importance of families. Much of the money raised during 1999 will be spent on advertising as the primaries grow closer.

Campaign Financing

Prominent candidates in both 1992 (Perot) and 1996 (Forbes) chose to use their personal fortunes to campaign, and thus were not bound by the constraints of the campaign finance laws. In 2000 Forbes and Bush will not have to observe the spending limits of the other candidates, as they are not accepting matching funds. Though there is evidence that public disgust with the campaign finance system is growing, particularly regarding the use of "soft money," and new efforts to pass legislation are expected in the House and Senate in the fall of 1999, when this book went to press there had not yet been any strengthening of the laws.

Having a huge bankroll doesn't guarantee anyone's nomination—witness the cases of Perot and Forbes, as well as Governor John B. Connally of Texas in 1980 and Senator Phil Gramm of Texas in the 1996 primaries (Connally spent $13 million in the primaries and gained only one delegate; Gramm raised at least $20 million but failed to win over voters, withdrawing before the New Hampshire primary). But such wealth can create the impression that no one else has a chance. For a time that was the situation in the summer of 1999, when Bush was treated as the actual nominee, long before anyone had voted.

PRINCIPLES FOR CHANGE

Many reforms have been proposed for the primaries. Reformers strive for a campaign context encouraging "thoughtful discussion of alternative solutions" to societal problems (Andersen and Thorson, 1989, p. 274). They maintain that these conditions do not exist at present, that the present system of primaries is "madness," "a high-speed demolition derby" (Broder, "Marching," *Washington Post*, in the Schenectady, New York *Gazette*, March 3, 1996).

Proposals for change take two main forms, either reforms in the scheduling of the primaries or changes in the basic principles underlying the primaries. Those who would change the primaries' schedule or timing generally oppose both the compression of the schedule and the early caucuses and primaries of states like Iowa and New Hampshire, arguing that these states are too small and idiosyncratic. Scheduling reforms include a national primary, regional primaries, or grouped primaries. In a national primary everyone would vote on the same date. An example of the grouped primary plan is that of Representative Morris K. Udall to hold primaries on the first Tuesdays of March, April, May, and June; the states could choose any of these dates. In the regional primary system, uniform primary dates would be designated for states in each region of the country (such as four regions), with a break in time between them (Mann, in Grassmuck, 1985; Geer, 1989). Another proposal is to schedule the primaries much later, perhaps starting in late May or early June 2000 for six to eight weeks (Patterson, 1993). (Note: States do seem to be moving toward a kind of highly compressed and early regional primary system by their own choice, but it looks nothing like any of the more stretched-out regional reform proposals.)

A second major approach to reform is more fundamental; it would return to the strong party system of nomination, shifting away from strong primaries. Advocates of such reforms want to reestablish the power of the parties and reduce the power of candidates. They would do this by such measures as increasing the number of caucuses (which parties are better able to control) and of state party conventions (Patterson, 1993; Busch, 1997), by decreasing the number of primaries, and giving more of the choice of candidates to party leaders (David Broder, in John Charles Daly, moderator, *Choosing Presidential Candidates* [Washington, DC: American Enterprise Institute, 1980], pp. 2–3), and by increasing the number of unpledged convention superdelegates, who are party leaders and elected officials, as a way to better screen the candidates (Al From, Democratic Leadership Council, "Current System," on C-SPAN, June 13, 1988; Michael R. Beschloss, "Let's Have Conventions with Cliffhangers," *New York Times*, August 11, 1996, Sect. 4, p. 13).

The author is doubtful that any of these proposals would succeed. First, any plan for the specific sequencing of groups of primaries overlooks the fact that *the early primaries lead the way.* Whichever primaries come first, in whichever reform plan, will frame the election and undoubtedly establish the nominee early. Furthermore, though the party leaders might prevail over the passionate objections of Iowa and New Hampshire and force them to change their caucus and primary dates (earlier efforts have failed), there is a serious question about the wisdom of this change. The voters in early primaries like New Hampshire have a long record of paying close attention to the primaries and subjecting the candidates to more intensive scrutiny than other states. They have earned their role as a kind of "advance guard" which tests the mettle of the candidates.

Second, the proposal to return to the dominance of party leaders ignores the power of habitual behavior, including the growing democratization of the nominating process, the habits of the media in investigating and describing the candidates, and the habits of the candidates in running their own campaigns. Just as new Republican Party incentives to stretch out the primaries failed in 2000, so would any party attempt to overthrow or dilute the primaries run into strong resistance. Defenders of the primary system would surely arise again to defend the "voice of the people" against the "bosses." Do the parties want to fight that battle again?

The course of action the author proposes is to make no sweeping changes in the present primary rules. What can and should be changed, however, are the ways in which voters are informed about the primaries and the laws regarding campaign finance. With multiple candidates running, it is difficult for voters to make an intelligent choice. With such loose and ineffective laws regarding campaign finance, independently wealthy candidates and the favorites of special interests have an unwarranted advantage. The author will focus on *the need to improve communication with the voter*. The topic of campaign finance reform, while related, requires another book.

Thomas Jefferson expressed confidence in the wisdom of the public, who, he said, "may safely be trusted to hear everything true and false, and to form a correct judgment between them" (in Chaffee and Frank, 1996, p. 49). Certainly this is the ideal, an optimistic vision. In an ideal world of presidential primaries, (1) voters would learn enough about the primary candidates to feel that they could make a well-informed choice, (2) the candidates would be able to communicate with the voters, and (3) the media would assist both voters and candidates in this process, providing plentiful, timely, and accurate information and expert analysis.

Taken together, the media do meet these goals. Anyone making careful use of multiple news sources can learn enough to make a wise choice. Candidates supplement the news with paid advertising and Web pages that contain information about themselves and their positions.

However, there are large obstacles on the road to utopia. Busy voters catch their news when and where they can, responding best to subject matter that "is made interesting and relevant to them" (Graber, 1993; Fiske and Kinder, 1981). News media with tight time and space limits often reduce the candidates' messages to sound bites, and candidates lack money to advertise enough to keep their message salient. Voters say they are dissatisfied with the coverage of the presidential primaries; in April 1996, only 38% of respondents to a national survey said they were satisfied, and 60% said they wanted more attention to a candidate's stands on policy issues (*Media Monitor*, May 1996, pp. 3–4).

The solutions clearly must involve all three parties: voters, media, and candidates. From what we know about voter political interest and involvement, it is highest in forums such as presidential debates and talk radio and in situations such as close elections, scandals, and stories of personal lives. It peaks as Election Day draws near. One of the most successful campaign events of recent times was the presidential debates of fall 1992: four nationally televised debates in eight days, "like a television miniseries in order to build viewership" (Owen, 1995, p. 145). They were widely publicized, held in the last month before Election Day in a closely contested election, full of argument about policy and information about the individual personalities, and each one drawing an ever-larger audience. In exit polls, voters said that the debates were most influential in helping them make their voting decision.

The author's suggestions for change would try to capitalize on our knowledge of such successful examples of political communication. In the 2000 primaries, there should be several widely advertised and nationally televised candidate events early in the primary season, when the campaign is most contested. As with the fall debates, these events should be advertised as a package to attract maximum attention and scheduled to take advantage of the natural interest in certain key contests, such as just before the Iowa caucuses, just before the New Hampshire primary, and just before the March 7 bicoastal primaries. These might be debates, and *Meet the Press*–type interviews with the individual candidates (perhaps done back to back so that voters could make comparisons). The goals would be to attract and hold public interest, to provide information valuable for voting decisions, and to help the candidates get their messages to the voters in their own words, free.

There are some excellent proposals for improving communication with the voters already available, such as Kathleen Hall Jamieson's suggestions (1988), and the "Nine Sundays Plan" by John Ellis and the Joan Shorenstein Center on the Press, Politics and Public Policy at Harvard University. Paul Taylor and the Free TV for Straight Talk Coalition persuaded networks, PBS, and CNN to give free air time to the candidates in the fall 1996 campaign. Many of these ideas could be adapted to the primaries, and new ideas about ways to capitalize on the popularity of the Internet could be explored. But unless such events are planned so as to gain public attention and interest, they will suffer the fate of the free-time experiment of 1996: "Only about 22 percent of registered voters even knew the free-time effort existed" (Public Policy Center of the Annenberg School of Communication, in Lawrie Mifflin, "Free TV-Time Experiment Wins Support, If Not Viewers," *New York Times*, November 3, 1996, p. 38).

Whatever changes are adopted, they must take into consideration that some patterns appear to be enduring features of the presidential primary election ritual and its news coverage, recurring regularly across time. Primaries help shape the agenda for the rest of the election year, lead naturally to a focus on the personal traits of the candidates, provide dramatic conflict and negative attacks irresistible to the news media, and reward candidates who can best communicate with their audiences: the media, the party leaders, and the voters.

NOTES

1. Aldrich (1980) states that the 1960 Democratic race, in which Senator John F. Kennedy demonstrated to the party bosses that he could win in primaries against Senator Hubert H. Humphrey, "was the first nomination in which primary victories were undeniably the keystone of success" (p. 10). Even so, 1960 is still seen as a year of strong party domination of the nomination process.

2. Kefauver, winner of 12 of the 15 preference primaries, led in the polls just before the 1952 Democratic Convention: Kefauver, with 45%, Alben Barkley, 18%, Adlai Stevenson, 12%, Richard Russell, 10%, Averill Harriman, 5%. The Democrats, however, chose Stevenson as their nominee (Busch, 1997, p. 133).

3. The author examined one news broadcast each evening in the January 24–March 13, 1996 period, from early evening television coverage by ABC, CBS, NBC, and CNN ("Prime Time News"), varying the order every four nights. Of 50 broadcasts studied, there were 15 lead stories on the primaries (30% of the total). The next most frequently mentioned lead stories were four each on Whitewater and the Clintons, winter weather in the United States, and the shooting down of unarmed American civilian planes by Cuba.

4. Kendall (1993) found that the State of the Union Address was the only speech given lead stories by the evening network news programs in the 1992 presidential primary period.

Selected Bibliography

ARCHIVES AND SPECIAL COLLECTIONS

George A. Ball Papers, Seeley Mudd Library, Princeton University, Princeton, NJ
Papers of Henry Cabot Lodge II, Massachusetts Historical Society, Boston, MA
George McGovern Papers, Seeley Mudd Library, Princeton University, Princeton, NJ
Edmund S. Muskie Papers, Bates College, Lewiston, ME
Richard M. Nixon Project, National Archives
Paramount News Newsreels, National Archives
Political Communication Center, University of Oklahoma, Norman, OK
Franklin D. Roosevelt Library, Hyde Park, NY
      Papers of the Democratic National Committee
      Franklin D. Roosevelt Speech File
Sound Division, Library of Congress
Robert A. Taft Papers, Library of Congress
Universal International Newsreels, National Archives

TELEVISION NEWS BROADCASTS

1972: Vanderbilt Television Archives
      Richard M. Nixon Project, National Archives
1992: *ABC World News Tonight, CBS Evening News, NBC Nightly News*
1996: *ABC World News Tonight, CBS Evening News, CNN Prime Time, NBC Nightly News*

BOOKS, ARTICLES, INTERVIEWS

Adams, Val (March 7, 1952). "Eisenhower Group Cancels TV Series." *New York Times*, p. 14.

Adams, William C. (1987). "As New Hampshire Goes. . . ." In Gary R. Orren and Nelson W. Polsby, eds., *Media and Momentum: The New Hampshire Primary and Nomination Politics*. Chatham, NJ: Chatham House Publishers, pp. 42–59.

"Al Smith Proposes 4 P. C. Beer and Prosperity Bonds" (April 1, 1932). AP, in *Philadelphia Inquirer*, pp. 1, 6.

Aldrich, John H. (1980). *Before the Convention*. Chicago: University of Chicago Press.

Aldrich, John H. (1992). "Presidential Campaigns in Party and Candidate-Centered Eras." In Mathew D. McCubbins, ed., *Under the Watchful Eye*. Washington, DC: Congressional Quarterly Press, pp. 59–82.

Alexander, Lamar (Winter 1997). "Let Us Speak for Ourselves." *Media Studies Journal* 11, no. 1, pp. 31–34.

Alger, Dean (October 1994). "The Media, the Public and the Development of Candidates' Images in the 1992 Presidential Election." Research Paper R-14, Joan Shorenstein Center on the Press, Politics and Public Policy, Harvard University.

Alger, Dean E. (1989). "The Media in Elections: Evidence on the Role and the Impact." In Dean E. Alger, *The Media in Politics*. New York: Prentice Hall. Reprinted in Doris A. Graber, ed., *Media Power in Politics*. Washington, DC: Congressional Quarterly Press, 1990, pp. 147–160.

Ambrose, Stephen E. (1983). *Eisenhower*. New York: Simon and Schuster.

Ambrose, Stephen E. (1989). *Nixon, Volume Two: The Triumph of a Politician, 1962–1972*. New York: Simon and Schuster.

Andersen, Kristi and Stuart J. Thorson (1989). "Public Discourse or Strategic Game? Changes in Our Conception of Elections." *Studies in American Political Development* 3, pp. 263–278.

Apple, R. W., Jr. (March 3, 1972). "For Muskie, Mild Support; For McGovern, Intensity." *New York Times*, p. 18.

Apple, R. W., Jr. (March 5, 1972). "Muskie Lagging But He Still Holds Edge; First Vote Tuesday in New Hampshire." *New York Times*, p. 33.

Apple, R. W., Jr. (March 7, 1972). "Debate Without Winner." *New York Times*, p. 26.

Apple, R. W., Jr. (March 8, 1972). "Two Senators Issue Claims of Triumph in the Primary." *New York Times*, pp. 1, 26.

Apple, R. W., Jr. (March 12, 1972). "Humphrey Says He's Even with Muskie and Has '3 Chances in 7' of Being Nominated." *New York Times*, p. 43.

Apple, R. W., Jr. (March 15, 1972). "Democratic Race Widens: Muskie Concedes Setback." *New York Times*, pp. 1, 32.

Apple, R. W., Jr. (March 31, 1972). "Bellwether Town in Wisconsin Favors 3." *New York Times*, p. 18.

Apple, R. W., Jr. (April 3, 1972). "Muskie Slips in PA; McGovern Counts on Bay State." *New York Times*, p. 22.

Apple, R. W., Jr. (April 4, 1972). "Muskie Pins Hopes on Polish District as Aides Voice Concern." *New York Times*, p. 36.

Apple, R. W., Jr. (April 5, 1972). "Victor Discerns Vote of Protest." *New York Times*, pp. 1, 32.

Arendt, Hannah (August 12, 1960). Unpublished radio script, WBAI, New York, in Library of Congress. Cited in Joanna Vecchiarelli Scott, "Hannah Arendt, Campaign Pundit." *New York Times,* July 27, 1996, p. 23.

Aristotle (1954). *The Rhetoric and the Poetics of Aristotle.* W. Rhys Roberts, trans. New York: The Modern Library.

Arterton, F. Christopher (1984). *Media Politics: The News Strategies of Presidential Campaigns.* Lexington, MA: D.C. Heath.

Arterton, F. Christopher (1993). "Campaign '92: Strategies and Tactics of the Candidates." In Gerald M. Pomper et al., *The Election of 1992.* Chatham, NJ: Chatham House Publishers, pp. 74–109.

Asher, Herbert B. (1992). *Presidential Elections and American Politics,* 5th ed. Pacific Grove, CA: Brooks/Cole Publishing Company.

Atkin, C. K. (1980). "Political Campaigns: Mass Communication and Persuasion." In M. E. Roloff and G. R. Miller, eds., *Persuasion: New Directions in Theory and Research.* Beverly Hills, CA: Sage, pp. 285–308.

Atkin, C. K. and G. Heald (1976). "Effects of Political Advertising." *Public Opinion Quarterly* 40, pp. 216–228.

Auer, J. Jeffery (1962). "The Counterfeit Debates." In Sidney Kraus, ed., *The Great Debates: Kennedy vs. Nixon, 1960.* Bloomington, IN: Indiana University Press, pp. 142–150.

Bain, Richard C. (1960). *Convention Decisions and Voting Records.* Washington, DC: The Brookings Institution.

Baker, Ross K. (1993). "Sorting Out and Suiting Up: The Presidential Nominations." In Gerald M. Pomper et al., *The Election of 1992.* Chatham, NJ: Chatham House Publishers, pp. 39–73.

Baker, Russell (June 8, 1996). "Observer: Reading for Bill and Bob." *New York Times.*

Barkin, Steve M. (Fall 1983). "Eisenhower's Television Planning Board." *Journal of Broadcasting and Electronic Media* 27, no. 4, pp. 319–331.

Barone, Michael (1990). *Our Country: The Shaping of America from Roosevelt to Reagan.* New York: The Free Press.

Bartels, Larry M. (1988). *Presidential Primaries and the Dynamics of Public Choice.* Princeton, NJ: Princeton University Press.

Becker, Samuel L. and Elmer W. Lower (1979). "Broadcasting in Presidential Campaigns, 1960–1976." In Sidney Kraus, ed., *The Great Debates: Carter vs. Ford, 1976.* Bloomington, IN: Indiana University Press, pp. 11–40.

Beniger, James R. (Spring 1976). "Winning the Presidential Nomination: National Polls and State Primary Elections, 1936–1972." *Public Opinion Quarterly* 40, pp. 22–38.

Bennett, W. Lance (1996). *News: The Politics of Illusion,* 3d ed. White Plains, NY: Longman.

Bentivegna, Sara (August 1998). "Talking Politics on the Net." Research Paper R-20, Joan Shorenstein Center on the Press, Politics and Public Policy, Harvard University.

Bernstein, James M. (1996). "The Use of Nontraditional Media in Campaign '92 and Its Implications." In James B. Lemert et al., *The Politics of Disenchantment.* Cresskill, NJ: Hampton Press, pp. 41–55.

Black, Charlie (December 9, 1997). President and CEO, Black, Kelly, Scruggs &

Healey, and Republican political strategist. Personal conversation with author.

Blankenship, Jane (1976). "The Search for the 1972 Democratic Nomination: A Metaphorical Perspective." In Jane Blankenship and Hermann G. Stelzner, eds., *Rhetoric and Communication: Studies in the University of Illinois Tradition*. Urbana, IL: University of Illinois Press, pp. 236–260.

Bonafede, Dom (March 18, 1972). "Report/New Hampshire, Florida Primaries Highlight Powers and Limitations of Media." *National Journal* 4, no. 12, pp. 461–471.

Brandenburg, Earnest and Waldo W. Braden (1955). "Franklin Delano Roosevelt." In Marie Kathryn Hochmuth, ed., *A History and Criticism of American Public Address*, Vol. III. New York: Longmans, Green and Co., pp. 458–530.

Broder, David (1976). "Political Reporters in Presidential Politics." In Charles Peters and James Fallows, eds., *Inside the System*, 3d ed. New York: Praeger, pp. 211–222.

Broder, David S. (April 27–May 3, 1992). "No Way to Pick a President." *Washington Post National Weekly Edition*, p. 4.

Broder David (March 3, 1996). "Marching into the Mad Primary Season." *Washington Post*, in *The Gazette* (Schenectady, NY), p. F2.

Buell, Emmett H., Jr. (1996). "The Invisible Primary." In William G. Mayer, ed., *In Pursuit of the White House*. Chatham, NJ: Chatham House Publishers, pp. 1–43.

Burgchardt, Carl (1995). "Herbert Clark Hoover." In Halford Ryan, *U.S. Presidents as Orators: A Bio-Critical Sourcebook*. Westport, CT: Greenwood Press, pp. 134–145.

Burke, Kenneth (1972). *Dramatism and Development*. Barre, MA: Clark University Press.

Burke, Sheila (1997). Senior Adviser, Dole/Kemp '96. *See* Institute of Politics (1997).

Burnham, Walter Dean (1997). "Bill Clinton: Riding the Tiger." In Gerald M. Pomper et al., *The Election of 1996*. Chatham, NJ: Chatham House Publishers, pp. 1–20.

Busch, Andrew E. (1997). *Outsiders and Openness in the Presidential Nominating System*. Pittsburgh, PA: University of Pittsburgh Press.

Busch, Andrew E. and James W. Ceaser (1996). "Does Party Reform Have A Future?" In William G. Mayer, ed., *In Pursuit of the White House: How We Choose Our Presidential Nominees*. Chatham, NJ: Chatham House Publishers, pp. 330–352.

C-SPAN (July 10, 1996). "1996 Presidential Primary Commercials."

"California Judge Backs Open Primary Election" (November 18, 1997). *New York Times* (AP), p. A18.

Cantril, Hadley (1951). *Public Opinion, 1935–1946*. Princeton, NJ: Princeton University Press.

Cappella, Joseph N. and Kathleen Hall Jamieson (July 1996). "News Frames, Political Cynicism, and Media Cynicism." *The Annals* 546, pp. 71–84.

Cappella, Joseph N. and Kathleen Hall Jamieson (1997). *Spiral of Cynicism: The Press and the Public Good*. New York: Oxford University Press.

Carcasson, Martin (Spring 1998). "Herbert Hoover and the Presidential Campaign of 1932: The Failure of Apologia." *Presidential Studies Quarterly* 28, no. 2, pp. 349–365.

Carville, James (December 9, 1997). He is senior political adviser to the president, and author, "Forum: An Historic Look at Presidential Campaign Practices: Have They Changed?" John F. Kennedy School of Government, Harvard University, and personal conversation with author.

Ceaser, James W. (1979). *Presidential Selection: Theory and Development*. Princeton, NJ: Princeton University Press.

Ceaser, James W. (1982). *Presidential Selection and Reforming the Reforms: A Critical Analysis of the Presidential Selection Process*. Cambridge, MA: Ballinger.

Ceaser, James W. and Andrew E. Busch (1993). *Upside Down and Inside Out: The 1992 Elections and American Politics*. Lanham, MD: Rowman and Littlefield Publishers.

Ceaser, James W. and Andrew E. Busch (1997). *Losing to Win: The 1996 Elections and American Politics*. Lanham, MD: Rowman and Littlefield Publishers.

Chaffee, Steven and Stacey Frank (July 1996). "How Americans Get Political Information: Print Versus Broadcast News." *The Annals* 546, pp. 48–58.

Chaffee, Steven H., Xinshu Zhao, and Glenn Leshner (June 1994). "Political Knowledge and the Campaign Media of 1992." *Communication Research* 21, no. 3, pp. 305–324.

Churgin, Jonah R. (1972). *From Truman to Johnson: New Hampshire's Impact on American Politics*. New York: Yeshiva University Press.

Cigler, Allan J. (1991). "Should Political Parties Govern the Presidential Selection Process? No." In Gary L. Rose, ed., *Controversial Issues in Presidential Selection*. Albany, NY: State University of New York Press, pp. 266–279.

Clark, David G. (Summer 1962). "Radio in Presidential Campaigns: The Early Years (1924–32)." *Journal of Broadcasting*, pp. 229–238.

Collins, Reba, ed. (1993). *Will Rogers Says . . .* Oklahoma City, OK: Neighbors and Quaid.

Congressional Quarterly Weekly Report (August 3, 17, 1996).

Cook, Rhodes (1989). "The Nominating Process." In Michael Nelson, ed., *The Election of 1988*. Washington, DC: Congressional Quarterly Press.

Coolidge, Calvin (October 3, 1931). *Saturday Evening Post* 204, pp. 3–5.

Corcoran, Paul E. (1990). "Language and Politics." In David L. Swanson and Dan Nimmo, eds., *New Directions in Political Communication*. Newbury Park, CA: Sage, pp. 51–85.

Corcoran, Paul E. and Kathleen E. Kendall (May 1989). "Communication in the First Primaries: The 'Voice of the People' in 1912." Presented at the International Communication Association, San Francisco, CA.

Corcoran, Paul E. and Kathleen E. Kendall (Winter 1992). "Communication in the First Primaries: The 'Voice of the People' in 1912." *Presidential Studies Quarterly* 22, pp. 15–29.

Cottin, Jonathan and Andrew J. Glass (February 26, 1972). "Report/Democrats Depend on Speechwriters for Their Ideological Images." *National Journal* 4, pp. 350–357.

Crotty, William J. and John S. Jackson III (1985). *Presidential Primaries and Nominations*. Washington, DC: Congressional Quarterly Press.

Crouse, Timothy (1972). *The Boys on the Bus*. New York: Ballantine Books.

Cummings, John M. (March 20, 1932). " 'Stop Roosevelt' Drive Proves Dud." *Philadelphia Inquirer*, p. 6.

Daughton, Suzanne M. (November 1994). "FDR as Family Doctor: Medical Metaphors and the Role of Physician in the Domestic Fireside Chats." Presented at the Speech Communication Association, New Orleans, LA.

David, Paul T., Ralph M. Goldman, and R. G. Bain (1964). *The Politics of National Party Conventions*. New York: Random House.

David, Paul T., Malcolm Moos, and Ralph M. Goldman (1954). *Presidential Nominating Politics in 1952: The National Story*. Baltimore, MD: Johns Hopkins Press.

Davis, Douglas (January 3, 1993). "The American Voter Mounts the Stage." *Newsday*, Nassau edition.

Davis, James W. (1980). *Presidential Primaries: Road to the White House*. Westport, CT: Greenwood Press.

Davis, James W. (1997). *U.S. Presidential Primaries and the Caucus-Convention System: A Sourcebook*. Westport, CT: Greenwood Press.

Davis, Richard (1999). *The Web of Politics*. New York: Oxford University Press.

Denton, Robert E., Jr. and Gary Woodward (1990). *Political Communication in America*, 2d ed. New York: Praeger.

Devlin, L. Patrick (1992). "1992 Presidential Primary Campaign Ads." Devlin Archive, University of Rhode Island.

Devlin, L. Patrick (January–March 1994). "Television Advertising in the 1992 New Hampshire Presidential Primary Election." *Political Communication*, 11, pp. 81–99.

Devlin, L. Patrick (1996). "1996 Presidential Primary Campaign Ads." Devlin Archive, University of Rhode Island.

Devlin, L. Patrick (August 1997). "Contrasts in Presidential Campaign Commercials of 1996." *American Behavioral Scientist* 40, no. 8, pp. 1058–1084.

Diamond, Edwin and Stephen Bates (1984). *The Spot: The Rise of Political Advertising on Television*. Cambridge, MA: MIT Press.

Diamond, Edwin and Robert A. Silverman (1997). *White House to Your House: Media and Politics in Virtual America*. Cambridge, MA: MIT Press.

Dinkin, Robert J. (1989). *Campaigning in America: A History of Election Practices*. Westport, CT: Greenwood Press.

Dooley, Patricia L. and Paul Grosswiler (Summer 1997). " 'Turf Wars,' Journalists, New Media and the Struggle for Control of Political News." *The Harvard International Journal of Press/Politics* 2, no. 3, pp. 31–51.

Eaton, Allen Hendershott (1912). *The Oregon System. The Story of Direct Legislation in Oregon*. Chicago: A. C. McClurg & Company.

Ehrlichman, John (1982). *Witness to Power: The Nixon Years*. New York: Simon and Schuster.

Elder, Charles E. and Roger W. Cobb (1983). *The Political Use of Symbols*. New York: Longman.

Ellis, John (1991). *Nine Sundays: A Proposal for Better Presidential Campaign Coverage*. Cambridge, MA: Joan Shorenstein Center on the Press, Politics and Public Policy, Harvard University.

Fabrizio, Tony (1997). He was chief pollster, Dole/Kemp 1996. *See* Institute of Politics (1997).

Fahrenkopf, Frank (1997). Co-Chair, Commission on Presidential Debates. *See* Institute of Politics (1997).

Farley, James A. (1938). *Behind the Ballots*. New York: Harcourt, Brace and Company.

Fenton, John H. (March 6, 1952). "Eisenhower Held Vital to the G.O.P." *New York Times*, p. 15.

Fiske, S. T. and Kinder, D. (1981). "Involvement, Expertise and Schema Use: Evidence from Political Cognition." In N. Cantor and J. F. Kihlstrom eds., *Personality, Cognition, and Social Interaction*. Hillsdale, NJ: Lawrence Erlbaum Associates, pp. 176–181.

Fitzgerald, Vincent M. (May 1996). "Polls and Issues: Television News Coverage of Presidential Campaigns." Paper presented at the International Communication Association, Chicago, IL.

FitzSimon, Martha (June 1992). "What the Polls Say About Campaign Coverage." In *Covering the Presidential Primaries*, The Freedom Forum Media Studies Center, New York, pp. 51–61.

Fontenay, Charles L. (1980). *Estes Kefauver: A Biography*. Knoxville, TN: University of Tennessee Press.

Fox, Sylvan (March 30, 1972). "Snowfall Disrupts Wisconsin Primary Schedules." *New York Times*, p. 32.

Frankel, Max (April 5, 1972). "Pivotal Moment in the Campaign." *New York Times*, p. 32.

Frankovic, Kathleen A. (1993). "Public Opinion in the 1992 Campaign." In Gerald M. Pomper et al., *The Election of 1992*. Chatham, NJ: Chatham House Publishers, pp. 110–131.

Freedom Forum Media Studies Center (June 1992). *Covering the Presidential Primaries*. New York: The Freedom Forum Media Studies Center.

Freedom Forum Media Studies Center (April 1996). *The Media and Campaign '96*, Briefing No. 1. New York: The Freedom Forum Media Studies Center.

Friedenberg, Robert V. (1990). *Theodore Roosevelt and the Rhetoric of Militant Decency*. Westport, CT: Greenwood Press.

Gardner, Alan (March 24, 1972). Vice president of an advertising agency and director of the Association of Political Consultants; worked on Robert Kennedy's campaigns for Senate and president, and 1968 Humphrey–Muskie ticket. Interview, Reel No. 31, Tape Transcripts, Box 5, McGovern Papers, Seeley Mudd Library, Princeton University.

Geer, John G. (1986). "Rules Governing Presidential Primaries." *Journal of Politics* 48, pp. 1006–1025.

Geer, John G. (1989). *Nominating Presidents: An Evaluation of Voters and Primaries*. Westport, CT: Greenwood Press.

Glass, Andrew J. (June 10, 1972). "Campaign '72: Report/Effective Media Campaign Paved Way for McGovern Win in California." *National Journal* 4, no. 24, pp. 966–974.

Goldman, Peter, Thomas M. DeFrank, Mark Miller, Andrew Murr, and Tom Mathews (1994). *Quest for the Presidency, 1992*. College Station, TX: Texas A & M University Press.

Golson, Barry and Peter Ross Range (November 21, 1992). "Clinton on TV." *TV Guide*, pp. 14–18.

Goodman, Walter (December 26, 1991). "Critic's Notebook: Seeking Ways to Elevate the Presidential Race." *New York Times*, p. D18.

Gorman, Joseph Bruce (1971). *Kefauver: A Political Biography*. New York: Oxford University Press.

Graber, Doris A. (1976). *Verbal Behavior and Politics*. Urbana, IL: University of Illinois Press.

Graber, Doris (1984). *Mass Media and American Politics*, 2d ed. Washington, DC: Congressional Quarterly Press.

Graber, Doris A. (1988). *Processing the News*, 2d ed. New York: Longman.

Graber, Doris A. (November/December, 1993). "Making Campaign News User Friendly." *American Behavioral Scientist* 37, no. 2, pp. 328–336.

Grassmuck, George, ed. (1985). *Before Nomination: Our Primary Problems*. Washington, DC: American Enterprise Institute for Public Policy Research.

Greenberg, Stanley B. (December 13, 1997). President, Greenberg Research, Washington, DC, and London, and pollster and adviser in Bill Clinton's 1992 campaign. Personal correspondence with author.

Griffith, Lanny (1997). Senior Strategist, Alexander for President. *See* Institute of Politics (1997).

Gronbeck, Bruce E. (March/April 1989). "Mythic Portraiture in the 1988 Iowa Presidential Caucus Bio-Ads." *American Behavioral Scientist* 32, no. 4, pp. 351–364.

Gronbeck, Bruce E. and Arthur H. Miller (1994). "The Study of Presidential Campaigning: Yesterday's Campaigns and Today's Issues." In Arthur H. Miller and Bruce E. Gronbeck, eds., *Presidential Campaigns and American Self Images*. Boulder, CO: Westview Press, pp. 3–11.

Guide to U.S. Elections (1975). Washington, DC: Congressional Quarterly Press.

Haldeman, H. R. (1994). *The Haldeman Diaries*. New York: G. P. Putnam's Sons.

Hallin, Daniel C. (Spring 1992). "Sound Bite News: Television Coverage of Elections, 1968–1988." *Journal of Communication* 42, no. 2, pp. 5–24.

Handlin, Oscar (1958). *Al Smith and His America*. Boston: Little, Brown and Co.

Harris, John (April 28, 1952). "Lodge Jibes Ike Foes as 'Antique Shoppers.'" *Boston Globe*.

Hart, Gary Warren (1973). *Right from the Start: A Chronicle of the McGovern Campaign*. New York: Quadrangle.

Hart, Roderick P. (Summer 1982). "A Commentary on Popular Assumptions about Political Communication." *Human Communication Research* 8, pp. 366–379.

Hart, Roderick P. (1987). *The Sound of Leadership: Presidential Communication in the Modern Age*. Chicago: University of Chicago Press.

Haskell, John (Spring 1996). "Reforming Presidential Primaries: Three Steps For Improving the Campaign Environment." *Presidential Studies Quarterly* 26, no. 2, pp. 380–390.

Hellweg, Susan A. and S. W. King (1983). "Comparative Evaluation of Political Candidates: Implications for the Voter Decision Making Process." *Central States Speech Journal* 34, pp. 134–138.

Hellweg, Susan A., S. W. King, and S. E. Williams (1988). "Comparative Candidate Evaluation as a Function of Election Level and Candidate Incumbency." *Communication Reports* 1, pp. 76–85.

Hellweg, Susan A., Michael Pfau, and Steven R. Brydon (1992). *Televised Presidential Debates: Advocacy in Contemporary America*. New York: Praeger.

Herbst, Susan (1993). *Numbered Voices: How Opinion Polling Has Shaped American Politics*. Chicago: University of Chicago Press.

Herbst, Susan (1995). "On Electronic Public Space: Talk Shows in Theoretical Perspective." *Political Communication* 12, no. 3, pp. 263–274.

Hiebert, Ray Eldon, Donald F. Ungurait, and Thomas W. Bohn (1985). *Mass Media IV*. New York: Longman.

Hoefler, James M. (March 1991). "Advertising on Cable Television in the Presidential Primaries: Something to Look For in '92." *PS: Political Science and Politics*, pp. 45–47.

Hogan, J. Michael and James R. Andrews (1995). "Woodrow Wilson." In Halford Ryan, ed., *U.S. Presidents as Orators: A Bio-Critical Sourcebook*. Westport, CT: Greenwood Press, pp. 111–133.

Howe, F. C. (1912). *Wisconsin, An Experiment in Democracy*. New York: Charles Scribner's Sons.

Institute of Politics (1997). *The Campaign for President: The Managers Look at '96*. Hollis, NH: Hollis Publishing Company.

Iyengar, Shanto (1991). *Is Anyone Responsible? How Television Frames Political Issues*. Chicago: University of Chicago Press, 1991.

Iyengar, Shanto and Donald R. Kinder (1987). *News That Matters: Television and American Public Opinion*. Chicago: University of Chicago Press.

Jamieson, Kathleen Hall (1984). *Packaging the Presidency: A History and Criticism of Presidential Campaign Advertising*. New York: Oxford University Press.

Jamieson, Kathleen Hall (1988). *Eloquence in an Electronic Age: The Transformation of Political Speechmaking*. New York: Oxford University Press.

Jamieson, Kathleen Hall (1992). *Dirty Politics: Deception, Distraction, and Democracy*. New York: Oxford University Press.

Jamieson, Kathleen Hall and Karlyn Kohrs Campbell (1988). *The Interplay of Influence*, 2d ed. Belmont, CA: Wadsworth.

"Jersey G.O.P. Gets Three-Way Choice" (March 6, 1952). *New York Times*, p. 16.

Johnson-Cartee, Karen S. and Gary A. Copeland (1991). *Negative Political Advertising: Coming of Age*. Hillsdale, NJ: Lawrence Erlbaum Associates.

Johnston, Richard J. H. (April 9, 1952). "Taft Takes Lead in Illinois Vote; Stassen Is Second." *New York Times*.

Jones, David A. (November 1997). "Political Talk Radio as a Forum for Intra-Party Debate." Paper presented at the Southern Political Science Association, Norfolk, VA.

Jones, James L. (December 1968). "Alfred E. Smith, Political Debater." *Quarterly Journal of Speech* 54, pp. 363–372.

Jones, T. (July 17, 1994). "Hot Air on the Air: Talk Is Not Only Cheap, It's Calling Out to More and More Listeners, Radio Stations Are Discovering." *Chicago Tribune*, p. 1.

Josephson, Matthew and Hannah Josephson (1969). *Al Smith: Hero of the Cities*. Boston: Houghton Mifflin Co.

Joslyn, Richard (1984). *Mass Media and Elections*. New York: Random House.

Just, Marion R. (1997). "Candidate Strategies and the Media Campaign." In Gerald M. Pomper et al., *The Election of 1996* (pp. 77–106). Chatham, NJ: Chatham House Publishers.

Just, Marion et al. (1996). *Crosstalk: Citizens, Candidates, and the Media in a Presidential Campaign*. Chicago: University of Chicago Press.

Kaid, Lynda Lee and John Ballotti (November 1991). "Television Advertising in Presidential Primaries and Caucuses." Paper presented at the Speech Communication Association Convention, Atlanta, GA.

Kaid, Lynda Lee and Anne Johnston (Summer 1991). "Negative Versus Positive Advertising in U.S. Presidential Campaigns." *Journal of Communication* 41, pp. 53–64.

Kalb, Marvin (July 3, 1992). "From Sound Bite to a Meal." *New York Times*, p. A-25.

Kalb, Marvin (October 16, 1997). Director, The Joan Shorenstein Center on the Press, Politics and Public Policy, and Edward R. Murrow Professor of Press and Public Policy, Harvard University. Personal interview.

Kamarck, Elaine Ciulla (1991). "Should Convention Delegates Be Formally Pledged? No." In Gary L. Rose, ed., *Controversial Issues in Presidential Selection*. Albany, NY: State University of New York Press, pp. 67–77.

Kendall, Kathleen E. (November/December 1993). "Public Speaking in the Presidential Primaries through Media Eyes." *American Behavioral Scientist* 37, pp. 240–251.

Kendall, Kathleen E. (1995). "The Problem of Beginnings in New Hampshire: Control Over the Play." In Kathleen E. Kendall, ed., *Presidential Campaign Discourse: Strategic Communication Problems*. Albany, NY: State University of New York Press, pp. 1–34.

Kendall, Kathleen E. (August 1997). "Presidential Debates through Media Eyes." *American Behavioral Scientist* 40, no. 8, pp. 1193–1207.

Kendall, Kathleen E. and June Ock Yum (1984). "Persuading the Blue-Collar Voter: Issues, Images, and Homophily." In Robert N. Bostrom, ed., *Communication Yearbook* 8. Beverly Hills, CA: Sage, pp. 707–722.

Kennamer, J. D. and Steven H. Chaffee (1982). "Communication of Political Information during Early Presidential Primaries: Cognition, Affect, and Uncertainty." In Michael Burgoon, ed., *Communication Yearbook* 5. New Brunswick, NJ: Transaction, pp. 627–650.

Kerbel, Matthew Robert (1994). *Edited For Television: CNN, ABC, and the 1992 Presidential Campaign*. Boulder, CO: Westview Press.

Kern, Montague (1989). *Thirty-Second Politics: Political Advertising in the Eighties*. New York: Praeger.

Kern, Montague (1995). "The Question of a Return to Basic American Values: 'My Mother and Winston Churchill' in the Heroic Narratives of Ross Perot's Infomercials." In Kathleen E. Kendall, ed., *Presidential Campaign Discourse: Strategic Communication Problems*. Albany, NY: State University of New York Press, pp. 157–177.

Kern, Montague (May 1997). "Social Capital and Citizen Interpretation of Political Advertising, News, and Web Site Information in the 1996 Presidential Election." Paper presented at the International Communication Association, Montreal, Quebec.

Kern, Montague and Robert H. Wicks (1994). "Television News and the

Advertising-Driven New Mass Media Election: A More Significant Local Role in 1992?" In Robert E. Denton, Jr., ed., *The 1992 Presidential Campaign: A Communication Perspective*. Westport, CT: Praeger, pp. 189–206.

Kiewe, Amos (November 1993). "George Bush's 1992 State of the Union Address as a Crisis Speech: Challenges to the Generic Approach." Paper presented at the Speech Communication Association Convention, Miami Beach, FL.

Kirby, Alec (Winter 1996–1997). "Harold Stassen and the Politics of American Presidential Nominations." *Minnesota History* 55/4, pp. 150–165.

Klien, Stephen A. (November 1994). "Pat Buchanan's 'Old Republic': Mythic Narrative and the '92 Campaign." Paper presented at the Speech Communication Association Convention, New Orleans, LA.

Kneeland, Douglas E. (March 30, 1972). "Fickle Wisconsin: A Crucial Testing Ground." *New York Times*, p. 32.

Kneeland, Douglas E. (April 2, 1972). "Candidates Spur Wisconsin Race as Voting Nears." *New York Times*, pp. 1, 41.

Kneeland, Douglas E. (April 3, 1972). "Long Head Start Is Vital to McGovern's Wisconsin Drive." *New York Times*, p. 22.

Kneeland, Douglas E. (April 4, 1972). "Governor Lucey Sees McGovern Victory." *New York Times*, pp. 1, 36.

Knight, Peter (1997). Campaign Manager, Clinton/Gore '96. *See* Institute of Politics (1997).

Kolbert, Elizabeth (May 1, 1992). "As Political Campaigns Turn Negative, the Press Is Given a Negative Rating." *New York Times*, p. A18.

Kovach, Bill (March 5, 1972). "New Hampshire: Round One—And a Big Stake for Muskie." *New York Times*, Sect. 4, p. 1.

Kovach, Bill (April 3, 1972). "Muskie Slips in Pennsylvania; McGovern Counts on Bay State; South Dakotan May Campaign 15 Days in Massachusetts." *New York Times*, p. 22.

Kovach, Bill and Tom Rosenstiel (1999). *Warp Speed: America in the Age of Mixed Media*. New York: Century Foundation Press.

Kramer, Michael (February 3, 1992). "Moment of Truth." *Time*, pp. 12–14.

Kramer, Michael (July 3, 1992). "The Political Interest: On TV, It's All Deja Vu." *Time*, p. 27.

Krock, Arthur (May 25, 1952). "South Dakota Primary May Tell G.O.P. Story." *New York Times*, p. 3.

Kruse, Doug and Kathleen E. Kendall (1995). "A Rashomonian Approach to the Study of Image Construction." In Kenneth L. Hacker, ed., *Candidate Images in Presidential Elections*. Westport, CT: Praeger, pp. 145–152.

Lanoue, David J. and Peter R. Schrott (1989). "The Effects of Primary Season Debates on Public Opinion." *Political Behavior* 11, no. 3, pp. 289–306.

Lanzetta, John et al. (1985). "Emotional and Cognitive Responses to Televised Images of Political Leaders." In Sidney Kraus and Richard M. Perloff, eds., *Mass Media and Political Thought: An Information Processing Approach*. Newbury Park, CA: Sage, pp. 85–116.

Lawrence, W. H. (February 1, 1952). "Truman Bars Test in New Hampshire." *New York Times*, pp. A1, A10.

Lenart, Silvo (1994). *Shaping Political Attitudes: The Impact of Interpersonal Communication and Mass Media*. Thousand Oaks, CA: Sage.

Lengle, James I. (July 1980). "Divisive Presidential Primaries and Party Electoral Prospects, 1932–1976." *American Politics Quarterly* 8, pp. 261–277.

Lengle, James I. and Byron Shafer (1976). "Primary Rules, Political Power, and Social Change." *American Political Science Review* 70, pp. 25–40.

Leubsdorf, Carl P. (September 1976). "The Reporter and the Presidential Candidate." *Annals of the American Academy of Political and Social Science* 427, pp. 1–11.

Lichter, S. Robert, Daniel Amundson, and Richard Noyes (1988). *The Video Campaign: Network Coverage of the 1988 Primaries.* Washington, DC: The American Enterprise Institute for Public Policy.

Lodge, Henry Cabot (1973). *The Storm Has Many Eyes: A Personal Narrative.* New York: W. W. Norton and Company.

Loevy, Robert D. (1995). *The Flawed Path to the Presidency, 1992: Unfairness and Inequality in the Presidential Selection Process.* Albany, NY: State University of New York Press.

Louden, Allan Dean (1990). "Image Construction in Political Spot Advertising: The Hunt/Helms Senate Campaign, 1984," Ph.D. Dissertation, University of Southern California.

Lucy, William H. (November 1973). "Polls, Primaries, and Presidential Nominations." *Journal of Politics* 35, pp. 830–848.

Lydon, Christopher (April 2, 1972). "Celebrities Rally Behind McGovern." *New York Times*, p. 28.

Macaulay, Thomas B. (June 1859). In *Harper's New Monthly Magazine*, cited by Russell Baker, "Observer: Reading for Bill and Bob." *New York Times*, June 8, 1996.

Magruder, Jeb Stuart (1974). *An American Life.* New York: Atheneum.

Marsh, Pamela S. (April 1995). "A Structural Analysis and Comparison of the Televised Political Advertisements of the 1992 Presidential Democratic Primary." Paper presented at the Eastern Communication Association Convention, Pittsburgh, PA.

Marshall, Thomas R. (1981). *Presidential Nominations in a Reform Age.* New York: Praeger.

Marshall, Thomas R. (1983). "The News Verdict and Public Opinion during the Primaries." In William C. Adams, ed., *Television Coverage of the 1980 Presidential Campaign.* Norwood, NJ: Ablex Publishing Corp., pp. 49–67.

Martin, John Bartlow (1976). *Adlai Stevenson of Illinois.* Garden City, NY: Doubleday and Co.

Matalin, Mary and James Carville (1994). *All's Fair: Love, War, and Running for President.* New York: Random House.

May, Ernest R. and Janet Fraser, eds. (1973). *Campaign '72: The Managers Speak.* Cambridge, MA: Harvard University Press.

Mayer, William G. (1996a). "Caucuses: How They Work, What Difference They Make." In William G. Mayer, ed., *In Pursuit of the White House: How We Choose Our Presidential Nominees.* Chatham, NJ: Chatham House Publishers, pp. 105–157.

Mayer, William G. (1996b). "Forecasting Presidential Nominations." In William G. Mayer, ed., *In Pursuit of the White House: How We Choose Our Presidential Nominees.* Chatham, NJ: Chatham House Publishers, pp. 44–71.

Mayer, William G. (1996c). *In Pursuit of the White House: How We Choose Our Presidential Nominees*. Chatham, NJ: Chatham House Publishers.

Mayer, William G. (1997). "The Presidential Nominations," in Gerald M. Pomper et al., *The Election of 1996* (pp. 21–76). Chatham, NJ: Chatham House Publishers.

McCombs, Maxwell E. (1981). "The Agenda-Setting Approach." In Dan D. Nimmo and Keith R. Sanders, eds., *Handbook of Political Communication*. Newbury Park, CA: Sage, pp. 121–140.

McCombs, Maxwell E. and Donald Shaw (1972). "The Agenda-Setting Function of the Mass Media." *Public Opinion Quarterly* 36, pp. 176–187.

McCubbins, Mathew D. (1992a). "Party Decline and Presidential Campaigns in the Television Age." In Mathew D. McCubbins, ed., *Under the Watchful Eye*. Washington, DC: CQ Press, pp. 9–58.

McCubbins, Matthew D. (1992b). *Under the Watchful Eye*. Washington, DC: CQ Press.

McGee, M. C. and J. S. Nelson (1985). "Narrative Reason in Public Argument." *Journal of Communication* 35, pp. 139–155.

McGovern, George (1977). *Grassroots: The Autobiography of George McGovern*. New York: Random House.

McGovern, George, Papers of (1948–1978). MC#181. Seeley Mudd Library, Princeton University, Princeton, NJ.

McLaughlin, John (1997). Pollster and Consultant, Forbes for President. *See* Institute of Politics (1997).

Medhurst, Martin J. (1995). "Dwight D. Eisenhower." In Halford Ryan, ed., *U.S. Presidents as Orators: A Bio-Critical Sourcebook*. Westport, CT: Greenwood Press, pp. 190–209.

Media Monitor (March/April 1996). "The Bad News Campaign." Center for Media and Public Affairs 10, no. 2.

Media Monitor (May/June 1996). "Whose Campaign Did You See?" Center for Media and Public Affairs 10, no. 3.

Meyrowitz, Joshua (1995). "The Problem of Getting on the Media Agenda: A Case Study in Competing Logics of Campaign Coverage." In Kathleen E. Kendall, ed., *Presidential Campaign Discourse: Strategic Communication Problems*. Albany, NY: State University of New York Press, pp. 35–67.

Miller, A. H., M. P. Wattenberg, and O. Malanchuk (1985). "Cognitive Representations of Candidate Assessments." In Keith R. Sanders, Lynda Lee Kaid, and Dan Nimmo, eds., *Political Communication Yearbook 1984*. Carbondale, IL: Southern Illinois University Press, pp. 183–210.

Miller, Norman C. (April 3, 1972). "Muskie Struggles for a Comeback." *Wall Street Journal*.

Miller, Warren E. (1985). "Participants in the Nominating Process: The Voters, the Political Activists." In George Grassmuck, ed., *Before Nomination: Our Primary Problems*. Washington, DC: American Enterprise Institute for Public Policy Research, pp. 60–71.

Morris, Dick (1997). *Behind the Oval Office*. New York: Random House.

Muir, Janette Kenner (1994a). "Clinton Goes to Town Hall." In Stephen A. Smith, ed., *Bill Clinton on Stump, State and Stage: The Rhetorical Road to the White House*. Fayetteville: University of Arkansas Press, pp. 341–364.

Muir, Janette Kenner (1994b). "Video Verite: C-Span Covers the Candidates." In Robert E. Denton, Jr., *The 1992 Presidential Campaign: A Communication Perspective*. Westport, CT: Praeger, pp. 227–245.

Murphy, Richard (1955). "Theodore Roosevelt." In Marie Kathryn Hochmuth, ed., *A History and Criticism of American Public Address*, Vol. III. New York: Longmans, Green and Co., pp. 313–364.

Myers, David S. (Spring 1996). "Editorials and the Economy in the 1992 Presidential Campaign." *Presidential Studies Quarterly* 26, no. 2, pp. 435–446.

Napolitan, Joseph (September 1976). "Media Costs and Effects in Political Campaigns." *Annals of the American Academy of Political and Social Science* 427, pp. 114–124.

Naughton, James M. (January 5, 1972). "Muskie Formally in Race; Pledges 'A New Beginning.' " *New York Times*, pp. 1, 23.

Naughton, James M. (March 13, 1972). "Muskie, In Shift, Pledges to Name His Fund Sources." *New York Times*, pp. 1, 28.

Nimmo, Dan (1994). "The Electronic Town Hall in Campaign '92: Interactive Forum or Carnival of Buncombe?" In Robert E. Denton, Jr., ed., *The 1992 Presidential Campaign: A Communication Perspective*. Westport, CT: Praeger, pp. 207–226.

Nimmo, Dan and James E. Combs (1990). *Mediated Political Realities*, 2d ed. New York: Longman.

Nimmo, Dan and Robert L. Savage (1976). *Candidates and Their Images*. Pacific Palisades, CA: Goodyear Publishing Co.

Nolan, Martin F. (November 8, 1997). "TV's Finest News House." *Boston Globe*, p. A17.

Nordheimer, Jon (April 4, 1972). "Wallace's Traveling Show Pulls Crowds in Wisconsin." *New York Times*, p. 36.

Orren, Gary R. and Nelson W. Polsby, eds. (1987). *Media and Momentum: The New Hampshire Primary and Nomination Politics*. Chatham, NJ: Chatham House Publishers.

Oudes, Bruce, ed. (1989). *From: The President. Richard Nixon's Secret Files*. New York: Harper and Row.

Overacker, Louise (1926). *The Presidential Primary*. New York: Macmillan.

Owen, Diana (1991). *Media Messages in American Presidential Elections*. Westport, CT: Greenwood Press.

Owen, Diana (1995). "The Debate Challenge: Candidate Strategies in the New Media Age." In Kathleen E. Kendall, ed., *Presidential Campaign Discourse: Strategic Communication Problems*. Albany, NY: State University of New York Press, pp. 135–155.

Page, Benjamin I., Robert Y. Shapiro, and Glenn R. Dempsey (1994). "What Moves Public Opinion?" In Doris A. Graber, ed., *Media Power in Politics*, 3d ed. Washington, DC: Congressional Quarterly Press, pp. 123–138.

Paletz, David L. and Martha Elson (Spring 1976). "Television Coverage of Presidential Conventions: Now You See It, Now You Don't." *Political Science Quarterly* 91, pp. 109–131.

Patterson, James T. (1972). *Mr. Republican: A Biography of Robert A. Taft*. Boston: Houghton Mifflin Co.

Patterson, Thomas and Robert McClure (1976). *The Unseeing Eye*. New York: Putnam.

Patterson, Thomas E. (1980). *The Mass Media Election: How Americans Choose Their President*. New York: Praeger.

Patterson, Thomas E. (1993). *Out of Order*. New York: Alfred A. Knopf.

Pavlik, John and Mark Thalhimer (June 1992). "From Wausau to Wichita: Covering the Campaign Via Satellite." In The Freedom Forum Media Studies Center, *Covering the Presidential Primaries*, pp. 36–46.

Payne, J. Gregory, John Marlier, and Robert A. Baukus (March/April 1989). "Polispots in the 1988 Presidential Primaries: Separating the Nominees from the Rest of the Guys." *American Behavioral Scientist* 32, no. 4, pp. 365–381.

Peel, Roy V. and Thomas C. Donnelly (1973; first edition, 1935). *The 1932 Campaign, An Analysis*, 2d ed. New York: DaCapo Press.

Pew Center for the People and the Press (May 13, 1996). *TV News Viewership Declines*. Washington, DC: Pew Center for the People and the Press.

Pfau, Michael (Fall 1988). "Intra-Party Political Debates and Issue Learning." *Journal of Applied Communication Research* 16, no. 2, pp. 99–112.

Pfau, Michael, Tracy Diedrich, Karla M. Larson, and Kim M. Van Winkle (Summer 1993). "Relational and Competence Perceptions of Presidential Candidates during Primary Election Campaigns." *Journal of Broadcasting and Electronic Media* 37, pp. 275–292.

Pfau, Michael and Jong Geun Kang (Summer 1991). "The Impact of Relational Messages on Candidate Influence in Televised Political Debates." *Communication Studies* 42, pp. 114–128.

Pfau, Michael, Kathleen E. Kendall, Tom Reichert, Susan A. Hellweg, Wai-Peng Lee, Lyle James Tusing, and Theodore O. Prosise (Autumn 1997). "Influence of Communication during the Distant Phase of the 1996 Republican Presidential Primary Campaign." *Journal of Communication* 47, no. 4, pp. 6-26.

Pfau, Michael and Henry C. Kenski (1990). *Attack Politics: Strategy and Defense*. New York: Praeger.

Polsby, Nelson W. (1983). *Consequences of Party Reform*. New York: Oxford University Press.

Popkin, Samuel L. (1991). *The Reasoning Voter: Communication and Persuasion in Presidential Campaigns*. Chicago: University of Chicago Press.

Pringle, Henry F. (1927; republished, 1970). *Alfred E. Smith: A Critical Study*. New York: AMS Press.

Protess, David L. and Maxwell McCombs (1991). *Agenda Setting: Readings on Media, Public Opinion, and Policymaking*. Hillsdale, NJ: Lawrence Erlbaum Associates.

Public Papers of the Presidents. Washington, DC: U.S. Government Printing Office.

Ranney, Austin (1975). *Curing the Mischiefs of Faction: Party Reform in America*. Berkeley, CA: University of California Press.

Ranney, Austin (1977). *Participation in American Presidential Nominations, 1976*. Washington, DC: American Enterprise Institute Studies, #149.

Reagan, Joey and Richard V. Ducey (Summer 1983). "Effects of News Measure on Selection of State Government News Sources." *Journalism Quarterly* 60, pp. 211–217.

Reed, Scott (1997). Campaign manager of the Dole/Kemp 1996 campaign. *See* Institute of Politics (1997).

Reinsch, J. Leonard (1988). *Getting Elected: From Radio and Roosevelt to Television and Reagan*. New York: Hippocrene Books.

Reiter, Howard L. (1984). "The Limitations of Reform: Changes in the Presidential Nominating Process." Essex Papers in Politics and Government, No. 20 (Department of Government, University of Essex, Wivenhoe Park, Colchester, England). Cited by Mathew D. McCubbins (1992), *Under the Watchful Eye*. Washington, DC: Congressional Quarterly Press.

Republican National Convention (August 12, 1996). *The Rules of the Republican Party*. San Diego, CA.

Reston, James (March 13, 1952). "Eisenhower, Kefauver Vote Seen as Two-Party Demand for New Era in Government." *New York Times*, pp. 1, 20.

Reston, James (March 5, 1972). "Help! Help! Help!" *New York Times*, Sect. E, p. 13.

Rich, Frank (May 29, 1996). "Journal: Cradle and All." *New York Times*, p. A19.

Ridout, Christine F. (1993). "News Coverage and Talk Shows in the 1992 Presidential Campaign." *PS: Political Science and Politics* 26, pp. 712–716.

Roberts, Marilyn S. (1995). "Political Advertising: Strategies for Influence." In Kathleen E. Kendall, ed., *Presidential Campaign Discourse*. Albany, NY: State University of New York Press, pp. 179–199.

Robinson, Douglas (March 11, 1972). "Jackson Expects to Finish Near Top in Florida Vote." *New York Times*, p. 12.

Roosevelt, Theodore (1954). *The Letters of Theodore Roosevelt, The Days of Armageddon, 1909–1919*, Vol. VII. Elting E. Morison, ed. Cambridge, MA: Harvard University Press.

Rosenman, Samuel I. (1952). *Working with Roosevelt*. New York: Harper and Brothers.

Rosenstiel, Tom (1993). *Strange Bedfellows: How Television and the Presidential Candidates Changed American Politics, 1992*. New York: Hyperion.

Royer, Charles T., ed. (1994). *Campaign For President: The Managers Look at '92*. Hollis, NH: Hollis Publishing.

Rubin, Richard L. (1981). *Press, Party, and Presidency*. New York: W. W. Norton and Company.

Ryan, Milo (1963). *History in Sound: A Descriptive Listing of the KIRO-CBS Collection of Broadcasts of the World War II Years and After, in the Phonoarchive of the University of Washington*. Seattle: University of Washington Press.

Sabato, Larry J. (1992). "Open Season: How the News Media Cover the Presidential Campaigns in the Age of Attack Journalism." In Mathew D. McCubbins, ed., *Under the Watchful Eye*. Washington, DC: Congressional Quarterly Press, pp. 127–152.

Safire, William (November 6, 1997). "The Theodore H. White Lecture." The Joan Shorenstein Center for Press, Politics, and Public Policy, Harvard University, John F. Kennedy School of Government, Cambridge, MA.

Sanger, David E. (July 1, 1996). "Clinton Leads Rites for Dead in Saudi Blast." *New York Times*, p. 1.

Saussure, Ferdinand de (1959). *Course in General Linguistics*. W. Baskin, trans. New York: Philosophical Library. (Originally published in 1916.)

Savage, Robert L. (1981). "The Diffusion of Information Approach." In Dan D.

Nimmo and Keith R. Sanders, eds., *Handbook of Political Communication.* Beverly Hills, CA: Sage, pp. 101–119.

Savage, Robert L. (1986). "Statesmanship, Surfacing, and Sometimes Stumbling: Constructing Candidate Images during the Early Campaign." *Political Communication Review* 11, pp. 43–57.

Scott, Walter (July 14, 1996). "Personality Parade." *Parade,* p. 2.

Shannon, W. Wayne (1991). "Should Political Parties Govern the Presidential Selection Process? Yes." In Gary L. Rose, ed., *Controversial Issues in Presidential Selection.* Albany, NY: State University of New York Press, pp. 251–265.

Shannon, William V. (April 3, 1972). "The Three-Man Race." *New York Times,* p. 37.

Shapiro, Michael and Robert Rieger (Spring 1992). "Comparing Positive and Negative Political Advertising in Radio." *Journalism Quarterly* 69, no. 1, pp. 135–145.

Sherwood, Robert (1949). *Roosevelt and Hopkins.* New York: Harper and Brothers.

Short, Brant (Spring 1991). "The Rhetoric of the Post-Presidency: Herbert Hoover's Campaign Against the New Deal, 1934–1936." *Presidential Studies Quarterly* 21, no. 2, pp. 333–350.

Shyles, Leonard (1984). "The Relationships of Images, Issues, and Presentational Methods in Televised Spot Advertisements for 1980's American Presidential Primaries." *Journal of Broadcasting* 28, no. 4, pp. 405–421.

Silvestri, Vito N. (1987). "John F. Kennedy: The Evolving Catholic Issue in His Campaigns, 1956–1960." In Richard J. Jensen and John C. Hammerback, eds., *In Search of Justice: The Indiana Tradition in Speech Communication.* Amsterdam: Rodolpi, pp. 205–228.

Simons, Herbert W. (1986). *Persuasion: Understanding, Practice, and Analysis,* 2d ed. New York: Random House.

Smillie, Dirk (June 1992). "The Public Opinion Beat." In The Freedom Forum Media Studies Center, *Covering the Presidential Primaries,* pp. 47–50.

Smith, Alfred E. (May 24, 1930). "Spellbinding." *The Saturday Evening Post* 202, pp. 3–5.

Smith, Craig Allen (1992). "The Iowa Caucuses and Super Tuesday Primaries Reconsidered: How Untenable Hypotheses Enhance the Campaign Melodrama." *Presidential Studies Quarterly* 22, pp. 519–529.

Smith, Craig Allen (May 1994). " 'It Was the Jeremiad, Stupid': The Focus Fallacy in Clinton's First Year." Paper presented at the Eastern Communication Association Convention, Washington, DC.

Smith, Craig R. (1995). "George Herbert Walker Bush." In Halford Ryan, ed., *U.S. Presidents as Orators: A Bio-Critical Sourcebook.* Westport, CT: Greenwood Press, pp. 344–360.

Sobel, Richard (Spring 1998). "Portraying American Public Opinion Toward the Bosnia Crisis." *The Harvard International Journal of Press/Politics* 3, no. 2, pp. 16–33.

Solberg, Carl (1984). *Hubert Humphrey, A Biography.* New York: W. W. Norton and Co.

Stebenne, David (January 1993). "Media Coverage of American Presidential Elections: A Historical Perspective." In *The Finish Line: Covering the Campaign's*

Final Days. Research Group of the Freedom Forum Media Studies Center, Columbia University, pp. 79–91.

Stiles, Lela (1954). *The Man Behind Roosevelt: The Story of Louis McHenry Howe*. Cleveland, OH: The World Publishing Co.

Sullivan, Mark (April 27, 1952). "Must Eisenhower Talk?" *New York Herald Tribune*, Sect. 2, p. 7.

Sullivan, Ronald (April 3, 1972). "Hughes and Williams of Jersey Shy from Muskie." *New York Times*, p. 22.

Summers, Harrison B. (1971). *A Thirty-Year History of Programs . . . Radio for 1951– 2*. New York: Arno Press.

Swanson, David L. (August 1997). "The Political-Media Complex at 50." *American Behavioral Scientist* 40, no. 8, pp. 1264–1282.

Swanson, David L. and Paolo Mancini (1996). *Politics, Media, and Modern Democracy: An International Study of Innovations in Electoral Campaigning and Their Consequences*. Westport, CT: Praeger.

Swerdlow, Joel L., ed. (1987). *Presidential Debates, 1988 and Beyond*. Washington, DC: Congressional Quarterly Press.

Traugott, Michael W. (1985). "The Media and the Nominating Process." In George Grassmuck, ed., *Before Nomination: Our Primary Nominating Problems*. Washington, DC: American Enterprise Institute for Public Policy Research, pp. 101–115.

Trent, Jimmie D. and Judith S. Trent (1995). "The Incumbent and His Challengers: The Problem of Adapting to Prevailing Conditions." In Kathleen E. Kendall, ed., *Presidential Campaign Discourse: Strategic Communication Problems*. Albany, NY: State University of New York Press, pp. 69–92.

Trent, Judith S. (1986). "They Keep Running and the Rules Keep Changing: An Overview of the Early Campaign From 1972 to 1988." *Political Communication Review* 11, pp. 7–17.

Trent, Judith S. and Robert V. Friedenberg (1995). *Political Campaign Communication: Principles and Practices*, 3d ed. Westport, CT: Praeger.

Trent, Judith S., Paul A. Mongeau, Jimmie D. Trent, Kathleen E. Kendall, and Ronald B. Cushing (November/December 1993). "The Ideal Candidate: A Study of the Desired Attributes of the Public and the Media Across Two Presidential Campaigns." *American Behavioral Scientist* 37, pp. 225–239.

Troester, Rod (November 1994). "Read Our Plans: The Books of the Perot and Clinton-Gore Campaigns." Paper presented at the Speech Communication Association Convention, New Orleans, LA.

Troy, Gil (1991). *See How They Ran: The Changing Role of the Presidential Candidate*. New York: The Free Press.

Tyndall, Andrew (September 1996). "Why Network TV Campaign Coverage Is Down in 1996." Briefing no. 3. New York: The Freedom Forum Media Studies Center, pp. 4–7.

Vanocur, Sander (March 15, 1972). "Wallace Views the Vote: Interview with Governor George C. Wallace." *New York Times*, p. 32.

Waldron, Martin (March 12, 1972). "Wallace's Rivals Fight to Prevent Sweep in Florida." *New York Times*, pp. 1, 37.

Warner, Emily Smith, with Hawthorne Daniel (1956). *The Happy Warrior: A Biography of My Father, Alfred E. Smith*. Garden City, NY: Doubleday and Co.

Wattenberg, Martin P. (1985). "Participants in the Nominating Process: The Role of the Parties." In George Grassmuck, ed., *Before Nomination: Our Primary Problems*. Washington, DC: American Enterprise Institute for Public Policy Research, pp. 47–59.

Wattenberg, Martin P. (1991). *The Rise of Candidate-Centered Politics: Presidential Elections of the 1980's*. Cambridge, MA: Harvard University Press.

Wayne, Stephen J. (1992). *The Road to the White House 1992*. New York: St. Martin's Press.

Weaver, Warren, Jr. (March 13, 1972). "Jackson, Lindsay and Askew Dominate Florida TV Politics." *New York Times*, p. 28.

Weaver, Warren, Jr. (April 3, 1972). "Lindsay's Radio-TV Spending Increased." *New York Times*, p. 22.

West, Darrell W. (1993). *Air Wars: Television Advertising in Election Campaigns, 1952–1992*. Washington, DC: Congressional Quarterly Press.

West, Darrell W., Montague Kern, and Dean Alger (1992). "Political Advertising and Ad Watches in the 1992 Presidential Nominating Campaign." Paper presented to the American Political Science Association, Chicago, IL.

Whillock, Rita Kirk (1994). "Easy Access to Sloppy Truths: An Analysis of the '92 Presidential Campaign." In Steven Smith, ed., *Bill Clinton: On Stump, State, and Stage*. Fayetteville, AR: University of Arkansas Press.

White, Theodore H. (1961). *The Making of the President 1960*. New York: Atheneum.

Wicker, Tom (March 14, 1972). "Thoughts on the Primaries." *New York Times*, p. 43.

Winkler, J. K. (October 31, 1925). "Al Smith Tells How He Gets the Crowd." *Colliers* 76, p. 20 (cited in Jones, 1968, p. 364).

Witcover, Jules (December 9, 1997). He is a syndicated columnist and author, "Forum, An Historic Look at Presidential Campaign Practices: Have They Changed?" and personal conversation with author. John F. Kennedy School of Government, Harvard University.

Witt, Evans (August/September 1983). " 'Here, There, and Everywhere': Where Americans Get Their News." *Public Opinion* 6, no. 4, pp. 45–48.

Wolfe, A. C. (1966). *The Direct Primary in American Politics*. Ph.D. Dissertation, University of Wisconsin.

Wolfsfeld, Gadi and William Gamson (May 1992). "Media and Movements: A Transactional Analysis." Paper presented at the International Communication Association Convention, Miami, FL.

Woodard, J. David (1994). "Coverage of Elections on Evening Television News Shows: 1972–1992." In Arthur H. Miller and Bruce E. Gronbeck, eds., *Presidential Campaigns and American Self-Images*. Boulder, CO: Westview Press, pp. 109–127.

Yum, June O. and Kathleen E. Kendall (Spring 1988). "Sources of Political Information in a Presidential Primary Campaign." *Journalism Quarterly* 65, pp. 148–151, 177.

Zhu, J., J. R. Milavsky, and R. Biswas (1994). "Do Televised Debates Affect Image Perception More Than Issue Knowledge? A Study of the First 1992 Presidential Debate." *Human Communication Research* 20, pp. 302–333.

Index

Adams, Sherman, 48

Advertising, primary: activation, 107, 108; addressograph role in, 100–101; all-purpose, 107, 116; biographical, 94, 114–115, 127; campaign developments and, 121; campaign paraphernalia, 120; candidate values and, 99; changes in, 125–126; colloquial use in, 120; comparative, 98–99, 122; computer letter, 111; condensation symbols in, 95, 99; constants in, 126–127; customized video, 123; deductive nature of, 98; direct mail, 100, 101, 111, 114; documentary, 120; dovetailing in, 94, 99, 105, 123, 124, 127; dramatic, 114; drawing attention to, 98; 800 numbers, 122–123, 126, 183, 194; emotional associations in, 94; endorsement, 116; fighting image, 116, 120, 189, 192–193, 208, 215–216; focus of, 126; horse race metaphor in, 126–127, 132, 173–174, 181, 185; ID spots, 94; image and, 94, 99, 105, 106, 112, 120, 123; influence of, 92–93; infomercials, 123, 126; innovations in, 122–124; issues and, 94, 108; language use in, 115–116, 132; length of, 108–109; limits on, 43; media attention to, 126; in multi-candidate field, 91–127; myths in, 95; name recognition and, 95, 109, 113–114, 117; narrative in, 94, 95, 121, 125; narrowcasting, 123; negative, 96, 98–99, 118, 122, 124; newspaper, 102–103, 105, 106, 108, 110, 116; in 1912 primaries, 97–100; in 1932 primaries, 100–102; in 1952 primaries, 102–108; in 1972 primaries, 108–121; in 2000 primaries, 220; party reference, 98, 125; personal qualities and, 93, 99–100, 125; person-to-person, 114; platform, 94, 122; political portraiture in, 95; print variety in, 98; production techniques, 121; radio, 102, 103, 111, 120; recordings, 120; referential symbols in, 95; research on, 92–96; retaliatory, 118; slogan, 94, 122, 126–127; smiles in, 110; as source of information, 96, 100; in Spanish, 118; specificity to states, 124; "studio declaration," 120; styles, 109; by telegram/telephone, 101; telethon, 117; television, 103, 104, 109, 111, 112, 114, 116, 118, 120, 125; testimonials in, 95, 97; unique characteristics, 124–125; viability, 105, 116; watches, 121, 122, 133–134, 180; "winnability" and, 105, 124, 126

Agran, Larry, 23, 25, 121, 130

Aiken, George, 172–173

Alexander, Lamar, 206, 207, 211, 213

Anderson, Jack, 167

Ashbrook, John, 21, 110, 172

Azbell, Joe, 120

Babbitt, Bruce, 123

Barkley, Alben, 27 n.7, 224 n.2

Bauer, Gary, 213, 216

Begala, Paul, 48, 49, 85

Bell, Steve, 169–170

Bentsen, Lloyd, 23

Berlin, Irving, 19

Beveridge, Albert, 55

Black, Charles, 82, 83

Bradley, Bill, 23, 213, 214

Brandeis, Louis, 55

Bremer, Arthur, 22

Brinkley, David, 160

Broder, David, 3, 130, 161–162, 176, 180

Brokaw, Tom, 185, 207

Broun, Heywood, 147

Brown, Jerry, 23; advertising by, 121, 122–123, 183, 193–194; agenda setting by, 193–194; in Connecticut primary, 10; debates by, 86; in Illinois primary, 25; in New York primary, 25; in 1992 primaries, 193–194

Brown, Ron, 46, 85–86, 86

Bryan, William Jennings, 55

Buchanan, Bay, 196

Buchanan, James, 24

Buchanan, Pat, 24, 115, 129, 212, 214–215; advertising by, 121, 196–197; agenda setting by, 196–197; in California primary, 11; images of, 189; media coverage of, 189, 196–197; in New Hampshire primary, 9, 48, 131, 208; in 1992 primaries, 24, 25, 26; in 1996 primaries, 206; in 2000 primaries, 213, 214–215; speaking style, 81–82; speeches by, 81

Bull Moose Party, 34

Bush, George: advertising by, 121, 122; agenda setting by, 197; campaign strategies, 135; loss of confidence in, 24, 48, 84; media coverage of, 189–190; in New Hampshire primary, 48, 189–190; in 1988 primaries, 30; in 1992 primaries, 23, 24, 25, 26, 122, 189–190; nonverbal style, 84; post-war approval rating, 24; in South Carolina primaries, 48, 49; speaking style, 83–84; speeches by, 83; voter knowledge of, 8; winner-take-all rules and, 40

Bush, George W., 213, 215, 217–218

"Busing" (Jackson), 118

"Busing" (Wallace), 120

Butler, Dan, 123

Butt, Archibald, 56

Caddell, Patrick, 114

California primary, 22, 27 n.8; Buchanan in, 11; Garner in, 16; Humphrey in, 23, 74, 118, 166; McGovern in, 23, 40, 74; media coverage of, 168, 187

"A Call to Economic Arms" (Tsongas), 123, 195

Camel News Caravan (television), 150

Campaign: advertising, 91–127; compression of news cycle in, 211; financing, 220; language of reporting in, 132; media coverage, 173–174; negative, 141, 142, 159; news, 135–136; persuasive, 98; spending laws, 109; stages of, 98, 130; strategies, 131, 132

Campaign HOTLINE, 183

Candidates: adaptation to media, 89; advertising and, 91–127; agenda setting by, 193–197; campaign organization, 10; character of, 131; characterization of primaries, 172–173; conflict among, 134, 141–142, 146; control of media by, 175–178; control of speeches, 81; differentiating among, 88; favorite-son, 16, 42; fund-raising, 9; images of, 71–73, 93, 94, 95, 120, 131, 165–172, 175–178; influence on media, 134–135; interaction with voters, 85, 183, 184; media interpretation of, 81, 87, 130–132, 150, 161, 162, 179–180; media noncoverage of, 130; multiple, 8–9, 159; name recognition, 92, 113–114, 117; "packaging" of, 91; personal characteristics, 10, 93, 207; policy issues and, 88; predetermined nominees from, 42; regional, 2; relational perceptions of, 93; selectivity on primaries, 36; stands on issues, 108; state convention system and, 14, 20; strategies, 131; third party, 25, 26, 34; values of, 99; voter assessment of, 93; wives' role, 140

Carlson, Frank, 63, 150

Carter, Jimmy, 40, 43; campaign strategies, 135; in New Hampshire primary, 9; in New Jersey primary, 133; in Ohio primary, 133; as "outsider," 135

Carville, James, 211

Caucuses, 2, 31, 35, 38, 51 n.4; voter turnout in, 2

Chancellor, John, 160

Chisholm, Shirley, 78, 111

A Citizen Views the News (radio), 157

Clark, Champ, 98, 99–100; media coverage of, 139; in 1912 primaries, 12, 139; use of advertising, 98, 99–100

Clay, Lucius, 103

Cleveland, Grover, 12

Clinton, Bill, 10, 24, 183; advertising by, 121, 122, 123, 126, 195–196; agenda setting by, 195–196, 208; campaign strategies, 208–210; in Connecticut primary, 10; in Florida primary, 25; in Georgia primary, 24; in Illinois primary, 25; images of, 190–191; media coverage of, 190–191, 195–196, 207, 208–210; "New Covenant" of, 82; in New Hampshire primary, 24, 133, 190–191; in New York primary, 25; in 1992 primaries, 24, 26, 46, 122, 123, 190–191, 195–196; in 1996 primaries, 205–206; public response to, 83; as "Slick Willie," 25; in South Carolina, 24; speaking style, 81, 82–83; speeches by, 81, 82, 83, 90 n.6; Super Tuesday and, 24

Clinton, Hillary, 183

Cochrane, Jacqueline, 19

Cole, Ralph, 55

Coll, Edward, 77

Colorado primary, 48, 49

Colson, Charles, 69, 177

Commission on Party Structure and Delegate Selection, 38

Common Cause, 209

Communication: campaign developments and, 121; computers in, 121, 211–212, 218–219; direct mail, 121; 800 numbers, 26, 122–123, 126, 183, 194; image and, 121, 165–172; impact of primary rules on, 29–50; interpersonal, 100; language use in, 115–116, 132; media with voters, 130; patterns in primaries, 83, 203–224; primaries and, 2, 5, 7; technological developments in, 137; by telegram/telephone, 101, 137; town meetings, 26, 184, 193. See also Advertising; Radio; Television

Connecticut primary, 10

Connor, Fox, 63

Connor, Kevin, 183

"Conversation with Nixon" (television), 170

Coolidge, Calvin, 16

Cousins v. Wigoda, 47

"Crime" (Jackson), 118

Cronkite, Walter, 174

Cuomo, Mario, 24, 129, 153

Daniel, Clifton, 114

Debates, 9, 53–89; changes in role/nature of, 88–89; characteristics of, 87–88; by Dewey, 67; differences among, 86; failures, 77; formats, 86; by Humphrey, 78, 79, 87, 168; as "joint appearance," 78, 86; by Kefauver, 67, 68; by McGovern, 77, 78, 79, 87, 168; multi-candidate, 9; by Muskie, 77; in 1952 primaries, 62, 67–68; in 1972 primaries, 77–78, 168; party-sanctioned, 86; on radio, 68; reduction in number of, 86; requisites for, 76–77; similarities among, 86; as "special edition," 78; by Stassen, 67; television, 67, 77, 78; time allotments, 86

Dees, Morris, 114

Delegates: allocations, 47; at-large, 34; bonus, 45; congressional district system, 39, 44; demographic representation of, 38, 44; fidelity to instructions, 35; independent, 43; light instructions to, 35–37; party leaders as, 42–43, 45, 46; public identification of, 38; quotas for, 38; selection of, 7, 11, 20, 21, 30–35, 38, 39; specific district, 34, 44; super, 45, 46; uncommitted, 42, 45

Democratic convention: Clinton and, 25; Commission on Party Structure and Delegate Selection, 38; Humphrey and, 38; Johnson in, 37; Roosevelt and, 17, 18; Stevenson and, 19; Wilson and, 13

Democratic National Committee, 17, 35, 43, 46, 60, 82, 85, 134, 209

Dewey, Thomas: in debates, 67; in 1952 primaries, 19

Dewson, Mary, 101

"Disarmament" (Humphrey), 118

Dixon, Joseph, 32

Dole, Bob, 49, 207, 209, 210–211; media coverage of, 207; in New Hampshire primary, 9, 208; as regional candidate, 2; in South Carolina primary, 48, 49, 207; voter knowledge of, 8

Dole, Elizabeth, 213, 216–217

Dovetailing, 94, 99, 105, 123, 124, 127

"Drugs" (Jackson), 118

Duff, James, 104

Dukakis, Michael, 11, 46, 82, 190

"Echoes" (Harkin), 91, 92, 121

Ehrlichman, John, 178

Eisenhower, Dwight: advertising by, 102, 103–106, 125, 126; in Illinois primary, 36; media coverage of, 150, 152–154, 155, 157, 158; media use by, 20; in New Hampshire primary, 20, 36, 48, 104; in New Jersey primary, 103; in 1952 primaries, 18, 19, 21, 103–106, 150, 151; speaking style, 63–64; speeches by, 63, 64

Election, general: finance rules, 43; national committees in, 43; party backing for, 9; Roosevelt and, 18; Wilson in, 13

Face the Nation (television), 71, 77

Farley, James, 17, 65, 100, 101

Federal Election Campaign Act (1974), 8, 44, 109

Federal Election Commission, 209

Florida primary, 6, 9, 22, 24, 27 n.8; advertising in, 109, 112, 118, 120; busing issue, 22; Clinton in, 25; Humphrey in, 117, 166; importance of, 164; Jackson in, 22, 118, 166; Lindsay in, 22, 167; McGovern in, 116; media coverage of, 164, 187; Muskie in, 22, 169; Tsongas in, 25; Wallace in, 22, 74, 75, 120, 164

Flowers, Gennifer, 24, 180–181, 184–185, 190

Forbes, Steve, 206, 207, 211, 213, 216; agenda setting by, 208

"Forgotten Man" speech, 59, 61, 89, 159

France, Joseph, 16

Fraser, Donald, 38

Garner, John Nance, 16, 148

Georgia primary, 24; Clinton in, 24, 48, 49

Gephardt, Richard, 23, 43

Gillett, James, 55

Gingrich, Newt, 209

Gore, Al, 23, 43, 213, 214; in Iowa pri-

mary, 11; in New Hampshire pri-
mary, 11
Gramm, Phil, 206, 207, 208, 211
Grandmaison, Joseph, 114
Greenberg, Stan, 82
Guggenheim, Charles, 109, 114, 115
Gwirtzman, Milton, 71

Haig, Alexander, 1
Haldeman, H. R., 69, 178
Harkin, Tom, 23, 80; advertising by,
    91, 92, 121, 194; agenda setting by,
    194; in Iowa primary, 11; leaves
    campaign, 25; in 1992 primaries,
    194; as regional candidate, 2; in
    South Dakota primary, 48, 49;
    speaking style, 81; speeches by, 81,
    85
Harkness, Richard, 157
Harriman, Averill, 27 n.7, 66, 67, 151,
    156, 224 n.2
Hart, Gary, 40, 72, 73, 78, 79, 115, 161;
    evaluations of, 8; in New Hamp-
    shire primary, 8
Hartke, Vance, 77
Hatch, Orrin, 213
Hawley–Smoot Tariff Act, 148
Healey, Robert, 161
Hearst, William Randolph, 16
Heatter, Gabriel, 156
Hecht, Gerry, 118
Herblock, 151
Herlihy, Ed, 154
Herman, George, 172
Hilles, Charles, 141, 142
Hoffman, Earl, 67
Hoffman, Paul, 63
Hoover, Herbert, 10, 15, 16, 18;
    speeches by, 59, 62
Howe, Louis, 17, 100
Humphrey, Hubert, 37, 42, 72, 147,
    148, 224 n.1; advertising by, 110,
    111, 117–118; in California primary,
    23, 74, 118, 166; campaign strate-
    gies, 73–74; debates by, 78, 79, 87,
    168; in Florida primary, 117, 166;

images of, 165–166, 175–176; media
    coverage of, 143, 166, 175–176; in
    Nebraska primary, 118; in New
    Hampshire primary, 165; in 1968
    primaries, 26 n.2; in 1972 primaries,
    21, 65, 73–74, 117–118, 175–176; in
    Pennsylvania primary, 39; relations
    with press, 175–176; speaking style,
    62, 73–74; speeches by, 73–74; in
    West Virginia primary, 117; in Wis-
    consin primary, 22, 117, 164
Huntley, Chet, 160

"I Like Ike" (song), 19
Ickes, Harold, 147
Ifill, Gwen, 210
"Ike and Problems and Issues" (Ei-
    senhower), 104
"Ike the Man" (Eisenhower), 104
Illinois primary, 24, 25; Brown in, 25;
    Clinton in, 25, 46; Eisenhower in,
    36; Kefauver in, 35; media coverage
    of, 164; Muskie in, 164, 166; rules
    of, 33; Stassen in, 36; Stevenson in,
    35; Taft in, 36; Tsongas in, 25
Image, 71–73, 92–95, 97, 99, 105–106,
    112, 116, 120–121, 123, 131, 143, 165–
    172, 175–178, 189, 191–193, 208, 215–
    216
Incumbents, 88; advantages of, 4, 32,
    144, 155, 178; defeat of, 15; images
    of, 170; late decisions by, 18, 36; na-
    tional party backing for, 10, 32; sec-
    ond nominations for, 15–16, 24;
    speeches by, 87; strategies of, 135;
    support for, 21, 24
Inside Politics (television), 121
Iowa caucus, 2, 44, 45, 206, 213; Dole
    in, 49; Gore in, 11; Harkin in, 11;
    media coverage of, 132; Robertson
    in, 49
Issues: in advertising, 94; affirmative
    action, 25; agreement among candi-
    dates on, 93; busing, 22, 68, 69, 75,
    108, 118, 120, 170; corruption, 66, 68;
    crime, 66; draft, 24; drugs, 118;

economy, 24, 74, 91, 108, 122, 123, 207; embodiment of, 94; environment, 112; farm support, 118; health care, 81, 86; housing, 24; income redistribution, 59; inflation, 110; information on, 54; monopolies, 57; Prohibition, 59; recall, 56; tariffs, 57, 61; taxes, 24, 25, 75, 108, 112, 120, 194, 207, 208; trusts, 57; unemployment, 24, 61, 62, 91, 92, 122; Vietnam, 24, 68, 71, 73, 76, 110, 112, 171, 176; welfare, 75, 79, 108, 120, 168

Issues and Answers (television), 77

Jackson, Brooks, 121
Jackson, Henry, 74, 76, 172; advertising by, 118–119; in Florida primary, 22, 166; images of, 166; media coverage of, 166; in 1972 primaries, 21, 118; speaking style, 76; in Wisconsin primary, 118
Jackson, Jesse, 24, 43, 194; evaluations of, 8
Johnson, Lyndon, 26 n.2, 37

Kalb, Marvin, 172
Kaltenborn, H. V., 156–157
Kasich, John, 213
Kefauver, Estes, 18, 27 nn.7, 8, 36, 204, 224 n.2; advertising by, 107; in debates, 67, 68; in Illinois primary, 35; media coverage of, 157, 158; in New Hampshire primary, 20, 27 n.8, 48, 65; in 1952 primaries, 18, 19, 35, 65, 107, 151; speaking style, 65–66
Kefauver, Nancy, 66
Kennedy, Edward, 46, 82, 111
Kennedy, John F., 37, 164
Kentucky primary, 30
Kerr, Robert, 18, 36, 67
Kerrey, Bob, 10, 24, 80, 81, 129; advertising by, 121, 123, 194–195; agenda setting by, 194–195; leaves campaign, 25; in 1992 primaries, 194–195; in South Dakota primary, 48, 49; speeches by, 85

Khachigian, Ken, 115
Korean War, 105
Krock, Arthur, 35, 103, 153

LaFollette, Robert, 12, 55; media coverage of, 138, 139; in 1912 primaries, 12, 34, 138; in North Dakota primary, 14, 139–140; in Wisconsin primary, 165
Larmon, Sigurd, 103
Larry King Live (television), 182, 183
Leynane, Jim, 121
Limbaugh, Rush, 212
Lindley, Ernest K., 59
Lindsay, John, 37, 41, 76; as "charisma candidate," 167; in Florida primary, 22, 167; images of, 165, 167; media coverage of, 167; in 1972 primaries, 21, 41, 77; speaking style, 76
Lippman, Walter, 19, 152–154
Lodge, Henry Cabot II, 19, 36, 63, 104, 150
Lodge, John, 36
Lugar, Richard, 207

MacArthur, Douglas, 63, 104, 105
McCain, John, 213, 215–216
McCarthy, Joseph, 19
McCloskey, Paul "Pete," 21, 110, 111; images of, 166
McCormack, John, 108
McCrary, Tex, 19, 150
McGinnis, Joe, 163
McGovern, George, 38, 161; advertising by, 109, 113–116; in California primary, 23, 40, 74; campaign strategies, 72, 177; debates by, 78, 79, 87, 168; in Florida primary, 116; images of, 71–73, 167–168; as leading candidate, 22; in Massachusetts primary, 40; media coverage of, 167–168; in Nebraska primary, 40, 118; in New Hampshire primary, 22, 48, 70, 164, 165, 167; in 1972 primaries, 21, 42, 71–73, 113–116, 167–168; in Ohio primary, 116; in Pennsylvania primary, 39; radical portrayal, 118;

relations with press, 177–178; reporter identification with, 167; speaking style, 71–73; speeches by, 70, 71–73; use of rules by, 23, 29–30, 38–41, 51 n.4; winner-take-all rules and, 40; in Wisconsin primary, 22, 40, 116, 164, 165, 167

McGovern–Fraser Commission, 4, 11, 12, 21, 23, 29–30, 38–41; effects on primary reform, 41–44

McKinley, William, 32

Magruder, Jeb, 117, 171, 178

Maine caucus, 33, 45

Mansfield, Mike, 173

Marrou, Andre, 121

Marshall, George C., 63, 64

Marshall, Thomas, 56

Maryland primary, 30, 48, 49; advertising in, 97–98; effect on polls, 5; General Election Law, 31; media coverage of, 148; rules of, 33; Tsongas in, 25; Wallace in, 22

Massachusetts primary, 30, 31; advertising in, 103; McGovern in, 40; media coverage of, 148; Muskie in, 40; Smith and, 17

Matalin, Mary, 48, 49

Media: agenda setting by, 164–165, 186; ambiguity and, 133; analysis of advertising, 121, 122; attracting, 7; campaign activities, 55; campaign coverage, 173–174; candidate adaptation to, 89; candidate control of, 175–178; candidate image and, 165–172; candidate importance decisions by, 165, 188; candidate influence on, 134–135; candidate portrayals, 189–192; changing needs of, 158; characterization of primaries, 172–173, 185–186; citizens' use of, 135–136; collegial influence in, 135; columnists' opinions, 147; communication with voters, 130; coverage decisions, 130; coverage of 1912 primaries, 137–143; coverage of 1932 primaries, 143–149; coverage of 1952 primaries, 149–158; coverage of 1972 primaries, 161–169; coverage of 1992 primaries, 179–200; coverage over time, 199–200; defining winners/losers, 131; depth of primary coverage, 132–133; description/prescription by, 131; distribution of, 9; dominance, 186; editorials, 152–154; effect of technology on, 200; frontloading and, 48, 49, 206; impressions of contests by, 163; information in, 9; interest in scandal, 85, 129, 184; interpretive role, 81, 87, 130–132, 150, 161, 163, 179–180; junkyard dog journalism by, 131; lapdog journalism and, 131, 145, 147; local, 136; negative coverage by, 133–134, 142, 159, 180; new technologies, 181–184; noncoverage of candidates, 130; outsiderism and, 135; pack journalism, 135; partisan stance of, 139, 141, 152; personal impressions of candidates, 81; personal interviews by, 156; policy issue coverage, 148, 187; political party professionals and, 135; poll use by, 174–175; power of, 130–132; pre-television era, 129–160; primary importance decisions by, 164–165, 186–187; primary shaping by, 129–200; public confidence in, 184; public opinion and, 92; reform efforts, 180; restriction of coverage, 135; securing attention of, 134–135; standards for news coverage, 158–160; telegraph use, 58; television era, 160–200; Vietnam coverage, 171; watchdog role, 131, 133–134, 180

Meet the Press (television), 65, 70, 77, 151, 156, 175, 176

Michigan primary, 24, 25; Brown in, 25; Clinton in, 25, 46; rules of, 33; Tsongas in, 25; Wallace in, 22

Miller, Zell, 24–25, 48, 49

Mills, Wilbur, 111

Minnesota primary, 31; Eisenhower in, 36; write-in votes, 36

Missouri primary, 31

Mitchell, Andrea, 186

Moley, Raymond, 59

Mondale, Walter, 46, 47; in New Hampshire primary, 8
Montana primary, 51 n.5
Montgomery, Robert, 157
Morris, Richard, 209
Morrison, Frank, 118
Morrow, Dwight, 16
Moynihan, Daniel Patrick, 194
Mudd, Roger, 69
Murrow, Edward R., 156
Muskie, Edmund, 42, 161; advertising by, 111–113; in Florida primary, 22, 169; in Illinois primary, 164, 166; images of, 71, 165, 168–169, 176–177; as leading candidate, 21–22, 111; leaves campaign, 22; loss of confidence in, 22, 112–113, 168–169; in Massachusetts primary, 40; media coverage of, 168–169, 176–177; in New Hampshire primary, 22, 48, 70, 164, 165, 176; in 1972 primaries, 21, 68, 70–71, 111–113, 168–169, 176–177; object of "dirty tricks," 68; relations with press, 176–177; speaking style, 70–71; speeches by, 70, 71; stands on issues, 88; winner-take-all rules and, 40; withdrawal from campaign, 70

NBC Radio Masterbook (radio), 156
Nebraska primary: advertising in, 118; Humphrey in, 118; McGovern in, 40, 118; media coverage of, 158; Taft in, 139
New Hampshire primary, 7, 14, 19–20, 22, 24, 31, 36, 44, 45; advertising in, 102, 103, 104–105, 107, 108, 109, 110, 112, 121; Buchanan in, 9, 48, 131, 208; Bush in, 48, 189–190; Carter in, 9; Clinton in, 24, 133, 190–191; Dole in, 9, 208; effect on polls, 5; Eisenhower in, 36, 48, 104; Gore in, 11; Hart in, 8; Humphrey in, 165; importance of, 48, 49, 80; influence of, 4; Kefauver in, 27 n.8, 48, 107; McGovern in, 22, 48, 70, 164, 165,

167; media coverage of, 132, 147, 156, 158, 165, 167, 187; Mondale in, 8; Muskie in, 22, 48, 70, 164, 165, 176; Nixon in, 110–111; Stassen in, 104; Taft in, 104; Truman in, 48; Tsongas in, 24, 48, 133, 192; Wallace in, 165
New Jersey primary: advertising in, 103; Carter in, 133; Eisenhower in, 103; newspaper coverage in, 138; Smith in, 17; Taft in, 58
New York primary, 24; advertising in, 97, 98; Brown in, 25; Clinton in, 25; media coverage of, 187; newspaper coverage in, 138; Roosevelt in, 97, 141, 142; rules of, 33; Smith in, 17
Newman, Edwin, 69
News: advertising, 97–100, 102–103, 105, 106, 108, 110, 116; columnists' opinions, 147; coverage decisions, 130; editorials, 152–154; electronic gathering of, 161; length of story in, 130; media interpretation of, 81, 87, 130–132, 150, 161, 162, 179–180; negative coverage, 133–134, 142, 159, 180; newsreels, 144–145, 154–156; policy issues, 148, 187; radio, 156–158; reporter hierarchy, 160–161; restriction of coverage, 135; speech transcripts in, 89; story placement in, 130; television role in, 136–137
Newsreels, 144–145, 154–156
Nixon, Richard: advertising by, 110–111; campaign strategies, 78; in China, 21, 87, 172, 178; Federal Election Campaign Act and, 43; images of, 170–172, 178; media coverage of, 160, 170–172; in New Hampshire primary, 110–111; in 1960 primaries, 37; in 1972 primaries, 21, 68, 69, 110–111, 170–172, 178; relations with press, 178; in Soviet Union, 21, 68, 69, 87, 172, 178; speaking style, 68–69; speeches by, 69, 70, 87

Nordheimer, Jon, 163
North Dakota primary: LaFollette in, 14, 139; 1912 primaries, 14; Roosevelt in, 34
Novak, Robert, 79, 178

Ohio primary: Carter in, 133; McGovern in, 116; media coverage of, 158; newspaper coverage in, 138; Taft in, 58
On the Line with Bob Considine (radio), 156
Operation Wintergreen, 18, 26 n.6, 153
Oregon primary, 6, 30; debates in, 62; Dewey in, 67; Stassen in, 4, 67; Taft in, 139

Paramount News, 154, 155
Pearson, Drew, 152–154, 156
Pegler, Westbrook, 152–154
Pennsylvania primary: advertising in, 102; Humphrey in, 39; McGovern in, 39; media coverage of, 148; Smith in, 17; Taft in, 140; Wallace in, 39
Perot, Ross, 26, 134, 182, 183; infomercials, 94; in 1992 primaries, 25
Persian Gulf War, 23
Pierce, Franklin, 24
Pinchot, Gifford, 147
Polls, 7, 141–143; media use of, 174–175; in 1912 primaries, 141–143; in 1972 primaries, 23; straw, 46
Presidential Timber (television), 66
Primaries: advisory, 35–37; candidate characterization on, 172–173; change proposals for, 220–224; closed, 43; communication patterns in, 2, 5, 7, 203–224; context of, 11–12; creation of, 1, 2, 6, 30–35; delegate selection and, 7, 11, 20, 30–35; direct system, 29; disagreement over, 2, 3–4; early, 5, 7, 20, 30–35, 41, 45, 48, 49, 186–187; effect on nominations, 4–5; frontloading, 7,

48, 49, 206; growth of, 6; heaviest coverage of, 132–133; importance of, 4, 5, 6; intraparty issues, 41, 88, 134; media characterization of, 129–160, 172–173, 185–186; momentum over time in, 3–4, 6; multiple, 8; negative advertising in, 96; nomination decisions and, 4, 6; nonbinding, 16, 34, 98; open, 43, 51 n.5; opportunities for candidates in, 5; party leaders and, 4, 32, 34, 39, 47–49; personal character in, 10; preferential, 6, 16, 30–31, 33, 48; proportional, 39, 44; reform of, 3, 6, 11–12, 29, 37–50; regional, 204; rhetorical situation of, 6–11; rules of, 29–50; semi-closed, 43; seriality of, 10–11; soap box, 33; symbols in, 2, 31; television coverage, 4; timing of, 24–25, 30, 45, 48, 49; as "voice of the people," 15, 31, 32, 33, 36, 50, 205; volunteer, 33; voter turnout, 5, 43, 50; weak, 15, 20, 37; winner-take-all, 30, 38, 39, 44, 45, 46; winnowing in, 11
Primaries (1912), 12–15; advertising in, 97–100; character and image in, 143, 165–172; Clark in, 12, 13, 139; experimentation in, 29; importance of, 204–205; LaFollette in, 12, 34, 138; media coverage of, 137–143; newspaper coverage in, 97–100, 137, 138; number of, 8, 31; political imagery in, 97; precedents of, 13; Roosevelt in, 12, 15, 31, 32, 33, 34, 136, 137, 139, 141, 142; speeches in, 54–58, 97; Taft in, 12, 15, 31, 32, 33, 34, 136, 137, 139, 140, 141, 142; Wilson in, 12, 13
Primaries (1932), 15–18; advertising in, 100–102; delegate selection in, 17, 34; importance of, 204–205; invisibility of, 143; media coverage of, 143–149; newspapers and, 145–147; newsreels of, 144–145; number of, 8; press conferences in, 144; radio use

in, 58; Roosevelt in, 16, 17, 58, 145–147; rules in, 34; Smith in, 16, 17, 145–147; speeches in, 58–62

Primaries (1952), 18–21; advertising in, 102–108; debates in, 62, 67–68; delegate selection in, 20; Dewey in, 19; Eisenhower in, 18, 19, 21, 36, 63, 64, 103–106, 150, 151; importance of, 204–205; Kefauver in, 18, 19, 35, 65, 107, 151; media coverage of, 149–158; newspaper coverage in, 152–154; newsreels in, 154–156; number of, 8, 18; Operation Wintergreen in, 18, 26 n.6, 153; press conferences in, 156; radio in, 156–158; speeches in, 62–68; Stassen in, 19, 36; Stevenson in, 18, 151; Taft in, 18, 19, 21, 36, 64, 107–108, 150, 151; television in, 150–152; Truman in, 18, 65, 108

Primaries (1960), 37

Primaries (1972), 21–23; advertising in, 108–121; debates in, 77–78, 85; delegate selection in, 21; Humphrey in, 21, 73–74, 117–118, 175–176; image as issue, 165; importance of, 204–205; issues in, 175; Jackson in, 21, 76, 118; Lindsay in, 21, 41, 76, 77; McGovern in, 21, 42, 71–73, 113–116, 167–168; media coverage of, 161–169; Muskie in, 21, 68, 70–71, 111–113, 168–169, 176–177; Nixon in, 21, 68, 69, 110–111, 170–172, 178; number of, 8, 21; reforms in, 29, 37–50; rules in, 37–41; speeches in, 68–80; Wallace in, 21, 43, 69, 74–76, 120–121, 169–170

Primaries (1992), 23–26; advertising in, 121–124; Brown in, 193–194; Buchanan in, 24, 25, 26; Bush in, 23, 24, 25, 26, 122, 189–190; Clinton in, 24, 25, 26, 46, 122, 123, 190–191, 195–196; Harkin in, 194; Kerrey in, 194–195; media coverage of, 179–200; number of, 8; Perot in, 25, 26; speeches in, 80–87; Tsongas in, 24, 25, 123, 195

Primaries (1996), 205–212; media coverage of, 205–212; number of, 12

Primaries (2000), 212–220; advertising in, 220; media coverage in, 217–218; new technologies in, 218–219; speeches in, 214–217

Progressive movement, 6, 13, 56

Prohibition, 17, 59

"Property Tax" (Humphrey), 118

Public opinion: media and, 92; personal characteristics and, 93; polls and, 141–143; primaries and, 5; speeches and, 54, 82; television and, 130–131

Pure Oil News Time (radio), 157

Pyle, Ernie, 152–154

Quayle, Dan, 213

Radio, 160; advertising, 102, 103, 111, 120; speeches on, 58, 62; talk shows, 183, 212; use in 1932 primaries, 58, 145; use in 1952 primaries, 156–158; voter use of for news, 135–136

Raskob, John, 17

Rather, Dan, 69, 170, 171, 190

"Read My Lips" (Buchanan), 124

Reagan, Ronald, 10, 48, 49, 134, 136

Reasoner, Harry, 165, 172–173

Reconstruction Finance Corporation, 19, 62

"The Relationship of Business to Government" (Wilson), 57

Republican convention, 4, 12–13, 21

Republican National Committee, 84, 137, 153, 210

Reston, James, 66

Rhode Island primary, 31

"Right to Know" (McGovern), 115

Robertson, Pat, 49, 123

Rockefeller, Jay, 23

Rockefeller, Nelson, 79

Roosevelt, Franklin, 34, 35; "Forgotten Man" speech, 59, 61, 89, 159; media coverage of, 158; in New Hampshire primary, 147; in 1932 primaries, 16, 58, 145–147; primary advantages, 16–17; Prohibition and, 17; "rose garden" strategy, 58; speaking style, 58–60; speeches by,

59–60, 89, 89 n.1, 144–145; stands on issues, 88; use of advertising, 100–101

Roosevelt, Theodore, 55, 99, 204; Bull Moose Party and, 34; media coverage of, 137, 138, 139; in New York primary, 97, 141, 142; in 1912 primaries, 12, 15, 31, 32, 33, 34, 139, 141, 142; in North Dakota primary, 34; object of "dirty tricks," 99; speaking style, 56; speeches by, 55, 56, 58; use of advertising, 99; in Wisconsin primary, 34

Rosenman, Samuel, 59

Rugaber, Walter, 163

Russell, Richard, 18, 27 n.7, 36, 67, 68, 157, 224 n.2

Safire, William, 19

Schieffer, Bob, 186

Schorr, Daniel, 69

Schrum, Robert, 71

"Score Card" (Humphrey), 117–118

Scott, Hugh, 63

Scott, Joseph, 55

Senate Crime Committee, 151, 155

Severeid, Eric, 77, 160, 161, 165

Shouse, Jouett, 17, 35

60 Minutes (television), 183

Smith, Al, 10, 17, 34, 35; in Massachusetts primary, 17; in New Hampshire primary, 147; in New Jersey primary, 17; in New York primary, 17; in 1932 primaries, 16, 145–147; in Pennsylvania primary, 17; Prohibition and, 17; speaking style, 60–61; speeches by, 60–61, 144–145; stands on issues, 88; use of advertising, 101–102

Smith, Howard K., 160, 166

Smith, Robert, 213

South Carolina primary: Bush in, 48, 49; Clinton in, 24; Dole in, 48, 49, 207; importance of, 48, 49; Reagan in, 48, 49

South Dakota primary, 45; Harkin in, 48, 49; Kerrey in, 48, 49

Speeches, 9, 53–89; agenda setting and, 88; assertion and, 54; by Buchanan, 81; by Bush, 83; candidate control of, 81; ceremonial, 90 n.6; changes in, 54; changes in role/nature of, 88–89; characteristics of, 87–88; cliches in, 82; by Clinton, 81, 82, 83, 90 n.6; damage to candidates through, 85; distinctions among candidates through, 84–85; by Eisenhower, 63, 64; eye contact and, 71; "Forgotten Man" (Roosevelt), 59, 61, 89, 159; by Harkin, 81, 85; by Hoover, 59, 62; by Humphrey, 73–74; importance of, 87; by incumbents, 87; as introductions to media, 81; issues in, 64; by Kerrey, 85; length of, 54, 89; by McGovern, 70, 71–73; media attendance at, 80–81; by Muskie, 70, 71; network news coverage, 89; in 1912 primaries, 54–58, 97; in 1952 primaries, 62–68; in 1972 primaries, 68–80; in 1992 primaries, 80–87; by Nixon, 69, 70, 87; personal representatives for, 55, 63; personal style of, 81; public opinion and, 82; question periods and, 85; on radio, 58, 62; by Roosevelt, 55, 56, 58, 59–60, 89, 89 n.1, 144–145; by Smith, 60–61, 144–145; soundbites and, 54, 85, 162, 163, 179; specificity to states' issues, 87; speech modules in, 65; by Stevenson, 66, 67; by Taft, 53, 54, 55, 56, 57, 58, 64, 65; television, 53, 62, 65, 66, 68, 81, 88; thematic, 82, 83, 163; timing of, 80–81; by Tsongas, 81, 85; in 2000 primaries, 214–217; voter interaction and, 85; by Wallace, 74–76; whistle-stop, 80; by Wilson, 57; writing, 57

Spivak, Lawrence, 151, 175

Sprague, Bill, 157

Stassen, Harold: in debates, 67; in Illinois primary, 36; media coverage of, 155; in New Hampshire primary, 104; in 1952 primaries, 19; in Oregon primary, 4

Stearns, Rick, 40, 161

Stevenson, Adlai, 27 nn.7, 8, 224 n.2;
    in Illinois primary, 35; media cover-
    age of, 153, 154, 158; in 1952 pri-
    maries, 18, 35, 151; speaking style,
    66–67; speeches by, 66, 67
Stewart, Richard, 177
"Stop-Roosevelt" movement, 17, 148
Sumner, William Graham, 59
Super Tuesday, 8, 24, 46, 48, 49, 180,
    187, 212
Swope, Ken, 91
Symbolism: competitive sports, 56;
    condensation, 95, 99; fighting, 56,
    106, 120, 134, 189, 192–193, 208, 215–
    216; horse race, 126–127, 132, 173–
    174, 181, 185; referential, 95

Taft, Robert: advertising by, 102, 105,
    106–107; in Illinois primary, 36; me-
    dia coverage of, 152–154, 153, 155,
    158; media use, 20; in New
    Hampshire primary, 104; in 1952
    primaries, 18, 19, 21, 64, 107–108,
    150, 151; speaking style, 64–65;
    speeches by, 53, 64, 65; stands on
    issues, 88
Taft, William Howard, 10, 20, 99; me-
    dia coverage of, 137, 139, 140; in
    Nebraska primary, 139; in New Jer-
    sey primary, 58; in 1912 primaries,
    12, 15, 31, 32, 33, 34, 139, 140, 141,
    142; in Ohio primary, 58; in Oregon
    primary, 139; in Pennsylvania pri-
    mary, 140; speaking style, 56;
    speeches by, 54–55, 56, 57, 58; use
    of advertising, 99
"Tax Structure" (Wallace), 120
Teeter, Robert, 110
Television: adaptation to, 89; advertis-
    ing, 103, 104, 109, 111, 112, 114,
    116, 118, 120, 125; agenda setting
    by, 164–165; cable, 123, 126, 179,
    182; candidate image and, 165–172;
    candidate speeches, 9; changes in
    primary coverage, 179–181; channel
    increases, 182; debates on, 67, 77, 78;
    effect on nomination process, 4; in-
    fluence of, 93; interpretation of can-

didate's words, 81, 130–132, 150,
    161, 162, 179–180; MTV, 26; news-
    magazines, 218; ownership growth,
    160; primary importance decisions
    by, 164–165, 186–187; production
    techniques, 121; public access, 193;
    public affairs programming, 182;
    public opinion and, 130–131; satel-
    lite technology, 181–184; simulation
    of intimacy in, 95, 137; soundbites
    on, 54, 85, 162, 163, 179; speeches
    on, 53, 62, 65, 66, 68, 81, 88; sum-
    maries of information on, 85; talk
    shows, 26, 179, 183, 195, 196; video
    news release, 181–184; video tech-
    nology, 161, 181, 182; visual factors
    in, 136–137; voter use of for news,
    135–136
Television Plans Board, 63, 150
Texas primary, 31, 34
Thomas, Lowell, 156
Threlkeld, Richard, 183, 192
Truman, Harry, 154; advertising by,
    108; late running decision, 18, 36; in
    New Hampshire primary, 20, 48, 65;
    in 1952 primaries, 18, 36, 108; views
    on primaries, 66
Tsongas, Paul, 1, 10, 23; advertising
    by, 121, 123, 195; agenda setting by,
    195; in Florida primary, 25; in Illi-
    nois primary, 25; images of, 191–
    192; leaves campaign, 25; in
    Maryland primary, 25; media cov-
    erage of, 191–192; in Michigan pri-
    mary, 25; in New Hampshire
    primary, 24, 48, 192; in 1992 pri-
    maries, 24, 25, 123, 191–192, 195;
    speaking style, 81; speeches by, 81,
    85

Universal Newsreels, 154, 155, 156

Vermont primary, 45
"Vets" (McGovern), 115
Vietnam War, 24, 68, 71, 73, 76, 110,
    112, 171, 176
Virginia primary, 37
Voters: assessments of candidate com-

petence, 93; communication with media, 130; impression of primaries, 4; informing, 8; interaction with candidates, 85, 183, 184; media interviews with, 175; primary turnout, 5; relational perceptions of candidates, 93, 130; turnout, 43, 48, 49; use of media for news, 135–136

Voting: candidate's image and, 93, 165; crossover, 38, 39; influence on media coverage, 132–133; instructions on, 97, 102, 105–106; majority, 9; past party, 38; plurality, 9, 30; straight population, 38; write-in, 25, 36

"Wages" (McGovern), 115

Wallace, Cornelia, 22

Wallace, George, 42, 161; advertising by, 110, 120–121; in Florida primary, 9, 22, 74, 75, 164; images of, 120, 169–170; in Maryland primary, 22; media coverage of, 169–170; in Michigan primary, 22; in New Hampshire primary, 165; in 1972 primaries, 21, 43, 69, 74–76, 120–121, 169–170; as "outsider," 135; in Pennsylvania primary, 39; "Send them a message theme," 75; shooting of, 22, 23, 76, 170; speaking style, 74–76; speeches by, 74–76; in Wisconsin primary, 22, 120

Wallace, Mike, 168

Walters, Barbara, 178

Warren, Earl, 67

Wattenberg, Ben, 166

"Welfare" (Wallace), 120

"Welfare #2" (Humphrey), 118

Wenograd Commission, 44

West Virginia primary, 37, 117

White, Theodore, 10, 37, 132, 163, 179

Wicker, Tom, 172–173

Wilder, Douglas, 23

Willkie, Wendell, 4

Wilson, Woodrow, 30, 34, 55, 98; in 1912 primaries, 12; presidential nomination of, 13; speaking style, 56; speeches by, 57

Winchell, Walter, 152–154, 156

"Wisconsin Farm" (Jackson), 118

Wisconsin primary, 6, 22, 30, 37, 51 n.5; advertising in, 118, 120; effect on polls, 5; Humphrey in, 22, 117, 164; influence of, 4; Jackson in, 118; LaFollette in, 165; McGovern in, 22, 40, 116, 164, 165, 167; media coverage of, 158, 164, 167; Roosevelt in, 34; Wallace in, 22, 120; Willkie in, 4

World News Roundup (radio), 157

Yorty, Sam, 77, 78, 111

"Youth Conservation" (Jackson), 118

About the Author

KATHLEEN E. KENDALL is Associate Professor and Graduate Director in the Department of Communication, University at Albany, State University of New York. She is the author of numerous articles on political communication in journals such as *Presidential Studies Quarterly, Journal of Communication, American Behavioral Scientist,* and *Communications Quarterly,* and editor of *Presidential Campaign Discourse: Strategic Communication Problems* (1995).

ISBN 0-275-94070-5

9 780275 940706

HARDCOVER BAR CODE